SPECTERS OF
GOD

SPECTERS OF GOD

An Anatomy of the Apophatic Imagination

—ɯ—

John D. Caputo

INDIANA UNIVERSITY PRESS

This book is a publication of

Indiana University Press
Office of Scholarly Publishing
Herman B Wells Library 350
1320 East 10th Street
Bloomington, Indiana 47405 USA

iupress.org

© 2022 by John D. Caputo

All rights reserved
No part of this book may be reproduced or utilized in any form or by any means, electronic or mechanical, including photocopying and recording, or by any information storage and retrieval system, without permission in writing from the publisher. The paper used in this publication meets the minimum requirements of the American National Standard for Information Sciences—Permanence of Paper for Printed Library Materials, ANSI Z39.48-1992.

Manufactured in the United States of America

First printing 2022

Cataloging information is available from the Library of Congress.

ISBN 978-0-253-06300-7 (hardback)
ISBN 978-0-253-06301-4 (paperback)
ISBN 978-0-253-06302-1 (ebook)

To Jodi,
For her ever-faithful love and our ever-amazing grandchildren

CONTENTS

Preface: The Apophatic Imagination ix

Acknowledgments xv

Introduction: Specters of God   1
1. Theopoetics: A Phenomenological Genesis   16

PART ONE: *The Ontotheological Imaginary*

2. From an Edifying to an Anxious Apophatics: Aquinas, Eckhart, and Luther   41
3. Hegel at the Foot of the Cross: Understanding the Death of God   74
4. Schelling and the Metaphysics of Evil   101
5. The Philosophical Meaning of Satan   121
6. Why Is There Something Rather Than Nothing at All? Schelling and the End of Idealism   139
7. Schelling's Either/Or   153
8. Hegel and Schelling: The Critique and the Scarecrow   169

PART TWO: *The Hauntological Imaginary*

9. Theism Transcended: The Post-Theism of Paul Tillich   185
10. Violence and the Unconditional: The Politics of the Apophatic   213
11. Haunting Tillich: Spectralizing the Ground of Being   242
12. The Devil Is In the Dissemination   264

PART THREE: *The Posthuman Imaginary*

13. Angelology—Posthuman Style: Would You Rather Be a Cyborg, a Posthuman, or an Angel?   277

14. Ruinology: Why Will There Be Nothing at All Rather Than Something? *304*
15. Axiology: A Mortal God, A World without Why *318*
    Conclusion: The Name (of) "God" *335*

Notes 345

Index 383

PREFACE
The Apophatic Imagination

THERE WAS A TIME IN my life when I suffered from angel envy—pure spirit, an intellect bathed in light, a will confirmed in good, immortal, united with God for all eternity. What's not to envy? I lived in a world of early morning mass and meditation, musing under towering trees, silence and Latin liturgies, black robes and books, "leaving the world," entering "religious life," taking a "religious name." They called me "Brother Paul." In those days, I thought what I was seeking was called "religion," but it was something going on *in* religion that had gotten hold of me. Whatever it was, at the time, Brother Paul and I thought the angels had it, purely, perfectly. Indeed, they *were* it, and Jesus said that in heaven we would live like the angels. What's not to envy?

Ever since it landed on me, when words were not available to me, in words that were not quite right, I have lived my life under an obscure imperative, a call of some sort, that I have been trying my best to answer. Call it the mystical sense of life, the "mystical element" *in* something—in whatever it was, not just religion, in whatever I was studying, teaching, lecturing, writing about. My first book, *The Mystical Element in Heidegger's Thought*, about Heidegger and Meister Eckhart, was what the bookkeepers and auditors of professorial rank and tenure call a "research program."

I called it my calling, the passion of my life, my vocation, even my "religious vocation," but not the same sort of religion I had started with. The mystical "element" is not a thing but a quality *in* things, in anything, in all things, great or small. If something does not pass through the discipline, the asceticism, the criticism, the prism, the exigency of the mystical, then I am not interested. I never was.

But let me be clear. *Mystical* is also the wrong word; it is, at best, the least bad word. I make no pretense to being "the man from whom God concealed nothing," which they said Meister Eckhart said. Quite the opposite: I am here to confess all that has been concealed from me. I make no pretense to speak from the heart of God or impart a vision that has been granted me in the heavenly sphere, as mystics are wont to do. I am not insinuating a secret gnosis, and I do not number myself among those who have scaled the steep ascent of the *via negativa*. I am serving up not peace and light but the sword of nonknowing. I do not valorize rest but the restlessness of our *cor inquietum*. I have no desire to be one with the One. I would rather be many with the many, large with multitudes.

Call it rather "the apophatic": the apophatic element, the apophatic imperative, the apophatic imagination. This means the multiple attempts we make to construe the shadows and specters of our being, to interpret what lies at the limits of our understanding. The apophatic arises from a kind of archiexperience of something unencompassable, an encounter with something that lays claim to us before we make any claims to it. Call it the concealed depths, the unlit core, the nocturnal powers. I am describing a passage to the limits, exploring that horizon beyond which we can see no more, where things become indistinct, uncertain, beyond our ken, beyond our reach.

But let me be clear. I am not advancing the occult arts and Satanic cults, not promoting obscurantism and attacking knowledge, not lending any credence to QAnon conspiracies. I have spent my whole life seeking knowledge and have spent a small fortune on books. I am all for knowledge; the more knowledge, the better. Indeed, what I have in mind is the very dim and obscure regions into which we are led by taking the hand of knowledge itself, a *docta ignorantia*. Today, for example, after the most disciplined investigations, the physicists have concluded that this vast universe, with its billions of galaxies, is just the visible part, only about 5 percent, while the remaining 95 percent is in the dark. That is a thought worth pondering, at once of scientific, poetic, philosophical, and theological import, a thought we think at the limits of thinking, at that point where these disciplinary distinctions disappear. There thinking is nothing other than itself, beyond the safety afforded by invoking a disciplinary method, which is why physics today is a breeding ground for mystics.

But let me be clear. Even *apophatic* is not the right word; it is, at best, the least bad word. While this all started for me in a world that was inundated with edification, where the nonknowing was the mystery of God, and God is light and truth, I am not proposing an exercise in piety. I am not trying to be edifying, not trying to offer assurance, comfort, and consolation to world-weary souls. I am not announcing a light so bright it blinds us. I am confessing we are deprived of light, plain and simple. When I speak of mystery, I am confessing that I am mystified and do not know what to do next. I am feeling around with a stick, writing a memoir of the blind. I mean the limit we run up against in our search for light, security, truth, and good counsel. I have in mind a kind of nocturnal phenomenology, wrestling with shadowy figures, like Jacob and his angel, describing a condition in which I am genuinely lost, hounded by doubts and insecurity. The power of being for me means being overpowered by it. If I say "I," I mean the I who could never say I, the we who cannot say we, but with this addendum: that *is* who I am, a self with no right to say "I" or "we." *Quaestio mihi magna factus sum.* I am still an open question for myself, even at my age. I have an identity card, several of them, but I am not identical with myself. If I say "radical," I am not posing as a foundationalist digging down to the root. I am confessing to being radically *uprooted*, exposed, at risk. The ground for me is a groundless ground, an abyss. When I say "deep," I do not mean I have fathomed the depths. I mean that I am almost drowning, that I am in over my head, out of my depth, excrementally deep, as Žižek does not fear to say rather more frankly.

Having mistaken the apophatic for religion, I left the "religious life," the institutional one, and abandoned religion and theology in any dogmatic sense for philosophy, where I thought I would not be pulled over by the police of orthodoxy, not annoyed by all that surveillance and a pathology that confuses itself with theology. If there can be a religion of the apophatic, where the apophatic is the *event* that is going on *in* religion, that is the only religion, the most religion, I can tolerate. Today, religion in the empirical sense—the word and the thing—is more and more the recourse of the reactionary, the resentful, the under-educated, the anti-scientific, an alibi for white supremacism and sexism, packing its guns, standing its ground against immigrants and people who look different, instead of welcoming "the widow, the orphan, and the stranger," as the prophets enjoin. Today, religion cannot save anyone. Someone needs to save religion from all the harm it does, which would require radicalizing it, submitting it to the discipline of the apophatic. I have always been working on the radicalization of something, of hermeneutics and phenomenology, of religion and theology, which has meant feeling about for their apophatic core. That is the story of my life. Thinking and acting are always already overtaken or disturbed by something, exposed to unsettling nocturnal powers, faced with an irreducible *mysterium*, which is the remaining cash value of the word *religion*. That is what fascinates me about Eckhart's *Gottheit* and Luther's *Deus absconditus*, which send the theologians rushing to the microphone like campaign press secretaries trying to reassure us that the candidate really did not mean what he seems to have said.

The task here is to find a discourse for the apophatic that *does it no injury*, that tries neither to sweeten or attenuate it nor to turn it into an abyss of despair. I have lately been willing to call this discourse "theology," meaning a weak theology or a radical theology, a theology worthy of the name, a theology that thinks, tout court, *simpliciter*, deeply, undogmatically, without the adornments of authority and supernaturalism, all in the service of keeping us open to the mystery. This is not to be confused with seminary theology, the confessional sense of theology. It is stationed at a point where the distinction between philosophy and "revealed theology" has come undone; it has been dissolved, suspended, swallowed up by thinking. If the word *theology* is getting in the way, then consider it a theo*poetics*, where the -*ology* is crossed out, pierced, wounded, crucified. Then why call this theology at all? There is no need. *It* does not care what you call it. When I say "theology," it is for *strategic* reasons. I am following the tracks of a kind of radical thinking *in dialogue* with confessional theology and religion, with which such thinking communicates but is not to be confused. When it comes to religion and theology, I follow Tillich: if we were all alive to the depths of being, we would have no need at all for religion, which exists solely as a remedy for our present distraction and inattentiveness. Religion is plan B.

ACKNOWLEDGMENTS

My thanks to the excellent readers of this manuscript who made several helpful suggestions for its improvement and to the always excellent staff of Indiana University Press; to Klaus Ottmann for sharing an advance copy of his translation of Schelling's *Philosophy of Revelation (1841–42) and Related Texts*; and to B. Keith Putt, for invaluable help with the index. While the great majority of this book is previously unpublished, portions of some chapters have appeared in earlier versions, which I am happy to acknowledge:

Chapter 1: "The Theopoetic Reduction: Suspending the Supernatural Signified," in *Literature and Theology* 33, no. 3 (September 2019): 248–54; "Being and Beings: The Ontological/Ontic Distinction," in *50 Concepts for a Critical Phenomenology*, ed. Gail Weiss, Ann Murphy, and Gayle Salamon (Evanston, IL: Northwestern University Press, 2020), 25–30.

Chapter 10: "Violence and the Unconditional: A Radical Theology of Culture," in *Journal for Continental Philosophy of Religion* 1 (2019), 170–90.

Chapter 12: "Gadamer and the Postmodern Mind," in *The Gadamerian Mind*, ed. Theodore George and Gert-Jan van der Heidne (London: Routledge, 2021), 435–48.

Chapter 13: "Cyber Spirits," in *The Human Soul: Essays in Honor of Nalin Ranasinghe*, ed. Predrag Cicovacki (Wilmington, DE: Vernon, 2021), 213–25.

SPECTERS OF
GOD

INTRODUCTION
Specters of God

A GHOST DANCE

In a scene from *Ghost Dance*, a 1982 French film in which Derrida played himself, an actress asks Derrida whether he believes in ghosts. He replies that his very "appearance" in this film is turning him into a ghost, an apparition in which, long after he is dead, we will be able to "see" and "hear" him, although he is no longer there. "I think that the future belongs to ghosts," he says, "that technology increases greatly the power of ghosts [*fantômes*]." When asked, in turn, by Derrida whether she believes in ghosts, she replies, "Yes, now I do, yes." As fate would have it, the young actress herself died two years later, and Derrida recounts the eerie experience of watching the film later on and hearing her say, "*now I do, yes.*" Does she mean now that she is dead?[1]

In the study that follows, I take up Derrida's belief in ghosts as a deadly serious way to frame the question of God, a very holy ghost indeed. I, too, believe in ghosts, not in the innocent way Brother Paul and I believed in angels many years ago, but the way Derrida does, where being is haunted by time and the spectral is the figure of the instability and undecidability of being, never identical with itself, especially today, when information technology has filled the air with ghostly voices and visions. I wonder if Derrida himself, who died three years before the rollout of the first iPhone, could have fully appreciated how truly he spoke. I believe in ghosts the way the physicists do, where what presents itself to us as a solid thing is but an evanescent event, the excitation of a field, a happening—a hologram, some say, which is the sort of spooky speculation that annoyed Einstein. Maybe the universe is information all the way down! Maybe, as Max Stirner said, *"es spukt in der ganzen Welt,"* the whole world is spooked.

I acknowledge that adopting these spirits as a leitmotif runs the risk of ridicule. How many angels can dance on the head of a pin? Thus did the moderns famously mock the premodern belief in these fantastic creatures. Nonetheless, throwing all (modernist) caution to the wind, as is my wont, what I am presenting here can be viewed as a ghost story, as a history of these ghosts. This is a typically teasing trope, even a bit of a taunt, whose seriousness can be seen in the prescience of Derrida's forecast. Today, information technology has greatly increased the power of ghosts, of cyber-spirits, immersing us in a world of virtual reality where, as we often hear, the physical presence of something—say, a business—is "immaterial," leaving the distinction between the material and immaterial to tremble. I track an uncanny continuity from medieval angelology to virtual reality that is signaled by the word *angelos*, a messenger, angels being the first instant message system. This may seem like happenstance, but it happens to be serious. As Michel Serres has shown, there is an important correspondence between medieval angelology and contemporary information technology, between angels floating on clouds and the "cloud." Today we ask, how much information can be stored on an increasingly miniaturized microchip? Mock that.

So, however much this looks like a merely literary conceit, a whimsical way to make a more straightforward point, I am also perfectly serious. My subject matter is God—that is certainly serious—and my claim, which I make with no expectation that this will reassure the orthodox, is that God is to be thought spectrally, that what is going on in and under the name (of) "God" is a spectral effect. By a specter I mean a phenomenon that neither is nor is not but in either case cannot be dismissed. A specter wavers between being and nothing, is almost there but not quite, is almost nothing but then again nothing that can be ignored. Specters do not exist; specters haunt existence, calling upon us in the night, leaving us to wonder if anyone was there. To speak of the specters of God is not to dismiss the name (of) "God" in the spirit of modernity or to ridicule it with an impish trope. This is not a game, and if it is a game, it is one I keep losing. The name (of) "God" is the name of something by which I have been haunted, and in this, my wager is, I am not alone. The spectrality of God, by which even those who rightly pass for atheists will admit to have been occasionally spooked, is everything that modernity wished to exorcize and we, with no little fear and trembling, dare to conjure up and engage in conversation. If I am right, hauntology—the discourse on specters—taken seriously is the only way to approach what is going on in and under the name (of) "God."

The theologically minded may think of what follows in these pages as a slightly heretical gloss on the New Testament, which is a serious book, in which I draw upon its central drama—the battle waged between the prince of peace and the prince of lies, between Christ and Satan, between the heavenly powers and the "principalities" and "powers"—and ask, *what is the philosophical meaning of this mythic contest?* Unlike Anselm, who wanted to embalm the New Testament, to drain out the living blood of the mythology and replace it with the lifeless serum of a scholastic syllogism turning on the logic of satisfaction, I want to read it, understand it.

To the complaint that all these angels and demons, ghosts and specters are figures of our imagination, my considered, technical, philosophically precise response is, so what? Only a ham-fisted rationalism would dismiss the work of imagination. The creators of the great works of science, art, and literature do not. Einstein certainly did not. A poetics is a work of imagination and as such is always conducted in the subjunctive, asking *what it would be like* to be an angel (Aquinas) or a cockroach (Kafka) or *what it would be like* if God ruled in the world instead of the powers and principalities (the New Testament). Einstein conducted his most famous thought experiment by asking *what it would be like* to hitch a ride on a particle of light. Imagination is not a purely subjective buzz but the way we resonate with the world itself before the functionaries of calculative thinking arrive on the scene. The apophatic imagination steps in when we run up against our limits, on the margin between knowing and nonknowing, where these boundary figures—angels and demons, ghosts and specters, string theory and superpositions, dancing at the borders between reality and unreality, life and death—come into play. Kant himself, the master surveyor and cartographer of the regions of "pure reason," said that at the limits of reason, we stand before an "abyss." As Plato pointed out long ago, when we reach the outer limits of understanding, we have recourse to myths and images in which, he held, if what they say is not true, something like it is true. Myths are stories meant to be *read*, not dismissed by the demythologizers.

In radical apophatics, which is an exercise in radical reading, a radical hermeneutics, we treat these specters as messengers from the deep, the contact that has been made with things for which we have no adequate concept, *before* the operations of conceptual thinking have arrived on the scene or *after*, when thinking finds itself confounded. When the astrophysicists speak of "dark matter" and "dark energy" to describe something they know they do not know, when Einstein casts his complaint about quantum entanglement in hauntological terms ("spooky" actions), these tropes are not idle fancies but the stuff of a *poetics*, an exercise of *poiein*, of creative, inventive making and, in this case, the issue of supremely sophisticated, expertly trained intellectual imaginations.

I am not playing around with truth; rather, I am trying to say how things are, in truth, without disguise or attenuation—the cold truth, not warmed over. The point of the hauntological model is to prompt a spirited search for truth, not to promote a dispirited skepticism or despair about attaining it. We think of truth as a light, which presumes a prior unlit core, a prior concealment, *lethe*, Heidegger said, which is the apophatic. This implies the instability of our beliefs and practices, the limits of our models, and the revisability and contingency of the traditions we have inherited, all of which is enabling, not disabling, otherwise things would be rigidified, sedimented, solidified. This is true of everything, even of the most commonplace things, but it is never more true than when we explore the outer limits of our experience, even and especially when it comes to God. The spectrality of God is here taken as the paradigm of the apophatic, famously enunciated by Paul as seeing in a dull and cloudy mirror, enigmatically (1 Cor. 13:12). That enigmatic, paradigmatic status does not mean that God is a master name, a transcendental signifier, that arrests the play of signifiers. It means that it is a placeholder permitting us to keep the play in play. In hauntology, the God of the gaps does not mean the gaps God fills but the gaps God opens, the abyss, the groundless ground.

THE GHOST OF UNDECIDABILITY

My anatomy of the apophatic imagination requires some distinctions. I identify an *edifying apophatics* of piety and peace, of praise and adoration, of divine comfort and consolation—a classical *theologia negativa*, let us say an *angelic* hermeneutics. This I distinguish from a *radical apophatics*, a more anxious apophatics of the concealed depths, of nonknowing—let us say a spectral apophatics, a *devilish* hermeneutics. In an edifying apophatics, negation, concealment, and nonknowing are a form of *praise* for a light that exceeds knowledge, for being beyond being, for God beyond God. In a more restless and anxious apophatics, however, we are not praising anything. We are deprived of light, genuinely adrift, bedeviled by the shadows, spooked and menaced by demi-beings, unable to get as far as being.

But in hauntology, if you come across a distinction, deconstruct it; every distinction is haunted by the ghost of undecidability. My *premise* is that the one apophaticism is embedded in the other, that it is not possible to keep the one safe from the other. Edification is always already inwardly disturbed by a "dark night of the soul" (John of the Cross), by a latent anxiety, by something for which piety is unprepared. Just so, there is something honorable and earnest about coming to grips with anxiety, being "ready" for it (*Angstbereit*), as Heidegger says, dealing with finitude and mortality without disguise, adornment, or attenuation. So, just as piety and trust are haunted by anxiety and suspicion, there is also something liberating and uplifting in a genuine and lucid anxiety. When Camus laments the absurd, we applaud a heartfelt search for meaning. The forces of deconstruction (*Abbaung*) and edifying construction (*Erbauung*) communicate with each other. There is an *undecidability* between the two, a possible confusion, an indiscernibility, a spooky interaction, a spectral indeterminacy, a mutual contamination, each one an incognito for the other.

Just as undecidability does not permit peace to have the last word, neither does it award anxiety the final say. Just as there is a danger in always avoiding danger, the macho chest-thumping of a knight of the abyss is no less to be avoided. Just as I am not writing a book of peace and consolation, so I am not writing a manual for phallic heroes of the abyss. So, alongside Heidegger's advice to be "ready for anxiety," instead of fleeing it, we juxtapose Catherine Keller's counsel to love the deep ("tehomophilia") as our mother, *matrix*, not simply a destructive vortex. To Heideggerian facticity, we join Hannah Arendt's "natality," being grateful for being born. If undecidability is the rule in the realm of specters, that means that, at bottom, there is neither pure being nor pure nothingness, neither pure light nor pure dark, neither pure life nor pure death, neither pure peace nor pure war. We live in the distance between the two, a spectral distance, a twilight, a play of entangled possibilities and impossibilities. Undecidability implies irreducible *risk*, an ambiguous promise/threat. The deep is beautiful but dangerous. Loving the deep is risky business. So let us speak of a bracing love, a beautiful risk.

All this is important because the concealed depth of the apophatic is everywhere, in everything, for better *and* for worse, and it is the source of a radical ambiguity. It constitutes the restless heart of philosophy and theology, of art and science, of theory and practice, of mysticism and politics. The apophatic gives the ethical its binding power, the political its power to incite; it gives the beautiful its depth, the sublime its height; it gives knowledge its mysteries, evil its power to tempt, religion its lure, the everyday its profundity. Far from being the captive of monastic solitude, otherworldly ecstasy, or exotic experiences, the apophatic is the stuff of everyday life, found on every register, in every place. It is the uncommon in the most commonplace, the abyss opened by a cup of tea and a madeleine, putting the exceptional within the reach of everyone. It is also why we can be so violent. It gives war its fury, hatred its rage, self-seeking its passion. It is the best of us; it is the worst of us. It is the source of our wisdom and our foolishness, our faith and our incredulity, our hope and our despair.

If we understood the apophatic, we would understand everything, but then we would understand that it is less a matter of understanding it than of standing under its sway, exposed to its influence, open to its powers, all in an attempt to discern an indiscernible imperative, interpreting it, where interpretation goes all the way down. The apophatic imperative is not a terrifying inquisition, promising us heaven or threatening hell, but a quiet question, who are you? It asks not what you want to have but what you want to be. It is not a booming command but a silent voice prompting us to embrace the riskiness of life, to *make ourselves worthy of what is happening to us*, instead of constantly searching for what worth things are to us. The apophatics I advance here is an axiology of worthiness, of leading a life worthy of the name, *digne dicitur*, not searching for a good deal or staying out of trouble.

AN OUTLINE

My argument for the spectrality of God is both *historical* and *structural*, where the history embodies the structural point and the structure interprets the history. I trace the *historical spectralization* of being starting from the angelic imaginary, the privileged paradigm of immaterial being in medieval metaphysics and mystical theology, up to the dematerializing simulations and virtual realities of today. But in the process, I am also working out a *structural spectralization*, an argument that lays out the genetic constitution of the hauntological *discourse* proper to the apophatic imagination, which I call theopoetics, and with which I begin. The main body of the work is the historical analysis, which is divided into three parts: (1) the onto-theological imaginary: from medieval angelology to the German idealist ontology of the Spirit; (2) the hauntological imaginary: from idealist ontology to Derridean hauntology; and (3) the posthuman imaginary, the contemporary complex of cyber-spirits and what Karen Barad calls "quantum hauntology," where "the future belongs to ghosts."

Theopoetics is the discourse proper to the apophatic imagination, the discourse that does it no harm and makes no pretense to be a master discourse or dominating metanarrative. Theopoetics is an inflection of phenomenology with its own characteristic *epochē* and reduction. In the *epochē* we weaken theo*logy*, a work of *logos*, into theo*poetics*, a work of imaginative construction, by suspending the supernatural attitude and bracketing the supernatural signified. The *epochē* effects the shift into the theopoetic attitude, in which revelation is treated not as a supernatural intervention but a phenomenological invention or inbreaking of a new vision of life. In the theopoetic *reduction*, we weaken the Supreme Being of classical theology into the event that takes place in and under the name (of) "God," which is the proper subject matter of theopoetics, its *Sache selbst*. The reduction is twofold: an ontological reduction, which deprives the Supreme Being of separate subsistence, and a hauntological reduction, which deprives the resulting ground of being of its depth and discloses it as an event, as a spectral call, like a sound that wakes us in the middle of the night (chapter 1).

The Angelic Imaginary

If Kafka became famous by imagining what it would be like to be a cockroach, Thomas Aquinas famously imagined what it would be like to be an angel, a pure spirit, an immaterial being, beyond space and time, a *substantia separata*. Having to explain how the perfection of angelic being could still be limited was the occasion of his fundamental intuition into the unlimited being (*esse subsistens*) of God. Angels are the keystone of the architectonic of the *Summa Theologica*. Because the metaphysics of the Angelic Doctor—his medieval nickname—leads right up to the borders of mystical theology, I link Aquinas with Meister Eckhart. Eckhart, a mystical theologian who respected metaphysics, and Aquinas, a metaphysical theologian who respected the mystical, locate the summit of mysticism and metaphysics in immediate union with God, in living like the angels—but with a difference! Aquinas became a sainted icon of orthodoxy while Eckhart was condemned by the pope. His concealed Godhead (*Gottheit*) was not only a figure of divine consolation, but it was also dangerous. His *Gottheit*, veiled from both faith and reason, opened the door to the *Deus absconditus* of Luther, a highly unnerving Godhead, suggestive of an undecidability between God and Satan. That influenced Jacob Boehme, Hegel, and especially Schelling, through whom it made its way into masters of suspicion like Schopenhauer, Freud, and Nietzsche and into theologian Paul Tillich, where it ended up in upper Manhattan speaking in English, its venerable lineage in tow (chapter 2).

The Onto-Phenomenology of the Spirit

In medieval metaphysical theology, God is an eternal transcendent immaterial spirit (theism). German idealism is a *post-theistic* philosophy of Spirit (*Geist*), in which the Spirit abdicates its transcendence to dwell on earth, incarnated in nature and inspiring history. In Hegel we find both the first (ontological) reduction, a radical post-theism, where the death of the God of theism means its rebirth as Spirit in the world, the death of the Supreme Being and its rebirth as being itself, and also a version of theopoetics, where religion represents the Spirit in the form of an imaginative figure (*Vorstellung*), which it is the task of reason to explain. But, of course, as we know, Hegel explained too much, and while his post-theistic credentials are impeccable, his motives were deeply anti-apophatic. His "Concept" was too strong, and Hegel ended up doing injury to the apophatic, exorcising its spectral side in the name of the self-thinking thought (chapter 3).

So it fell to Schelling, a metaphysical voluntarist, the great maestro of what he called the "dark ground" (*der dunkle Grund*), to restore the rights of what he also dared to call the "barbarian principle." Schelling gets to the heart of the anxious apophatics of which I am in pursuit; a lot of what I am arguing is a rewiring of Schelling, with constant reference to deconstruction. Schelling held that God *becomes* God by overcoming the "dark ground," boldly located *in* the divine being itself—a nocturnal power humanity inherits from God, where it unleashes evil, so the ultimate reason for human evil is that there is something ungodly in God. Human freedom is the power to choose *evil*, not a pale privation but an ominous power inherent in being itself, which Heidegger labelled Schelling's "metaphysics of evil" (chapter 4). Alone among the philosophers, Schelling sought "the philosophical meaning of Satan" as a figure of the abyss in being, the *Abgrund*, the *Ungrund*. In his Satanology—a prism in which his metaphysics can be seen, the way angelology is the key to Aquinas's metaphysics—he audaciously argued Christ was free to cut a deal with the devil and become the Lord of creation independently of the Father (chapter 5)! Called to Berlin to put down the perils posed by Hegel and the "young Hegelians," Schelling announced the "positive" philosophy, the philosophy of the "unprethinkable," of the priority of "existence" over essence, of "facticity"—*that* the world is rather than not over *what* the world is. In these hugely influential lectures (Kierkegaard was in the audience), I single out a *tension* between an edifying Schelling who trusts in divine providence to contain the "dark ground" and a radical Schelling, who says that the fate of history and of the divine being itself are exposed to risk by the nocturnal powers (chapter 6). For Schelling, adopting the philosophy of freedom is itself a matter of freedom, not of thinking, an either/or, in which we decide who we want to be—free or a piece of fate, free or a mere pawn of the blind actuality of the "that" (chapter 7). I conclude by sorting out the "scarecrow Hegel" (Žižek), meaning the caricature of Hegel which Schelling inspired in Kierkegaard, from the genuine criticism Schelling made of Hegel (chapter 8).

From Ontology to Hauntology

Paul Tillich serves as the "boundary" between modernity and postmodernity, between classical theology and radical theology, between edifying and radical apophatics, between ontology and hauntology. To my tastes the most important theologian of the twentieth century, he made the dialectic between the demonic and the divine central. He considered that the challenge posed to theology by a modern world steeped in anxiety, doubt, and meaninglessness had been better addressed by the expressionist artists than by German theology. Drawing upon his two student dissertations on Schelling, Tillich launched a watershed investigation into religion as a matter not of doctrines and rites but of being seized by something of ultimate and unconditional concern, by the "ground of being" (the *Geist* in German idealism). After presenting Tillich's project of transcending theism (the ontological reduction) (chapter 9), I turn my attention to the practical and political import of his notion of the "unconditional" by exploring its downside, its implication in violence. By describing the battle pitched between the better angels of our nature and the "powers" and "principalities" of the world, we have all along been talking about politics, not just ontology. Radical theology is political theology; theopoetics demands theopraxis. The apophatic is the excess in ethics and politics, and it is responsible for its excesses, for better *and* for worse (chapter 10).

The "reduction" of ontology to a hauntology of a groundless ground is carried out by allowing Tillich, my favorite official theologian, to be haunted by Derrida, my favorite unofficial theologian, a slightly atheistic a-theologian. I pit Tillich against a radical Tillich by *weakening* or *spooking* the ground of being by bringing it in contact with Derrida's unconditional *without* being, "without sovereignty," without the power of being to back it up. The hauntologic of the specter is that it neither is nor is not, that it does not simply exist but cannot be simply dismissed. That is the spectrality of the *sans*, which elicits the dynamics of an unconditional faith—a *foi* not to be confused with propositional beliefs (*croyance*)—by striking something out but in such a way that the thing crossed out is still legible, *sous rature*. For Derrida, the Spirit, no longer an ontological ground of being, hauntologically reduced to an "event," is a spectral *call* or *imperative*. In Hegel the apophatic is rationalized, in Schelling and Tillich it is valorized and protected from the withering light of reason, but all three proceed on onto-theological grounds, be they intellectualistic (Hegel), voluntaristic (Schelling), or existential (Tillich). While theology has become theopoetics (interpreting a *Vorstellung*, myth, or symbol), what is still required is the spectralization (chapter 11). In deconstruction, the devil is in the dissemination, where we twist free of the classical axiom of the infinite depth, inexhaustibility, and assured destination of the Spirit in favor of drift, dissemination, and *destinerrance*. In deconstruction, we relieve the apophatic (the "concealed depths") of any suggestion of esoteric knowledge, onto-theological foundationalism, or religious edification (chapter 12).

Cyber-Spirits and Quantum Hauntology

That brings us to the hauntological today, when "technology increases greatly the power of ghosts," when "the future belongs to ghosts." Beyond the postmodern, the greater challenge today is the specter of the "posthuman," when we wonder whether we have *ever been human*. This I address by asking whether you would rather be a cyborg, a posthuman, or an angel, which is a riff on a famous line from Donna Haraway. Does contemporary AI, which flirts with the idea of transcending biology itself, suffer from angel envy? Is it the ancient desire to live like the angels? The analogy with the angels of classical theology is uncanny—does AI mean angelic or artificial intelligence? Is the "immortality of the soul" a problem to be solved by uploading? Are biological bodies replaced rather than resurrected? Is this the end of theology? Will it turn out that we cannot be theological without a body? In addition, just as the distinction between the human and nonhuman is being unsettled in AI, the spooky findings of quantum physics are unsettling the fundamental distinction between matter and spirit upon which theology has always relied. The uncanny thing in "quantum hauntology" (Karen Barad) is that it is not spirit that is being spooked but matter. If God is dead, a funny thing happened on the way to the funeral; it is not God who was buried but cold, dead, inert matter (chapter 13).

To bring this exploration of the apophatic imagination to a head, I conjure up the spookiest specter, the most apophatic prospect of all, an *inhumanism* (Lyotard) beyond even posthumanism. The unimaginable immensity of the universe, shrinking the earth to a tiny fleeting sliver of cosmic stuff, has reduced us poor existing individuals to even less. Now for the bad news. The universe is out to kill us. The physicists tell us that this vast universe is expanding at an increasing rate of acceleration headlong into oblivion. This turns Leibniz's question on its head: "Why will there be nothing at all, rather than something?" Facing star death and entropic dissipation, the end of all the theological eschatologies and philosophical teleologies, in the final "age of the world," the "dark ground" triumphs over the light (Schelling) and nonbeing triumphs over being (Tillich), representing the victory of dissemination itself (Derrida). That in which we live and move and have our being will end up as nothing at all. Is that the unknown God, the ultimate apophasis? Is cosmology a ruinology (chapter 14)?

Since the prospect of oblivion is a cheerless note on which to conclude, I turn instead to joy, a more austere joy in a "mortal God"—a thought unconventional, even unthinkable, to classical theology. Here, where mortality does not refute panentheism but redefines it, God is taken not in the ontological terms of unconditional being but in the "axiological" terms of what is *worthy* of being unconditionally affirmed, while we are tasked, in turn, with making ourselves worthy of what is happening to us. In affirming a "world without why," joyfully, unconditionally, untethered from teleological and eschatological conditions, we see the workings of the undecidability, the permeability, of the two apophaticisms. Firm in our affirmation of the world, calm and clearheaded about finitude and mortality, we do not try to flood the nocturnal powers with light. Instead, we embrace the rhythms of life/death, the seasons of the cosmos, with a reverence for their majesty, even a prayerfulness, which differs from the white-on-white mythology of the mystics' simpler angelic imaginary. Ruinology issues in axiology (chapter 15).

In the conclusion, I ask why we worry about God at all if God too is mortal. After all, in speaking of God theopoetically, cosmopoetically, hauntologically, and axiologically, it is clear that I do not think God is some superbeing somewhere, a Supernatural Somebody who can Save us. But I also think this desire to personify God, the theopoetic trope, springs from sources deep in our imaginary. I chose the name (of) "God" because I had no choice; it chose me first. It serves not as a master name but a placeholder, a *focus imaginarius* of the apophatic imaginary, an incognito in which I think I hear the heartbeat of the world. If I knew all the languages in the world, I could make a list of all such names. Perhaps the coming posthumans will look back upon this word with smiling condescension, as we do on the four humors, and "God," drained of its poetic power to galvanize a form of life, will have given way. What then?

Then the spectrality of God will mean that God has become a holy ghost of the past.

Then the apophatic imagination, ever groping for the ungraspable, will move on to the unimaginable immensity of the universe itself, including the spooky thought that it all ends in naught.

Then the name (of) "God" will have been a transient sonic effect of the ancient supersonic harmonies of the spheres when, for a while, in a remote corner of the cosmos, there could be heard a great doxology to the glory of the world, however it was in the beginning, however eerie its end, world without why, Amen.

ONE

THEOPOETICS
A Phenomenological Genesis

IN ORDER TO DO THE apophatic no harm, we require a discourse proper to the apophatic imagination, one that does not purport to be a master discourse or in any way to dominate it and probe its depths. To that end, theo*logy*, a work of *logos*, must be weakened into theo*poetics*, a work of imaginative construction. As a methodology, theopoetics represents an inflection of phenomenology. Accordingly, it has its own characteristic *epochē* and reduction, the combined effect of which, driven by an apophatic reserve, is to weaken the Supreme Being of classical theology into the event that takes place in and under the name (of) "God." That event is its proper subject matter. By suspending the supernatural attitude and bracketing the supernatural signified, the theopoetic *epochē* effects the shift into the theopoetic attitude and gains admittance to the matter itself (*die Sache selbst*) of theology, which is the poetics. Thereafter revelation is taken not as a product of a supernatural intervention but of a phenomenological invention in the sense of an inbreaking phenomenological vision.

The *reduction* is a twofold process of weakening or attenuation. The *ontological* reduction leads beings back (*reducere*) into their Being, depriving God of the eminence and subsistent independence of the Supreme Being and relocating God on and as the ground of Being. The *hauntological* reduction deprives the ground of Being of its ontological depth and prestige and redescribes it as the event that takes place in and under the name (of) "God," as a desubstantialized specter that troubles our spirit—a call that solicits us in unsettling ways, like a sound waking us in the middle of the night, which sets the apophatic imagination in motion.

THE THEOPOETIC *EPOCHĒ*

Theopoetics begins by suspending the supernatural attitude. Just as theopoetics does not ask nonbelievers to believe in angels and demons but rather to suspend their disbelief (naturalism), it is, at the same time, asking believers to suspend their belief (supernaturalism). This represents an *epochē* in the Husserlian sense, one that gains entry to the discursive space in which the apophatic imagination is in play, which I call theopoetics, where the figures and the narratives of revelation are protected from being believed or disbelieved, each of which is injurious.

Theology, as it is classically conceived, which I call "strong theology," is a logic, a coherent body of concepts, propositions, and arguments that serve to clarify, as far as possible, a supernatural revelation considered in principle mysterious and beyond the reach of natural reason. Theopoetics, which I like to call "weak theology,"[1] is a poetics, a loose coalition of discursive resources—paradoxes and parables; metaphors and metonyms; striking sayings and memorable stories; songs and prayers; homilies and letters; figures and images; semantic detours, deflections, and indirections; and hyperboles and ellipses—all of which, collectively, seek to evoke the force of what is going on in the name (of) "God."

Theopoetics represents a reinterpretation of theology that relieves theology of its supernaturalism and thereby allows it to speak in its proper voice, adopt its proper discursive mode, and find its proper truth. In theopoetics, the classical distinction between the natural light of reason and the supernatural light of revelation is reinterpreted as a distinction between a prosaic discourse and a poetic one. In theopoetics, revelation is beyond the reach of reason, not because it enjoys the benefit of an intervention into natural human affairs on the part of a supernatural being but because it represents a shocking poetic insight or gripping poetic revelation unavailable to the concepts, propositions, and arguments of logical thought.

In theopoetics, as it is *classically* conceived, the world is a poem of which God is the poet, which we find in Schelling's aesthetic idealism. In theopoetics as it is conceived here, classical theopoetics gives way to a more *radical* theopoetics, which suspends the operations of the metaphysical theology and treats both God and the world as poems. Here the texts and songs, and the prayers and practices, of the several historical religious communities are the work of theopoets, providing the discursive resources in which figures like "God" and "creation" come to words.

In the language of phenomenology, a theopoetics is made possible by an *epochē*, which *suspends* the supernatural *attitude* in order to allow the theopoetic attitude to come into play, which *brackets* the supernatural *signified* and allows the properly theopoetic phenomenon to make an appearance. This suspension of supernaturalism in theology frees up the matter itself (*die Sache selbst*) of theology, which is the poetics. But this also requires the suspension of the natural attitude, which is reductionistic, reducing theopoetic phenomena to subjective fantasies. Naturalism is a hermeneutic misunderstanding, a failure to know how to read theological texts and understand theological discourse. Both naturalism and supernaturalism block the appearance of the properly theopoetic domain.

A poetics is the unique discourse that brings to words the lived experience of the call by which we are addressed in the narratives and songs, and in the figures and forms, of theology's founding texts. Theopoetics follows their lines of force, allowing these images and narratives to speak for themselves and from themselves, to stand on their own feet and enjoy their own authority. It releases them from the armature of the supernaturalist assumptions in which they are encased and by which they are mystified and distorted and protects them from the attacks of naturalism, by which they are misunderstood. It releases the power proper to these images and narratives, which is neither naturalistic nor magical nor supernatural but strictly, rigorously theopoetic. A poetics exerts the powerless power of a story or saying that cuts through prosaic life and leaves us shaken, disturbed, and solicited, having revealed to us an alternate way to live. Relieved of the misunderstanding, deprived of the magic, their supernatural credentials revoked and their theological backup weakened, these images are forced back upon themselves. They are reduced to speaking on their own behalf—as the image of a crucified body, say, where a shocking forgiveness triumphs over the brutal power of the executioner. Images like this are not logically verified but existentially witnessed to; they are not logically falsified, but they can die off, become moribund, if and when they lose their grip on us.

In speaking of theology's "founding" texts, I am referring to the first-order and prereflective theopoetics characteristic of a text like the New Testament, which constitutes a primal, originary archipoetics around which a subsequent tradition is consolidated. This is distinguished from the second-order theopoetics, which *reflects* upon the founding texts and requires the cautious and circumspect use of language to examine, explain, and protect the archipoetics. As a reflective, explicative discourse, theopoetics is a hermeneutics, which J. J. Rambach long ago called the *subtilitas intelligendi*—having the right touch in reading a text, a light touch that does no injury to its subject matter.[2] This distinction is analogous to the distinction between poetry and poetics.

In the New Testament, Jesus is a poet, not a theologian. If we press Jesus for his theology, for what he says about God, we get mustard seeds, not metaphysics. He does not speak so much of God as of the Kingdom of God, and he does not speak directly about the Kingdom of God but of prodigal sons, treasures hidden in the field, and weddings feasts. The sayings of Jesus systematically *deflect* us from God to the most ordinary things of daily life, which have been given theopoetic force, entered into theopoetic space and time. In the kingdom sayings and the parables, the most common material objects are charged with a deeper significance; they have subjunctive power, evoking how the world *would* look *were* God's rule to come about. They "reveal" another "world," but this does not mean they disclose another physical (or metaphysical) location—that is, the misunderstanding, the reification, the supernaturalist mystification—but that they open another realm of meaning and significance. Think of how coming upon a family keepsake, like the old pipe smoked by one's father, now long dead, opens up the "world" of our childhood, which comes flooding over us, or the way a painting of a haystack by Van Gogh opens up the "world" of rural life. Accordingly, while theopoetics is a discursive operation, it is a paralogical one, inasmuch as it is being pressured to put into propositions a sphere of experience that precedes propositions. The stress this paradoxical situation puts on prosaic thinking and speaking, the distress it causes, is called a poetics.

If the Kingdom of God is a poem of which Jesus is the poet, it is misunderstood if it is viewed in terms of prosaic space and time—as a description of a distant place or the prediction of a coming state of affairs. The coming year of Jubilee that Jesus announces is the fiftieth year, the year that follows seven times seven, a Sabbath of Sabbaths. But nobody is counting. This is not a calculation. As simple as it is, it could never be counted by a computer. This year does not occur in calendar time but in theopoetic time. The *truth* of the kingdom Jesus announces is not refuted by the fact that it has been two thousand years and counting and it still has not arrived. It is not a prediction; it is a prayer. May your kingdom come. It is not an existence; it is an insistence, in the optative. You are to be the salt of the earth; you are the one God has been waiting for to make it happen! It is a hope, a sigh, a dream for a world in which God rules, not the powers that be, not the *imperium Romanum*, and in which the peace of God reigns, not the *pax Romana*. It does not chronologically forecast a future event but happens kairologically, episodically, whenever and wherever its call is answered. It is verified every time an offense is forgiven, the hungry are fed, and the afflicted are comforted; it is falsified every time mercy is withheld, like separating the children of illegal immigrants from their parents.

Theopoetics describes a sphere where the rules governing the prosaic world of space and time are suspended and the impossible is possible, a sphere that does not exist but insists.[3] We suspend the existence of the supernatural realm in order to expose ourselves to the insistence of these stories, the event to which they give words, which are read for what they have to say. Here we are invited to enter a world where offence is greeted with forgiveness, hatred with love, and suffering with compassion—an impossible and topsy-turvy world where things appear under their opposite, *sub contraria specie*, as Luther said, where the first are last and the last are first. Here there are no guarantees that we will win in the end or be rewarded in another world for our troubles. By removing all such misunderstandings, theopoetics releases the *truth* of these figures and stories, giving them their head, allowing them their proper force, and leading them back (*reducere*) into their proper element. We release them from reification and mystification by suspending the transcendental-supernatural signified, some authoritative being or metaphysical authority behind the scenes pulling all the strings. Searching for such a supernatural signified is like looking for the real Hamlet who lies concealed behind the texts in order to settle the interpretation of the text authoritatively. The powerless power of these texts means they are not backed up by a sovereign power who has passed them along by way of supernatural messengers. All such transcendental supports have been suspended. Lord, when did we see you hungry and give you to eat? Period! No Son of Man coming to separate the sheep from the goats. No hidden reward for doing what mercy requires of itself, without the threats. Just the works of mercy, no mercenaries of celestial goods.[4]

None of this is said as an assault upon theology. On the contrary, theopoetics is the only way to make theology worthy of the event that happens to it.[5] Theology is not about making propositional claims but about being claimed, not about proposing but about being exposed to something that is beyond the reach of propositions. Every attempt to contract this discourse into a fixed doctrine, to draw up a canon of orthodox and heterodox propositions, does injury to theology. Far from a modernist critique of theology, theopoetics is a postmodern or postcritical attempt to protect the truth of theological thinking. We can experience the force of the "good news" announced in the New Testament only if we understand that "good news" is not a journalistic but a theo-literary genre, a unique and powerful form of *literature*. Whenever it is taken as a historical, evidence-based report of supernatural episodes, like the preposterous proposal that Jesus is either a liar, mad, or God, it invites suspicion or even outright scorn, the familiar *odium theologiae*. The theopoetic reduction does not reduce theology to a subjectivistic projection with no purchase on reality; theopoetics effects a reduction to its truth. The subjectivist view of literature and religion alike is the fruit of the poisonous tree of modernist objectivism.

Like a work of art, a theopoetics is astir with truth, but not the representational truth of propositions. Poetic making (*poiesis*) does not mean merely "making things up"; it is a primal founding that gives creative form or figure to something *not* of our own making. It comes in response to something inbreaking, incoming, revelatory, world reforming, and self-transforming, something that does not yield to the prosaic form of propositions and the standards of representational truth. On this point, *pace* Luther, theopoetics stands with Aristotle: not the Aristotle who helped put the word *theologia* on the map—a "pagan" word signifying the science (*episteme*) of the highest being (*theos*)—but the Aristotle who claimed that being and truth are said in many ways. For the truth of particular facts of the matter, we turn to history, but for truths of a more universal sort, we turn to the poet. That we locate novels in the "fiction" section of the library says nothing against their truth. Theopoetics also makes its own what Aristotle said of ethics, that it has a rigor of its own—a *subtilitas intelligendi*—which is not to be confused with the exactness we find in mathematics.

In order to identify Jesus the poet and disburden him of all the supernaturalist baggage, let us refer to him by his Aramaic name, Yeshua. Beyond being a poet, Yeshua very quickly became himself a poem. After they killed him, Yeshua, a first-century Aramaic-speaking preacher, healer, exorcist, and teller of parables, became himself a parable, a figure, an *icon* of God. The particular body of this particular first-century Galilean man became an iconic body, like the two bodies of the king: this gout-ridden, unpleasant, and miserably unmajestic man and His Royal Majesty,[6] in which we catch sight of God, of what is going on in the name (of) "God." The theopoetic reduction is not a reductionist attempt to dismiss the Incarnation, to replace the Christ of Christian faith with Yeshua, who is all but lost in the fog of ancient history. It is not an attack upon the Incarnation but a more persuasive rendering of it. Yeshua becomes the Christ, but without the supernaturalism, without the mystification, without an unbelievable mostly Neoplatonic metaphysical theology that has the impossible task of negotiating between this world and another one, between matter and spirit, between the human nature and the divine one, and other metaphysical conundrums. Instead of theology from above, where an Eternal Logos comes down to earth, the Incarnation is redescribed from below, as the way a historical community *elevates the real spatiotemporal body of Yeshua into theopoetic space and time*, where he becomes the Christ, an icon of the event that is harbored in the name (of) "God." The Christ is a theopoetic phenomenon.

When Jesus "ascended into heaven," that does not mean he attained orbital altitude, which is—if, as the councils want to maintain against the Docetists, the *resurrected* body is a *real* body[7]—the inconvenient but unavoidable implication of replacing first-century with twenty-first-century cosmology. It means, instead, that Jesus was elevated into theopoetic space, where, over and above the body of flesh and blood that occupied a bit of space and time in ancient Galilee, he became an iconic body. They killed him, but he would not stay dead.[8] They could kill the man but not the poem. He lives on in and as the "dangerous memory"[9] of his unjust suffering, which condemns the injustice of the world, and he lives on in and as the promise of what the world *would look like* if the parables came true. The Kingdom of God occurs in the subjunctive. This is accomplished by way of a text that became part not only of world literature but also of the living and ongoing community that both produced this text and gathered around it, thereby preserving his memory and his hopes, without which Yeshua, son of Miriam, would have disappeared entirely from the memory of the world.

When Paul speaks of the *logos* of the cross (*logos tou staurou*) (1 Cor. 1:18), this *logos* is not a theo*logical concept* but a prelogical, paralogical, theo*poetic message*, a transforming word about the life-transforming power of the image of the unjust death of Jesus on the cross. This *logos* has all the irony and paradoxicality of a theopoetics—a God who, against all ancient expectations, is executed by his enemies. In the face of a Greek intelligentsia who looked with scorn upon the saints at Corinth, Paul offered a vision of a topsy-turvy world in which the foolishness of the cross is wiser than the wisdom of the world and the weakness of God is greater than human strength.[10] This is not a supernatural revelation but a theopoetic one, a startling, striking, and life-changing unveiling of another way to be, a vision of an alternative to the ways of the "world," which is ruled by the "powers and principalities." Once again, the powers and principalities are to be construed theopoetically, not as metaphysical-theological demons but as figures of the demonic, of structural evil, of the powers that be, which are, alas, always with us, which is the reason the poor are always with us.

Finally, in speaking of a theopoetics, I do not mean a *supplementary* rhetoric or poetry that *ornaments* or *illustrates* a prior theological concept, proposition, or argument.[11] On the contrary, the theopoetics is a primal discourse, a founding act, an architheology; it attempts to give words to the event by which it is called into being *in the first place*. The theopoetics—the constellation of figures and forms, narratives and sayings—is the way the matter, the substance, the *Sache*, comes to words *to begin with*. Theopoetics precedes, founds, and provides the prolegomenon to any possible future theology by supplying it with its subject matter. Any possible theo*logy* purporting to offer a logic would be at best a secondary quasi-conceptual clarification of the founding images, giving the faithful inside the community a certain clarity but with little or no purchase outside the community. Epistemologically, absent the theopoetic reduction, theology risks sounding like the technology required to *really* fire up the starship *Enterprise* or to *really* beam Scottie up, speculated about in a panel discussion at a *Star Trek* convention. The substantive content, the *Sache* of theology, its truth, can make itself understood more widely, outside the community, only by way of the theopoetic reduction, just the way we try to understand the literature and languages, the lifeworld, of other cultures. The theological distinction between a "general revelation" and a "special revelation" (always ours!) is reinterpreted in theopoetics as a distinction between nature and culture, which are the respective subject matters of a cosmopoetics and a theopoetics. There are as many special revelations—theologies of culture—as there are cultures. There is never a theology that is *not* a theology of culture.

THE ONTOLOGICAL REDUCTION

In the genesis of the theopoetic imaginary, the *epochē*, the suspension of the supernatural *attitude,* opens up the theopoetic field. The next step is the *reduction* of a strong theology of the Supreme Being to a weak theology of the event. In Husserl, an *epochē* is executed on the noetic (or subjective) side of the noesis-noema correlation as "suspending" the natural (transcendent) *attitude* and adopting a properly phenomenological (transcendental) attitude. The result on the noematic or objective side is that the transcendent object is "bracketed," and the phenomenological object comes into view as a phenomenon. Proceeding on the basis of the *epochē*, a *reduction*, which concerns not the subjective attitude but the constitution of the object, next traces or "leads back" (*re + ducere*) the objective structure to the transcendental subject in which it is constituted. In Heidegger, whose lead we are following here, the phenomenological reduction was shifted from the Husserlian domain of consciousness to that of Being, to the *Sein* of *Bewusstsein*.[12] For Heidegger, the reduction does not turn on an epistemic difference—the noetic-noematic (subjective-objective) distinction, which Heidegger rejects because of its Cartesian baggage—but on what he called the "ontological difference," which reflects the Aristotelian standpoint he is restoring. For him, reduction means leading beings back into their Being.

The *theopoetic* reduction I am proposing here, which turns on the theological distinction between God and the world, means the reduction of the being of God as Supreme Being to Being itself. This reduction deprives the Supreme Being of its eminence and independent subsistence as the first among beings on the plane of beings and reimagines God on and as the ground of

Being. Without employing the language of phenomenology, this "reduction" is exemplarily carried out in theology by Tillich (and by the German idealists before Tillich, from whom he inherited it), but the formal operation of the reduction itself is set out with methodological rigor in Heidegger, who had worked closely with Husserl himself. While tracking the fortunes of the ontological difference in Heidegger's work provides a valuable insight into the much-debated development of his thought, it also articulates the logic of a post-theistic theology, of what we call nowadays "panentheism," which is my interest here.

But beyond the ontological reduction found in Heidegger and Tillich, the theopoetic reduction requires a second step, which I describe as "the hauntological reduction," using Derrida's famous trope. My point is to show that and how the ontological difference, under the pressure of the apophatic, must yield to the hauntological difference. My point is also to show that and how theopoetics is the *spectralization* of the ontological difference. It should not go unnoticed that even in the later Heidegger himself, the word "ontological" was weakened and displaced, as was its near kin "onto-theo-logical," both coined in modernity and consigned by him to the "history of metaphysics." Heidegger eventually pushes past the "ontological difference" to more exotic and evocative formulations that, while certainly not hauntological in Derrida's sense, suggest the need to weaken the grip of ontology. If Tillich's theological purpose is to free the name of God from supernatural mystification, Heidegger's is to free it from onto-theological distortion.

The ontological difference, the distinction between Being (*Sein*) and beings or entities (*Seienden*), is central to *Being and Time*, but the expression itself does not appear there, having evidently been reserved for "Time and Being," the famous missing part,[13] and ultimately it is replaced by more radical and poetic formulations in the 1940s. Being and beings are distinct: Being is not a being. But they are not separate: Being is always the Being *of* beings, and beings are only beings only *in* their Being. They belong together in a circular relation. Being is not a first being, like God. To God, as to every being, there belongs a proper Being, in virtue of which it appears. Being does not differ from beings ontically, as one being differs from another, but ontologically, as the condition under which beings appear. Without Being, no beings appear; when beings do appear, there is no additional being to reckon with. Nor is Being the sum total of all beings. Being is the horizon or framework within which beings are encountered, the "clearing" (*Lichtung*) where the light breaks through, the "open" where beings are "freed" or "released" into appearance. We say of Being not that it "is" but that "there is" (*es gibt*) Being. Marking the difference between Being and beings puts a stress on language, which is oriented to beings and their ontical relationships. Anything we say about Being is prone to distortion, the way anything theologians say about God is prone to idolatry. This is a structural feature: Being of itself withdraws, and we are inclined to be preoccupied with beings. This "forgottenness" or "oblivion" (*Vergessenheit*) of Being's difference from beings is an ontological rather than a psychological point. But even while Being remains out of explicit cognizance, it is implicitly presupposed. Thinking Being makes the implicit explicit, re-cognizing it, recollecting it.

The ontological difference is *phenomenological*, concerned with how beings are given and with the ontological sense of truth (disclosedness), where phenomenology means letting (*legein*) things appear in their proper light (*phainomena*). It is *hermeneutical* since any given understanding of Being determines whether beings appear *as* this or that. It is *transcendental*, in both the Aristotelian sense, where Being crosses over all the regions of beings, and the Kantian sense, where Dasein's understanding of Being provides the condition under which phenomena (beings) are possible. In "What Is Metaphysics?" (1929), Heidegger exploits the paradoxes invited by his line of thinking.[14] Since Being is *not* a being, this *not* is no thing, hence "nothing," and Dasein's transcendence means to be stretched out into (the) Nothing. This essay aroused the ire of Rudolph Carnap, whose attack—along with the "Nazi affair"—forever scorched Heidegger's reputation in Anglo-America.

But Carnap was mistaken. Positivism proved to be epistemologically bankrupt while the ontological difference proved to be immensely fertile. The various disciplines, like physics or history, are organized under "basic concepts," understandings of the Being proper to their field, which are the subject of the "regional ontologies." The advances that take place *inside* the regional field without disturbing the prevailing framework (ontic changes) differ from more radical changes in the basic concepts themselves (ontological shifts). This distinction cuts across *all* disciplines— Luther in theology, Einstein in physics—and undercuts the old divide between the *Geisteswissenschaften* and the *Naturwissenschaften*.[15] Thomas Kuhn's theory of the revolutionary change occasioned by (ontological) "paradigm shifts" effectively confirmed Heidegger's analysis, one of the most important insights afforded by the ontological difference.

Beyond the "regional ontologies" lies the question of the meaning of Being as such, the subject of "fundamental ontology." This introduces a third thing: beings, their Being, and its "meaning," which is called the "upon which of a projection," a time function that fixes the parameters of the projection of the Being of beings. Hence, the "meaning of Being" is *time*. That meaning is an *ontological* rather than an *ontic* determination; it is a *transcendental* answer, not a transcendent one, like love or God.

Being and Time is unfinished, but Max Müller reports a first draft of "Time and Being," the most important missing part, which distinguishes *two* forms of the ontological difference: (1) "the '*transcendental*' or ontological difference in the narrow sense: the difference of beings from their beingness [*Seiendheit*, abstracted, universalized is-ness]" and (2) "the '*transcendentisch*' (*transcendenzhafte*) or ontological difference in the wider sense: the difference of beings *and* their beingness from Being itself."[16]

Heidegger's path of thought is a search for this third thing, the root of the ontological difference, variously named Being itself, or *Seyn* (with a *y*), or Being crossed out, or Being's "unconcealment." Interestingly, Müller further reports a third difference, "the '*transcendent*' or theological difference in the strict sense: the difference of God from beings, from beingness and from Being." The discourse on God takes place entirely outside the jurisdiction of the ontological difference in either sense, which Heidegger abandoned. What Heidegger would have meant by this is far from clear. He might have merely meant what Husserl meant—that God is simply transcendent to phenomenological experience—but I suspect he meant what Luther (Heidegger knew Luther well) or Karl Barth meant—that we should never mention "God" and "Being" in the same breath, for that is paganism, the vanity of the "theology of glory."

The published part of *Being and Time* is largely taken up with working out the difference between the Being of Dasein, whose essential being (*Wesen*) is "existence" (*Existenz*), and its ontical (*existentiell*) characteristics. That caused huge confusion. The French assumed that *was* the ontological distinction, and, after the war, Heidegger became the guru of French existentialism, remarkably enough, given the National Socialist affair. By 1940,[17] the ontological difference came to constitute the very metaphysics of which it is the task of thinking to overcome. Metaphysics reduces Being to some version of beingness—*eidos*, *ousia*, *actus*—but the difference as such, "infinitely different from Being,"[18] is left unthought. "Difference" is then detached from the expression, dropping the "ontological," in order to think the differing *itself*, the Dif-ference (*Unter-Schied*) or the *Austrag*. *Austrag*, ordinarily meaning the issue of a decision, literally translating the Greek *dia* + *phorein* and the Latin *dif* + *ferre*, to carry off, to carry out, describes the ontological circle. Being is carried over or "comes over" (to) beings (*Überkommnis*), thereby unconcealing (*ent-bergend*) beings in their Being, even as beings arrive or "come into" Being (*Ankunft*) while concealing Being. Being and beings "are borne away from and toward each other" (*auseinander-zueinander-tragen*).[19] Metaphysics is the issue of the *Austrag*, itself unthought. Thinking takes the "step back"—as opposed to Hegel's step up (*Aufhebung*)—into this unthought Dif-ference, which "sends" (*Geschick, schicken*) Being to beings, the "event" (*Ereignis*) that "gives" Being (*es gibt*) to beings.

Metaphysics is onto*theo*logical. In ontotheology, *logos* degenerates into *ratio* and *Grund*, an explanatory ground, calculative thinking. Being provides the common ground of beings (ontology) while the Supreme Being supplies the causal ground of other beings (theology). To the God who enters the ontotheological circle, the *causa sui*, "humanity can neither pray nor sacrifice," "neither fall to its knees in awe nor play music and dance." A "godless thinking" would be closer to "the truly divine God (*dem göttlichen Gott*) than onto-theologic would like to admit."[20] But this time we can be sure that the truly divine God is not the crucified God of Luther's theology of the cross because Heidegger's Christianity had become a thing of his prewar past. Now he means the God of the poets, Hölderlin's Greek divinities.

Whatever Heidegger meant, contemporary theologians have made much of this suggestive remark. A godless atheism closer to the truly divine God is, in particular, a felicitous introduction to the theology of Paul Tillich, whose post-theistic views were independently developed in dialogue with Schelling and German idealism—not with Heidegger, despite their deep similarity on the logic of being as a groundless ground. For Tillich, God is not a being (ontic) but Being itself, the inexhaustible (ontological) "ground of Being" from which beings emerge and into which they pass away. For him, the Supreme Being is a "half-blasphemous and mythological concept" to which "atheism is the right religious and theological reply."[21] The blasphemy is to reduce Being itself to a being; the mythology is to think God an inscrutable superperson with whom we negotiate about our salvation.

Atheism about the *causa sui* is not the end of theology but the beginning—of a radical post-theistic theology, of a pan*en*theistic God-in-all and all-in-God (the circularity between Being and beings described by Heidegger). For Tillich, the radicalization of theology is *ontologization,* and religion means entering that ontological force field. "God" as a first or supreme being is at best a "symbol" of the ground of being and at worst (if taken literally) myth and blasphemy.

In my view the great debate in twentieth-century theology is the divide between Tillich and Karl Barth. When Heidegger said that theology is a "positive" science,[22] he did not mean that it is an *empirical* study but that it is an *ontic* one. Theology is a *logos* about God as the Supreme Being and as such draws upon ontological sources, upon a prior understanding of the Being of the Supreme Being. Theology, the sometimes "queen of the sciences," is subject to "correction" by the ontological inquiry, which supplies the conditions under which its understanding of beings (God among them) is possible. That sets the stage for a debate about the range of the *ontological difference* and the status of the *theological difference,* of which three versions deserve notice:

- For Thomas Aquinas (see chapter 2), the theological difference *is* (or *absorbs*) the ontological difference because the Supreme Being, God, is *subsistent being itself* and creatures are God's really distinct and analogical similitudes. Aquinas, who antedates Suarez by three centuries, would have regarded the idea of "general metaphysics" as a mental fiction because its purported subject matter, "being in general" (*ens commune*) prior to God and creatures, is a purely mental construction, an *ens rationis,* a way of speaking (*modus significandi*), but not the way it is in the order of being (*modus essendi*), where God *is* Being itself subsisting in itself.
- For Tillich (chapter 9), contrariwise, the ontological difference *is* (or *absorbs*) the theological difference because the

name of God is a symbolic way to speak of being-itself or the ground of Being, but it is only one name, the symbol found in religion and theology. God is being-itself, but being-itself is not God.
- For Kierkegaard and Barth, contrary to both Aquinas and Tillich, the ontological difference is *abolished* by the theological difference! God neither absorbs nor is absorbed by the ontological difference. The transcendence of God breaks absolutely free from the ontological difference, which, like the analogy of being, is idolatry.

For Barth, who is closer to Paul's and Luther's *theologia crucis*, God is not contaminated by Being *at all*. His entire theology is a great howl of pain, a sustained *Nein* to the ontological difference, a *Nein* that echoes the scornful laughter of Kierkegaard's pseudonyms. God is other than beings and other than the Being of beings. God is wholly other, and every attempt to subordinate God's difference, the absolute transcendence of God, to Being is paganism. Theology is neither supplemented nor corrected by ontology but is a great *no* to the foolish wisdom of this world (ontology). For Barth, theology is the*ology*, where the emphasis falls on God, not on any human word. It is *God* who speaks, not the evangelists, not Aristotle, and not Being (*die Sprache spricht*). Bibliolatry, a literalist reading of the scriptures, forgets the theological difference between the human language of the scripture and God's inbreaking Word.

For Tillich, on the other hand, theology is the*ology*, the ground or logos of Being, and the ontological difference is the way *out of* idolatry and blasphemy. God is the ontological depths of being. Religion, too, undergoing a correspondingly profound ontological shift, means being seized by a matter (*Sache*) of ultimate concern (what Heidegger called *Sorge*).[23] Religion in the ordinary or narrow sense is an *ontic* and regional matter, which differs from and too often finds itself at odds with religion in its deeper *ontological* register. The "regional" hostilities between one religion and another, and between the religious and the secular, religion and art, religion and science, religion and politics, and even theology and philosophy themselves, should cease, arising as they do from a misunderstanding. Barth's neoorthodoxy faced backward, and Tillich faced forward, forging a religion for the emerging postmodern world. But what remained intact in Tillich was his residual German idealist metaphysics.

THE HAUNTOLOGICAL REDUCTION

For Derrida, the sheer "differential space" between signifiers (ring/king/sing), let us say the *grammatological difference*, is the most formal and irreducible difference. In his view, the ontological difference is one—binary—difference among many (dialectical, transcendental, sexual,[24] etc.); it is another "signified," one more effect produced by a rule-governed use of signifiers. Derrida nicknamed the grammatological difference by means of his famous "little *a*," *différance*, which can only be read and written, not spoken and heard. This signaled that even speaking is a kind of coded spacing. So, although *différance* of itself is prior to both empirical speaking and writing, he also called it "archi-writing"—an extraordinarily prescient decision in light of the role of the coded systems and "programs" (programmatology) of the current "information age" (chapter 13). The misspelling of *différance* is meant not to produce another effect of the linguistic system but to point to its constituting, quasi-transcendental condition. But, paradoxically, once it is used and repeated, it too joins the system as another constituted effect.[25] This strictly formal ineffability led to the charge (why not a congratulation?) that this is all negative theology, which is false. *Différance* is not mysticism but antiessentialism. *Différance* is not transcendent being but a quasi-transcendental condition of any coded system. *Différance* is not the truly divine God. "Being" and "God," like Husserl's "consciousness," are all constituted differential effects, not stable essences. They are all alike subject not to a pure transcendental (Husserlian) or ontological (Heideggerian) reduction but rather to a "grammatological reduction,"[26] as effects produced in neither consciousness nor Being but *différance*.[27] Just so, once constituted, these effects tend to sediment. The process of desedimentation is called *déconstruction*, a word Derrida coined as a French transcription of Heidegger's *Destruktion* of "the history of ontology" on the basis of the "ontological difference" (which for him becomes the "deconstruction" of the "metaphysics of presence" on the basis of *différance*).

The theological implication is not Christian Neoplatonic negative theology but a quasi-Jewish messianic without a Messiah, a structural expectancy, whatever the particular historical context. The effect of *différance* is to expose the contingency of any purportedly stable presence, which keeps the future open-ended, open to the limits of the possible, to the possibility of *the* impossible. Its effect is to attach an apophatic reserve, an irreducible nonknowing, to all our constructions. Of course, he was not saying that the pure messianic *really exists* somewhere or that it is an *ideal essence* to be pursued. It describes an inbuilt constitutive structural disturbance or provocation of whatever exists or purports to have a stable presence and exposes its historical construction—its contingency, contextuality, and endless recontextualizability—which keeps it in permanent unrest. The opposite of deconstruction is to arrest this unrest (which is what is truly destructive), which is the role played by "God" in classical ontotheology. The Messiah means the coming of what we cannot see coming, the "event" (*événement, l'à venir*) shattering the horizon of expectation. This suggests another possibility for "God," not as a "transcendental signifier" but as a placeholder, one of our best names for the possibility of the impossible itself, let us say a God "to come," which demands a faith (*foi*) in an event irreducible to any doctrinal belief (*croyance*). This is the stuff of what he called "religion without religion," found wherever the inbreaking possibility of the impossible may break out.

Like Tillich, this religion is not an ontic or regional structure because it is—again like Tillich—concerned with the "unconditional" ("undeconstructible") that can be found anywhere in the culture, in art or politics or everyday life. But unlike Tillich, the unconditional for Derrida is not an ontological category, a ground of being, but a hauntological one. The unconditional is a trace of a promise and a memory, of a call and a recall, of an "event," coming to us "without sovereignty," without any ontological ground to secure it or teleological warranty to ensure it. Any given (conditional, constructed) order is inwardly and structurally exposed to disturbance, made restless by the expectation and memory of something unconditional, just as Augustine's "restless heart" (*cor inquietum*) is made restless by an unconditional desire. In Tillich, the unconditional is an ontological ground that buoys up beings in their Being. In Derrida, the unconditional represents the weakening of Being into may-being, although, as we will see, this weakening does not reduce but intensifies *our responsibility*. It does not imply anemia or spineless indecision on our part. This is what Walter Benjamin calls a weak messianic force, where the Messiah cannot change the past but calls upon us to change the meaning of the past because *we* are the messianic generation, the ones the dead have been waiting for.[28]

In Derrida, the *ontological difference* between Being and beings has become the *hauntological difference* between being (*être*) and may-being (*peut-être*). The unconditional is not a *Geist* but a ghost, not a Spirit but a specter, the issue of the in/stability of *différance*, of the *memory* and the *promise* lodged in a complex legacy. Derrida describes an archireligion of the unconditional, without the support of the Spirit of German idealism (Tillich) or the Neoplatonic metaphysics of the One (negative theology). We are disturbed by an uncanny (*unheimlich*) visitor, an unanticipatable *tout autre*. This "unconditional without sovereignty" is neither a being nor Being itself, neither Being nor nothing, neither finite nor infinite. It does not exist; it insists, it calls for existence. The promise is a pure promise, exposed in all its powerless power, without a panentheistic ground, without theistic omnipotence to protect it. The promise promises nothing other than itself. The promise is nothing more than the open-endedness of what is being promised and recalled in constituted effects like "God," "justice," and "the gift," what is stirring within any word of elemental suggestiveness, wherever it is found, having passed through the prism, the discipline, of the apophatic. *Die Sprache verspricht*, language promises, and that promise, coming without ontotheological backup, cannot be immunized or protected from the threat. Some of the worst violence is committed in the name of justice, love, or God.

In sum, theopoetics arises from an *epochē* that suspends the supernatural attitude and from a twofold reduction: (1) The ontologization of the ontic (Tillich): God as the First Being yields to the ontological ground of being, demythologizing the Supreme Being; religion as an ontico-regional category yields to a matter of being seized by something of unconditional depth. (2) The deontologization of the ontological: the ontological ground of being is spectralized, yielding to an unconditional call without sovereign authority. Theopoetics is a radical apophatic discourse, a "weak" theology coming after the death of *both* an omnipotent theistic superbeing and a deep ground of being, a theology not of the Almighty but of the might-be, a theology of the event—of the dangerous, perhaps (Nietzsche). Theopoetics, the spectralization of the ontological difference, is the discourse proper to the apophatic imagination.

PART ONE

THE ONTOTHEOLOGICAL IMAGINARY

TWO

FROM AN EDIFYING TO AN ANXIOUS APOPHATICS
Aquinas, Eckhart, and Luther

TWO TROPICS OF NEGATIVITY

By triangulating Thomas Aquinas, Meister Eckhart, and Martin Luther, I construct an unconventional trio and venture where angels fear to tread. But I hope, in doing so, to gain an insight into the way an edifying apophatics is inhabited from within by an anxious apophatics. The radical in radical thinking implies, on the one hand, that we raise a theological question with no guarantee that we will get a theological answer (the old Enlightenment) and, on the other hand, that we raise a philosophical question with no guarantee that we will not get a theological answer (the new Enlightenment). This is all because of the undecidability that insinuates itself into limit questions. We have the right to ask any question, but we must be ready for any answer. We are prepared to admit that we will not know what to call the result. The radical means we risk running up against something radically unknowable, leaving us confounded. So, there is a quiescent apophaticism transcending doubt and uncertainty—the mystic as the man from whom God concealed nothing:[1] one of valorizing rest, which is perfectly achieved in death, and another inquiescent apophaticism, which is uneasy, perplexed, restless, and perfectly achieved in life.

There is no doubt that the medieval masters practiced a mysticism of piety, prayer, and praise,[2] one that was modeled after angelic unity with God. After all, Jesus said that in heaven we will live like angels (Matt 22:30). Accordingly, in medieval theology, metaphysics and mysticism fit hand in glove—or, better, like a head and its crown. According to the young Heidegger—it is hard to imagine, but in those days, he was a rising star in German Catholic philosophy—the complex and technical arguments of the medieval schoolmen are the "conceptual expression" of an "inner existence anchored in the primordial and transcendent relationship of the soul to God."[3] These schoolmen were not elbow-patched academics. They were members of religious orders, whose teaching day was punctuated by psalms and liturgy. Their academic discourse was kept afloat on a sea of piety, supported by the depths of the divine being, separating a medieval summa by an ocean of reverence from an eighteenth-century rationalist "system" of philosophy.

My claim is that there is an unnerving undecidability between the two apophaticisms and that it is not possible to insulate the piety of the one from the trouble created for it by the other.[4] Edification (*Erbauung*) is never safe from its disruptive deconstruction (*Abbauung*); the concealed depths are never far from the surface. I start with the first two angles in the triangle, Aquinas and Eckhart, where we must not be misled into thinking that Eckhart differs from Aquinas as mysticism differs from metaphysics. We must recognize both the metaphysical theology in Eckhart and the negative theology in Aquinas. The Meister in Eckhart's name is the scholastic *magister*, who a quarter of a century later held the same prestigious Dominican chair of theology at Paris as "Brother Thomas." While Aquinas did not share Eckhart's taste for conundrums, for which Eckhart was made to pay a price, he would have agreed with Eckhart that it is not what we say about God but what we do not say that is most true.[5] They were both elite professors of academic theology, but everything they taught was made to tremble from within by the mystical element by which it was inhabited, which left them wary of their own words.

Eckhart (1260–1327/29) advanced an ambitious metaphysical theological project that, because of his busy life as a preacher and high-ranking Dominican administrator, went largely unfinished; his fame rests upon his rhetorically explosive German sermons, replete with brilliant aphorisms, adventurous mystical-theological explorations, and experiments. Aquinas taught without interruption and in his short life (1225–74) left behind an imposing legacy of systematic theology—which put *scientia* before risky sayings and precision before poetic paradox—for which he became rightly famous. But at end of his life, as legend has it, he stopped writing and declared his theology to be like straw compared to what he had seen in mystical prayer. This suspicious Dominican dramatization,[6] likely aimed at promoting the cause for the canonization of a favorite son, was meant to assure the pope of the candidate's piety by insisting on the *theologia negativa* embedded in his metaphysical theology. In Aquinas, metaphysical theology and negative theology are held in an exquisite equilibrium intent on avoiding confusion, a kind of angelic lucidity that earned him his nickname. Eckhart had a more daring, dancing, and adventurous spirit, with a taste for paradox, for speaking *emphatice*, as he told his Inquisitors, which led him to say things that were speculatively risky in order to deliver their existential punch.

But beyond this difference of style, there is a substantive difference that explains the presence of Luther in this triangle. When Eckhart distinguished God (*Gott*) from the hidden Godhead (*Gottheit*), he unleashed a future that was no part of his intentions as an author. While Aquinas would become the preeminent doctor of the hierarchical church and the chosen spokesman for orthodoxy, Eckhart would be condemned as a spokesman for the unorthodox, the ecclesiastical outsiders, the anarchical, who bedevil the powers that be. As we will see here, Eckhart opened the door to an unnerving apophaticism, one that certainly made his Inquisitors nervous. I hope to show that there is a line that leads from Eckhart's hidden Godhead to Luther's *Deus absconditus* that would make anybody nervous! On that point, at least, the Inquisitors were not wrong about what was going on in Meister Eckhart.

AQUINAS: THE ANGELIC IMAGINARY

I like to think that Thomas Aquinas and Franz Kafka, as odd a couple as you can imagine, have something in common. The one became famous by imagining what it would be like to be embodied as a cockroach, the other by imagining what it would be like to be a disembodied angel. They represent paradigms of the two sides of the apophatic imagination, angelic and devilish, edifying and anguished, reassuring and unsettling. I would like to explore this unlikely pairing further one day, but in the present chapter I must confine myself to Aquinas, who produced a speculative metaphysical angelology, which we might describe today as an "imaginative variation" in the Husserlian sense—by conjuring up what it would be like to be a pure, disembodied intelligence, a project interestingly not dissimilar to AI research today (chapter 13). Angelology is medieval sacred sci-fi, the *sci-* meaning, of course, *scientia sacra*. As a faithful Dominican friar, innocent of modern biblical historical research, Aquinas simply accepted the *existence* of angels, as did everyone else. He bent his efforts on determining their *essence*, the makeup of their being, in a brilliant exercise of speculative inventiveness that holds the key to his entire metaphysical theology and tells us a great deal about the spirit of medieval theology. The medieval imaginary was filled with such spirits, angelic and demonic, but it is with the angelic imaginary in particular that we begin here in order to see how it would lead to the most unexpected results!

Beyond their literary function in the Bible as messengers (*angelos*) of God, angels pose a metaphysical problem: how such pure and immortal spirits could still be limited beings. Aquinas accepted the reality of angels on faith, and his philosophical argument that they exist is at best an argument "from convenience" (suitability).[7] But no matter. If there were no angels in his world, Aquinas would have had to make them up. By imagining what these (literary) creatures would actually *be*, Aquinas made two central metaphysical breakthroughs. The first concerns *esse*, and the other concerns *intelligere*, the "superintelligence" of the angels (a word I am borrowing from Nick Bostrom for reasons to be made plain later) (chapter 13).[8]

Aquinas provides a précis of his panoramic view of the great chain of being early on in his career in a brilliant little treatise entitled *De ente et essentia* (*On Being and Essence*), which sorts out what he means by *essentia*, *esse*, and *ens*.[9] It is no exaggeration to say that the keystone in his theological architecture is the metaphysical status of angels. The question is how angelic being, pure and everlasting, is still limited. The Franciscans maintained that angels must have some sort of materiality but of an incorruptible sort, like the fiery-airy substance of the "celestial bodies." Aquinas maintained that they were pure forms without matter and hence entirely immaterial. Their being is limited not by matter but by *form*! As creatures, they are not pure act. Their *esse* (act-of-existing) is received in a limited form of being (*modus essendi*, *forma essendi*), which is not a matter/form composite but a pure form. Here Aquinas's central insight is on full display. Pure act is pure *esse*. *Essentia*, be it material or immaterial, limits *esse* to a particular *form* of being. One then may say of God, alternately, either that God is *esse tantum, esse purum, esse infinitum*—purely, infinitely, and only *esse*—or, given the irresistible inclination to speak of *what* God is, that in God *essentia* is identical with *esse*. God's *esse* is unlimited because there is no separate *forma* or *essentia* to determine it. Form or essence confines or defines *esse*, which of itself, left to itself, is unlimited perfection. There is the whole thing in a simple formula, Aquinas's $e=mc^2$: the self-subsisting act-of-being as distinguished from limited entities whose *esse* is received. The language of act and potency here is not the best. Better to distinguish unlimited *esse* and limited *ens*, entities, Being and beings. Notice the sea change: "form" and "limit" are now *imperfections*, in contrast to the Greeks, for whom the *lack* of form is *me on*, imperfection, *apeiron*, indeterminacy and nonbeing.[10] Material beings are doubly limited—by matter, which exposes them to corruption, and by being created, being actualized by a separate act-of-existence (contingency). The angels are incorruptible but created. In angels, form is not limited by matter, but being is limited by form. The highest perfection is not found in being incorruptible but in the act-of-being itself.

Esse Is Not a Predicate but a Perfection

Like Kant, Aquinas would say that *esse*, the act-of-existence, is not a predicate. But the comparison ends there. *Esse* is a much *richer* notion than Kant's notion of existence as the mere *positing* of a thing, the *mere fact* of being there. In modernity (and this goes for modernist scholastics like the Spanish Jesuit Suarez) existence is reduced to the empty or *contentless* positing of some *essential content*. In the Kantian rendering, all the excellence lies on the side of essence, whose properties spell out the intelligible perfection, while existence is added on like an appendix, a literal afterthought, to posit that all this perfection is really there (a view that goes back to Avicenna, who treated existence as an accidental perfection of a substance). For Aquinas, *esse* is not a *predicate*, but it is a *perfection*. The act-of-being left to itself is unlimited perfection, while essence *limits* the perfection, restricts, constricts, and modulates the act-of-being to a specific form or mode (*modus essendi*). *Essentia* is a *negative principle*; it delimits and determines *esse*, which is a positive or active principle. This is a particularly striking point in the light of Schelling's "positive" philosophy and its critique of the philosophy of essence (Hegel) as "negative" philosophy, an issue we will revisit later (chapters 6–8). Essence is a determination and, in the famous dictum of Spinoza, *omnis determinatio est negatio*. The intuition of being the angels occasion is that perfection lies not in *form* or *essence* but in the *excellence* of *esse*, the unchecked upsurge of the *act-of-being*, which left to itself is infinite and all-encompassing, an infinite matrix in which we live and move and have our *being*.[11] *Esse* is not contentless; it is uncontainable excess. *Esse* is not the stasis of form—here is the debate with process theology—but the dynamic of pure act. *Esse* is not *lacking* in form but an unformed excellence *exceeding* form, *epekeina tes ousias* if *ousia* implies form. Notice that the language of potency and act, cut to fit the Aristotelian explanation of changing material things, is more of a hindrance, suggesting as it does some free-floating essence waiting to be actualized, like matter waiting for a form. Better to think in terms closer to Heidegger's "ontological difference," Being and beings, and hence to distinguish not potency and act but *esse* and *ens*, the act-of-being and the concrete entity that limits and receives *esse*.[12]

Intuition of Being

The extraconceptual, nonessential perfection of *esse* means it is given in what Jacques Maritain (a reader of Bergson) called an "intuition of being," of the upsurge of existence: *esse*, the "to-be"—which is not an inert fact but an act, an achievement, a triumph of being over nonbeing. This intuition can be occasioned by anything from a single blade of grass to the implacable presence of the universe at large. Without it the philosopher is condemned to merely talking "about" being with a "precarious and sterile knowledge, however freighted with erudition it may be," going "round and round the flame without ever going through it."[13] Metaphysics clarifies this intuition, conceptualizes what is given to us in a preconceptual, prescientific way that Aquinas called *scientia connaturalis*. This is a paradoxical task because concepts befit essences, answering the question, "What is it?" But existence is not an essence, not a what-it-is but a that-it-is. It is not unintelligible but intelligible with an intelligibility that exceeds essence, defies definition, extends beyond quiddity or what-ness to the sheer intelligibility of be-ing. *Esse* is not a blind fact, a mere *that*, a *factum brutum*. *Esse* is the correlate not of a concept but of an intellectual affirmation (judgment) that something is, exists, rather than not, belonging to an intelligibility of "another order." *Esse* signifies coming to ex-ist, *ex-sistere*, by standing outside its causes, *extra causas*, outside nothingness, *extra nihil*, as "the mysterious gushing forth of the act of existing."[14] The metaphysics does not *prove* this intuition; it is not the outcome of an argument. But without this intuition, the arguments are futile, weak, and completely contestable. The metaphysics *supports* the intuition by *elaborating* it, like an *intuitus quaerens intellectum*, raising its preontological verity to the level of ontology.

Critique of Aristotle

This puts Aquinas at odds with Aristotle. Aquinas defends a metaphysics of creation, and, while his is surely a Christian metaphysics, it is more broadly a monotheistic metaphysics, on this central point equally available to Jewish and Islamic theologians. In Aristotle, there is no act-of-being, not because Aristotle missed it but because the Greeks just did not have the problem of which *esse* is the solution. Instead of *creatio ex nihilo*, they taught the opposite, *ex nihilo nihil fit*. Like everyone else in the ancient world, including the book of Genesis and the early Christians,[15] they explained the origin of the world in terms of a creative power forming preexisting elements. For both Plato and Aristotle, form is the highest principle of being, while formlessness is the mark of imperfection and nonbeing (*me on*). What has definition is more perfect than the indefinite. The "infinite" is the imperfection of the indeterminate (*apeiron, tohu wa-bohu*), which is why Derrida speaks of two tropics of negativity. For both Aquinas and

Aristotle, to be is to be in act (*energeia, actus*), but for Aristotle, *pure act* meant *pure form*, while for Aquinas *pure act* meant *pure esse*; form would only determine *what* a thing is but not *that* it exists. For Aristotle, *that* the world is was never an issue. It just never comes up. Individual things come to be and pass away, but the world itself, what there is, is necessary and everlasting. The problem is *what* it is, which Aristotle, like Plato, took to mean of enduringly present form (*ousia*), which Heidegger called standing, steady presence (*stetige Anwesenheit*). Aristotle did not think in terms of "creatures" but of "substances" and their categories. Material substances are corruptible, but some substances are incorruptible, having no potential principle; they are pure act, pure form, pure intelligence. These he associated with what the poets call the gods, the immortals. For Aquinas, a Christian theologian living a millennium and a half later, the operative distinction is not between changing and unchanging substances but between "creatures" and their "creator." Created beings have been given existence (*esse*); their potential to exist (essence) has been actualized. The creator is the causal source of their existence, a moving or "efficient" cause, not only a final cause, as in Aristotle. God is pure act, not pure form, but pure *esse*, subsistent *esse*, existence itself, *ipsum esse*, subsisting through itself, *per se subsistens*, beyond any "form" of being.

Platonism: Ipsum Esse per se Subsistens

But if God is the unchecked upsurge of being itself, *ipsum esse*, pure being, only being, then is God the being of all of things, the being of beings? Is this pantheism? Panentheism? The source of this concern is not metaphysics but Aquinas's biblical faith. The problem is not merely metaphysical; it is also *theo*logical. Creation is something *somebody* does, and we are unique somebodies before a personal God, a father, a judge, the interlocutor of our prayers. This problem is resolved in the second half of the expression, *per se subsistens*. God is not only *ipsum esse* but *ens*, *subsistens*, being subsisting in and through itself (*per se*)—as opposed to being *in* another (*in alio*) or through another (*per aliud*). But here Aquinas proceeds with a caution of which Tillich, as we see in the following, appears to be oblivious. God is not "an" *ens*, "a" subsistent entity. That implies limitation, making God an individual in a genus, who shares being with other beings but differs from them because he enjoys the biggest share. To be sure, God is the *primum ens*, the first, highest, and supreme being, but *not* as if God is a *primum inter pares*. God's being is "incommunicably" its own, subsisting independently in itself, whether or not there is a world at all. But if God is incommunicably self-subsistent, is God at an infinite remove from the world? Are creatures deprived of real being or blocked from having being at all? If God is, it seems that creatures cannot be; if creatures are, then God must be something other than being, a point that is famously taken up by Eckhart in his Latin works (following).

As the great mid-twentieth-century commentators on Aquinas have shown, at this very crucial point, the move Aquinas makes is *Platonic*, not Aristotelian.[16] He calls upon Plato's theory of participation. What God is subsistently (*esse*) creatures are by *participation* (*ens*). God is that in which we live and move and have our being—in the Platonic sense. Now the more elemental ontological difference (*esse/ens*) is raised up into a more elaborated ontotheological difference—between *Esse subsistens* and *ens per participationem*. Participation means taking part in the divine being in the mode of a real likeness or similitude. The status of creatures is modeled after the relationship between the forms and sensible things in Plato. Creatures are finite, limited likeness of God's unlimited being. The Platonists are right—not right about sensible things, not right to say that the true tree is found in a supersensible form of which particular sensible trees are a likeness, but right about being itself, *ipsum esse*, which subsists of itself, of which finite things are concrete likenesses, particular participations. When it comes to the "transcendental" names, like being, the true, and the good, the Platonists are right.

Analogy

Then do creatures have being the way the image of the face in a mirror has being, not as a real face but only as an image? Again, this addresses a point of biblical piety, for a personal God counts every hair on our head, and the reality of each individual is special "before God" (*coram Deo*). Enter the theory of analogy, where being is said in many ways. To say that God is our rock is a metaphorical predication, but to say that God is wise or good is not a metaphor. God is wise, properly speaking (*proprie*); this is a transcendental predicate based upon the wisdom of finite things that we attribute to God analogically, in a higher way (*eminentiore modo*). We know that God is wise because Socrates is wise, *not* wise the way Socrates is wise, but in a higher way, of which Socrates is a finite image. Wisdom is not something that God *has* but what God *is*, and while we can see *that* this must be so, we cannot see *how*. The positive content of our knowledge of God as subsistent being itself is drawn from the finite beings all around us, whose reality is not in question (Rom. 1:19). We attribute this being to God analogically but properly, not merely by "attribution," the way we would say clean air is "healthy" not because the air is in good health but because it contributes to our health. God and the world have being in ways that are different but *proper* to themselves, the one subsistently, the other by limitation and participation.[17]

Negative Theology

Accordingly, in a very precise and delimited sense, Aquinas could make his own the venerable Platonic and Neoplatonic notion that God is "beyond being," *epekeina tes ousias*, by which he meant *supra ens*, beyond *ens*. This means, *pace* Tillich, that God is not a *particular* subsistent being (*ens*) but subsist*ent* being (*esse*).[18]

But God is not beyond *esse*, since *esse* is what God is subsistently. This not only permits but also requires negative theology. We may know *that* God is and *that* in God essence and *esse* are the same thing, but it is well beyond our capabilities to grasp *how*, to "see" it directly. We know more about what God is *not* than what God is. *Ipsum esse subsistens* does not yield a comprehensive grasp of God's being; it describes the whole God (*totum*), but not wholly (*non totaliter*). It is the *least limiting* way we have to speak of God's *unlimited* being.[19] We can show that certain things are true of God without "comprehending" them—getting our head around, "grasping" (*capere, greifen*) them round about (*com*). So to describe God as *ipsum esse per se subsistens* is not to have a *Begriff* in Hegel's sense; it is to have a concept that God is inconceivable. The legend his Dominican brothers came up with to advance the cause of his canonization has a *fundamentum in re* because a *theologia negativa* lies at the heart of his metaphysics and his piety.

The Ontological Argument

Aquinas holds that God's essence is existence itself without being tempted by Anselm's argument. Like Kant, but with a different understanding, he too thought that *esse* is not an (essential) predicate. But Aquinas thought it *would* be a valid argument if we had a direct intuition into the essence of God, which we do not. But then again, if we did have such an intuition, that would, in turn, eliminate the need for an *argument*. We would just *see* it. We do have an intuition of *being*, but our intuition is too weak (*debilis*), too imperfect, to extend to God, to an intuition that *God* is being. Our intuition of being is like someone who sees Peter coming off in the distance but cannot see that it is Peter. Our human intuition of being concludes with the claim that God is being itself, but it cannot start there. That claim is a discursive elaboration of the intuition.

Ratio et Intellectus

The angels can see that it is Peter. The ontological argument arises from angelicism, angel envy. Angels just intuitively "see"; they do not construct *arguments*. That might even serve as a defining feature of angels. That brings us to the second contribution angelology makes to Thomistic metaphysics. By imaginatively constructing a concept of angelic being as purely immaterial, as possessed of "superintelligence" (Bostrom), Aquinas was able to cast important light on *human* intelligence. Angels possess pure *intellectus*, the very intellectual intuition Aquinas and Kant alike say we are denied. Angels do not need to piece reality together by abstracting general concepts from sensible things, fitting these abstract concepts together into propositions and finally stringing the propositions out into arguments. That step-by-step (discursive) work is the mark of *ratio*, which arises from the *debilitas, ex debilitate intellectus*, from the weakness of the intellectuality of human reason, our "weak thought."[20] As purely immaterial beings, angels enjoy *instant perfect insight*, which might serve as a periphrasis for *intellectus*. As such, they simply "share" their thoughts with each other in a kind of mind-to-mind "instant communication" system, the way computers on the same network can exchange information, except that angels do not need computers and are faster and smarter than smartphones. They have no need to communicate thoughts through sensible signs, no need for any kind of semiotic system or language. I return to the link between angels and advanced information technologies later (chapter 13). Medieval sci-fi is closer to contemporary sci-fi than we think. AI comes in two versions, angelic and artificial.

Human reason does not altogether lack *intellectus*; it participates in it in a limited way. According to Pierre Rousselot,[21] the concepts, propositions, and arguments reason constructs are little "sparks" in us where *intellectus* is the fire. Reasoning step by step is a "substitute" or "remedy"[22] or, we are tempted to say, the "dangerous supplement" (Derrida) of *intellectus*. These sparks, what we call a "flash of intuition," are not merely cognitive but range over the whole of life, including moral intuition (*phronesis, prudentia*); scientific, logical, and artistic intuitions; background knowledge (Polanyi's "tacit" knowledge); and so on. So by this off-putting word *intellectualism*, Rousselot actually meant something very fetching, better described as intuition (Maritain), insight (Lonergan), a direct and simple awareness, an artful discernment, as distinguished from the laborious and error-prone argumentation of *ratio* (*logos*). So human intelligence (*ratio*) is a limited version of angelic (*intellectus*). *Ratio* is a *debilitas intellectus*, the weakest form of *intellectus*, "weak thought," centuries before Vattimo's *pensiero debole*. Maybe it is something about us Italians.

Rousselot disabuses us of the stereotypical image of the *Summa*. Rather than a sea of arguments that are too subtle by half, Aquinas's *quaestiones* are better approached with an aesthetic sensibility. Like logicians and mathematicians who take the "elegance" of an argument seriously, the architectonic, the "system" of the *Summa*, has a limpid elegance and beauty of its own which does service for the work of art, whose proper depth Aquinas himself held in "slight esteem."[23] Aquinas, Rousselot said, was a "poet who dreams and a scientist [*savant*] who proves," producing a "logical poem, better at charming someone who already believes than useful for controversy."[24] Rousselot comes very close to treating theology as theo*poetics*, to the "theopoetic reduction." Aquinas has a fundamentally different concept of reason than is found in modernity. For Kant, reason means a "faculty of principles," of subsuming concrete individuals under abstract rules of universal formalizability. For Aquinas, reason, which is our share in angelic and ultimately the divine intelligence, is a *capax dei*, and this because it is a capacity for being. Human reason is driven by an underlying intellectual *dynamism* (Rahner), a drive for intuitive understanding that is helped along the way by intermittent sparks or flashes of intuition. Reason is disturbed from within by its own dynamics, which orient it toward the vision of the divine being, representing an "ec-static" reason, as Schelling called it, a reason exposed to the excess of reason, touched by what exceeds reason.

This becomes clear in the other property of Thomistic *intellectus* singled out by Rousselot. Beyond its *intuitive* dynamics, *intellectus* is a *unitive* power, and consequently it is the seat of the *unio mystica*. The classical notion of truth as *adequatio*, he argues, obtains only in the lower register of *ratio*, where the soul achieves a weaker *intentional* unity with things—Aquinas had a theory of intentionality, not of modernist representationalism[25]—by way of a transparent mediating similitude (*species*) that aims the intellect at the thing (*res*) while respecting its distance (*extra mentem*). In its highest (or strongest) registers, however, this unity is immediate; *adequatio* gives way to *assimilatio*.[26] The will is the power of desiring unity and taking joy in its possession, but it is in the intellect that the unity is *formally achieved*.[27] The higher the level of knowledge, the greater the unity of knower and known. Knowledge is a way of becoming other, becoming one (*fieri unum*) with the other.[28] The *crown of this intellectualism*—and this is where the whole account is headed—is immediate unity with the divine being, which Aquinas defined as the "beatific *vision*,"[29] which we desire with a desire beyond desire.[30] Human intelligence is a dynamic for unity with God, beyond the likeness of concepts or propositions to the very substance of God's own being. *Then we will be like the angels*; we will *see* what the ontological argument claimed we already saw. The ontological argument is less wrong than precipitous. In this life, short of the beatific vision, the "crowning point" of the intellectual life involves intermittent moments of ecstatic or mystical experience.[31] Reason, in Aquinas, remains on guard against closing itself inside its own ratiocinations, always "open to the mystery," as Heidegger puts it. The next chapter explores how the distinction between *ratio* and *intellectus* is reconfigured in the German idealist distinction between (analytic) *Verstand* and (synthetic) *Vernunft* and is also reworked in Heidegger's distinction between calculative reason and *Denken*.

Rousselot confirms what was never in doubt, that Aquinas offers an edifying and angelic rather than an anguished apophaticism, that reason's *debilitas* is ordered to mystical light as to its crown. The genius of Rousselot is to have adroitly identified the mystical element in what looks like the dry bones of the *Summa*, but his analysis needs to radicalized, *weakened* still further, by being led (reduced) back to the phenomenological and theopoetic experiences he identified so well.[32]

MEISTER ECKHART: *GOTTHEIT* AND GOD

The opening for a more unprotected, bedeviling, anguished apophaticism is created in Meister Eckhart, who was of a different frame of mind than Brother Thomas.[33] He was also a "master" of scholastic discourse at the pinnacle of medieval academic success in Paris, and our interest in him today is centered on his German sermons. But the extant Latin writings tell us he was working out a sophisticated and daring metaphysical theology of his own. The mystic and the "Meister," the *Lebemeister* and the *Lesemeister*, the German sermons and the Latin treatises, fit together, and both are audacious.

God Is a Pure Nothing

If anything, Eckhart carried Dominican "intellectualism"—and therefore the angelic paradigm—further than the Angelic Doctor (Aquinas), arguing for the primacy of intellect not only over the will but also over *esse* itself. In the *Parisian Questions*, Eckhart defended the thesis of the "nothingness of the intellect."[34] Eckhart based this conclusion, in part, on Aristotle's *tabula rasa*,[35] where the soul must itself be free from admixture with the objects known; since being is what is known and the soul is in a way all beings, it follows that the intellect as intellect is free of being.[36] Aquinas would have rejected this formulation—he would simply call it *esse intentionale*—but not the underlying point. Eckhart goes on to say that *esse* is not only *outside* intellect but that it is *derived* from intellect: "I declare that it is not my present opinion that God understands because he exists, but rather that he exists because he understands."[37] This is said against his earlier view and that of Brother Thomas, for whom *intelligere* in God follows upon *ipsum esse subsistens*, in which every perfection is precontained. Here Eckhart is not drawing upon Aristotle but upon the Neoplatonic *Liber de causis* where being (*esse*) is what the creator creates while the creator is beyond being. When Eckhart says in the German sermons that God is a pure nothing, not even a little bit, he is actually reformulating more boldly a classical Christian Neoplatonic patristic teaching that the creator is beyond created being.

Esse est Deus

The challenge is that Eckhart also defended the opposite thesis. In the Prologue to his planned masterwork, the *Opus Tripartitum*, the foundational axiom is *esse est deus*,[38] which is, tellingly, the converse of Aquinas's *deus est suum esse*. The difference is that Aquinas is careful to conserve the *reality* of created *esse* while Eckhart stresses its utter *tenuousness and derivativeness*. Eckhart holds that God differs from creatures as being itself (*ipsum esse*) differs from this or that (*esse hoc aut hoc*), as whiteness itself differs from white things. God is the fulness and purity of being (*plenitudo esse, puritas essendi, purum esse*) while creatures are "absolutely nothing" (*nihil penitus*) and, in the German sermons, *ein reines Nichts*, not even a little bit. Eckhart meant they are absolutely nothing *of themselves*, that everything they have has been "lent" to them by God (*ab alio*), the way the air has light, which would disappear were the sun blocked, which is why he says *esse est Deus*, not the other way around. Creatures exist but not with their *own* act of being but with the being of God.[39] That position is either pan*en*theism or very close to it, God *in* all as their sustaining act-of-existence, as the soul sustains the body, as the sun sustains the heat in the air. This looks very much like the view struck by Schelling (chapters 5–6). For both Schelling and

Eckhart, without God's support, the world would vanish back into God, but God, like the sun blocked by a cloud, would be left standing; in a more radical view, they would be interdependent.

But how could he hold two contrary positions? Because they are the *same* position, the utter dependence of creatures upon God, in alternate if contrary formulations. We can see this in the ambiguity of the expression *puritas essendi*,[40] which can mean either purity *of* being, being subsisting purely (as it does for Aquinas and the *Opus Tripartitum*), or purity *from* being, without the admixture of being (as it does in Neoplatonism and the *Parisian Questions*). Eckhart has nothing invested in the language of being or nothingness; all his stock is invested in the relationship, in the transcendence of God and the utter dependence of creatures, in *either* formulation. If we treat the language of being as stable (univocal) and from that standpoint look up, then God is nothing (meaning *beyond* being, not below; being does not reach that far). If we take the language of God as stable and from that standpoint look down, then creatures are nothing (of themselves). Either standpoint does service to demonstrate the same point: the utter dependence of creatures on God, which is so complete that one without the other looks like nothing. The language we use about God is endlessly recontextualizable. Either way, language is used to *praise* God as the holy undecidability of the *puritas essendi*. It is all very radical, but the radicality is in the service of edification, a hymn sung by a heavenly choir of angels, and the life of piety that implies.[41]

Difference between Eckhart and Aquinas

The difference between these two sons of St. Dominic is twofold. First, Aquinas's use of Neoplatonism was filtered through a robustly realist, analogical Aristotelianism, while Eckhart's Aristotelianism was preponderantly Neoplatonic. Eckhart thought the hold that creatures had on existence was frail and fleeting, next to nothing, like an image in a mirror. Second, Aquinas's language is sober, careful, and scientific, and he distrusted the use of poetic language in science; for Eckhart, language is a plastic and poetic medium, capable of multiple transmutations and recontextualizations, and will never render a fixed result, on this point closer to Derrida.[42] Words are effective when they are deployed felicitously within a given framework, and—as the variety of frameworks he himself deployed illustrates—there is no one normative framework. Because God is *un*namable, God is *omni*namable and the scriptures are bottomlessly rereadable. As long as we inscribe a zone of absolute respect around the depths of God, any vocabulary—being itself or a pure nothing, the Latin language of the university or the German vernacular of the pulpit—can be worked to good ends. What interested Eckhart was the power of any given formulation to transform our lives. If you do not understand what I am saying, he told his hearers, do not trouble yourselves about it; just *be* this truth in your life and you will understand everything.[43] That is why he was a great preacher and, it is fair to say, without the German sermons, would have remained an obscure scholastic master. As it is, he is numbered not only among the mystics but also among the founding geniuses of the German language, where he teases, twists, and torments language to wring from the Gospel stories their meaning for our lives. I am speaking *emphatice*, he told the Inquisitors, a word we might translate today as "existentially."[44] The truths of our faith are existential imperatives meant to transform our lives, not to sit in libraries gathering dust, accessible only to those Latinate, literate, and leisured enough to understand them.

God and the Godhead

This bring us to my central interest, his distinction between God (*Gott*) and the Godhead (*Gottheit*), the context in which Eckhart uttered one of his most striking sayings, "I pray God that he may make me free of God."[45] He appeals to the personal God whom he addresses in prayer as a Dominican friar to grant him access to the God beyond this God, which he calls the Godhead, or the *Gottesgrund*, the deeper ground of God. The God he meant to transcend is not only the God accessible to us by reason, the God of metaphysical theology, but also the God made accessible to us by *faith*, the God of *revelation*—the Trinity and the Incarnation—beyond both philosophy and theology. So then what is this *Gottheit*? Whatever it is, it is no "what," has no whatness, *quidditas*. Whatever it is, it is more an "it" than a what,[46] and the most we will be able to do is to say what it is *not*. Then what is it *not*? As Derrida would say, how not to speak of the Godhead, how to not-speak, how in speaking not to be in denial?

A good case could be made that, for Eckhart, the highest, deepest, or first name of God is the One, the absolutely simple *unum* behind every multiplicity.[47] The One is a perfectly negative name, the most perfect, because one means undivided, and since division is itself a negation, it names God as the negation of a negation. The *Gottheit* is a unity deeper than the tri-unity of the Trinity. It is the prepersonal ground of the persons, the prepersonal substance in which the processions of Father, Son, and Spirit are inscribed. This is devilishly tricky Trinitarian business. It inserts the personalism of the Bible within the framework of a prepersonal Neoplatonic One, which is the least imperfect name of the unnamable. Every name of God—including both the revealed names of the three persons and synonyms for the Godhead, like abyss (*Abgrund*) or desert (*Wüste*) or "naked being"—addresses God in *relation* to our knowledge (being, truth) or our desire (will, love) and leaves God in God's absolute unity, in absolved solitude, *in se*, alone with Godself, untouched, in unscathed holiness. "God," by contrast, is the God who is namable on the basis of a relationship to us. The Godhead is God before "God" comes to be, where there is as yet neither a creator, for that is the name of a causal relationship to the world, nor a creature, since "creator" and "creature" are interdependent and inseparable notions, neither possible without the other. Seen thus, unity with God, the "breakthrough to the Godhead," takes place for Eckhart as a process of uncreation, reversing creation, moving back to a point prior to creation and the distinction between God and creature. So the "Godhead" is *in principle* unnamable. Whatever we say or think of God, that is what the Godhead is not.[48] The names of God are veils; the Godhead is naked and unveiled. Unnameability is a conversation stopper, a disputation closer. It nullifies the debate between *esse* and *intelligere*, between *intellectus* and *voluntas*, between Aristotle and Neoplatonism, between Dominicans and Franciscans, between philosophy and theology, leaving all of them standing in the vestibule, outside the sanctuary of the Godhead, where even God gains no admittance.

There is nothing we can say or think or do to effect this unity, to gain us admission to the inner sanctuary of the Godhead. At the very moment a word is uttered, verbal or mental, or a desire is expressed or an action taken, the Godhead has fled the scene. Here the way must be way-less (*sine modo*), without a method (*hodos*), without a means of advancing, which is the paradoxical condition of possibility of being admitted. The will must be will-less, without will; the mind must be no-mind, thoughtless, free of all images and concepts. We must live and be "without why."[49]

The Birth of the Son

The Godhead is a hard pill to swallow in a historical religion where something of the true God has, by definition, been *revealed*. The austerity of the Godhead not only contrasts with philosophical discourse (where God is *esse* and/or *intelligere*) but also, and more strikingly, its impersonality contrasts with the personal language of the New Testament, in which God is love, *abba*, a fatherly love. *Gottheit* looks like the victory of Neoplatonism over Christianity, the One over the many, the deeper impersonal unity over the Trinity of persons, the still-concealed Godhead over the God revealed in the Incarnation, none of which was lost on the Inquisition. But if the Godhead is my central interest in Eckhart, thus far

I have said nothing about what is, for Eckhart himself, his central interest, which he calls the *Gottesgeburt*, the "birth of God" or the "birth of the Son" in the soul. As a Dominican friar and Christian theologian, what interested Eckhart above everything else is how the Son who is born in eternity is also born *in* the soul and *as* the soul, so that I too become that same Son, not merely *similar* to that Son. What good is it for the Father to bear his Son in eternity if I too am not also born that Son?[50] Eckhart is not about pagan Neoplatonism but a distinctly *Christian* spirituality, whose focal point is the letters and gospel of John, the gospel of love.

The birth of the Son is prepared for in the deepest point of the soul, in that region where the soul had abdicated all its powers (faculties), which Eckhart calls the *Seelengrund* (ground of the soul), which is the root from which the faculties spring. The *Seelengrund* is the counterpart to the *Gottesgrund*, and the point of their common convergence where the soul in its ground and God in God's ground are one. This unity, which is a function of the *unitative* quality of the *intellectual* substance of God and the soul, takes place in space cleared in the soul by "letting-be" (*Gelassenheit*) and "detachment" (*Abgeschiedenheit*), which are nothing we *do* but rather something we do *not* do.[51] We do things in our "faculties," but in the ground of the soul we must simply "be" without thinking or willing, "without why." "Now all God wants of you," he says, "is for you to go out of yourself in the way of creatureliness and let God be God within you."[52] Then we will live like the angels, in unity with God. It is here, in this *Seelengrund*—pure, poor, naked, virginal, cut off (*abgeschieden*) from everything created, when the soul lets God be God (*lassen*) in the soul—that the soul joins in the very life of God at its very source so that the "birth of the Son" takes place *in* the soul, indeed even *as* the soul, and indeed the soul can itself give birth *to* the Son. That is the heart of the Trinitarian spirituality of the German sermons that brings the austerity of this Neoplatonism to its Christian and Scriptural fruition.[53] Here the virgin becomes a fruitful wife; the prepersonal ground becomes the scene and setting of the play of the Trinity of persons. The point of all this, the very heart of Eckhart's spirituality, is to let both God and the creature vanish by occupying a place *before* the creator-creature relationship has emerged, before God becomes creator and we are created, in order to join in the perichoresis of the Trinity, where we become one, not with Jesus of Nazareth but with the eternal Son, in which the distinction between the uncreated Son, the biblical Christ, and the created soul is no longer in play.

LUTHER'S *DEUS ABSCONDITUS*

The opening Eckhart has created for a more disturbing apophaticism is found by asking a bedeviling question. If the *Gottheit* is unnamable, must it not remain absolutely *anonymous*? If so, why is thinking the Godhead as the unnameability of the "One," a vintage bit of Neoplatonic metaphysics, any less objectionable than any alternate way of thinking what is, in principle, unnamable? Why say the *Gottheit* is one, or the One, or still and quiet? Why not the many, the unmasterable multiplicity, noisy flux, the Multitude? *Khora*? *Tohu wa-bohu*? If it is completely indeterminate and indeterminable, why is it determined to be worthy of praise instead of fear and apprehension? If the *Gottheit* is beyond knowledge and naming, how can we say anything *at all* about it, including what it is *not*? Its only property is that it is without any identifying properties. If something is radically unknowable, we are not only blocked from saying what it is but also from saying what it is not because we cannot adjudicate the difference.

The problem is analogous to the old "patchwork" problem raised in Kantian scholarship concerning the *Ding an sich*. Hans Vaihinger showed years ago that in the *Critique of Pure Reason* Kant alternates between speaking of the "noumenal" thing concealed behind phenomenal appearances and of the unknowable "thing in itself."[54] The noumenon, which Vaihinger said belonged to the older, precritical manuscripts, is a dogmatic name, signifying how things are known (*nous*) by a supersensuous intuition unavailable to us. The noumenal is the intelligible being beyond the sensible being favored by metaphysics, to which critical philosophy denies us access because we, unlike God—and the angels—have only sensuous intuition. As Kierkegaard's Johannes Climacus said against the Hegelians, the world is indeed a system, but only for God, not for us.[55] Noumena are how things are *known* by God but *unknown* by us. But in the later manuscripts, Kant simply spoke more critically, skeptically, and circumspectly of the "thing in itself" as simply unknowable. This could be anything, God knows what. It could be intelligible or wildly unintelligible; it could be one or many. It could even be a Nietzschean play of forces or the depths of the "unconscious." These are not random suggestions but, via Schelling and Schopenhauer, some of its offspring. Noumena are a known unknowable; with noumena, we know what we do not know, and we know God knows it. With the thing in itself, we do not know anything; it is an unknown unknowable.

I think the same double trouble bedevils the *Gottheit*, which trembles with the undecidability of the two tropics of negativity. Eckhart knows what he does not know. Despite everything Eckhart says about the unknowability of the *Gottheit*, he knows what he means, and what he means is *edifying*, as he repeatedly reassured his Inquisitors, to the extent that if it is not, he rejects it. The *Gottheit* means the mystery, the depth dimension *in*, the unknowability *of*, what he knows about "God" from his scholastic life of study, from his Dominican life of prayer, and from the scriptures and the teachings of the church, and it is the basis of the birth in the soul of the Eternal Son. It is what is unknown *in* what he knows, the *Gottheit* in *Gott*, to which it is internally and *differentially* related. *Gottheit* and *Gott* are constituted by their differential distance from each other. The concealment of the

Gottheit is relative to the revelation of *Gott*, and conversely. When he talks about the unknowability of the Godhead, he means this as *praise*, not *apprehension*, as adoration, not anxiety, as a source of divine consolation (*göttliche Tröstung*), not fear or alarm over an ominous threat. He is not urging us to release ourselves into the nocturnal powers of an inscrutable, confounding, and unintelligible morass or *apeiron*. *Gottheit* for him is like an unknown *noumenal* sphere; it is how God is *known by God*, with which we seek without seeking to be united, not an utterly unknowable thing in itself. It is divine mystery, not inscrutable chaos. He is talking about the depths of the God whom he embraces with all his heart, for whose honor and glory he has lived a life of poverty, chastity, and obedience and served as a high-level administrator in a major Roman Catholic religious order. As he says as the end of the *Talks of Instruction*, "For as far as you are in God, you are at peace.... That is how you can tell how far you are in God or otherwise, by whether you have peace or unrest.... Nor is there anything to be feared in God: whatever is in God is to be loved. Likewise there is nothing in him to cause sadness."[56] He has dedicated his life and body not to an *unintelligible abyss* but to an *abyss of intelligibility* that far outstrips him, an excess of everlasting being, a sea of light and truth, of eternal goodness and love, which has laid claim to him unconditionally, long before he can lay any claim to it. Whatever its subsequent history, for Eckhart, his entire teaching and preaching is one extended *Book of Divine Consolation*.[57]

But the *Gottheit* is a more haunting and haunted notion than Eckhart is allowing (*lassen*); he cannot limit what he is letting-be. *Gottheit* does not get a pass. It too trembles in devilish undecidability. The door Eckhart has opened up with this unnerving notion cannot be closed; it cannot be contained, kept safe and stabilized like that. The disturbance it creates cannot be quelled by a reassuring mysticism, one that calms our fears and comforts the yearnings of our heart for peace. It spells trouble, which the Inquisition—of which, I hasten to add, I am not an admirer—picked up. The *Gottheit* signals a disturbance arising from within, not an external attack on God by a heartless atheist. It is an *auto*-deconstructive disturbance occurring *within* theology, formulated by one of the great geniuses of Christian spiritual life. There is a deconstructive force (*Abbaung*) disturbing this edifying construction (*Erbaung*), and it is doing so *from within*.

That is why it was already bedeviling Eckhart in his own lifetime. This is not because he was a "heretic," which is how the Inquisition judged about half of the propositions they cherry-picked out of his writings. Understood carefully, properly qualified, in virtue of several subtle formal scholastic distinctions found in the Latin writings, Eckhart showed the Inquisitors he was not serving up heresy but an edifying, if rhetorically daring, variant of Christian Neoplatonist mystical theology that was handed down to him from multiple sources in the tradition, both patristic and even Thomistic, and if anything about it were heretical, he said he would retract it. But the pope was right to say that many of the things Eckart said *sounded* dangerous, *a devil's workshop* for those who are not as loyal to the church as was Eckhart.[58] Even if Eckhart could explain how he understood these sayings, they were liable to be misunderstood—I would have said understood *differently*—by others when he was not around to explain them. The pope was referring to what Derrida calls the "ear of the other," the way it will be heard. That is good hermeneutics; once something is written down, it can no longer be governed by the "intentions of the author." What was written down by a devout fourteenth-century Dominican friar, theologian, preacher, and provincial general of the German Dominican province, who lived a life of poverty, chastity, and obedience (Eckhart), was capable of taking on a subsequent life of its own. That is exactly what happened, especially since, after the condemnation, his sermons circulated anonymously for centuries. A written text can detach itself from the original context and grow legs—or angelic wings—of its own, including the wings of the "bad angels," producing a history of its own effects, a *Wirkungsgeschichte*, over which the author has no say. The subsequent history of the *Gottheit*—which is pretty much the subject matter of this book—is a case in point.[59] As I suggest, one of the distant descendants of the *Gottheit* may even be showing up today in what contemporary physicists are saying about the universe.

The tipping point from an edifying to a more anxious apophaticism is found in Luther, the third tip of my triangulation. A line can be drawn from *esse absconditum*,[60] as Eckhart once put it, passing through Tauler and the *Theologia Deutsch* to Luther's *Deus absconditus*,[61] but with this difference. Where Eckhart said there is nothing to fear in the Godhead, Luther said there is everything in the world to fear from it. Luther introduced the notion of the *Deus absconditus* in a well-known debate with Erasmus, where he distinguished it from the *Deus revelatus*. For Luther, the Godhead is a lot more ominous than for Eckhart. Luther dared to say very shocking things about the "hidden" God because he descended from the Augustinian-Franciscan-Ockhamist line of voluntarism. The seemingly arcane scholastic distinction between intellectualism and voluntarism has explosive consequences. Eckhart is not Luther. Eckhart had undertaken a mystical radicalization of the intellectualist tradition that meant the *Gottheit* was an abyss of intelligibility (*esse, intelligere, unum*), although not an unintelligible abyss, but his German sermons were a minefield for orthodoxy. When Luther said we have every reason to fear the worst from the *Deus absconditus*, he was drawing upon medieval Franciscan sources to which Eckhart himself was opposed. Far be it from Luther to say what a hidden, omnipotent, and sovereignly *free* power like God was capable of. If you think of God primarily in terms of unchecked, unknowable freedom, anything is possible. The *Grundstimmung* in Eckhart is *Gelassenheit*, which is a serene calm, a scene of comfort and consolation, but in Luther it is *Anfechtung* and *Angst*, and his anxiety lay in not knowing what the hidden God would do. In the eleventh century, Peter Damian had even suggested that God could make it to be that Rome was not founded even though Rome was founded—that is, God could change past time, were God so minded. Of what is such a God capable? Well, literally everything and anything. God only knows!

So when Erasmus says that God does not will the eternal death of a just man, Luther replies that he is far from sure about that.[62] Remember the hypothesis—quite astonishing for Luther himself, who literally risked his life trying to retrieve Christian theology from scholastic metaphysics and return it to divine revelation—that the *Deus absconditus* is the *Gottheit*, the God who remains hidden behind the *Deus revelatus*, hidden not only from *reason* but also from *revelation*. This represents a more disconcerting sense of the hiddenness of God, not a God hidden *in* the cross, *sub contraria specie*, as he argued in the *Heidelberg Disputation*, but a God hidden *behind* the cross.[63] The God of revelation may not will the eternal death of a just man, but, for all we know, the inscrutable and hidden God may very well have double predestination up the divine sleeve. As Alistair McGrath writes, "*Deus incarnatus* must find himself reduced to tears as he sees the *Deus absconditus* consigning men to perdition."[64] We are reminded of the English poet William Blake, who said that we reach a point where it is difficult to tell the difference between God and Satan.[65] Once we say that the Godhead at the heart of God is a concealed and inscrutable abyss, there is no way to shut down this possibility. Here, pretty literally, all hell breaks out. It was a Lutheran theologian, Rudolf Otto, who would describe this God in terms of the *mysterium tremendum et fascinans*, meaning not only the edifying mystery, the one that attracts us (*fascinans*) by its depth, but also the anxiety-inducing mystery, the one that repels us and fills us with fear and trembling (*tremens*) like a roaring storm at sea.

For the most part, Luther scholars tend to close ranks and try to contain the damage of this text by attempting to show that the revealed God and the hidden God are one and the same, constituting what is not yet revealed in the revealed God, which makes the idea safe and resembles what I am proposing about Eckhart. I agree with McGrath that, in this text, Luther is saying something different, something more disturbing and devastating, that the *Deus absconditus* is capable of contradicting the *Deus revelatus* and nullifying what has been revealed, which reflects Luther's voluntarism. But if McGrath thinks we should simply write the text off as errant, as a mistake that Luther should retract, I treat the text not as a breakdown but as a breakthrough, a point where Luther exposes the ruthless logic, or alogic, of the divine *Gottheit*.[66] I think that at this point the radical theologian in Luther has broken through the confessional theologian and managed to show his face. To be sure, Luther's radicality was more than enough for any one lifetime, but here we encounter a still *more* radical streak in his thought, where the apophatic is not a place of rest and praise but one of tremors and groundlessness, leaving us nowhere to hide. At this point, thinking, be it theological or philosophical, scientific or poetic, touches bottom, all converging at its ground, baring the roots of our being-in-the-world and leaving them exposed. This uprooted condition belongs not to a reassuring apophaticism that is consummated in eternal glory but to a discomforting mysticism that is the stuff of a more difficult glory. As Nietzsche once said, the ability of an idea to give comfort is not a criterion of its truth.[67]

But there is more. However radical Luther's reply may be, it is still theoanthropomorphic. Luther, for whom the cosmic battle between Christ and Satan held center stage,[68] personifies the *Gottheit* as a mythological and wrathful divine will, a God who under the form of Satan himself would put us to the test (*tentatio, Anfechtung*). But if the *Gottheit* is concealed from both reason and revelation, we have no basis saying anything about it other than that it is an unknown it. We can no more say with the intellectualists that it is an infinite sea of intelligibility than we can say with the voluntarists that it is an abyss of unintelligible freedom. We can no more say that it is love than that it is wrath. Might it be that the element in which we live and move and have our being is not concerned with *us* at all and this because it is not in the least bit *personal*? Might it be that we are on our own, left to our own resources to sort things out for ourselves, by forces that do not know we are here and could care less, that do not "know" or "will" or "care for" anything? Might it be that what there is, is *indifferent* to us, an "it" that does not care what we call it—*esse, intelligere* or *velle, Gott* or *Gottheit, Deus sive natura*, good or evil, $e = mc^2$, or simply "it," *es gibt, il y a, Ça*? Might its namelessness be nothing deep and divine but simply nothing more than some anonymous power, force, or energy? Might it be nameless because it has no name? Might the anonymous be its proper name? Might there be, at the bottom of things, *neither* a generous will and loving intelligence, as the theologians of glory like to think, *nor* a wildly inscrutable will who consigns us to infinite torment, as in Luther's tormented imagination? Then what? Perhaps an absolute indifference, prior to the distinction between consciousness and its object, in the manner of Schelling. Perhaps a totally indifferent "it," a completely innocent force, whose majesty and divinity, such as it is, *s'il y en a*, lies in working itself out according to mathematical laws with intentions neither benign nor malign. Might there be an array of forces such that human good fortune is not the fruit of love and human misfortune is not born of wrath, where no one is trying to be generous or malicious? Might it all be a matter of the fortuitous play of chance and that the mystification lies in the personification, which is the mythologization?[69]

As I said at the outset, to raise theological questions without the assurance of getting a theological reply represents a *radical apophatic imagination*, a radical account of our encounter with the world in which we take a long, cold, hard look at how things are without needing them "attenuated, veiled, sweetened, blunted and falsified."[70] When we try to enter into the depths of experience, who knows what we will find? That is why I began the present analysis by framing radical theology within the radical phenomenological terms of a theopoetic *epochē* and reduction. Given that premise, one could predict that results like this would show up in phenomenology itself, which, left to its own devices and without any theological motivations, should hit upon the anonymous substratum I am trying to describe. In fact, it would be surprising if it did not.

I do not mean to grant myself an easy grace and call into evidence Heidegger's famous analysis of anxiety and *das Nichts*, which has manifest Lutheran-Kierkegaardian roots. I cite a completely untheological place—Husserl's analysis of what he calls the "destruction of the world."[71] Husserl imagines—by way of an extraordinary imaginative variation—what the world would be like if the orderly sequence of noemata simply collapsed, if we could no longer rely upon the order of empirical experience. When I open my front door, I expect to find my home within, not a roaring storm at sea. Otherwise, Husserl argues, it would be impossible to "constitute" a unity of meaning, like my entrance hall or my home or *anything*, even my own embodied self, because a unity of meaning is formed by a set of intentional expectations that are regularly fulfilled. That is why I mentioned Kafka at the beginning of this chapter. What if I woke up one morning, looked in the mirror, and saw *ein Ungeziefer*! Absent this order, Husserl says, transcendental consciousness would be left to preside over chaos, reduced to a sheer flux of experiences (*Erlebnisse*), a breakdown of true experience (*Erfahrung*). The radical possibility—shall we say, the devilish possibility?—of the "destruction of the world" is intrinsic to the possibility of constituting that contingent unity of experiences we call our "world." The constitution of the world is made possible by conditions that also provide for the possibility of its destruction, its deconstitution, its deworlding, which inhabits it from within. Husserl's transcendental consciousness weakens into a *quasi*-transcendental status.

It was possibly with this text in mind that Levinas, whose Jewish theological sensibility is attuned to the rhythms of the opening passages of Genesis, made a famous analysis of the *il y a*, the "anonymous rustling" of the world. His *il y a* is born of a reduction to a pure anonymous existence prior to the constitution of any definite existent, a kind of brutal fact-of-the-world, which Levinas describes as the *remue-ménage*, the stirring hubbub, the "incessant bustling of the *il y a*, the horrible eternity at the bottom of essence,"[72] which Levinas says falls into a "possible confusion" with the illeity of the Most High.[73] For Levinas, this is the anonymous rumbling not of being or of the beyond being but of something *less* than being, beneath being, the formless void and darkness preceding creation, the *chaos*, the *tohu wa-bohu*, the *apeiron*,[74] or, in Derrida's analysis, the virgin/mother/nurse *khora*.[75]

Whether cast in the language of Husserl's dispassionate transcendental science or in Levinas more biblical, evocative, and poetic language, the same or a very similar phenomenon—the undecidability, the possible confusion, between the two apophaticisms, the two tropics of negativity—is on full display. Either way, these are discourses that have been deontologized, detheologized, demythologized, deanthropomorphized. They are images of neither angels nor demons, love nor wrath, but of a kind of radical protoindifference, constituting a nontheological reply to a theological inquiry. We reach a level of experience where there is, at bottom, neither *intellectus* nor *voluntas*, neither good will nor ill, no "who" at all, in the sense of somebody doing something with love or wrath on their mind, but rather something that simply happens, simply is, that is because it is, that is, as Eckhart himself said, "without why." Might it be the case—and this is what I argue—that living "without why" is the right *response* but for reasons quite unimaginable to Eckhart? Might it be that living "without why" is the answer to a question Eckhart had no intention of asking? The Inquisitors were right to be worried. They thought it was the devil's workshop.

THREE

HEGEL AT THE FOOT OF THE CROSS
Understanding the Death of God

IF ANYTHING LOOKED LIKE THE work of the devil, it was a group of young radical theologians back in the 1960s who successfully if briefly gained national attention for a somewhat esoteric theology they brazenly and a bit flamboyantly called the "death of God."[1] In the process they rightly invoked the name and the words of Nietzsche, who was for many the devil himself, with whom they yoked the name of Hegel—in that order. They were reading Hegel through the lens of Nietzsche, not the other way around, so with Hegel they got it only half right. Hegel does indeed have a notion of the death of God as a *moment* in the ongoing *life* of God, the moment in which this Supreme Being abdicates its transcendence and manifests itself in space and time on the way to becoming Spirit in the world. So, Hegel is not Nietzsche. Hegel is not excoriating religion from without like Nietzsche (or debunking it like an *Aufklärer*) but *rethinking* religion from within. He undertakes a "speculative hermeneutic"[2] of *how* religion should be *understood as* a manifestation of the absolute Spirit in the world.

The particular form religion takes he calls a *Vorstellung*, an imaginative figure, of which the "death of God" is a good example. He does not mean religion is purely subjective, like a fairy tale to be read to children at bedtime—a point he shares with Schelling—but something more serious, like a work of art, which is revealing something important. A *Vorstellung* has both a subjective side and an objective side. On its subjective side, it is a work of religious imagination, a representation, a figurative way of understanding being, which, on the objective side, is presenting itself (*stellen*) before (*vor*) our sensuous selves. This correlation is a metaphysical counterpart to Husserl's correlation of the noematic and the noetic sides of a conscious act, not however as a *pure* phenomenology (of pure consciousness), as in Husserl, but as a speculative phenomenology of being's ascent to self-consciousness. Hegel's *Lectures on the Philosophy of Religion* are a speculative hermeneutic of religion, an ontological phenomenology of the self-presentation of being, where being, as Aristotle said, is to be understood on many levels. Hegel replaces the classical natural/supernatural distinction with a series of phenomenological levels or strata. There are not two worlds, natural and supernatural, but one world, which can be understood in different ways because it presents itself on different levels—art below, philosophy above, religion in the middle. The content of art, religion, and philosophy is the same; it is the form that differs.[3] So religion is neither debunked nor absolutized but redescribed or, as Hegel would prefer to say, thought through. Seen thus, to stop with the "death of God" in Hegel would be like leaving at intermission without hearing how the play ends. Were Hegel to be found at the foot of the cross, he would offer the women who were keeping watch there the consolation that however terrible this moment is, it is only a moment in a larger story in which God will finally be all in all, for God is that in which we live and move and have our being.

What we will find in Hegel is both a theopoetics and a posttheism (chapter 1) of decisive historical importance, both, however, with speculative *anti*-apophatic motivations that are singled out for criticism by Schelling (chapters 6–8), which lays the ground for the post-theism of Paul Tillich (chapter 9).

THE REVOLUTIONARY SIDE OF HEGEL

Hegel is at once a profoundly *revolutionary* figure and yet in a deep *alliance* with classical theology, which explains why, after his death, both "left-wing" (atheistic) and "right-wing" (orthodox) versions of his thought would emerge. In his own day, he was accused of "pantheism," which amounts to "atheism," since to a theist, there is no significant difference. Either way, God does not exist, meaning there is no *entity* "up there" called "God." The theists have no patience with the ontological difference, with the post-theist proposal emerging in German idealism that God might *be* by being *otherwise* than an existent entity, that God might indeed not be separately but by coinciding with being-itself. For Hegel himself, the term *pantheism* refers to something either absurd—that every finite being is God, a view that does injury to the divine being and no one has ever held—or mistaken—that God is the substance of things where particular beings are ephemeral, accidental, near nothings (Spinoza), which does injury to finite beings like us.[4]

The task of the philosophy of religion is to show just how God and being coincide in such a way as to do justice to both God and finite beings. The basic formula, that finite beings come and go, whereas God is infinite and eternal, sounds like the soul of orthodoxy until we examine it more closely. What Hegel meant reveals the two sides of Hegel, the revolutionary *rethinking* (the radical side) of the most fundamental assumptions of *classical theology* (the alliance). I say "rethink" to signify that this is a redescription, what Heidegger would call a creative repetition (*Wiederholung*) of the classical tradition rather than a simple critique, dismissal, or rationalistic destruction. In Hegel's terms, "speculative" thinking does not proceed by way of propositions representing a fixed state of affairs (representing *beings*), proving the true propositions and disproving the false ones; that is the way of the Enlightenment ratiocination (*Verstand*, calculative reason). Speculative thinking describes how things unfold into their truth, from their still untrue form into their true form, which is the way of *Vernunft*, the power of unifying reason rooted in understanding *being-itself*, a distinction in some ways foreshadowed by the *intellectus/ratio* distinction.

Hegel reroutes the analytic misunderstandings of *Verstand* to the synthetic comprehending ways of *Vernunft*, redirecting statements about beings to an understanding of being. *Vernunft* means the power of insight into truth's unfolding into itself, the power to see the truth, the true being, in the *transition* between being and beings. So, for Hegel, the infinite and eternal being of God does not refer to an otherworldly entity residing in an eternal realm standing outside, over and against time (*atemporal*), but the unfolding of the eternal *in* time called history (and also the spacing of the eternal called nature). Eternal does not mean no-time but everlasting time, the *omni*temporal, meaning that God is now, always was, and always will be world without end, Amen. In his terms, the *in*ternal and eternal idea of God is an abstract, ideal portrait painted in the *Logic*, while God achieves *ex*ternal *ex*istence in history and nature, and especially in human history, where, as finite, incarnate Spirit, God becomes conscious of God-self. God is ever changing because God is ever-*becoming* God (radical), but the idea of *what* God is becoming does not change (classical).

The classical image of God, as transcendent, absolute, and eternal, is not "false" but one-sided and "abstract." By this he meant that it was drawn out of or separated off from real movement, like pausing or freezing the action in a video or like a frozen waterfall. The pause is not a random pause but a carefully selected idealized portrait, like a picture of an athlete at the peak of a performance, at a moment of supreme effort and mastery for all to admire and emulate; or like a great portrait painting, which captures the "eternal essence" of a peasant or a merchant or a queen; or the way that Keats's "Ode on a Grecian Urn" captures the lovers as they are just about to kiss and renders it "eternal." By bringing the rush of time to a standstill, a freeze-frame affords us the opportunity to pause over and admire its perfection, contemplate its essence, examine its logic, study its form, and spell it out in words. But we must not forget this is an abstraction; we must not misplace the real concreteness. We must remember that the athlete's moment of perfection is itself part of a larger motion, that the picture was snapped at its peak. We could not ask the athlete to reassume that position and hold it, please, until we take a picture. It was only possible, only *real* and actual, as a *moment* of a motion that keeps on moving. Reality is not made up of freeze-frames. Concrete reality is a flowing motion, not the sum total of stops. A stop is an abstraction, and a proposition representing the stop is a distortion (*Verstand*). God in his eternity apart from the world is a stop, an abstract essence, a still, capturing the "logic" of God's "perfections," the divine names, omniscience, and so on, but the *existing* and *really* eternal God is found unfolding in motion and matter, in space and time.[5] What is "dead" is the misunderstanding that this static freeze-frame God is a real being somewhere. Put in the form of a *Vorstellung*, that God died the day Jesus was born.

Hegel did not so much deny the old version of the idea of eternity as redescribe or reinvent it so that the eternal works itself out *in* time. That is the radicalization. That is also why, for the sake of clarity, it is more accurate to describe his view as "panentheism," God-in-all, all-in-God, the eternal-*in*-time, the temporalizing-of-the-eternal, drawing upon the power of *Vernunft* to *see* God *in* all things. The goal of thinking is "reconciliation," to honor both the finite and infinite, both temporal and eternal, and to do no harm to either, without embracing the illusion of two different worlds or collapsing the two into unmediated self-identity (which is the misunderstanding promoted by "pantheism"). Hegel honors space and time by treating it as the plane on which the divine being is realized (and in that sense, Spirit is radically incarnational), and he honors God by releasing the activity (*actio*) of the divine being from the abstract static one-sidedness (*actus purus*) in which it was held captive by classical theology (*Verstand*). This is a predecessor form of the distinction I have elsewhere made between insistence and existence.[6] In Hegel it was variously called the distinction between essence and existence, implicit and explicit, logic and nature, the ideal and the real, in itself and for itself, referring to the way the inner logic expresses itself in external reality.

This is not free-floating speculation. This is a matter of hard metaphysical necessity: the *only* way God *could* be *real* is in space and time (otherwise God would "lifeless and alone"[7]), and the *only* way reality could *make sense* is if it is driven by the inner logic supplied by God (otherwise it would be chaos). At the same time, Hegel said he was just being a good phenomenologist, simply observing the factual course of *history*, its actual unfolding. In Hegel, the course of an idea and the course of reality are the same route, at different stages of development. If it is real, it must be because it was all along rational; if it is rational, it will necessarily find a way to be real. For *Vernunft*, the true should be distinguished not so much from the false as from the *still un*true, meaning that things are in varying degrees in a still nascent, implicit, unformed, undeveloped, imperfect form. Like Aristotle, Hegel thinks organically, biologically, in terms of seeds, germination, maturation, in dynamic categories, not like Plato, mathematically, in terms of fixed forms, in static categories. So, when his lecture course gets to Christianity, which he regarded as the "true" religion, he calls it the "completed" or "perfect" (*vollendet*) religion, where other religions were not precisely false but incomplete and imperfect anticipations of Christianity, one-sided, abstract, immature. In Christianity, the truth of religion is consummated, and in it the Greek religion of the beautiful and the Jewish religion of the sublime are superseded as one-sided. The God of Judaism, for him, is a pure law, transcendent, other, and alien, his very name unutterable, in which God is located at a distant remove from humanity and humanity from God. (Hegel, we should recall, was a German Lutheran and was not averse to saying unkind things about the Jews.) What is untrue has not yet realized its innermost being and truth, from which it cannot be separated. The truth, to paraphrase Tillich, is not alien to the thing, but the thing is (still) alienated from its truth.[8] Of course, Hegel's story is completely Christocentric. Today we would insist that there are as many religious revelations as there are cultures, each representing their own form of life. Nonetheless, Hegel opens the door—this is a threshold position—to a more radical pluralism that made the Christian orthodoxy of his day nervous by embedding the God of Christianity in history and culture.

Hegel's view that the divine being is the real truth and genuine substance of finite things was found in the tradition, where it went under the name of *unio mystica*, the fundamental religious feeling of *unity with God*. The task of philosophy was to make this mystical feeling clear to itself. Hegel is not making war on mysticism and feeling. He does not disdain the affectivity of religion, like the Enlightenment *philosophes*. Everything, feeling included, has its inner truth. Hegel would understand the passion of the Bible thumpers; they are not wrong but still in a state of untruth. Philosophy *is* this feeling come *true*, brought to its truth in the clarity of reflective thought. Religion is philosophy in a form that fits those who are not quite fit for philosophy. Philosophy is religion in its philosophical form, its truest form, its truth. There can be, *in principle*, no conflict between them—between the infinite and the finite, between reason and revelation, which requires closer attention.

THE FINITE AND THE INFINITE

Religion means knowledge of God, but to base our knowledge of God upon the traditional proofs for the existence of God represents a misunderstanding because, for Hegel, a being named God does not exist and the proofs do not actually prove anything, as Kant had shown. The proofs are pure *Verstand*: confined to accounting for beings by means of other beings, with no understanding of being-itself. They start out with a finite thing and attempt to prove an infinite thing, but the proofs can never cross an infinite distance. From the finite only other finite things follow but not the true other of the finite, which is the infinite.[9] Moreover, the infinite is not a thing, because a thing is determined by the limits that define it as this thing rather than that thing—that is, render it finite. The infinite cannot be an infinite *thing*. Being itself is not another being. God has being (*Sein*), not determinate existence (*Dasein*). So when classical theology speaks of the "existence of God," it is speaking figuratively, subjectively, imaginatively—it is not "false" but still imaginative—since, to be conceptually precise, the being of God is not contracted to determinate existence.[10] God is not less than existence; existence can never get as far as God, which is being-itself. Still, it belongs to the being of God to particularize or realize itself concretely, in and through finite things, and in that sense, the expression "the existence of God"—now Hegel uses the Latinate *Existenz*—is true enough, so long as we are cautious. I have called that the exist*a*nce of God.[11]

How then are being-itself and God properly conjoined? The problem with the proofs is that they are a "distortion," not that they are "rubbish,"[12] and "our task is to restore the proofs of God's existence to a position of honor by stripping away the distortion."[13] The restoration is the radicalization, not Enlightenment critique but speculative hermeneutics. The distortion arises not from the *content* of the proofs but from their *form* as proofs, which is a *Vorstellung*, a subjective figure. We all seek what the proofs seek, the passage, the transition, from the finite to the infinite, the elevation of the mind from the finite to the infinite, in which we ourselves feel lifted up, and that is the content, the deeper truth and substance, of the proofs. In religious consciousness, the finite gives way to the infinite. The finite thing perishes. It does not stand on its own ground; it has no truth within itself.[14] While that is true, the distortion is to turn this movement of the human Spirit into a proof. That is the distorted way of *Verstand*, held captive by the interplay among beings, the results of which are creations of an intellectual imagination on holiday, logical illusions comparable to perceptual illusions, which furthermore have no power to touch our heart.[15]

The truth is, rather, to allow the finite thing, which is nothing in itself, to *vanish* into the infinite, which is its truth, its true being and ultimate ground. The truth is to *see* (*Vernunft, intellectus*) the being *in* its being (which we are calling here the "ontological reduction"). The religious heart does this affectively, unconsciously, implicitly, but in philosophy this must be made clear, conscious, and conceptually explicit. In the proofs, the finite is made to serve as the ground or foundation of the infinite. This it can never do because the ground gives way. In Hegel, the finite serves as a starting point, not as a ground but by vanishing into the infinity by which it is sustained. We do not move linearly, from one being to another, highest being, but by vertical descent, sinking into the depths of being-itself. In the proofs, the being of the finite is affirmed, and God is affirmed on that basis as the result; in speculative thought, the finite is a negativity that gives way to the affirmation of the infinite within. In the proofs we move from one actual existent positivity to posit another, but entities are not positivities; they are negations, limitations, whose negativity thinking negates. In speculative thought finite beings give up their claim to genuine positivity and confess that only God has genuine being, that "*the infinite alone is.*"[16]

It is not enough to say that we can never build a bridge from a finite actuality to an infinite one.[17] While that is "correct," it is still *Verstand* talking; it makes no contact with the inner truth of the proofs and could lead to simple atheism or skepticism. But for *Vernunft*, the finite has no truth in itself; it is only a limit inscribed within the unlimited. The truth of the negation (finite) is its negation (infinite), the negation of a negation. The truth of the finite is its *transition* into the infinite. *Verstand* objects that we cannot build a bridge to cross an infinite distance. *Vernunft* replies that that there is no need for a bridge because the two, the finite and the infinite, are not really two. We do not need to cross over because we are already there, or better still, the infinite is already here, for it is that in which finite beings live and move and have their being, their truth. That is the underlying insight (*Vernunft*) into the truth of being, which has all along been understood by the mystics, and by Paul preaching in the Areopagus, and by our affective nature, of which the proofs are the distortion (*Verstand*).

The philosophy of religion restores the honor of the proofs by rerouting them from *Verstand* to *Vernunft*. Where the cosmological proof imagines the existence of a separate and necessarily existent "first cause," *Vernunft* understands the underlying necessity of being-itself. Where the teleological proof imagines the existence of an intelligent Governor of the Universe, *Vernunft* understands an inner logic, a *logos* and a *telos*, inscribed immanently in the world itself. But the "most profound"[18] of all the proofs, the one that comes closest to the truth itself, is the most hotly contested, Anselm's "ontological proof." This proof is rightly rejected because it invalidly passes from mere subjective thought to actual being, its point of departure being a priori, unlike the cosmological and teleological proofs, which are a posteriori. Cast in the form of a proof, it is but a futile work of the *Verstand* misled by propositions. But for *Vernunft*, Anselm has caught sight of the truth that being and thinking are the same. This was known to the mystics like Meister Eckhart, who said that the eye in which I see God is the same eye in which God seem himself.[19] God is the self-thinking thought, which means that God divides himself into subject and object, thinking and what is thought, in just the way that the Father in knowing himself knows the image of himself, which is the Son. This is a complex move in which

Hegel merges mysticism, Aristotle's notion of God as the *noesis noeseos*, and Trinitarian theology, to which we return in the following. Anselm has, in a vague and confused way, caught sight of the fact that in the finite Spirit's thinking of God, God thinks himself—the "thought of God" is both a subjective and an objective genitive—but he has distorted this insight of *Vernunft* by turning it into an invalid argument constructed by *Verstand*.

In short, in classical theology, the necessity, the order, and the intelligibility (thinkability) of being-itself are imaginatively attributed to a Supreme Being who bears these properties as divine names, as predicates of a divine subject. While that serves the purposes of the pulpit and of a simpler piety, it is a product of an intellectual imagination gone astray. Kant called them Ideals of pure reason, the subject matter of a "dialectics" that is futile (formally invalid) but suggestive, because *Vernunft* has an "interest" in them. Metaphysics is invalid as science, Kant said, but our metaphysical tendencies are ineradicable—because our honor as members of the "kingdom of ends" is at stake. But for philosophy (thought), the proofs belong to a kind of mythologizing or anthropomorphizing understanding (*Verstand*) in which an ontological property is personified as a property of an exceptional superbeing, the way in natural religion thunder is personified as an angry god. That is the central gesture of *supernaturalism*. In truth, the divine names are the names neither of many beings (polytheism) nor just one being (monotheism) but of being-itself (pan*en*theism). They are not the names of "somebody," although the needs of piety are met in imagining it so, but of something that is not less than a somebody but prior, greater, and deeper, making itself explicit in existing entities.

REASON AND REVELATION

In classical theology, the *natural* light of human *reason* (philosophy) is restricted to establishing certain universal truths, like proving the existence of God, the freedom of the will, and the immortality of the soul, matters debated by the Greeks in a purely rational way. But reason cannot say or gainsay anything about the doctrines of *revelation*—like the Trinity, Incarnation, and Resurrection—which are revealed by the *supernatural* light of faith. This distinction had already been established in the scholastic theology of the middles ages, where a close integration of faith and reason, *fides quaerens intellectum*, and a keen respect for the majesty of God took care to do no injury to piety. Hegel is more focused on the Enlightenment philosophers, who disdained religious piety. But in either its scholastic or modern form, Hegel rejects this distinction and redescribes it in terms of what I am calling theopoetics. For Hegel, there are not two different domains, one of which is off limits because of some supposed supernatural provenance, but one and the same domain of being that is understood *differently*, each of which is equally open to philosophical reflection. Indeed, theology enforces this distinction at the cost of its own well-being. Hegel held that in his day, the theologians, intimidated by the Enlightenment, had drained the lifeblood out of theology by restricting themselves to matters of rational demonstration and excluding the materials of revelation, which are the most important and spiritually nourishing elements of theology. If matters of revelation were raised at all, it was by historians of theology discussing the thought of past generations. Theologians, he quips, have become like cashiers counting other people's money. They no longer engage "the needs of our Spirit"; the truth of revelation has been forgotten.[20]

The theologians allowed the Enlightenment to drag Christ down to a merely human level, treating him as a man of great honor and courage, in which case, Hegel says, we have no need of Christ at all—for that much we already have Socrates.[21] For Hegel, "reason" (*Vernunft*) does not mean reducing the Christ of faith to a Jewish prophet, healer, and exorcist by way of rational-historical criticism. If this sounds like Kierkegaard, that is because, so far, it is. They both reject a rationalistic, reductionistic Enlightenment criticism of revelation, and they both maintain the important thing is not the historical Jesus but the *revelation* taking place in the Christ of faith. The difference is that Kierkegaard thinks the revelation is reached by confessing the God/man to be a rational absurdity that requires us to abandon reason and make a leap of faith (made possible by a supernatural booster shot from God). Hegel thinks the God/man is the deepest and most revelatory figure in the history of the world, far surpassing Socrates in just the way Christianity is the fullness of what the Greeks are only partially. For this, we require another idea of revelation and a richer idea of reason than Kierkegaard's. *Vernunft* is thinking, reflecting spirit, which reads the Bible with the eyes of the Spirit, not in a *literal* interpretation, of course, which is opposed to the Spirit (2 Cor. 3:6), but in a *speculative* interpretation.[22] Speculative hermeneutics is the art of seeing the workings of the Spirit everywhere, in everything, albeit differently.

Seen thus, the Incarnation, Crucifixion, Resurrection, and Ascension in the New Testament are a *Vorstellung*, a *story*, and not just any story but the greatest story ever told. In Christ we are given an "intuition" of the divine, of the *unity* of the divine and the human, in the striking form of an amazing man, a man of marvels and miracles—they killed him but he didn't stay dead—whose empirical death gives way to and permits the sending of the Spirit into the universal community of humankind.[23] The life and death of the *historical* Jesus, insofar as that can be reconstructed at all, is an empirical point, and about that let the chips fall where they may. If biblical archeologists someday discover his bones, so be it. Knowing that Jesus was a devout Jew, who never heard of Paul or Augustine, of Christianity or the Trinity, and had no intention of founding a successor religion to his own deeply held Jewish one, is ultimately of no more matter than knowing who the historical Hamlet or the historical King Arthur were; what matters is the formation of the Spirit that took shape. The important point is not the empirical-historical fact but the speculative-historical meaning, the point that is being made by the ongoing, unfolding *history of the Spirit* (what Gadamer would call "the history of effects"), which is that in Jesus we gain an insight into the unity of the divine and the human, which is elaborated into the Incarnation and the Trinity by later theological reflection. The story of Jesus recounted for us in the Scriptures is an image (*Vorstellung*) of something going on *in* the divine being, which is being mediated to us in and with the *figure* of Jesus in the New Testament and the subsequent rise of Christianity. On the side of conscious human subjects, we enter a higher stage of consciousness, catching sight of the deeper truth of the divine than found in the Jews, Greeks, Romans, and nature religions, a new consciousness of the unity of God and the world. On the side of the object, something is going on in the divine being-itself. In Jesus, the Spirit is spiraling into a higher form, morphing, shape-shifting. In Jesus, the divine being both realizes and reveals itself in a higher form, no longer as a distant abstract alien presence but in the concrete form of flesh and blood, here and now. In Christianity, humanity rises to a more mature consciousness because the Spirit itself matures into a higher form. God and humankind are growing together (*con* + *crescere*), not side by side, but as two sides of the same Spirit; that is the genuinely "concrete" universal.

What is "revelatory" in the Christian story, then, is not a supernatural intervention into space and time disclosing information about a series of supernatural events no mere mortal could ever obtain. Revelation means a burst of creative figuration that is "beyond reason" not inasmuch as a higher truth is revealed to a lower faculty but insofar as a work of imagination, like a poem, outstrips the analytics of abstract *Verstand*. Hegel was saying that the story of an Eternal Logos coming into time and assuming the form of a baby born in a manger while angels sing on high is a striking figure, an unforgettable *Vorstellung*. The New Testament is like a poem in which a speculative point can be discerned. It was clearly bold business that Hegel was about, neither an empirical history nor the business as usual of orthodox Christology. It was an audacious interpretation of Christianity. God is divested of the celestial sanctuary that once sheltered the divine being from time and becoming even as we are divested of an escape hatch into eternity after our personal death (there being no "where" to go). To declare matters of revelation off limits to the philosophers would force them to philosophize with one hand tied behind their back, quarantining them to the quarters of the Enlightenment, where no one had any appreciation of poetics, the figurative and the metaphoric, the epic and the narratival. The true philosophers of the Spirit take a special interest in the powerful *manifestation* of the Spirit taking place in Christian "revelation." Everything is available to the eagle eye of philosophy. That does not mean that there is no difference between philosophy and theology; it just means the difference has to do with form, not content.

In what sense, then, can Hegel speak of the "mystery" (*mysterion*) of revelation? [24] Revelation is a mystery or secret for the imagination and the understanding (*Verstand*), which sees one thing here, the world, and another thing there, God—or the finite here and the infinite over there—and it counts up one, two. It does not understand the transition. It does not understand that the infinite is the transition into the finite and the finite is the transition from the infinite. The infinite *is* its becoming-finite *in* particular things, and the finite *is* the becoming-finite *of* the infinite. The infinite is always expressing itself *in* the finite, and the finite is always the expression *of* the infinite. The one cannot be without the other, and so we do not have two things, or even just one, because we are not *counting*; we are *thinking*. We are not counting up beings, we are thinking being; we are not numbering beings, we are describing the process of beings emerging in their being. To the imagination and the understanding this is a great mystery, and it is inexpressible, but in Christianity the mystery is finally and after a long historical preparation no longer concealed but revealed, no longer inexpressible but expressed.

Of all the classical dogmas of revelation, the one of supreme importance for Hegel, the very touchstone, is the doctrine of the Trinity, so much so that it would be no exaggeration to say that, with all due respect to the patristic theologians who worked it out in the first place, Hegel was the greatest, the most radical, and the most consistent of the Trinitarian thinkers! For in this doctrine, the very meaning of being is revealed. There it is revealed that "God," to speak as if God were a discrete object over there, is in fact an autogenerative process in which the Father distinguishes himself from himself not by producing something totally other than himself but by externalizing himself for himself in his Son and then reconciling himself in and for himself in the Spirit of love. Here the mystery is revealed. Here the secret is told. Here the meaning of being and the history of the world reach their summit, their consummation.

While this praise for Christianity was received with nodding ministerial heads in high places, especially when adding that this was all coming to a head right here in Prussia, what Hegel meant requires a gloss. This is all true in the form of a *Vorstellung*, a set of figures, because fathers, sons, and their mutual love are all images of the Spirit drawn from family life and the natural world. That permits us to say that the Father does this and the Son does that, the Spirit is love, and in the Jewish religion there is the Father but without the Son. But this is all figurative talk, using the categories of finitude, where the understanding (*Verstand*), with a puzzled look on its face, counts one, two, three, wondering how it can all be. Describing this as a process among persons is a still more profound figure because the character of a person in love is being-for-others, which surrenders itself in its isolation to the other. In love, I win myself back by giving myself up.[25] So these figures are all figures; they must be "actively received"—that is, interpreted, speculatively, in and by *Vernunft* (the Spirit), which brings them to reflective clarity. The theologians, Hegel says, are like Moliere's Englishman who did not know he was speaking prose.[26] The theologians do not know what they know. They do not quite appreciate what they are saying in their exegetical work. But we (philosophers) know that, in truth, what in religion is called "God" is the entire process of being in itself, for itself, in and for itself, the onto-hermeneutic circle, or shall we say, the circum-incession of being and beings.

In other words, for Hegel, the distinction between reason and revelation is not a *regional* one but a *modal* one. It is not a difference in regional responsibilities, assigning reason to rule this natural region down here and revelation to reign in that more exotic and inaccessible supernatural region up there, to "reason" on this level and to "faith" on the other one. Hegel has undone *supernaturalism*, undone the distinction between the "natural" and the "supernatural," the two-stories theology that places natural reason on the first floor and theological faith on the second floor. The genuine difference between reason and revelation is a difference of angles of entry or interpretation of one and the same thing. It is not a *content distinction* between the material accessible to unaided reason and the revealed materials to which faith alone has access, as if we could draw a boundary line marking off the limits between them. It is *formal* distinction between the different *forms* taken by the same content. Philosophy and religion have the same content. The doctrines of Christology and the Trinity are the deepest, most profound truths of all time, the very soul of the divine revelation, of the self-manifestation of being that takes place in Christianity—in the *form* of a *Vorstellung*, of images and stories, of striking sayings and dramatic narratives, of paradoxes and parables, all gathered together into the figurative concepts of Christian theology. In sum, Hegel has shown that theo*logy* is theo*poetics*, and it is in philosophy that we get the straight talk. That is the radicalization.

But why does the absolute not simply reveal itself point-blank, without taking intermediate forms like religion? Because this is all part of the absolute's self-development and our education. In matters of the Spirit, nothing is shot from guns; being is becoming. These are all so many forms the absolute Spirit takes in order to make itself fit to the people, because religion is as much philosophy as most people can assimilate, as much Spirit as their finite spirits can admit. In philosophy, however, the very same content is given the form of philosophical concepts, indeed of *the* Concept (*Begriff*). So the revealed doctrines of Christian religion are the figurative forms of the same content that takes the form of thought in philosophy, where the figures of religious revelation are revealed in their full clarity. The task of the philosopher of religion is to read these doctrines with a subtle Spirit, with a light touch (*subtilitas intelligendi*), and to undertake a *speculative interpretation* of the figures of the Christian religion (*subtilitas explicandi*), which does them no injury. They are not off limits to philosophy but the very heart and soul (content) of philosophy in figurative form. Without them, the philosopher of religion has no subject matter. In the light of such an analysis, Tillich's famous claim in his theology of culture that religion is the content of culture and culture is the form of religion makes perfect sense.

Indeed, there is a third party to this discussion yet to be mentioned, which is art. In art the same content is given still another and this time more sensuous form. Religion is more conceptual than art (it has explicit precepts and concepts, or quasi-concepts) but more sensuous than philosophy (which is purely conceptual), but they all have the same content. These forms are rank ordered by their proximity to the concept, the increasingly, explicitly more conceptual form they give to their underlying content. The distinctions are not *regional* or *material*—they all address the same thing—but *formal*, providing formally different and ascending degrees of conceptual clarity and self-consciousness of the self-same content. Art, religion, and philosophy are the three degrees of self-consciousness of the absolute Spirit in which it presents itself sensuously, figuratively, and conceptually. Hegel assigns the middle ground to religion, which is lush with sensuous imagery, telling fetching stories that groan to be *re*told conceptually, stories that calm our heart and bring peace to troubled souls, religion being the Sabbath of life.[27] Art, religion, and philosophy—a Renaissance painting of Madonna and child, a Christmas liturgy where the Introit is *puer natus est*, a philosophical treatise on the unity of the finite and the infinite—these are *three stages of the same thing*, in rather the way that in science, material substances can be found in any of three states, solid, liquid, and gaseous. Art is the most earthy-solid state, religion more liquid, and philosophy the most airy and spiritual—which for the furious mockery of an outraged Kierkegaard meant that philosophy is mostly gas and hot air. Hegel left Kierkegaard howling in pain and evoked the biting wit of his pseudonyms, who sent out a great collective *Nein* to ontology and its being, as did a latter-day Kierkegaardian.

THE CLASSICAL ALLIANCE

Hegel planted a stake in the heart of supernaturalism, of the classical two-worlds architecture of theology. Hegel has, as Tillich says, relieved theology of the *blasphemy* of contracting the infinite depth of being-itself to a superbeing on high and of the *mythology* that reduces religion to a series of supernatural communications from a superbeing. Hegel's breakthrough—the radical Hegel—can be summarized as follows:

> *From theism to panentheism:* Hegel rethinks the distinction between God and the world, the infinite and finite, so that "God" is a not the Supreme Being (classical theism) but immanent in the spatiotemporal world (pane*n*theism).

From theology to theopoetics: Hegel breaks down the regional distinction between the supernatural revelation and natural reason and rejects the notion that the characteristic doctrines of revelation are off limits to philosophy. Revelation is not a supernatural intervention but an imaginative figure (theopoetics) requiring philosophical clarification.

Hegel did not deny what Aquinas called *ipsum esse subsistens*, but he did deny that it could take the form of a separately subsistent being, *per se subsistens*—that was a demand of piety, a conceptual *Vorstellung*. He thought it subsisted in and through finite entities that were finite modulations of its infinite absolute being, in varying and increasingly higher degrees of perfection, constituting a transcendence-in-immanence, an infinite-in-the-finite. This was an advance over traditional theism, but it remained in alliance with the classical assumption that being and thought are absolutely commensurable and even contemporary. So with Hegel we reach a radically anti-apophatic result, which evokes our Lyotardian incredulity.[28] The difficulty that comes up with respect to almost anything Hegel had to say is his notion of *absolute knowledge*, the all-encompassing grip of the concept (*Begriff*), which leads him to conclude that speculative thinking can get its head around the infinite process of the Spirit or that the absolute Spirit can fit inside the head of finite Spirit. As Heidegger says, in anxiety the world is lit up as a whole—all the world seems to tremble with nonbeing—but it is one thing to come to realize the world is the whole in which we find ourselves and quite another to say we understand it wholly. *Befindlichkeit* means finding ourselves *in*, being *in*, a world totality (*totum*), but not that we understand it totally (*non totaliter*).[29]

When Hegel said that religion is the Sabbath of life, he was assuring us that he was in *alliance* with the heart of Christian theology and its ultimate work of edification, of offering divine consolation. The entire vocabulary of classical theology, the pantheon of divine predicates, and all the old divine names are still available to him, but with a difference. These funds have now been transferred from their heavenly account and deposited in a worldly account, made to do service in space and time. His assumption is that the classical categories of philosophy and theology, by being distinguished from the categories of finitude and the *Verstand*, can be so refitted and refashioned so as to do service in *comprehending* the length and breadth and depth of being, of that *in which* we live and move and have our being. That is the heart of the objection made by Schelling, which (with a crucial assist by Kierkegaard) changed everything thereafter (chapters 6–8).

HEGEL AT THE FOOT OF THE CROSS

To see how deep is this alliance, let us return to the death of God with which we began. For Hegel, God *is* not simply (immediately) God, but God must *become* God. Hegel means thereby to honor the contingency, the hazards, the harshness of life in space and time, the fortunes and misfortunes, the chance and the contingencies. The world is the stormy medium in which God becomes God, in which God's being emerges stronger and more truly itself, tested, tried, and found true by what he calls the "power of the negative." This much he and Schelling have in common. But the question put by radical apophatic thinking—which we also pose to Schelling himself—is this: how much *risk* does this negativity pose? Once God's being is exposed to space and time, is God exposed to the risk of nonbeing? The Greco-Christian God of classical theology is God eternally, purely, perfectly, and incurs no risk. But is the speculative God-becoming-God exposed by its spacing and timing to failing altogether? Might God suffer death itself? If history is God's autobiography in time, do not all biographies end in death? Might God's story end badly?

For Hegel, Jesus is a particular being, and like every particular being, his empirical reality must break up. But Jesus is not like every other human. He is the Christ, an icon of God, our intuition of God, the pivot of world history, a privileged place where the divine life is revealed. So at this point, citing an old Lutheran hymn composed by Johannes Rist in 1647 for Good Friday worship, Hegel says that with the death of Jesus on the cross, God himself dies.[30] Hegel is being bold, but he is not being Nietzsche *avant la lettre*. He means that death *touches* the life of God. Death does not have power *over* God, but death inhabits and *affects* God. Weakness, fragility, suffering, and death itself are within God, not outside, and God himself is involved in it, along with us, as one of us. Like Luther, Hegel insisted that this pain enters into the divine nature, in contrast to the Roman Catholic supernaturalist view that the suffering of Jesus was confined entirely to the human nature. Hegel is not anticipating Nietzsche or making any kind of sociological comment on secularization or the declining state of religion. He is engaging the theological debate between what is called the divine impassability (the Greek and Roman Catholic view) and theo-passionism (the Lutheran view).

This death is a moment of God's life, but it is a "vanishing moment" that gives way to a higher reconciliation of God and humankind called the Spirit.[31] The death of Jesus is a harsh, cruel, and dramatic moment in the greatest drama ever written. But it is still just a moment, one part of the longer, larger life of the Spirit, the point where the universal Spirit becomes visible in a particular individual (Incarnation) in order that the particular can break up (Crucifixion) and thereby allow the formation of the concrete universal (Pentecost). The truth is the whole story, and it does not end on Good Friday. The death of Jesus is the middle, mediating moment in the living movement from the distant Father to a Son who is born and dies among us in the flesh to the life of the Spirit. That is why the authors of the Gospel story have the risen Jesus say that he must now ascend to his Father up in the sky but is sending his Spirit to be with us down here on earth for all days, even unto the consummation of the world. It is also why the early church had to issue a patch to the final chapter of Mark about the resurrection. So Hegel (no more than the Lutheran hymnist) does not mean that the absolute Spirit is here executed by a contingent of cruel Roman soldiers, that the course God takes through time is here stopped dead in its tracks, that the idea of God sketched in the Logic is scratched out. Only finite beings die. Only finite individuals are conquered by death, but God is neither finite nor an individual. Death can never overtake the very substance of reality, the ground of beings, the Spirit itself. For Hegel, death finishes off the finite, but it cannot finish off the infinite, which is unfinished and unfinishable. It cannot extinguish the inextinguishable; it cannot call a temporal halt to the eternal. Death catches up to Jesus but not to the absolute Spirit. If Jesus gives up his Spirit, the Spirit does not. God is dead—long live God!

While Hegel's account of the speculative Good Friday,[32] the death of God, gets all the attention, it is in fact not Good Friday, or even Easter Sunday, that matters most to Hegel, but Pentecost, the feast of the tongues, of the fire hovering over the heads of the disciples. That is the first day in the rest of the Spirit's life, the holiest feast day on the Hegelian liturgical calendar, the feast day of the absolute Spirit, the day the disciples receive the Spirit and the Spirit commences the fullness of its life in the world. On this day, the Spirit becomes the Spirit. The treasure of divine names, once the property of a distant deity, is transferred into the account of humankind, which is the consciousness of its unity with the divine. This takes place in Christian Europe, which helps explain why Christian Europe felt called, like the world-historical Spirit on horseback, to march into every city around the world. Galileo named the moon he discovered revolving around Saturn "Europa." If you get caught up in Hegel's Spirit, the "European Union" would mean the whole world! This can and did serve as the metaphysics of empire building, and it is one of the ways that the politics of the Spirit's march through history can run off the tracks and leave a lot of dead bodies in its wake. It allowed European explorers to weaponize the medieval word *religio* so it could now be used to enforce the "*true* religion" with the power of the sword.

For Hegel, the death of Jesus was the life-giving pangs of childbirth. For as long as Jesus was alive, the manifestation of the Spirit was confined, contracted to this paradigmatic and focal individual. So it is necessary for this individual to break up, like a seed that breaks open in order to germinate, in order that the Spirit may spread across the face of the earth and enfold all people in its embrace. Individuals die. Entire cities, civilizations, movements, peoples, nations, and languages die, but the Spirit does not die. Aristotle said that individuals die but the species is immortal, that individuals come and go, but the species, supported by these changing individuals, is unchanging. Hegel said much the same thing, but he reset it to the music of time, recasting it all in terms of a philosophy of history. Humankind is not a static species, as it was for Aristotle, but a work in progress, a historical form of life passing from lower to ever higher forms, stages in the education of humankind and of the Spirit. History is a kind of *Bildungsroman* of the Spirit, or an epic poem.

The march of absolute thought through history cannot end up in the cosmic ditch. For Hegel, that would be absurd. God does not end badly, nor does history. This is Augustine's theology of history playing to the music of Hegel's philosophy of history, where eternity is inscribed in time and time puts eternity on display. If Hegel begins with Paul's notion of *kenosis* (emptying), he subordinates it to and fits it inside a larger story of *plerosis*, of the "*pleroma*," the fullness and completion (*Vollendung*) of time. If Hegel were at the foot of the cross, he would have said that this terrible thing is ultimately part of the wise work of the power of the negative. God is not defeated. The Logos is not illogical. Religion is the Sabbath of life.

BEYOND HEGEL: BREAKING THE GRIP OF THE CONCEPT

Clearly, then, the *risk* is contained. Every individual entity is at risk, including Jesus, *Eli, Eli, Lama Sabachthani*, but risk stops at the door of being-itself. The risk does not reach all the way down to the ground of beings, to the underlying substance out of which beings emerge and into which, in the end, they finally submerge. In the terrible drama of the life and death of vanishing individuals, God emerges as God, and the story of how God makes that appearance in the final act is what Hegel called the "phenomenology of the Spirit," meaning the science of those rising appearances and our rising consciousness of them. The Spirit becomes the Spirit, in Spirit and in truth, and we become who we are. Truth is the whole. The path is bloody but not blocked. God's head, as the poet says, is bloodied but unbowed. So Hegel's alliance with classical theology comes down to this. Any given finite being is contingent, but being-itself is necessary. Any given finite being is at risk, but being-itself is safe, assured, everlasting. There is contest and conflict among beings, but being-itself is not defeated. The idea of God inscribed in the *Logic* will not permit it. God can make his way by way of whatever particular beings come his way. The eternal idea of God is always working itself out. God will always become God. Reason permits *moments* of the irrational, but reason means the power to turn these moments to the purposes of Reason in the end. To that extent, Hegel's view is radical in the classical sense, radically foundational, since God is the deep ground in things that steers all things unto one, which is why he began his lectures by saying that religion is the Sabbath of life.

That is the point at which a radical apophatic breaks off from Hegel. While Hegel is right to treat theology as a *Vorstellung*, as a figurative form of life, it is a mistake to say that it is a figurative form of a *higher rationality*. Theology is a figurative form, period, tout court, and there are no philosophers waiting in the wings who hold the key, the *legendum*, the Concept governing these figures. It is not that the theologians do not realize they are speaking prose but that the philosophers do not realize they are speaking poetry. What a more radical Hegel would have discovered is that the*ology* is theo*poetics*, and like every great poem, it does not admit of a final telling but only of endless retelling. That is why I speak of a *headless* Hegelianism,[33] a Hegelianism without absolute knowledge, one that recognizes Hegel as a founding figure, an antecedent, a predecessor, in which the final concept is that there is no Concept, that the *Vorstellung* goes all the way down. The immensity and the density of that in which we live and move and have our being exceeds our grasp (our *greifen* and *begreifen*). We have no such prodigious head for absolute concepts. When it comes to absolute knowledge, we never get past a *Vorstellung*.

The radical apophatic view is that not only are "God," "religion," and "Christianity" figures of the Spirit, but even "Spirit" itself is a figure, a *Vorstellung* for which no one holds the hermeneutic key (radical hermeneutics). Each is a clue for which we lack the code. Religion, art, and philosophy represent so many fleeting and provisional forms, imaginative figures, suggestive words, and deconstructible concepts. Period. We lack the big story, the *grand récit* that can outrank them, rank order them, or purport to explicate them in a final or decisive way. Hegel assumes that thinking being means being is thinkable all the way down, which we greet with Lyotardian incredulity and even, as Lyotard also shows, with shock. For it is part of the scandal of Hegelianism that it is committed to an obscenity, to saying that Auschwitz, that every Auschwitz, anywhere in the world, belongs to a larger divine narrative.[34] In radical apophatics, the ground is made to tremble, the Spirit turns out to be a specter, the *Geist* becomes a ghost, the ontology a hauntology. In a radical apophatic theology, art, religion, and philosophy are all so many ways to recall something from time immemorial, to dream of something we know not what, of some impossibility beyond the possible, of the coming of what we cannot see coming, for which we pray and weep, but not without fear and trembling. We later return to the question of the death of God (chapter 15) to consider the possibility of understanding the God of panentheism otherwise, in a way that would not be opposed to the mortality of God but in fact constituted by it, which would be to press not only Hegel but apophatic thinking itself to the limits.

FOUR

SCHELLING AND THE METAPHYSICS OF EVIL

IN PORTRAYING THE GENEALOGY OF radical apophatics in terms of the leitmotif of angels and demons, I have, of course, been cribbing on the New Testament, its central drama, which is the battle pitched by the "principalities" and "powers" (Eph. 6:12) with the kingdom of God. There Christ and Satan are world-historical antagonists in a cosmic spectacle. Schelling, more than any other philosopher I know of, has captured—or, perhaps better, has been captured by—this scene. Anselm dismissed this as so much mythology, arguing that we need a "more rational" (*rationabilius*) account of "why God became human," his (in)famous "satisfaction" theology of the atonement. For Schelling, that reflects a hermeneutic failure, an inability to understand a myth. A myth is not a fantasy, a poetic ornamentation, in need of replacement by a logical argument but a way of accessing something to which logic cannot gain access. Myth is an echo bouncing off the ground of being, resounding with the depths, reverberating in our unconscious long before the functionaries of reason and consciousness arrive on the scene and unpack their bag of concepts, propositions, and arguments. In myths like the narrative of Satan, we are visited by the powers of the night; the task of philosophy is not to flood it with the light of the Concept, as in

Hegel, but to expose ourselves to it and experience the nameless powers by which we are assaulted.

THE RADICAL SCHELLING

Schelling alone sets out to find the "the philosophical meaning of Satan." Of course, unlike Aquinas, he thought that angels and demons were a myth, that they did not actually exist, but again unlike Aquinas, he thought that myths were of great philosophical importance. Schelling is the philosopher of the apophatic par excellence, the preeminent philosopher of the "dark ground"—this is his literal expression—which he once called the "barbarian principle."[1] While Schelling has contributed mightily to our understanding of mythology and the depths of indigenous culture, Schelling was not "woke." He never heard of Black Lives Matter. But in an age in which we are trying to sensitize ourselves to the systematic character of racism, we cannot pretend that "dark ground" is an innocent expression, that it does not associate evil with being dark and black. Metaphors matter, and if we want to change things, we have to change the metaphors. So after marking the philological point that Schelling's literal expression is *der dunkle Grund*, we will hereafter observe the philosophical point that just as by *Grund* he did not mean soil or earth but basis, so by *dunkel* he did not mean black but deep, concealed, denied the truth, something anarchical, unruly, a groundless ground or *Ungrund*. If Luther liked to speak, even to jest about, the *posteriora dei* (Ex. 33:23), the divine backside, Schelling had in mind a kind of divine underside, a place of recess, contraction, and concealment, rather like what Heidegger meant by *lethe*—in short, the apophatic principle, or unprinciple. So we will treat this image gingerly, use it sparingly, and remember that Schelling is referring us to the depths of our experience, not to skin pigmentation.

In Schelling we find a philosopher with a radically apophatic sensibility for the depths in which we live and move and have our being. This is out of character for metaphysicians who, ever since Parmenides, have been trying to explain to us why being is all truth and light, all the way down. For Schelling, by contrast, being, truth, and goodness are inwardly disturbed by nonbeing and evil. He is the author of what Heidegger called a "metaphysics of evil," which decidedly did not mean the standard fare *malum metaphysicum*, the usual evasion that declares evil to be a privation of being, thereby exonerating being and God, above all, of all wrongdoing. The bolder stance struck by Schelling is to say the groundlessness is inscribed in being itself, including in the being of God, where it constitutes the part of God where God is not being God with which God must contend. With Schelling, we hit radical apophatic ground.

Schelling does not think that being is simply being, truth is simply true, or good is simply good. He thinks that being is becoming and becoming is overcoming, that being is life and life is strife. Being is the process of overcoming nonbeing, of the good overcoming evil, of truth overcoming untruth, of life overcoming the immobile and inert. Forces come in pairs of opposition; *there is no such thing as one force*. Each thing is entangled with its opposite and becomes what it is only by overcoming what struggles against it. This applies universally—joy comes from overcoming sorrow, order from quelling disorder—everything, up to and including God, who must struggle with what is not God. Were this not the case, everything would be an inert, lifeless Parmenidean plenum or, rather, would never have come to be at all.

If there was one thing Hegel got wrong—Schelling and Hegel started out as seminary roommates but ended up as famous adversaries—it is his notion that being is reason all the way down, that reason is being all the way through. Hegel thought there was a reason—however long term, tortured, and difficult to discern—in all the violence, injustice, and bloodshed littering history. Schelling thought that was a ruse, a kind of obscene intellectualism. If we take a hard, close-up, unvarnished look at evil, we see an active force, a destructive power, nothing rational or merely privative about it. Auschwitz is not a privation but an odious, destructive, powerful agency. Just as with Aquinas's angelology, we can catch sight of Schelling's ontology in his Satanology. If Aquinas was known as the *doctor angelicus*, I will resist the devilish temptation to call Schelling the *doctor diabolicus*—as *diabolical* is a word with which we must be cautious—but I will say that he is the preeminent doctor of the powers of evil and the most important antecedent of radical apophatic theology before Tillich. His is an unnerving and uncertain business, a "negative" theology, not in the classical sense, where the negatives are high praise and add up to making positive theology even more positive, but in a radical sense, where things are risky, uncertain, unnerving, menaced, and disturbed from within by the powers of the night.

If this were the whole story with Schelling, he would probably not be an accredited member of the philosophers' guild. But notwithstanding all the exotic materials of which Schelling made use, including a rather large dose of theosophy, Schelling was a philosopher intent on constructing a "system of philosophy" from these unlikely materials. I number myself among those who think he did not succeed in this systematic task, that in fact he exploded the system from within. But I regard his failing as a happy fault. I think the side of Schelling that failed to construct a system is his more interesting side, that the Satanological side is more interesting than the systematic side, and that the radical Schelling is more interesting than the edifying Schelling who tried to keep one foot in traditional philosophy and classical Christian theology. In keeping with his own metaphysics, he had a kind of divided sensibility, an internal strife between a metaphysics of edification that respects the diurnal light of love and reason and a radical apophatic respect for the powers of the night, for both reason and the breakup of reason, condensed into the expression "ecstatic reason." His ambivalence is the source of his creativity. At any given moment, we might see the one side getting the better of the other. He enacts his own metaphysics: the radical Shelling emerges from overcoming the edifying Schelling.

While he meant his work to be philosophy, he did not think, as Hegel did, that everything comes to a head *in* philosophy itself. Of all the great idealists, Schelling's work clung closest to *art* and *nature*, the subject of Kant's third *Critique*, which is why he was a favorite of Coleridge and Romanticism. Early on in his work, he saw in art the intimate collaboration of conscious and unconscious forces, an interweaving of unconscious instinct with conscious design, even as nature gives the appearance of having been designed by conscious intent, acting purposively without purpose, as Kant said. Schelling influenced Freud, not directly, but through a book on Schelling's concept of the unconscious by Eduard von Hartmann that Freud read, which explains why Žižek is deeply interested in Schelling and made a major contribution to the revival of interest in Schelling today. In his later years, Schelling concluded that the focal cultural practice was found not in art but in *religion*, a "philosophical religion" that entertains radical ideas of God and the world, of reason and revelation. This religion is an antecedent of radical theology on the very grounds I set forth at the start—that it suspends the supernatural signified in the name of theopoetics and challenges classical theism with a position that he calls pantheism but today is called panentheism. Everything—science, ethics, and art; nature and history—comes to a head in religion in the deep sense, not the "stunted" and "puny" formulas of confessional religion but a religion that turns on an ecstatic sense of reason and what I am calling a radical apophatic imagination.[2]

Hegel treated religion as a lesser version of philosophy. Schelling saw the apophatic in religion, a deep encounter with the sheer fact of being rather than nothing that displaces philosophical thought. This religion lacks the comforts traditionally dispensed by religion, the religion that led Hegel to call it the Sabbath of life and led Lacan to lament that religion will "triumph" over psychoanalysis because the latter faces up to the lack in being that religion fills with false promises.[3] But Dr. Lacan needed to spend some time on the couch with Dr. Schelling, who would have instructed him about another kind of religion—full of demons and blind destructive forces that can be artfully raised up to productivity, unless they are not, with the result that it is uncertain whether God will prevail. That remains to be seen, a posteriori. God's rule may be *disproved* by experience,[4] because there is something ungodly in God and because being itself contains the "raw material" of infinite possibilities, of the worst as well as the best, both the divine and the demonic.[5]

Obviously, Schelling is rather more than what the standard histories portray, the bridge from Fichte to Hegel. He outlived Hegel and launched an explosive and influential critique of Hegel that brought "German idealism" to an end. He is a "protean" thinker, precocious, already a national figure in his early twenties, constantly rethinking his views, and almost impossible to summarize and distill, something I wisely refrain from attempting here. My focus here is on monitoring the tension between the opposing forces *within* Schelling, the struggle between the edifying Schelling and the radical one. In the present chapter, I examine the metaphysics of evil in the *Philosophical Investigations into the Essence of Human Freedom* (1809) and to a lesser extent in *The Ages of the World* (1809–15), and in the next chapter, I explore his Satanology. After that I turn to the Berlin lectures on the philosophy of mythology and revelation in the 1840s, which announce something he calls the "unprethinkable."

WHAT THEY DID NOT TELL US IN SEMINARY

If the author of the book of Genesis were a reader of the works of Schelling, Genesis might have sounded something like this:

> In the beginning without beginning, God resided in self-contented self-contemplation, enjoying perfect peace, except for the stirring of some vague gnawing at the divine being, some

obscure longing God could not quite put into words. Meanwhile, on the other side of God, there was a terrible turbulence, things blindly tossing about, a whirling *tohu wa-bohu*, all topsy-turvy, deep waters restlessly swirling round and round, winds howling—in all, an unruly restless chaos. All of which, God secretly confessed, looked rather interesting. Then, from out of a past that was never present, God said, "Fiat!" And it was done. That was the Word God was looking for. Then the turbulence settled into an order beautiful to behold. Then, for the first time from time immemorial, God felt really alive, thrilled by the throbbing rush of time pulsating through the divine body, delighted by the spread of space as God stretched the divine limbs, and all this in the divine companionship of humankind. "Free at last," God exclaimed. "Free at last!"

While this little riff on Genesis may seem like a whimsical way to treat a serious metaphysical thinker, it is in keeping with Schelling's own counsel in *The Ages of the World*, where he says, in the spirit of Plato, that when rigorously conceptual thinking (*pace* Hegel) hits a wall, tell a story or write an "epic poem."[6] That is why I think Schelling is the antecedent par excellence of theopoetics.

God yearns? God is lonely? The *ens realissimum* needs us? What anthropomorphic, mythological, and theosophical prattle! But Schelling is asking us to check our standard theological assumptions at the philosophy department door and be prepared to *think* about God and the world *differently*. Philosophy is not an apologetics course. Philosophy engages a world full of cruelty and injustice as well as peace and love, and the name of God is the name of something going on in that world, in us, all around us.

Be prepared to think of *God* not as the transcendent immutable deity of *theism* but as an autoengendering, self-birthing process of eternal becoming, where being-God means God *becoming* God. Think of God not as eternally unmoved but as a living matrix,[7] a moving, active process in endless contest with unfathomable forces. Think of the act of *creating* not as a pure presto *creatio ex nihilo* work of magic (it is not even that way in Genesis) but as a further spiraling out of God's being into the world of space and time, less as "making" something than as giving birth, without which God is incomplete and lonely; think of it as growth, expansion, the ongoing continuation of God becoming more fully God. Think of *created nature*, in turn, not as a collection of atoms moving around in empty space according to the laws of Newtonian mechanics but as a living body, an organic unity, an eco-organic system teeming with life, held together by way of a unifying world soul.

Think of *human being*—this is particularly confounding—not as the species of upright talking bipeds found on planet earth but as God's companion sphere, counterpart, or alter ego (the *alter Deus*), another God also free and conscious, not an entity but a realm of "spirit"—whose feet are planted in nature—in which God finds a confidante, a partner in dialogue, a correspondent,[8] God's offspring and fulfillment *as* God. Schelling is hardly talking about *anthropos* at all, or if he is, he is treating the anthropological as an ontological event taking place in the sphere of Spirit, of divine being, of God. Think of human *history* not as *human* history but as the history of God, as a stage in the "ages of the world," spanned between the absolute beginning, the beginning without beginning; the absolute past, that time immemorial when God was something of a divine yearling; and the absolute future, when God is fully matured as God. Human being, to borrow an image from Nietzsche's Zarathustra, is a rope strung between the self-enveloped eternal God and the fully developed God, tested and ripened by the course of history. We are the rope, and if the rope snaps, if we do not do our part, God will not make it. God will not be God. How so? Remember the forces of refusal, contraction, and concealment. Back at the seminary they whitewashed this as "theodicy," the "problem of evil." Remember, *evil* is not pure nonbeing, a negative *privatio boni*, but active powers that have been unleashed with creation and with which even God has to contend.

PANTHEISM, ATHEISM, MATERIALISM, AND NATURALISM

Critics of Schelling have "accused" him of pantheism, atheism, materialism, and naturalism. Are these insults against which he should be protected or bold positions for which he is to be congratulated? How to sort out all this name-calling? Schelling himself described his view as pantheism, and properly understood, it is. But the problem with the word *pantheism* is that it is almost impossible to understand it properly. As we saw with Hegel, this word has long been a term of abuse, a scandalous charge, and damaged almost beyond repair. Pantheism means there is *nothing outside of God*, but it inevitably suggests that each and every particular thing *is* God, and, in Schelling's time, it suggested Spinoza, which was a problem. Spinoza's mistake was his not his pantheism, Schelling said, but his mechanism and determinism. Spinoza's error was not to posit *all* things in God but to reduce them all to *things*, blind matter in motion, which is what Shelling meant by "realism" (from *res*).[9] For Schelling, human freedom is the issue of a free and living God, resembling God as a child resembles its parent, and so, far from being a form of fatalism, pantheism is the engendering matrix of freedom. We are free because we are *in God* just the way the hand is alive because it is part of the body. If pantheism is the system, then the system is not opposed to freedom; it is the *system of freedom*, of a living will, which is what he meant by idealism, which is itself a "higher realism." In pantheism we recognize the freedom in nature and the nature in freedom, where nature itself, understood in terms of life, not machines, prepares the necessary ground of freedom.

So Schelling had to spell out why *pantheism* is not a term of abuse. I accept Mary-Jane Rubenstein's argument about the value of the word and the well-deserved shock it delivers to theism (and atheism).[10] I accept its strategic use, its polemical punch. Anything that can scandalize classical theism is doing important work for post-theism. But I question its conceptual value—for Hegel, for Schelling, and in general. I think it is more precise and instructive to speak instead of pan*en*theism: not God is all but God is *in* all, God is *all in all*, a formula Schelling held close to his heart.[11] Confusion is avoided, Schelling contends, by properly understanding his principle of identity as "belonging together," not as simple unmediated identification. Individual things come and go, but God is their underlying ground. There is more to God than God, than the primal being. There is more God, God in a more extended form, more of God becoming God, where the history of the world is the history of God becoming God. Panentheism is the logic of Spirit, a universal force present *in* each thing but not simply identical *with* any one thing. The Spirit is *in* every individual; the individual must *have* the Spirit.

If we ask what Schelling means by the term *atheism*, the answer is mechanism and determinism. God is life, and so the denial of life is the denial of God; mechanism drives the life and Spirit out of everything. If God were reduced to a pure, blind, necessary being, God would be dead, Schelling says.[12] Any theory that makes life an epiphenomenon, explained away in lower nonliving and mechanistic terms, would be heartless death-of-God atheism. His panentheism could be described as a panvitalism, where God in all means life in all. All things are full of gods, Heraclitus said, means all things are alive—in varying and ever-graduated degrees of intensity climaxing in the life of the Spirit. It is not life that is an illusion; the illusion is "inert" matter (as any quantum physicist could tell us today), whose living energy (*energeia*), power (*dynamis*), and vitality are simply invisible to the naked eye but clear to the metaphysical eye.[13] The next closest thing to atheism for Schelling would be classical theism, if that means an absolutely transcendent, immutable, and detached being unmindful of us, like Aristotle's unmoved mover.

Then what does Schelling mean by the term *materialist*? That is the thing that interests Žižek and Habermas and a new generation of philosophers today.[14] Materialism would *not* mean atheism because the ground in God is, if not matter itself, the longing for matter, for God's own embodiment in the material world. His pantheism is a kind of naturalism, like an "ecstatic naturalism" (Robert Corrington), a "dynamic naturalism" (Iain Hamilton Grant).[15] Schelling is advancing a materialistic or naturalistic panentheism or, maybe better, a panentheistic naturalism, since *natura* literally means emergent life (from *nascor, nasci, natus sum*). The all, the *pan* in panentheism means nature, God in nature, nature in God. Nature is visible spirit; spirit is invisible nature. Dig deeply enough into either one and you inevitably hit the other. The two "belong together" (*zusammengehören*) in the unity of a deeper common ground (the principle of identity). The real contradiction to be resolved is not between nature and spirit but between necessity and freedom.

In sum, God is the father and the mother or matrix of all, the primogenitor of all things. The very being of God is giving birth, where God is threatened not with death but barrenness, no offspring, confined to celestial solitude, eternal sterility, a sad and lonely outcome for the Ancient of Days. But, in a world in which there is nothing outside of God, how can the world be such a mean, cruel, and bloody place?[16]

THE JOINTURE OF BEING

Schelling held that every being is composed of two opposing forces, two principles, which he called ground and existence.[17] This Heidegger labels "the jointure of being."[18] Forces are internally related to each other; their opposition belongs to their composition. By the *ground* he meant the substratum or basis of the being, its anchor in reality, the principle that contracts it to itself, a principle of individuation or what Schelling called egoism or self-ness. *Existence*, the opposing force, is a forward thrust, an expansive movement of the being out of (*ex*) and against the ground in which it stands (*sistere*). Overcoming the ground does not mean *extinguishing* it but successfully *engaging* it. Without the ground, existence would simply vanish, just the way the force exerted in lifting would vanish absent the opposing force of gravity. This is not just an analogy, because he thought gravity is the form ground takes in nature. Today physicists speak of a "black hole," where the gravitational force of matter is so great that not even light can escape. As the force that is straining to escape the contractive power of the ground, existence is the light. As the ground is self-concealing, existence is self-revealing. As the ground offers anarchical resistance, existence is the *arche* that establishes order. As the ground is unconscious, existence is the seat of consciousness and understanding.

So this jointure should not be reduced to traditional distinctions, like matter and form or essence and existence. This is an important observation because in Schelling's later writings (chapters 6–7), these categories do move to front and center, which is a case of the radical Schelling taking a back seat to a more edifying Schelling. Nor should the difference between ground and existence be confused with Heidegger's famous "ontological difference" between Being and beings. In Heidegger's vocabulary, Schelling would put the focus on the really real thing, the being (*das Seiende*), which is what really exists (*das wirkliche Existierende*), while Being (*Sein*) would be not the higher, prior horizon of possibility that makes the being possible, as in Heidegger, but its lower-lying self-concealing ground, its stuff, something to be overcome.

That this composition of existence and ground also applies to God puts Schelling's unorthodoxy in plain view, contradicting the classical simplicity of God. The ground is *within* God as the part of God where God is *not being God*.[19] This is where Schelling sounds a little theosophical. In part, what he is saying is biblical: as the "egoist" self-contracting side of God, the ground is God's "wrath"—the jealous, angry God bellowing out against Job, the furious burning fire, what Rudolf Otto called the *mysterium tremendum*, the God who terrifies us. But Schelling also says that the ground in God is called nature, which leads him to remark that, despite their other differences, on this point his view is the same as that of Spinoza, who famously spoke of *Deus sive natura*.[20] So God, the primal being, is both spirit (existence), where God is being God, and nature (ground), where God is not God. But *natura* here does not mean spread out in space and time but rather, as Heidegger says, something like Eriugena's uncreated *natura naturans*. God's nature, Schelling says, is a surface in which God can catch sight of his own image and possible likenesses, where God imagines, in an ideal way, endless possibilities for extending his being into the real natural world. Here the account goes mythopoetic, even theosophical. The ground in God is restless, yearning for the light, an infinite "longing" for existence, while God, on his side (existence), experiences the pain of solitude and divine loneliness. So it is that the understanding (existence) of God beholds the ground and is moved by it to flood it with light, to speak his word into its silence and by his "fiat" to create the world. Cast a little more philosophically, God sees in the divine being potencies that could be actualized by the divine will.[21]

Viewed from the side of existence, God's own being, Schelling is being edifying: God is Spirit, love, wisdom, and understanding; all knowing, all loving, all powerful, and so on. It is the other side that is radical—nature, the principle of ground, where God feels a lack or longing. This should not be sanitized; its pedigree is theosophical, originating in Jacob Boehme's notion of a swirling hurly-burly of forces. Thus, contrary to Cusa, Leibniz, and the classical tradition, this sea of possibilities is not in a state of eternal peace and passivity but is stormy in the extreme, and God's creative action is to pacify this unruly disorder. While this unruliness is contrary to classical metaphysical theology, it is not far from the poetic picture painted in the opening scene of Genesis. Furthermore, the ground in God has a certain independence of God, a certain ontological (not chronological) priority to God, who emerges as the first and primordial being by overcoming it. God is the first among beings, a kind of *primum inter entia*, but not absolute primordiality itself, not the absolute, unconditioned first. God is fully actualized in the existential principle, as the primary existing being, but not in the ground, where nature is present only as a yearning. God wills nature as his other, as his other self, so that God may fill space and time with still more divine life and satisfy the divine hunger. Schelling is close to saying that God is responsible for evil because human beings have descended from a heavenly parent who has a concealed and occluded side, that humanity has bad ontological genes, which, while recessive in our parent, are dominant in us. That, in a very real sense, is true, and explaining how is the purpose of the treatise on freedom.

But first a question on behalf of the radical Schelling. Schelling says that, beholding the possibility of a created world, God is moved by love to utter his famous fiat. But love, like life, like everything else, has no force unless it is overcoming something opposing it, and here it overcomes or resolves God's solitude. Creation makes for the *pleroma*, for the fullness of time, for the consummation of the ages of the world, for the eternal fulness of God and creation. *God's love is pleromatic, not kenotic.* That means it is not like the "greater love" of those who give up their life for a friend but are not around to enjoy the fruits of their deed, as Jesus says, or like a "pure gift" in Derrida's sense. God does not *empty* the divine being *into* creation without remainder. God *fulfills* the divine being *with* creation, which effects God's self-fulfillment.

God is a eudemonist seeking perfect eternal bliss where God ends up being all in all. In creation, then, God takes the risk that evil will come into the world, from which God does not shirk lest fear triumph over love. But this is a *limited risk* because God, in a very classical way, does not and cannot put the *divine being* itself at risk. If the world itself were to perish, God would be still standing (and still longing). At this point, a radical theology of the pure gift can ask, which one is the greater love?

THE METAPHYSICS OF EVIL

Schelling is not rehearsing the classical idea of *creatio ex nihilo* but proposing instead something like a *creatio ex profundis*, not a making but a birthing, engendering more being from out of the eternal womb of God, the way a plant grows from a seed.[22] Taking Genesis at its word, creation is a forming of pregiven and highly unruly elements that God brings to order and fills with life. Creation is the opening or awakening of the ground (actualizing its potency, ordering its disorder), where ground is not a passive, dumb, inert stuff but a *will*, albeit in an unconscious, unruly state. In the *Weltalter* manuscripts, it is a churning rotary stuck in what Nietzsche would have described as the eternal recurrence of the same.[23] God's understanding (existence) shines upon the ground, illuminates it, divides its contending forces, and names its namelessness. This brings the ground to life, arouses the ground to *assert itself*, to separate itself off, to say yes to itself, which goes hand in hand with the possibility of saying no to the divine source of its being. This ongoing process of contracting and expansion, of yes and no, is distributed across a graduated series of intensities extending from the lowest natural forces up to the emergence of the highest, human freedom (spirit). The greater the tension in the jointure of the being, the higher the being, which means the more spiritual its powers, *for better or for worse!* The more spiritual the being, the higher the stakes.

Love's desire in creation is to bring forth the *alter Deus*, the other God meant to be God's companion, made in the likeness of God. The *other* of God is to be *like* God, which means free, conscious, and independent. But love's creation thereby exposes itself to an irreducible *risk*: God's other becomes another God, *free* to say no to God, a rival, up to and including an antagonist or adversary (*Diabolos*, from *dia* + *ballein*). Creation means, taken in a rigorously ontological sense, all hell breaks loose. God is the eternal success of existence overcoming the ground, while creatures have both principles "but without complete consonance because of the *deficiency of what was raised from the ground*".[24] "If the identity of both principles were just as indissoluble in man's spirit as in God, then there would be no difference, i.e., God as spirit would not be revealed. The unity that is indivisible in God must therefore be divisible in man—and in this is the possibility of good and evil."

To create is to create something different, otherwise there is no revelation and expansion of the divine being, which is to incur the risk that creatures, who lack the power of God to maintain the consonance, the harmony, will allow the self-contracting ground to break out and assume the upper hand, overthrowing existence. This can be seen in everything from natural tsunamis to human tyrants—and this because of the isomorphism that obtains over all creation (the Son, nature, history). When that happens, creation itself is disturbed, the equilibrium of its forces is upset, its order is disordered, and the result is that what the being ought to be (existence) it is not and what it ought not to be (the ground, unruly, unconscious forces) is what it is. If that sounds like Saint Paul (Rom. 7:15–19), that is not an accident. This is topological topsy-turvy: the ground is where existence should be, the creaturely will is where God's will should be, the particular will is where the universal will should be, and a no is where yes should be.[25] In short, the creature acts as if it is God, absolutely free—which it is!—a position that, as Manfred Frank points out, also sounds not a little like Jean-Paul Sartre.²⁶ In evil, which is the perversion of order, the disjointure in the jointure, human being, the *alter Deus*, is a reversed God, an adversary of God—"the revolt of the adversary element against the essence of Being," as Heidegger puts it.²⁷ That is why Schelling's Satanology (the Adversary) is a prism of his ontology.

Note well, as Heidegger points out, that Schelling uses the conjunction good *and* evil, not the disjunction good *or* evil. Good *or* evil suggests that the triumph of good extinguishes the evil. Good *and* evil suggests the opposite: the evil is held in check, not extinguished, and this because the very being of the good *depends* upon the resistance thrown up by the evil, which implies the irreducible risk that the order will be overturned by the disorder ever simmering within the order. If spiritual power is "for better *and* for worse," we never know when the best will turn out to be the worst thing that could have happened or whether people we have known all our lives will betray us and reveal their real ("eternal") character (more about this later). A thin membrane separates the best and the worst, the martyr who is willing to die for the good and the terrorist who is willing to kill for it (chapter 10). "In man," Schelling says, "the whole power of the dark principle and, in him, too, the whole force of light. In man are the deepest abyss and the highest heaven, or both centers."²⁸

A STILLBORN SON

Is God Responsible for Evil?

No, not in the part (existence) in which God is incommunicably Godself.

Yes, in the part—the ground—in which God is not being God. This answer shocks the history of theology for whose "barren subtlety" Schelling has no time by allowing that God has an occluded side and an inarticulate longing that prompts God to "will nature" in search of fulfillment.²⁹ God is the eternal master of the ground, which he floods with life and love, but this worse side is an irreducible constituent of being itself, part of the jointure of being. Žižek is exploiting the full shock value of the position when he says that Schelling's answer to the problem of evil is that God "is" evil or defective, which is true enough, if we carefully understand this "is." The ground is not actually evil, but it is potentially evil. By creating the world, God is creating a troubling situation.[30]

The ground of evil is the ground in God, which is the original element of creation. So God could not avoid passing along the ground in a derived and received manner. God is dreaming of ways to actualize the divine being—but God is rolling the dice. When created being reaches the state of Spirit, which is what God wants—to have a companion like himself, another God, a being of understanding and will—things may go seriously wrong. Freedom is unpredictable, unprogrammable, unforeseeable—which is the problem Schelling has in proposing to construct a "system" of freedom. It is a contest with opposing powers, and things will go well unless and until they do not. We cannot blame it on "finitude," because the concealed depth of the ground is a universal feature of being itself, created and uncreated, and ground is an active principle of being, an opposing principle, not a lack or privation but an act of self-affirmation. Whatever is, God included, is because it has a concealed ground, and if it has a ground, then it has a problem, an inner turmoil, and if it does not have a ground, then it would not be at all, for there would nothing for it to overcome.

This essay on "human freedom" is not dealing with a merely human matter.[31] What is at stake is not merely ethics, good behavior, but a matter most metaphysical. The problem of evil poses a risk not only for human being but for the balance of being itself, for powers at work in nature and history, and so ultimately for God. God's fate, God's plans for expansion, hangs in the balance. In the realm of human "spirit," the struggle is of uncertain outcome, unlike the one found in God and unlike the one found in nonhuman nature, where the forces are blind and unconscious and regulated by natural law. The domain of human being lies in the very center of being. The struggle between *good and evil*, which is *freedom*, is the very meaning of *being*—for "primordial being is will" (*Ursein ist Wille*), which is the very meaning of God. If human being rises to the occasion, God's plan will work out. But if the self-asserting human will prevails, God's plan will fail, frustrating God's love, fueling God's wrath. It will have turned out that *God does not exist* (God will remain isolated in a primordial being, not existing in the world). Having put the divine being at risk, at the mercy of human history, as Habermas argues in an incisive analysis of Schelling,[32] God will not have existed. History will be a catastrophe, disease and pandemic, cruelty and violence, death and destruction. The barbarian principle will win out. Evil is ultimately the interruption of the unfolding birth of *God*, threatening a barren God, a stillborn son. This is *being's* struggle with itself, God's struggle with Godself. The fate of history and nature, of the entire cosmos, the outcome of the *Weltalter*, the history of God, the history of being—all this depends on it.

In the multiple manuscripts of *The Ages of the World*, this struggle is recounted as a great cosmic drama, a *grand récit* of being, a "deep history," not a merely empirical one. In terms alternately philosophical and theosophical—I would say theopoetic—especially in the first version, everything turned on a dénouement, a moment of decision, the decisive scission, on a power great enough to make the first principle a thing of the absolute past, to put the eternal, paternal power behind us in time immemorial, to reduce its power, its act, to potency. That allows the *alter Deus* to step forth in act, the Son, the Christ, the world, time, and humankind (all belonging to the second principle, power or potency), which is what we call the "present," the world, time as we know time. But all this, in turn, sets the stage for the final act, the age to come, the ultimate age of the spirit, the third principle, in which God will be all in all. In this, he says, we are reminded of the soaring cosmo-theo-drama sketched by Joachim of Fiore, which traverses the ages of the Father, of the Son, and of the Spirit, of which Gianni Vattimo made use.[33] That dramatic narrative, in Schelling's view, is, in fact, superior to any dialectical argument to back it up.

The question raised by the *radical* Schelling is whether this drama will have a sad or a happy ending and whether the third age *will ever dawn* or remain suspended in a pure ought-to-be, not the death of God but a stillborn God. This exposure to evil explains "the sadness clinging to all finite life," "the veil of despondency spread over all of nature, the deep, indestructible melancholy of all life."[34] How will it end? Only time—literally, metaphysically—will tell. It is not over yet. The answer we get from the *edifying* Schelling is not to fear, for God will be all in all, which sounds like Eckhart's *Book of Divine Consolation*, where there is nothing to fear in God, only to love.

FIVE

THE PHILOSOPHICAL MEANING OF SATAN

INSTEAD OF FURTHER ELABORATING SCHELLING'S metaphysics of evil in the abstract, let us follow it in action in his reading of the figure of Satan, starting with his exceptional rendering of the New Testament story of the temptations of Jesus found in his later writings on the philosophy of revelation.[1] Schelling's point is that this story is a sham unless Jesus *were really* tempted and not simply playing an assigned role in fulfillment of the scriptures and not merely in his human nature—Schelling rejects the classical Chalcedonian Christology—but in his divine being. Schelling's startling point is that Jesus must really have been free, which is, remember, the ability to choose good *and* evil, to take the devil's offer. This story—this is the radical Schelling speaking—has teeth only if something were really at risk, inwardly disturbed by the powers of concealment.

THE METAPHYSICS OF SATAN

Taking the temptation of Jesus seriously requires taking Satan seriously.[2] If so, then Satan cannot be merely a fallen angel. No created individual spirit could challenge the power of the Son of God. Satan, the tempter, signifies instead a "blind cosmic power" that rules over this world, a symbolic expression of what in the freedom period was called the "dark ground." In the later *Potenzlehre*, where I think it has been somewhat domesticated, it is simply called "B," the power that was originally obedient to the Father but was unleashed by the Fall and now rules over a fallen "world," a power that Schelling says is neither finite nor created. "You see here how deep, indeed back to the first beginning, the idea of Satan goes," he says, all the way back, to the blind power of the primordial ground.[3] Nothing depends upon whether or not this famous scene represents an actual historical episode in the "lower" empirical history that is the subject of historical-critical research. It would be a superficial misunderstanding to think this is a story about Jesus of Nazareth being tempted by a bad angel. This narrative is a profoundly revealing *Vorstellung*, a Christian narrative (he mostly reserves the word *myth* for the "pagans") in which Christ finds himself face to face with the nocturnal powers of being itself. This is not a contest between two entities, between a good man and a bad angel. This is not an ontic incident but an ontological event, a confrontation, a *polemos* in the powers of being itself, between being and nonbeing (Tillich), between the Pauline "powers and principalities" and the kingdom of God.

Schelling stresses what a timid orthodoxy (intimidated by the prestige of conceptual reason and the authority of rigid doctrine) has never dared imagine: that the Christ, the Son, is clearly free to enter into this bond with Satan.[4] The Son is now an independent power, the Father has withdrawn into the absolute past (*in potentia*), and the kingdom has been handed over to Christ. The second principle is now *in actu*, of one being with the Father (*homoousia*) but not of one *potency*. Had Christ, the lord of creation, accepted this bargain with the lord of this "world" (the prince of lies), he would have remained the lord of creation but would have severed the bond of the world with the Father, who is the first, true, and only lord of all things. Christ would then reign but in a state of independence from the Father, having seized the glory of the world for himself, instead of returning it to the Father. That would mean the second age of the world would be forever divided and the third age, the age of the Spirit, forever deferred, and God would not become all in all. Duality would overwhelm the unity of the Spirit. Freedom would have spoken its final word. That is the risk the Father took by retiring into potency. Otherwise, there would be no real test, no real freedom, and no real obedience to the Father—and no real risk! Anselm is turning in his grave. Of course, instead of self-assertion, the Son obediently surrendered to the will of the Father and returned the fallen creation to the Father, just as he does in the Garden of Gethsemane.

If Aquinas's angelology is cut to fit his metaphysics of creation, Schelling's Satanology is cut to fit his metaphysics of the *Potenzlehre*. As Schelling points out, the apostle's use of the word *powers* (*dynamesi*) confirms that he and the New Testament are on the same page. Schelling made no use of the Anselmian "satisfaction" theory of the atonement. His close reading of the Greek text of the New Testament brought him back to the view that prevailed for the first millennium of the church, the *Christus Victor* narrative, according to which the Father sent the Son into the world to bring the forces of Satan to heel. God, if not Anselm, took these powers seriously. Christ is the "savior" of the world by saving it from a demonic power, not by paying off a divine debt accumulated by human sin to appease the injured honor of God, as if the Father were an offended medieval lord. The Christ, a divine power sent on a mission to return a "fallen world" to the Father, does battle with a demonic power, his "adversary," the antagonistic principle, the *Diabolos* (from *diaballein*, to throw up obstacles in our way). Each is the worthy opponent of the other.[5] The central players in the dramatis personae of the New Testament are counterparts—there is never just one force, as forces come in pairs—at work on the same ontological level. We must not trivialize the enemy of Christ. Later on, Nietzsche—who took up Schelling's theory of a will proving what it is worth—thinking of Socrates, would say we should have enemies of whom we can be proud.

Who then is the Christ? Who is Satan?

The Christ

If we pose the Anselmian question to Schelling, *cur Deus homo?*, his answer is that Christ is the only one who can overcome the immense power of Satan, which requires an ontological reversal in the powers of being and restores their disturbed order. The atonement is an onto-Christological event taking place in the heart of being. Mythological religion addressed the symptoms of this disturbance, when the powers were still in a prepersonal, largely instinctive and unconscious state of nature; this prepared the way for the Christ, who alone could transform the very root and metaphysical substance of the disturbance. For by *freely* and obediently dying the death of an outcast, Christ carries out a metaphysical reversal on the level of *will as primordial being*. Only the will of Christ carries the ontological weight to occasion a realignment of the potencies or, in the language of the *Freedom* essay, to restore the subordination of the ground to existence. The sacrificial offerings found in pre-Christian religion could only work on the surface of being. Christ alone works in the ontological depths. The difference between revelation and mythology is not merely historical; it is ontological. It is literally the difference between the world as will and the world as representation (*Vorstellung*), as Schopenhauer would put it.

Schelling rejects the Chalcedonian view of the Incarnation as a union in one person of two natures, one human and one divine.[6] On that view the divine nature neither loses anything of its own nor truly becomes human. Instead, it assumes (*analepsis*) a second nature without injury to or effect upon the divine one, which allowed Aquinas to say that Jesus on the cross suffered in his human nature but was immediately united with God in his divine nature. Not only is this view "forced," but it contradicts the words of Paul, who speaks not of an *analepsis* but of *kenosis* when he writes, referring to Christ: "who, though he was in the form of God, did not regard equality with God as something to be exploited, but emptied himself [ἑαυτὸν ἐκένωσε], taking the form of a slave, being born in human likeness. And being found in human form, he humbled himself and became obedient to the point of death—even death on a cross" (Phil. 2: 6–8).

Focusing his analysis on the *morphe theou*, Schelling argues that Christ (who preexists from all eternity), having the form of God originally, now empties himself of that form in order to put on the form of man. For Schelling, the generation of the second person in the Trinity in Christ, the creation of the world, and the creation of humankind (Adam Kadmon) tend to run together—they are all, in the more radical view, the second principle, power, or moment in the unfolding life of God, the way God relieves the solitude of his being, creating divine companionship, and ventures into the world of space and time, of nature (mythology) and history (Christian revelation). Like Hegel, and unlike the later "death of God" theologians, Schelling thinks that *creation* is pleromatic, not kenotic. But he takes the *Incarnation* to be kenotic—again, Schelling's view is the more scriptural one—not a pleromatic or additive process. There is no union of two natures, no adding of a second nature to a first, but a transformation of natures, a *transformation of potencies*. The potency that once took the form of God now takes the form of man. The same one who was God is now a man, and not only a man but a servant (*morphe doulou*), which is a scandal to the Jews and a stumbling block to the pagans, where nothing of the like is to be found in their mythologies. Schelling rejects both the ancient heresies, which ascribed either too much or too little divinity to Jesus, as well as the orthodox Chalcedonian view, all of which presuppose two natures. He proposes an alternative view—a transubstantiation, a shape-shifting—according to which the divine being makes itself freely into man, where the man is the divine power in human form. What is dreamed of in the pagan mythologies, a divine man, becomes an actual historical fact.

Christ's free acceptance of death, his obedience, is the central moment in the history of being (the "ages of the world"), the reconciliation of the world to the Father on the level of knowledge and will.[7] Will must be met with will. The divine unwill, the divine wrath (the unruly side, the "nature" in God), can only be reversed by a reverse will, which places the world back in the hands of the Father. If there were not an ontological power (Satan) opposing the Father, Abelard would be right. God could have simply freely pardoned humanity out of love. But there is ontological disorder here—a perversion of the order of being, of ground and existence—that can be restored by neither God's forgiveness nor man's penance but only by a genuinely mediating metaphysical principle, the one who emptied himself of the form of God and took on the form of man.

Who Is Satan?

The fallen angel, the mischievous spoiler who roams the earth making trouble for other angels and then for human beings, is a mythological construction (but remember, a myth is an echo bouncing off the ground of being). If Satan were merely a creature, he could have been dealt with more easily than with the terrible sacrifice of Christ. If we remind ourselves of what an immense ontological event was required to combat Satan—the birth of God in the world culminating in a humiliating death—we will not underestimate his "dignity," and we will know to assign him an "even higher reality" or, to switch the figure of speech, locate in him a deeper source (ground). Still, if Satan is not a creature, neither is he an uncreated Manichean principle of evil. He is portrayed, like Christ, as one who rules over a kingdom, but a counterkingdom of evil and lies, a cosmic antagonist, a kind of Darth Vader of the New Testament in sinister touch with the Force. Satan is majestic (*kyriotes*), a prince, even a *theos* of this world (2 Cor. 4:4), a divine counterpower, a counter-divine power. What else, then, can Satan be than a *Vorstellung* of the unruly restlessness in being, in nature and human history (the unruly underside, the concealed ground, the principle B)? Once compliant and subordinate to the Father in eternity, it was reawakened, aroused anew in the creation by the Fall, the overcoming of which is the foundation of human consciousness even as it is capable of its destruction. "Satan," Schelling says, "is the B posited through the divine Unwill. He is the great might [*Macht*] of God in the fallen world."[8] This means that evil is not pure lack, pure indeterminacy, but an active principle of resistance and defiance, a constitutive element, force, or power of being.

The name of Satan is not the name of a being, created or uncreated, but the name of the power of the unruly ground, of infinite restlessness, which, left to its own devices, will stray beyond its defining limits and proper borders. *The concealed ground is not evil.* It is a power, the *potency* for good *and* evil that is Schelling's definition of freedom and spirit. Satan is a spiritual symbol of a law inscribed in being. So far from being evil itself, B is, in fact, necessary. B is a "law" of being, the very law of the "test" (*Probe*), which puts every power to the test, without which it cannot be realized or actualized (*potenziert*), whose fury has been unleashed upon the world. "For our struggle is not against enemies of blood and flesh," Paul says, "but against the rulers [*archas*], against the authorities [*exousias*], against the cosmic powers [*kosmokratoras*] of this present darkness, against the spiritual forces of evil in the heavenly places" (Eph. 6:12). There is arguably, for Schelling, no more important text in the New Testament than this. Dramatized as a terrifying individual (the mythological *Vorstellung*), the name of Satan is the name of an ontological power—"That is the authentic philosophical idea of Satan"[9]—an errancy in being itself that ultimately serves a divine purpose. Only in contest with this opposing power can blind necessity be turned into freedom. But once unleashed by the Fall of Adam ("humankind"), the principle

B becomes a monster, a "barbarian," the principle of "what should not be," the principle that makes of human life a constant struggle, tossed about by the antagonistic forces that are the stuff of freedom. The state of paradisal innocence for Schelling—for both God and man—is a nascent and undeveloped one, untried, untested, undeveloped, unrealized, risk free.

As a philological matter, in the text of Genesis, it is not that the Fall of Adam unleashes this principle but exactly the opposite; it is Satan who caused the Fall in the first place. In that text, says Schelling, Satan refers to the realm of possibility that antedates the deed, the ideal possibility to disobey that hovers before freedom, to which Adam and Eve succumb, thereby making it real, rousing the potential principle into action.[10] As Kierkegaard says in *The Concept of Anxiety*, freedom peers into the abyss of possibility and swoons.[11] Sartre was no less taken by this phenomenon. Freedom, the Fall, and the figure of Satan are all awakened in one and the same moment. Satan, thus, is not an angel who first existed in an innocent state and then, after his own fall, tempted humans. The name of Satan is not the name of unambiguous evil; it is the name of the ambiguous power of the groundless ground, which is the ground of both good *and* evil, creation *and* destruction, neither one without the possibility of the other.

Demons and Angels

The demons—Satan's minions, the "angels of destruction"—are mythological figures (*Vorstellungen*) of the disorder that spread throughout all of creation, including nature, by reason of the Fall, all the diseases, plagues, pandemics, and natural disasters. The good angels are symbols of the special bond humanity maintains with God, with the ground of its being, even now in this state of alienation from God, and so they are called "messengers" of God.[12] Finally, Schelling asks why the angels and demons are so prominent in the New Testament but nowadays not so much. The reason for this is that the apostolic age was a pivotal moment in a cosmic combat, a turning point in the "ages of the world," a time of an onto-seismic shift, an epochal crisis and transition in the eons. The New Testament describes an age when the power of Satan, after the long, slow, and still unfinished strife with the powers of unruliness in mythology, was finally put down by Christ. The demons, knowing they were under attack, struck back with all their fury. The apostolic age is the age in which mythology was giving way to revelation. Christ never paused to point out the positive role played by the figure of Satan, as the principle of the test; his attention was taken by the passion of the contest, not the ontology of the test.[13] He was a heavenly power, not a professor at the University of Berlin.

CHRISTUS VICTOR OR SATANAS VICTOR?

The radical Schelling would have rested his case at this point and said of this cosmic combat something like, "And the rest is history, time will tell." We can never count Satan out because he is a wily serpentine spirit who can be trusted to endlessly reinvent himself as the occasion demands.[14] Instead, the edifying Schelling inserts this remarkable analysis into the *grand récit* of the "ages of the world," according to which, having subdued Satan, the torch of time will be passed on from the Son (who will then go into potency) to the Spirit, opening the third age, the final florescence of the history of revelation. "Christianity" will be sublated, potentiated, broken up, and passed over to a higher form of universal religion itself. The church, having lived under the successive authority of the Petrine principle (Catholicism), which contains the content (*Sache*), and then the Pauline or Protestant principle (see Tillich), which puts the content to the test, culminates in the church of the future, of the Spirit, guided by the Johannine principle. This church—if we even want to call it a church, because the very word *ekklesia* suggests a bound and enclosed space—represents the universal spirit of humanity, the final unity, uniting Jews and pagans. No longer "a narrow, stunted, puny Christianity," a confessional body enclosed by dogmas and formulas, it will be a "public" religion (not to be confused with a "state church") of all humankind, uniting both the religious and the secular in a single culture.[15]

World without end, Amen. All things work unto good. We cannot help but notice that in the later Berlin lectures, God looks a little less panentheistic and a lot more orthodox, the God of theism—a personal and loving Spirit overseeing everything transpiring down below and seeing it to a safe and happy conclusion. The risk of history is defused by the eschatology, where it is taken out of human hands and entrusted to divine providence. As Habermas says, Schelling has purchased a "metaphysical life insurance" policy to guard and protect history.[16]

A WORD OR TWO FROM THE RADICAL SCHELLING

The radical Schelling is the more interesting Schelling, the one who emerges by overcoming the edifying one, by playing the part of an *advocatus diaboli* against himself. We can imagine this more radical Schelling stepping up and making himself heard on three points.

1. *The essence of human freedom*: A radical Schelling might argue that in the *Freedom* essay there really is no such thing as human freedom, not because there is no freedom but because it is not *human*. The essence of freedom is located in a decision made in eternity that is carried out in space and time. This speculative conceit reproduces everything that is objectionable about the Kantian dualism that idealism sets out to overcome. Instead of reconciling necessity and freedom, it simply redistributes them, assigning them to different spheres. Freedom is nothing *human* at all but rather the doing of a supersensible agent in the intelligible world. The

"spirit" that reigns over existence and the ground is rather more an angel or a demon than a human agent. Schelling backs away from his faith in nature as visible spirit, recognizing freedom in nature and the nature in freedom. He ushers freedom off the stage of space and time and escorts it to a supersensible safe house, a noumenal realm where it remains untouched by magnetism and electricity, gravitation and organic decomposition, lifted above the terrible rotary turmoil of time and space. Against this subterfuge, the radical Schelling holds that nature itself, considered closely, understood amply, and approached in nonmechanistic and nonreductionistic terms, is spirit enough, that nature itself suffices unto itself to allow for freedom and spirit. The only surviving cash value behind this metaphysical conceit is the deeper "character" that we reveal in times of crisis, when we show our "true colors," "what we are made of," but that is something that is *gradually forged* in space and time a posteriori, not decided in eternity a priori. Character is an effect, not a cause, something we dare pronounce only after the dearly departed is dead and cannot contradict us. While we are still alive, we are not who we are, and we do not know who we are—which is the stuff of a phenomenology of ambiguity, of the unruly ground, not of a dualist ontology.

2. *The system of human freedom:* The *Freedom* essay seeks to establish a "system" of human freedom, about which Schelling says, "In the divine understanding there is a system; however, God himself is not a system but a life, and therein lies the answer to the question concerning the possibility of evil with reference to God."[17] The understanding (existence) is a system, but God is a "life," and life is a strife—of existence and the ground. So the radical Schelling would argue that the system cannot accommodate both existence and the ground, that the system is subject to something of a Gödelian dilemma. The system is either consistent—and then it

is restricted to the divine understanding (existence)—or it is complete—and then it is no longer a system because it includes the unruly ground, a necessity of life, which is not a rule-abiding system. Even God's own existence cannot "annul" the ground, for then God would be inert and immobilized. So God dominates the unlit ground and floods it with his light and love, for the ground in God is perfectly integrated into God's being. While the ground is the source of God's vitality, it does not upset the divine order.[18] In creatures, by contrast, the concealed ground is received, on loan, independent of the creature, so that the bond with existence is weaker, breakable. Freedom, which is the power to break the bond of being and turn it upside down, is, while created, "unconditional" (we cannot be a little bit free) and therefore unpredictable, unprogrammable, and as a result *not* a system.

The radical Schelling would declare this mere zoning board philosophy; it is analogous to separating eternal freedom from factical life, and it is this disjunction—as will be seen in the next chapter—that leads Schelling to segregate negative philosophy from positive philosophy, confining the system of essential necessity to separate quarters of negative philosophy while housing factical experience in positive philosophy. Instead of isolating the system in a separate sphere, the radical Schelling would rethink the system as an "ecstatic" one, just as he does with reason. Then the system would be at best a quasi-system, an open-ended one, in which speaking of a "system" would mean that everything is "entangled" (shades of quantum physics) with everything else, as Catherine Keller has shown, or a "network" of actors and actants, as Bruno Latour argues, but in an open-ended and unprogrammable (ecstatic) way, so that nothing guarantees the system will hold forever or produce predictable events.[19] The Internet, for example, is a system, but no one is in charge (so far). That would result in what our radical Schelling might call "the Quasi-system of a Quasi-transcendental Not-quite-ideal Idealism."

3. *The highest point:* Toward the end of the essay on human freedom, just when we might have thought it was over, we are surprised to learn—something like the emergency patch issued for the last chapter of the Gospel of Mark to make sure everything ends well—that the originary strife is not really originary. After all that? How can that be? Because "when we finally reach the highest point of this investigation,"[20] it turns out that the primordial strife is not primordial at all but derivative; it is the disturbance of a primordial peace or *Gelassenheit*. The opposing forces of ground and existence are *modifications* of a prior *indifference*, of an *Ungrund* or *Urgrund* whose only predicate is that it has no predicates, or, in the language of the *Weltalter*, a primordial *Lauterkeit* of ineffable purity and light—perhaps we can call it, as Joseph Lawrence says, "the purity of the *Ungrund*" (or *Urgrund*). Whatever we call it, the fix is in. There is evidently enough predictability and discernibility to "divine just enough of a quiet joy (freedom from the burden of existence) to permit him the suggestion that it awakens the craving to be from the abyss of what absolutely is not."[21]

This absolute, unconditioned *Indifferenz* "decides" to "divide itself"—*mirabile dictu*, no mean accomplishment for something devoid of predicates and absolutely indifferent—into ground and existence, which turn out to be derivative forces. Strife, the play of opposing forces, which sustained the entire analysis hitherto, is, at the end, suddenly relieved of its command, reduced in rank, domesticated into a modification of a primordial peace, and then directed teleologically to return to a higher peace than the original one it disturbed. The strife is put to work, entered into a divine economy, where it is made to pay infinite dividends. The strife, and so the risk, turns out to be a vanishing mediator, a transition. Once we reach the "highest point," we can see the whole terrain: *From* a thin, untested peace *through* the trial of strife *to* a robust hard-won strife-free peace; from a bare, simple, innocent One through the many to the all-gathering One; from a lonely God through the God of all to the God who is all in all. The Jonas of strife is swallowed by the whale of Neoplatonism—not only by the Neoplatonism of the Trinitarian figure at work throughout but by the most classical Neoplatonic schema of *exitus* and *reditus*, a tired dyad reissued as a triad and orchestrated in the terms of the dialectics of German idealism but otherwise left completely undisturbed. This dialectical triad, found at every stage of Schelling's thought—early, middle, and late—as also in Hegel and Fichte, makes a critically important improvement on the dyadic schema. By introducing an irreducible mediating step, in dialectics—unlike Neoplatonism, which lacks this third element—there can be no immediate union of the finite and infinite. Mystical union is always mediated, never immediate, which is a welcome improvement. Nonetheless, dialectics remains a captive of Neoplatonism, which is trying to economize on difference. If there is an "essence" of German idealism, found in any and all of its varieties, this schema is it. In German idealism, difference has a glass ceiling. It does economic service in the cause of unity, which is its alpha and omega. Strife is derivative from originary peace, difference from originary indifference, and both are teleologically destined to reunite in a higher peace and differentiated unity. Difference can do no (ultimate) harm or pose an ultimate risk. This is a relapse that a radical Schelling would never tolerate.

Truth to tell, we should have seen this relapse coming. After absolute unconditioned *Indifferenz* "decides" to "divide" itself, however that is to be established, explained, or imagined—a feat I seriously doubt—Schelling immediately consolidates the resulting difference (the play of forces) into a *primal* being, a first among beings, submitting the forces to a first existing being who is what-is, who even turns out to be personal and loving. This represents both an ontotheological and a mytho-poetic relapse. The genuinely *radical* move is to see that difference is not derivative but originary, that what is productive is difference, not indifference. Unity is an *effect* of the play of difference. The radical move is, as Schelling says, to "allow the ground" its play, to think the play of forces as an irreducible field in which multiple and *non-hierarchical* effects are produced as excitations of the *field*, where every effect in the field is entangled with every other and no one effect is put in charge and authorized as the "Lord." The genuinely radical move is to see that difference, or rather differences in the plural, not oppositional or dialectical difference but purely *differential* differences, are, as Heidegger puts it, "equiprimordial" (*gleichursprünglich*), that linguistic difference precedes and makes possible all this talk of the "word" spoken into the abyss and the "vowel" and the "consonant"; in the radical view, essences are historical constructions, days in a life. It is just because difference is such an unlikely origin, because we like to think of origins as unitary, that Derrida coins a misspelling as a nonword for the "origin" of words and calls *différance* a "non-originary origin."

Reaching a more radical point, rather than a highest one, we would see that from something that would *actually be* absolutely neutral and indifferent, *nothing* would "emerge," because nothing would ever have the opportunity or the occasion to occasion anything or to be occasioned. Absolute indifference would be neither active nor passive nor even latently active or passive. Anything *genuinely lacking* in predicates would not be equipped in advance with latent life, love and personality, or purity and clarity, which for Schelling are terms of the *highest praise*, which is what *praedicatio* means in Latin. So the radical apophatics Schelling proposes is domesticated by an edifying apophatics of peace and praise. On his own terms, things "emerge" only in contest with an opposing force. Otherwise they are either eternally inert or, what amounts to the same thing, their force simply vanishes, pure and simple, in a *nihil negativum*. That is why Schelling has to assume that this absolute *Indifferenz* is implicitly *not* absolutely indifferent but simmering at a very low heat with some kind of barely discernable longing and unrest, which means *difference*, in which case it was *not* absolutely indifferent after all. Then, might there be something even *more* indifferent, even *more* devoid of predicates, that is the source of absolute *Indifferenz*? This is the very conceptual acrobatics typical of metaphysics that Kant did everything he could to stop. Why, one might ask, when it "divides itself," does it not "decide" to divide itself up differently? Why not produce different results? Why did it not divide up into mechanical parts? Why does it not divide itself up into warring parties, endless slaughter, and uninterrupted pain? After all, strife and duality do excellence service for war. Why does "love" get pride of place? Why is love prior to evil? Why must "strife" be for the sake of love? Why not strife, *agon, polemos* for itself until everything breaks down and is *utterly destroyed*? Because a system of reason cannot contradict the needs of the heart, this more pious Schelling says.[22] Really? Would not absolute indifference be "indifferent" to our needs, literally heartless? Where is it written that the ability of an idea to comfort our heart is a criterion of its truth?

THE THEOPOETIC REDUCTION

The right response to the Kantian dualism of phenomena and noumena is not German idealism but a richer, radical—phenomenological—sense of "phenomena" that pulls up dualism root and branch. I think that is what the radical Schelling was getting at, an experience taking place on a *phenomenological* register, and his claim that it enjoys metaphysical status is, to say the least, difficult to swallow. We see this plainly in the next chapter where phenomenology travels under the incognito of "metaphysical empiricism." This metaphysics of *Indifferenz* belongs, I think, to a phenomenology of the anonymous *il y a*.[23] On the *radical* rendering that I want to defend, all these materials have legitimate but strictly *phenomenological* credentials. They speak for themselves and do not require metaphysical certification. More radically conceived, this is the stuff not of a metaphysical theology but of a theopoetics. Its virtue is to tell a stunning story, to spin a magical "narrative," not a deep—meaning metaphysical—history of the life of God. It is not a dialectical argument but an "epic poem," as Schelling says in the *Weltalter*, where it can travel lightly, "without the burdens of existence."

Viewed thus, what we call "God" is an effect of the play of forces.

Viewed thus, the "Lord of Being" and the "God of love" are not ontotheological structures but theopoetic ones; they are a dream, a hope, a prayer, an aspiration—what Schelling would call a "longing" lodged deep in our heart, in the center of our being—that justice will prevail, that the "kingdom of God" will prevail over the kingdom of the "powers and principalities," which may or may not happen. His phenomenology of the "needs of our heart" belongs to a theopoetics, not a metaphysics. Being itself by his own definition does not know we have a heart, much less care (*Indifferenz*).

Viewed thus, in its more radical version, what he calls the third age of the world, the final epoch of being, when God will be all in all, is to be transcribed as a phenomenology of the "absolute future," an infinitival to-come, *l'à-venir*, which means that, grammatologically speaking, every noun and verb must be infinitivized, potentiated, raised up to the power not of infinity but of the infinitive, where every *x* is an *x*-to-come. Schelling is describing the coming of the "year of Jubilee" announced by Jesus, which so far has not arrived.[24] That is because this year does not belong to empirical calendar time or to deep metaphysical time but to *messianic* time, the time of hope and expectation, of prayers and tears. It is always and structurally *to-come*, and its coming (*venue*) is not to be confused with *presence*, not even a future presence.

Lauterkeit, Urgrund, Gelassenheit—these motifs are neither empirical, which says too little, nor metaphysical, which says too much, but precious imports by a poetic sensibility from a mythopoetics, a theopoetics, a kind of deep phenomenology, whose pedigree in Rhineland mysticism we reviewed previously (chapter 2). Indeed, they bear an interesting similarity to Heidegger's *Lichtung*, the "open" or "clearing," or even to *Ereignis*.[25] These words belong to the vocabulary of the apophatic imagination, arising in response to the apophatic imperative, and they are demeaned by enlisting them in the service of an ontotheological economy and given predictive, explanatory force.

The radical Schelling, who understood more about Satan than the rest of us, would have seen right through this business of reaching the "highest point," which is an old trick of Satan to lead the philosopher to the top of mountain or the temple and promise, "All this can all be yours." The radical Schelling would have made his excuses, pleading that he has no head for heights and that philosophy is conducted from below, down in the valley of tears.

SIX

WHY IS THERE SOMETHING RATHER THAN NOTHING AT ALL?
Schelling and the End of Idealism

ON JANUARY 16, 1842, KIERKEGAARD, who was attending Schelling's lectures in Berlin, wrote to his nephew Michael Lund to inform his uncle Peter (Kierkegaard's brother) that the "unprethinkable" has become Schelling's favorite expression and the answer to his philosophical prayers. With typical sarcasm, Kierkegaard put his finger on something serious that now demands our attention.[1]

ON NOT FORGETTING THAT WE EXIST

It was Hegel's misfortune to have been outlived by Schelling, who was called in 1841 to occupy the very chair at Berlin once occupied by Hegel, to rebut the left-wing "young Hegelians," a movement of radical atheists for whom Hegel had been an essential impulse. This was a time, Paul Tillich says, when fundamental decisions were made about the subsequent course of European thought.[2] Schelling's Berlin lectures, attended by many luminaries of the day, proved to be a hugely influential criticism of Hegel. Far from being a middle link between Fichte and Hegel, Schelling is better viewed as having brought the idealist project to a close. In these lectures, which prompted the brilliant mockery Kierkegaard made of Hegel, Schelling now argued for a new philosophy of "existence," which he said is ultimately *religious*. If a philosophy ends up irreligious, it has somewhere made a wrong turn. To be sure, this is a religion in touch with the nocturnal powers of the world and a suggestive contribution to the radical apophatic imagination.

Even in his final years, Schelling did not abandon his systematic aspirations, but now he thought it necessary to divide the system into two parts. The first part is a system of concepts he called "negative" philosophy, the philosophy of essence, of *what* things are (*das "Was*," the "what"), and the second, the "positive" philosophy, which addresses the fact *that* (*das "Dass*," the "that") things are, their actuality (*Wirklichkeit*). This is the "facticity" radicalized and made famous by Heidegger's "hermeneutics of facticity," which Heidegger described as the "naked 'that is it is'" (*nacktes "Dass es ist"*), where "the whence and the whither" of things are shrouded in darkness.[3] Kierkegaard, fresh from his broken romance with Regine, where "existence" had recently given him quite a thrashing, was taking furious notes that begin with the exclamation that when Schelling began to speak of *Wirklichkeit*, "the child of thought leaped for joy within me as in Elizabeth."[4] Schelling's "failure" to produce a system of existence led to two of the greatest works of European philosophy in the last two hundred years—Heidegger's *Being and Time* and Kierkegaard's *Concluding Unscientific Postscript*, where the "unscientific" was the impossibility of a system of existence.

The purely conceptual system would be the prolegomenon to positive philosophy, but the system of philosophy as a whole is made up of both parts, which is the Gödelian problem to which I referred in the previous chapter. The system is either consistent or complete but not both. Schelling thought it could be both, but the explosive things he would say about existence and facticity shattered his own systematic project. After dividing the system into two, it could never be put back together again. The radical Schelling could admit at most a certain "system"—and it is not inconsequential—in which all things are entangled with one another (like quantum physics) or linked up in "networks" (Internet, global economy, ecosystems, etc.), but in an open-ended way that admits unpredictability and unprogrammability. Such a "open" system is what Derrida meant by a "quasi-" or "ultra-transcendental" and what Schelling himself called an "ec-static" concept of reason,[5] one that is radically exposed to what exceeds reason, where the most reasonable thing to say is that there is no such thing as "Pure Reason." There is nothing for freedom to fear in the interconnectedness of all things; its only fear is programmability. Schelling's limit, his traditional side, was to think he could install someone who could control the system by flooding it with love, which I am saying is an idea that is rooted in piety and does service in theopoetics, not metaphysics.

Schelling thought that without the negative philosophy, we would never know what is possible, but without the positive philosophy, we would linger forever in an imaginary world of thought-possibilities. Enter Kierkegaard's lampooning of Hegel for constructing a castle of concepts while living in the humble hut of actuality. Hegelian philosophers "forget that they exist." I do not share all of Schelling's criticisms of Hegel, and I do agree with Žižek's complaint about the "scarecrow Hegel" created by Kierkegaard. But I think Schelling is quite right about the primacy of the positive philosophy, that existence precedes essence. Upon that, I would go so far to say, everything depends, for facticity is the source of the unruliness and the risk in radical apophatics. In Hegel, reason and the *Begriff* have the final word; in Schelling, in response to Hegel, existence has the final word, which means there is no final word—try as the more traditional Schelling might to supply one by means of an all-loving Providential Father who would tie up all the loose ends, world without end, Amen!

THE UNPRETHINKABLE

Schelling's ultimate complaint with Hegel, the one that sticks, is that being *precedes* thinking, that being arrives on the scene before thinking has a chance to prepare for its arrival, not just historically but structurally. Thinking will always arrive too late. That is what Schelling called *das Unvordenkliche*, literally the "unprethinkable."[6] Hegel's intellectualism overrides the facticity of being and makes light of the concealed depths of existence. Reason in Hegel, as Andrew Bowie says,[7] is something of a narcissist; whenever reason looks into the well of being, it sees its own image looking back. Being reflects the categories of reason, and reason articulates the categories of being. Being and thinking enjoy a kind of mutual admiration society. Starting on a level where the identity of being and thinking is obscure and implicit, where finite things appear opposed to one other, thinking ascends to ever higher levels in which these oppositions are seen as one-sided moments of a larger whole. This is less a positive argument than a negative elimination, negating these negations, letting the finite "vanish" into the infinite whole to which it belongs, where being thinks itself, as in Aristotle's *noesis noeseos*. We might say that in Hegel, being and thinking are contemporaries, whereas Schelling holds that no matter how early reason rises, being is "always already" there,[8] like Levinas's notion of the "absolute past"—a past that never was and never could be present, the shore we will never reach, where *Wesen ist gewesen* (being is having been). Like Levinas, the unprethinkable represent a sphere of absolute diachrony with which thinking can never establish a synchrony.[9] The unprethinkable priority of being is the true a priori, the *prius*. Being is not the reflection of reason; it is the unreflected, prereflective precondition that antedates reason. Thinking always takes place after the fact of being, *per posterius*, trying to clarify being.[10]

Being is the unconditional. It gets there before thinking is able to lay down the conditions under which being is possible. Schelling breaches the core idea of reason in German idealism by claiming a fracture or fault in *Vernunft*, which sees to it that *Vernunft* is not pure and cannot form a closed system—and to the extent that it does, it remains isolated in the sphere of thought without being. That not only inspired Kierkegaard, but it is also the defining gesture of post-structuralism—which claims that the structure is internally limited, at odds with itself, that it cannot close. For the radical Schelling, *das Unvordenkliche* does not imply antisystematic chaos; it simply means that systems cannot be formalized or axiomatized (closed). We are bound to being by bonds we cannot break or even see. As Heidegger effectively objected to Husserl, it is impossible to carry out a neutralizing reduction. As opposed to the Hegelian *Begriff*, we do not grasp being; being grasps us. As Tillich said, it is a matter not of conceiving or seizing but of being seized by something unconditional, which is what Tillich and Schelling mean by religion not in a narrow confessional sense but in a radical sense.

The positive philosophy can be viewed as an extended elaboration of Kant's refutation of the ontological argument. From thoughts only more thoughts follow, and no matter how long I persist in thought, at the end, I will still remain in thought. Jacobi proposed to span the gap by a leap of faith from thinking to being, but the unprethinkable means we are always already there, a standpoint worked out in magisterial fashion in Heidegger's *Being and Time*. The encounter with being is not the discovery of something new but the realization of something older than old, from time immemorial. As in hermeneutics itself—which I maintain it *is*—positive philosophy makes the implicit explicit, taking what we take for granted and making it a matter of wonder and astonishment demanding an elaboration. This task is paradoxical: to bring the unprethinkable to thought, just so far as that is possible, to catch the prephilosophical in act without turning it into more philosophy, to turn on the lights fast enough to see the dark, all of which is impossible. The unprethinkable belongs not only to a past we will never make present but also to a future we cannot foresee. That is the event, the stuff of which radical apophatics is made.[11]

Das Unvordenkliche represents the end of idealism so much so that it pushes back against Schelling's own idea of negative philosophy by putting the torch to the very idea of a *pure* rational science. The principle of the unprethinkable means that pure reason could never be pure, and pure reflection could never be possible, because being could never be really neutralized. We cannot stand outside being and come up with a table of the categories purified of experience. Being is life, and, as Kierkegaard would say, life does not have the patience to pause and allow us to step outside and inspect it. Once the negative or pure rational philosophy introduces anything other than the strictly formal relations of formal logic, it abdicates any such purity. Once it becomes a "dialectical" logic, its categories are datable and locatable, culturally constructed abstractions ultimately drawn from experience (Western Christian, white male, very German, and so on). The positive philosophy retroactively undermines the negative philosophy by subjecting it to the factical conditions of space and time. Negative philosophy could never be anything more than a field report sent back by correspondents embedded in a particular, locatable, datable moment in history about the then prevailing system of conceptuality—like Kant's twelve categories of the understanding that allegedly were universally valid everywhere, not just in dateline Königsberg, 1781. Every such purported "system" proves unprepared for the "event," the unforeseeable (unprethinkable) coming of what we cannot see coming. Hence the Gödelian paradox that besets Schelling—whether the positive philosophy is simply the existential instantiation of the essences analyzed in negative philosophy, which undermines facticity, or whether things might happen in the positive philosophy that ignore the advice of pure reason, which undermines the system. That paradox is resolved by being dissolved: the strong idea of a pure system of reason (negative philosophy) is an illusion (not an intuition!), a mistake, exposed by the unprethinkable (positive philosophy), even as it had been exposed earlier on by freedom. What remains is weak, quasi-transcendental open-ended interconnectedness.

WHY IS THERE SOMETHING RATHER THAN NOTHING AT ALL? 145

HOW TO MOVE ON FROM THE UNPRETHINKABLE

The instinctive response to Leibniz's question "Why is there something rather than nothing?" is to launch a search for causes, like God or the big bang. But the question cuts deeper than that. For even when we posit a first cause, and even if we say God is a necessary being, the question remains in place: Why God and his creation *at all*? Why the history of the universe *at all*? Why is there anything *at all*? The question is not about cause and effect but about being and *nothing at all*. The question gathers up everything in its sweep, including any possible primordial cause or primal existing being, be it in physics or metaphysics. We only feel its full force when we hold out being itself against the possibility of nonbeing, of *nothing at all*.[12]

That the world is *at all* is the mystical, Wittgenstein famously said. Enough said, he added, but, of course, explaining what this confession of not-saying means, knowing how *not* to speak of being or God, has always been the source of the wordiest treatises. Negative theologians are among our most prolific authors.

By such a force as this, Schelling says, thought is deprived of its freedom, taken by surprise; thinking cannot get out ahead of being, cannot see it coming. The temporal factor is central. Unprethinkable being is a priori, the prior, the absolutely *prius*, the first and most primordial *principium*. Being is too early, too much to take in, too strong for thought. As he likes to say, citing Aristotle, being is "stronger than thought."[13] Schelling, a century before Vattimo, already had a theory of "weak thought."[14] This pure fact of being is the pure act of being, without a trace of potency. Contrary to everything we learn from negative philosophy, being itself is not the actualization of a prior possibility.[15] If there is potency and possibility here, Schelling says, it comes later, not first. Here is an existence without an antecedent essence, an actuality without an anterior potentiality, being without a concept, which is why Schelling calls it "blind" being. In just the way that an action is blind if it is undertaken without foresight, he says, so being is blind if it is not preceded by a concept, an essence, a possibility either to be or not be.[16] It is impossible to think, to prethink, to outthink this being. Because it does not follow from a concept, it is "just there," seemingly accidental, unwilled, unforeseen.[17] We can understand essence without existence, a concept (like that of a unicorn) without having a corresponding (existing) object, but here thought is faced with the opposite, an existent without an essence, an actuality without a prior possibility. This turns thought inside out, leaving it literally ec-static, outside itself. Here then is the "wonder" that launches the work of philosophy: how what, prior to thought, is inconceivable can become conceivable a posteriori.[18]

But if this is to be the beginning of the positive philosophy, it is hard to see what or how anything could come next. The danger, Schelling says, is to get stuck with the unprethinkable, for blind being is so "rigid and immovable" that we cannot move on to anything that exists besides it, beyond it, or after it. However, experience teaches us that other things do exist, so there must be a way to get past it. But if we cannot prethink it, we can postthink it. While no potency can precede blind being, nothing says that something cannot follow it, that there cannot be a *potentia post actum*, a posteriori.[19] What is not possible beforehand is possible "afterhand" (*nach der Hand*). Something other-than-the-unprethinkable is actual and therefore must be possible.

Schelling symbolizes the unprethinkable as A and other things, "the other," as B. The movement from A to B is not a "fall" but an "elevation," a "liberation," for what he has in mind is nothing less than the creation of the world (the actualization of the power or potency B), which represents a further development or unfolding of the unprethinkable.[20] As noted previously, God's relation to the world is not kenotic but pleromatic. This also corresponds to the way pure *Indifferenz* "decides" to "divide" itself into ground and existence, but this time it is not a speculative hypothesis but a factical experience—that there is a world at all! In creation, the unprethinkable frees itself from the "holy necessity" (*ananke*)— shades of Rudolf Otto and the *mysterium tremendum et fascinans*— of its blind being; it is set in motion, giving life to what, left to itself, rests in itself in a completely actionless calm *Gelassenheit*.[21] As Kierkegaard records in his notes, "In positing B, it ushers A out of its *Gelassenheit*."[22] Schelling thinks of the unprethinkable rather the way Levinas speaks of the "otherwise than being": we are "trapped" in being, and freedom means to "escape" the inescapable (*existentia ineluctabilis*).[23] Unlike Aristotle and Aquinas, pure act for Schelling does not mean plenitude but inactivity. Pure act is purely inactive. The act (*actus*) must become activity (*actio*)—which is the founding axiom of process philosophy and theology. Pure act provides a base from which we start out, a ground for further actualizations. The result of "sublating" (which for Schelling means just negating) the unprethinkable is not a descent from pure act but an ascent to something higher— becoming, process, life, personality.[24] "The true God is the living God; living means to dispose of one's Being freely; the living God goes beyond Godself by God's own power and becomes something Other than God's unforethinkable Being"—the way God goes beyond (*praeter*) his own ground—"different from the Being in which he is *a se* [by itself]. To think of God without this power means to rob him of the possibility of any movement."[25]

BOLD THEOLOGY: MAKING EXISTENCE
WORTHY OF GOD

So, then, the unprethinkable is God? Not so fast. There is a difference between the unprethinkable and God, just as there is a difference in the *Freedom* essay and the *Weltalter* fragments between God as the primally existing being and the absolute, unconditioned *Indifferenz* or *Lauterkeit*. By beginning with unprethinkable being, Schelling has recast the question of God in an interesting way. What we learn from negative philosophy is that God is a necessary being, the *ens realissimum*—which supplies us only with an *idea* of God, provided that God exists at all. What we do not know and cannot say is that necessary being is God. That is why Kant said the cosmological and teleological proofs depend upon the ontological proof, of which he made a famous refutation, and Aquinas, having demonstrated the need for a first cause and realizing the gap, simply inserts the missing link, "and this everyone calls God." Well, Schelling thinks, maybe not everyone. The question is not, "Is God a necessary being?" The real question is, "Is God necessarily the necessary being?"

Blind being is indeterminate and undifferentiated (*Indifferenz*). The pure *Dass* does not know its opposite, does not know or desire itself. It did not choose to be pure being. It must prove itself worthy of anything we proceed to say about it, any further determination we make of it. The *prius* can show itself as "desirable" or "necessary" or "eternal"—or manifest its "divinity" (*Gottheit*)— only subsequently, after the fact, *per posterius*. Does God exist? We do not know yet, epistemologically, and—here is the radical point—that is because *it has not happened yet*, ontologically! This is not just "uncertainty" but "indeterminacy." Here we hit the heart of my interest in Schelling, upon precisely the argument I made in *The Insistence of God*, where God does not exist, God insists, and whether God exists depends on us, in a text I ask the indulgence to cite: "The responsibility for God's existence falls upon us and has to be cast in the future active participle: it remains to be seen whether God will have been or whether God will be stillborn, whether what will have been will be called God. . . . We will only be able to determine whether God exists after the fact. . . . We will only be able to tell afterwards if God has come. So theology will always be after the fact, and God's providential foresight will all be reconstructed retroactively, after we see what has come."[26]

Blind being for Schelling must prove itself as divine against its opposite. It may prove itself in some other—unforeseeable!—way. This is not epistemological caution; this is the law of being: nothing is what it can be unless it is tried, true, and tested, and it must be a real test, with a real chance of failing, like Christ and Satan.[27] The wellspring of infinite possibilities that emerge from the unprethinkable is filtered by the law of being, the law of the *test*. For Hegel, what is real is rational; for Schelling, what is real is a survivor, having survived the strife, the contest of oppositions. The existence of God will be determined by the test of unfolding historical experience. Schelling proposes a fascinating innovation on the ancient question of the existence of God. He wants to know not whether God exists but whether existence proves itself worthy of God, to slightly adapt Deleuze's notion of ethics as "making ourselves worthy of the events that happen to us."[28] The argument is "a posteriori," not merely epistemologically but *ontologically*! God has not happened yet! Only at the end of time will we be able to say whether there will have been God.

After defining the realm of pure thought as a sphere of immanence and that of being as transcendence, Schelling distinguishes a timid from a bold transcendence.[29] A "relative" or timid transcendence derives what exists necessarily from the concept of a necessary being, keeping "one foot in the concept." Here thought feels secure, "strong" enough to grasp (*greifen*) being in advance in a "concept" (*Begriff*). This is distinguished from an "absolute"—or we would say "radical"—transcendence, which has to do with *affirming existence itself* without the breastplate of a concept. Contrary to a strong concept-dependent theology (which Heidegger calls "onto-theology"), bold theology braves existence denuded of the concept, forced after the fact to find a concept for a bare, blind being that is prior to all thinking. In absolute, bold, or radical theology, existence must *prove itself divine*—and that is structurally undecided in advance. Any such determination comes after being. "The existence of God cannot be proven, only the godhood of that which has existence, of that which has Being *actu* by itself and eternally, though that, too, only *a posteriori*."[30]

Bold theology is willing to take its chances, which is the heart of Habermas's assessment of Schelling. Existence must prove what it is made of, and the outcome is not assured beforehand. It does not follow from any law of essence or necessity—*unless Schelling is willing to allow the negative philosophy to dictate in advance what takes place in the positive philosophy*, which would undermine the very idea of the unprethinkable, of the pure that, of facticity. That is the dilemma besetting the division of the system: if negative philosophy does not prescribe the course of existence, what purpose does it serve? If it does, then there is no such thing as the unprethinkable. The determination of "what" is subsequent, posterior to the unprethinkable—the upshot of activating the principle or potency B—is not governed in advance by any concept, essence, or necessity but by history and freedom. If the form that freedom presses upon this protean material of the world is too weak, the world will overflow the form and produce disharmony, a drunken riot. Thought is required to be both sober (well formed) and drunk (creative) at the same time, both Apollonian and Dionysian.[31] That is the bold theology of Schelling, the only concern being the extent to which it is compromised by a more pious Schelling.

The radical Schelling is willing to go very far in this direction, putting the very existence of God at risk. Of itself, the *Unvordenkliche* is *indifferent* to every property, earlier than every quality, prior to every name, anonymous, pre-nonymous, not a pro-noun but a *pre*-noun. If there is anything as open ended, risky, and indeterminate in the history of philosophy and theology that anticipates what Schelling is talking about, it is the *radical* version of the *Deus absconditus* in Luther and the dark ruminations of Jacob Boehme on the *Ungrund*—and further back still the Rhineland mystics' distinction between the *Gott* of reason and revelation and the abyss of the divine *Gottheit*.[32] However, the twist Schelling gives to the mystics was pointed out very early on by a contemporary, Hans Martensen[33]—the mistake the mystics make in praying God to be rid of "God" is to think that the ever-concealed Godhead is *better* than God. For Schelling, on the contrary, the higher perfection is found not in the absolute by itself, not in God in absolute solitude contracted to itself (the Neoplatonic figure), but in the living and personal God encountered in history and revelation.[34] Left to itself, being is bare, barren, naked; taken in itself, it dwells in solitude, lonely and in longing. The living, revealed God longs for the companionship of the world.[35] This is the same tension between the Neoplatonic One and the active Trinitarian life that we saw in Meister Eckhart (chapter 2). That is the difference between the kenotic and the pleromatic versions of God in the world.

God must "suspend" his unprethinkable being, break its grip—otherwise everything would be frozen in immobility— and transform blind being into something "desired" (*gewolltes*). Why do this? And for whom? For the *other*, for creation. Why? Because only in this being-for-the-other does God fully unfold the (active) potencies of God's being and become free and blessed (*selig*) as the Lord of Being.[36] So God is a eudaemonist. On this point, too, Schelling's "pure act" takes leave of Aristotle, whose aristocratic *theos* was entirely happy to think himself alone for all eternity. For Schelling, however, happiness, bliss, *Seligkeit* is not found in oneself, alone, self-contracted—that would be an *un*happy lonely life—but in expansion, self-transcendence, production, the ongoing and ever-new actualization of the potencies, positing something outside oneself. So the unprethinkable, the basis or ground, does not predetermine in advance the outcome but supplies something like the ontological raw material. But this potency is only there for God *if God desires it*.[37] At the end, in the final age of the world, the *actus purus* that was alone with itself, at rest in a kind of divine Edenic innocence, isolation, and inactivity, a divine *Gelassenheit*, is regained. But this time it is different.

Tested by the trials and tribulations of the world, it returns to itself fulfilled by the fulness of time, which is the circularity in a line of thought that Schelling likes to think is linear.

Schelling is trying to position himself precariously between theism and post-theism, between classical theistic transcendence of God and a pantheism in which God is emptied into the world. In the Berlin lectures, he emphatically rejects the view that God *needs* the world in order to become God,[38] which is Hegel's view and his own earlier view, and tilts to the side of classical transcendence of God in theism. Otherwise, he says, God is deprived of his sovereign freedom. In the Berlin lectures, God is a personal being free to remain in transcendent isolation, if "he" so willed, despite "longing" for companionship. In theism, God does not absolutely need the world (metaphysically), but God does "need" it morally (in terms of love). On the register of being, God is like the sun, which is still its same bright self if it does not have us to shine upon, but, on the register of love, that would be unfulfilling, so Schelling says God posits this desire in his desireless being.[39] God does not really (metaphysically) need humanity, but God *chooses* to need humanity, thereby breaking up the divine peace and internal harmony in order to invest in the risky venture of a divine expansion that will represent a successful divine economy. Schelling is straddling the fence between his radical and traditional sides.

SEVEN

SCHELLING'S EITHER/OR

IN POINT OF FACT, THE final word for Schelling is found in neither mythology nor revelation but in the *philosophy of* mythology and revelation, in what he calls a "philosophical religion," which is structurally very close to what we are calling radical theology or theopoetics and a predecessor figure of what Derrida calls a "religion without religion." Like Hegel, Schelling did not regard the distinction between reason and revelation as a distinction between the natural human order and a supernatural intervention. Both Hegel and Schelling make what we are calling the "suspension of the supernatural signified," which means not to treat revelation as something that dropped from the sky but to take revelation as seriously revealing something about our condition to anyone with the eyes to see or the ears to hear.

HERMENEUTIC PHENOMENOLOGY *AVANT LA LETTRE*

The only means available to Schelling to identify this philosophical religion was to call it a "metaphysical empiricism," a force fit that could not hold together very long. If, on the one hand, Schelling rejected purely rationalist metaphysics and limited the philosophy of pure reason to negative philosophy, he had nowhere else to turn for positive philosophy than to empiricism. But, on the other hand, he also rejected the truncated and atomistic conception of experience found in English empiricism, just as he rejected a mechanistic interpretation of nature. So the best he could do was qualify this empiricism as "metaphysical," by which he meant a philosophy of experience in its richest and deepest sense, one that starts with the unprethinkable facticity of being and builds upon it, always with an eye to the powers of being at work in experience.[1] Experience so conceived demands an understanding subtle enough to catch sight of the ongoing movement of Spirit in the world.[2] Neither theosophy nor paranormal experience, this empiricism feels about in experience for the spiritual lines of force by which it is penetrated.

To this metaphysical empiricism we must attach two cautionary notes. First, as an empiricism, as a posteriori knowledge, tethered to the contingent course of experience, we have to concede that things may not turn out well. History is not over until it is over,[3] and we cannot be assured of its outcome. Existence is not a predicate; existence is a test. Tellingly, Schelling is prepared to admit that in the process—since this is factual experience, not a geometric proof—*a contradiction could arise.*[4] Like what?

On God's side, perhaps the *prius* would decide to withdraw. God once regretted ever coming up with the idea of creation (Gen. 6:5–7). God is what God chooses to be. We might then slightly recast the standard translation of Exodus 3:14 to read, "I am who I choose to be" or even "I am free to be or not to be." As Robert Scharlemann points out, Schelling goes further than Anselm: "Which is greater—a God who must be, and cannot not be, so that he cannot even be thought not to be; or a God who, as Lord of being, is free to be or not to be and is thus free to be thought or not to be thought to be?"[5] Or, on the human side, even if God proves faithful, perhaps human freedom would prove faithless, so that nothing like the "kingdom of God" would ever appear! Evil's reign would be unchecked. As Habermas argues, Schelling is here entrusting the divine fate to human history—that is, to us—and we are notoriously unreliable, inconsistent, and prone to evil, as history bears ample and sorry witness. It is up to us to fill what is missing in the historical body of God and make the kingdom of God come true, and we might not come through. Either way, God would never get to be God, the Lord of Being. God would never get to "exist" but would remain behind, above, beneath, prior, concealed forever in eternal beyond-beingness. That is to strike a *radical view of the risk to which God*—the process of God becoming God, of proving the divinity inscribed in being—is exposed.

Second, this philosophical religion or metaphysical empiricism is not to be confused with "Christian philosophy" or a "religious philosophy," for the authority in play here has the authority of experience, not of any religious dogma, revealed book, or official teaching. Christianity is present here not as a supernatural authority but as another historical document, just like Greek art or the history of Rome. We must take account of the history of *everything*—from Stonehenge to the Rolling Stones—which means not excluding Christian and other religious sources (as is the wont of the philosophers), *all* of which are occasions of philosophical insight. We learn something from revelation not by supernatural intervention but in the way we are able to see a constellation in the sky only after someone has pointed it out to us.[6] This was also Hegel's goal, but his mistake was to think he could rationalize, systematize, and totalize it all.[7] So the philosophy of revelation means understanding revelation philosophically, which is the opposite of submitting philosophy to ecclesiastical surveillance.

Everything Schelling is saying about metaphysical empiricism comes to a head in the telling example he provides of a "metaphysical" experience—the other person. For English empiricism, the other person can be no more than a collection of sense data organized by the laws of association of ideas, issuing in an "animal faith," a conditioned belief, that "somebody" is "in" there or "out" there, which not only does damage to experience but also undermines the seriousness of ethics. In a more insightful rendering of this experience, we come to know other persons by *interpreting* what they say and do in the world, reaching an understanding of their moral and intellectual character, which is not known a priori or by intellectual intuition but made manifest in our concrete embodied encounters.[8] This, of course, is given a magisterial account by Husserl in his *Cartesian Meditations*.[9] Metaphysical empiricism turns out to be hermeneutic phenomenology, *avant la lettre*. The face of the other person is not a visible object, like a picture on the wall. We see the face of others seeing us; our seeing is also being seen. This basic insight funded both the atheistic phenomenology of Jean-Paul Sartre, where hell is other people, and the ethics of Emmanuel Levinas, the counter-Sartre, the Jewish philosopher, who sees in the face of the other the trace of God in the world, which is not far from Schelling. Sartre and Levinas are both drawing upon Husserl and together represent salient examples of a hermeneutic phenomenology for which Schelling lacked only the vocabulary, not the idea. Phenomenology was sent into the world to save us from having to use the word *empiricism*.

The objection to Schelling's language of a "metaphysical empiricism" is like Schelling's own objection to traditional Christology. It is a "forced" idea, jamming together two opposed natures without seeing clearly the *tertium quid*. The "metaphysical" says too much, the "empiricism" says too little.[10] The conflict between Sartre and Levinas is also an indicator of the possibility of conflict and contradiction that Schelling predicts for his empiricism, which is what Paul Ricoeur famously called the "conflict of interpretations," which Schelling would prefer to call a conflict of wills. On the one side, there is the hermeneutics of suspicion found in Marx and Freud, Schopenhauer and Nietzsche, representing a "history of effects" issuing from Schelling himself. On the other side, there is a more inspiring, inspirited reading of history in terms of God's loving providence—something he should have said we could speak about only after the fact, like the owl of Minerva, retrospectively—which is Schelling's own *interpretation*. For Schelling, the experience of the other is the experience of spirit in the world, of the other as an *infini* in Levinas's sense, an infinite depth whose concrete life flows from sources whose effects we experience but to whose depths we have no direct access. Schelling described these depths as "supersensible," which is to say too much, as metaphysics habitually does, just as empiricism's sense data impoverishes them. It is enough to say they are "invisible." As Schelling himself once famously said, nature is visible spirit, spirit is invisible nature. Period, perfect! Spare us, please, the metaphysics of the noumenal will.

So the claim that the *prius* proves itself to be God comes down to a *hermeneutic* rendering, once summarized by Gadamer as the *subtilitas intelligendi et explicandi et applicandi*, the subtle art of understanding, explaining, and applying—having *subtilitas*, the right touch, the light touch, when we approach something subtle, like the face of the other person.[11] The philosophy of revelation amounts to a hermeneutics of history in which we *read* the depths of history *as* (note Heidegger's "hermeneutic as") the unfolding life of Spirit in the world, in precisely the way we read the character of another person in and through their words and deeds and "body language." It is all a matter of interpretive reading, a *speculative hermeneutics*, of *taking* history—and nature—*as* God's unfolding being. This is a hermeneutic decision, as one could always decline this reading and maintain that it is just the brute facticity of being all the way down, just the density of matter, where freedom, God, love, and the beautiful are so many illusions. That is a choice we have to make. That, as we keep saying, is the *risk* Schelling has very nicely identified.

EITHER/OR

By saying this is a choice, Schelling admits—indeed, he insists—that this will be a proof only for the wise, for those who have the eyes to see, the ears to hear, and the subtility of spirit to understand, not for the fool who says in his heart there is no God, who is a ham-fisted, undiscerning reader of spiritual matters. "Whoever does not want it should just as well leave it alone . . . if one wants the actual chain of events, if he wants a freely created world, and so on, he can have all of this only via the path of such a philosophy."[12] Schelling's view can be saved from the blatantly decisionistic terms in which he casts it only if, as I am arguing, what he really has in mind is hermeneutics.[13] Schelling is here going back to Fichte's notion that the resolution of Kant's antinomy of freedom and necessity is found not in a rational argument—for speculative reason this is an irresoluble conflict—but in a choice about our eternal moral character. The choice comes down to who we want to be, to who is deciding, to the will that is willing—a moral one or an amoral one. The choice comes down to whether this primordial willing is a who (personal, free) or a what (impersonal, deterministic). Once again, we get some help from Deleuze; the question is not "What does this mean?" (negative philosophy) but "Who or what wills?" (positive philosophy).

From a strictly logical point of view, the very idea of the "unprethinkable" is that we do not know what to think of being, that we have no idea whether it is reason or will or some absolutely unintelligent and indifferent density, some great cosmic stupidity, as Nietzsche said. This choice represents a kind of existential test of what we are made of, of whether we will *make ourselves worthy of the will within us*. Are we life affirming—lovers of freedom, life, process, mobility, risk, and hidden depths—or, like the Stoics, Spinoza and Hegel, are we content to say that everything is measured by necessity and an unbroken, unbreached (nonecstatic) reason? Do we rejoice in setting sail on the risky waters of freedom? Or does nothing comfort us more than the thought that things cannot be otherwise? Are we life affirming or life denying?

As Tillich says, "To think the absolute is a necessity of reason; to think God is freedom, which, like all freedom, transcends necessity."[14] In Tillich's terms, Schelling is posing the question of whether we have the "courage to be"—the courage to be free, to be God-affirming spirits. For Schelling, in a philosophy of willing, it all comes down to the quality of the choice, to the depth of willing and consequently courage[15]—let us say the courage to love. Courage to be (Tillich) and courage to love (Schelling) are the way we make ourselves worthy of the will, while for Hegel, the highest courage lay in the courage to think, daring to think (*sapere aude*), just as the Enlightenment encouraged us. Schelling is thus posing for us a metaphysical either/or:

> *Either* we posit the absolute alone with itself and hold that all that exists is the dark, blind actuality of the that, of pure *prius*, holding that life and love, beauty and ethics, the whole constellation of ethico-aesthetico-religious categories, the realm of the personal, of Spirit, are pure illusions, merely phenomenal appearances.
>
> *Or* we say that the deep, overwhelming power and sublimity of the *prius* becomes beautiful, its concealed incomprehensibility makes itself known, its terrible strict law becomes gift and grace, and its solitary self-identical unity becomes the manifold of the world of space and time, holding that all this is real, that it all happens in nature and, still more perfectly, in human history.

Reason cannot settle this conflict. As with all such metaphysical disagreement, there is no cognitive way to adjudicate this dispute. Schelling thought, as a metaphysical voluntarist, that the God-affirming will is the only *honorable* course of action. It is the only way to make himself worthy of the will; otherwise, we turn the will against itself. If we want freedom and love to be genuinely real and not mere appearance, then we will affirm they have a *fundamentum in re*, a foundation in being, in the Being of beings (Heidegger), in the ground of Being (Tillich), in God, who is freedom. This is the very nub of God proving himself to be God in the world, of God's autobiography—indeed, of God's autoverification, autoidentification (God proving God is not a robot!). We remain free to dismiss the aesthetico-ethico-religious categories, the whole sphere of the living and the personal, the Spirit, by dismissing the personal God and reducing reality to a great cosmic stupidity, a blind play of forces, a mindless machine. For Schelling, we cannot have one, the true, the good, and the beautiful in human life, without the other, the personal God whose life is unfolding in it.

Of course, what is decisionistically affirmed can be decisionistically denied. So, Nietzsche drew the opposite conclusion—when the will does not kill me, it makes me stronger. The ability of an idea to comfort me is no assurance of its truth. Instead of backfilling the abyss with the God of the gap, he danced over it on a wire without a net.

The experience, Schelling adds, is not a particular experience but the entirety of experience, and the proof constitutes the entirely of positive philosophy, which means it is never finished. If we ask if God exists, the right philosophical answer is that we do not know yet. It is not over. Even if, as Schelling thinks, nature's work is finished (it now just repeats the same cycle, its whole purpose having been to produce humanity), history is the never-finished, ever-searching love, *philia*, of *sophia*.[16] A philosopher, a wisdom-seeker, is one who is prepared to be instructed by anything and everything, to put his ear close to the beating heart of being wherever it is found. Agreeing that it has something to learn from religion, philosophy makes the content of religion a part of its own (phenomenological) insight. Philosophy learns from both art and revelation. So, too, philosophy can now see things with its naked eye what Christianity as an historical phenomenon first pointed out, without doing harm to either philosophy or revelation.[17] Philosophy undergoes an "expansion" by way of revelation but an expansion based on a necessity within philosophy itself.[18] On this point, that philosophy cannot be denied access to revelation—which I have described as suspending the supernatural signified—Schelling and Hegel are agreed, and that, I think, is because, while their own intentions are metaphysical, they are both talking about revelation as a theopoetics, not supernatural legerdemain.

In short, the philosophy of revelation is theopoetics, and "philosophical religion" is a hermeneutic phenomenology, or so says Schelling in his bolder voice.

THE DIFFERENCE BETWEEN MYTHOLOGY AND REVELATION

With this philosophical religion in mind, let us revisit Schelling's distinction between mythology and revelation and see what it looks like under the hand of a bolder theology. Philosophical religion is religion in the deep sense. Religion in the deep sense is religion in the apophatic sense, and religion in the apophatic sense is the issue of our unbreakable bonds with being, of which the experience of facticity is not only a case in point but pretty much the whole point. On its objective side, the why-there-is-something-rather-than-nothing side, this means the mystery of being, and no one has put its subjective side, the why-I-am-rather-than-not side, better than (Kierkegaard's) Constantine Constantius, who asked, in reference to the fact of being born, "Why was I not asked about it? Is there no manager? To whom shall I make my complaint?"[19] In Schelling, mythology and revelation are drawn from the bonds of being in a graduated way: first, mythology, the lower natural stratum, immersed in deep natural forces, and then revelation, the higher one, bathed in the light of consciousness and freedom.

Schelling's work on mythology, while inevitably limited by the state of the scholarship of the day and by a widespread Christo- and Eurocentrism from which Schelling was by no means exempt, was both prescient and profound.[20] Insisting that mythological religion is not to be dismissed as a subjective, primitive poesy, he maintains that it is closer to the unprethinkable than is conscious life and hence more resonant with the inscrutable powers of being. Mythological religion springs from a natural, visceral, and preconscious or unconscious "attunement" (*Stimmung*) to being, to borrow a term from Heidegger, long before reflective thought arrives on the scene to sort things out. Hegel appreciated the value of the mythological *Vorstellung* as the sensuous embodiment of the Spirit in song and story, but Hegel went on to depreciate it as the way the Spirit can be felt by those by whom it *cannot be thought*. Hegel takes the measure of mythology by its proximity to the Concept, Schelling by its proximity to the unprethinkable. For Hegel, mythology can be translated without remainder into the clarity of absolute knowledge. The *Vorstellung* illustrates figuratively what is more clearly self-presented in the Concept. Religious images are the way the common folk get their philosophy, and as such they are less than thought. To Schelling they are deeper than thought, beyond the reach of thought, establishing nonconceptual contact with the unprethinkable. Myth is important not because it is a lower and more accessible version of absolute consciousness but because it puts us in touch with a dimension of our being to which reason and consciousness are otherwise denied access, whereas Hegel held that reason cannot be denied access to anything.

As Tillich says, for Schelling, myth is not to be understood psychologically but ontologically, "in terms of powers of being which grasp the human mind itself." Myths and symbols are rooted in things that are happening in the human soul but do not derive from the human soul, but "from the roots men [sic] have in the depths of reality itself," expressing "the different powers of being by which men are grasped." In the symbol, we have been seized by the depths of being itself, of the real. The reason "religion is the most glorious and the most cruel part of man's history," Tillich says, is that "religion is not a matter of wishful thinking, but a matter of powers of being which men encounter."[21] Instead of simply decoding the latent conceptual content of mythology, we should enter into it and expose ourselves to its unique power. The literalism of biblical fundamentalism, the allegoricism of literary theory, and the intellectualism of Hegel all deprive the myth of its depth. "Mythology is not allegorical; it is tautegorical."[22] A myth is not speaking about something else (*allos*) in the dispensable figures of the myth; it is not a figure that can be "figured out" and dispensed with, not a code to be decoded. It is speaking about itself (*to auto*) in terms that are indispensable to it. So a myth is like a sacrament; it is itself what it is signifying. As Tyler Tritten suggests, Deleuze can help us out here.[23] A myth is not a representation; it is a performance. We should not ask "What does it mean?" but "How is it to be played?" Do not just read it; do it, dance it. Far from an exercise in fancy or untamed imagination, mythology is being itself playing on the strings of our bodies and our unconscious life (whence the interest of Schopenhauer and Nietzsche in music).

Mythology must have begun, Schelling speculates, in a stage of undeveloped, untested monotheism, some kind of naturally implanted common knowledge of a single but completely undifferentiated divine power.[24] Of course, this would need to be put to the test, differentiated and articulated, by the various polytheisms, which represent the historical mythological traditions we know about, culminating in the Greek mystery cults, where the veil of the mystery they announce is lifted by the revelation of Christ, for which they provide the immediate preparation. Mythological religion engages the unruly powers set loose by the Fall on the level of song and rite, dance and sacrifice, a level that is largely naturalistic and instinctive. However undeveloped, this is a necessary stage of "potentiation" and provides a transition to the light and freedom of revelation, where the disturbance in the powers is addressed on the very level of being itself, which is not sensuous natural powers but the power of the will. Mythology, he thinks, seeks to reconcile the world to the divine power phenomenally, while revelation addresses it noumenally.

Revelation is already *implicit* in mythology. The eternal Christ first enters the world of time in the form of the natural powers, and so he is already operative in pagan mythology, where he begins his struggles against the powers of concealment. He comes into the light explicitly in the Incarnation, which Schelling explains in a remarkable rendering of the prologue to the fourth gospel,[25] Schelling's gospel of choice. "In the beginning"—that is, in the absolute past that was never present to thought, in a time before creation—was "the Logos"—that is, the *Unvordenkliche*, the *actus purus*, the facticity of being, the primordiality of blind being—"and the Logos was with God." The additional clause (*pros theon, bei Gott*) signifies that a difference between God and the Logos has set in, that the grip of the unprethinkable is loosened. Now the Logos is alongside (*praeter deum*), not simply identical with the Father, who is closest to the *das Unvordenkliche*. The Logos is still compliant with and dependent upon the Father but now distinct. The Father is in act, the Son is still in potency; this unity is less a matter of freedom than of essence. But now the Father steps back into potency and the Son steps forward into act, serving first a demiurgic function, for it is through the Son that the Father creates the world, and second, after the Fall, the salvific function, of descending into space and time to confront the powers of darkness under whose sway humanity has fallen. Thus begins the history of revelation, when the Son follows fallen man into time to do battle with the anarchic powers unleashed by the Fall. The "age of the Father" belongs to the absolute prototemporal past. The present age, what we call the world—the history of Being from the Fall to the Parousia—is "the age of the Son," when the Father had handed sovereignty over the world to the Son. "And the Logos was God": this describes the third age, history brought to completion, the age of the Spirit, after the mission of the Son is complete. The movement of the dialectic is not a circular Hegelian *Aufhebung* but a linear progression, in which each stage is overcome, sublated in the negative sense, by its successor. When one stage is highlighted, the others are grayed out.

At the culmination of revelation, the summit of time as we know time, the Logos has become the "Lord of Being," fully proven, potentiated, and personified—as God. At that point—as we have seen, an extreme implication of a voluntaristic theology—the Logos is free and could have remained independent of the Father but instead returns creation to the Father, thereby reuniting God and creation in mutual fulfillment. At the end of creation, the Logos is God (*theos*), and *das Unvordenkliche* has brought forth its divinity (*theios, Gottheit*), fully tested and actualized. But, Schelling notes, the gospel says *theos*, not *ho theos*. The Son is God, not *the* God. Only the Father is *the* God. The Son enters into a free and independent unity with the God, now as a work of freedom, not of essence. Put anthropomorphically, having lived in childlike subordination in his Father's house, the Son freely returns—as the "heir of the Father"[26]—now tested by the trials of this world. Having put down a challenge to the sovereignty of his Father over the family estate, he now lives with his Father in a free union. So the prologue sketches the life of the Trinity beginning from an ideal and still-untested state to its completion. The hidden powers of the *Unvordenkliche* first emerge in an initial but nonconflictual differentiation, in a kind of peaceful paradisal ring dance, what Hegel calls "the game of love with itself," which Schelling sarcastically calls "very edifying."[27] But this peace is provisional. God is not yet fully God; the infinite depths of the

Gottheit, the divinity, are still untapped, in potency, and a power cannot be potentiated unless it is put to the test.

This reading of Christian revelation is entirely dependent on the dubious metaphysical assumption that primordial being is will and that a change in being's fortunes can only be effected by a being of divine will, who can freely reverse the ill will of the Fall. Absent this metaphysical extravagance and relieved of its Christocentrism, the question is, "What is left of 'revelation'?" That, I propose, is its *mythological* content, the battle between the forces of evil and the kingdom of God, between the Christ and Satan, and that admits of a completely different reading of the death of Jesus, not as something he *voluntarily undertakes*—which plays into Anselm's hand that the Father's "wrath" has to be "satisfied"—but as an *innocent victim* of cruel empire, where the truly revelatory moment is that Jesus unexpectedly responds to his unjust execution with forgiveness! That, in turn, undermines any "deep" distinction between mythology and revelation. The New Testament turns on a *mythic* battle—that was Anselm's objection to it!—and the indigenous or so-called nature religions are deeply *revelatory* of our bonds with the natural world and the depth of our bodily life, a revelation of which we are singularly in need today as humankind is in the process of ravaging the earth for its spoils.

In other words, mythology is revelatory; revelation is mythological. Revelation is Christian mythology; mythology is non-Christian revelation. What does a revelation reveal? A form of life, a mode of being-in-the-world, a theopoetics; it does not deliver supernatural information. Revelation is found wherever there is factical-historical life—that is, a culture—not only in Christianity, which is the Christocentrism a bolder Schelling would shed. Religion—the deeper religion constituted by our bonds with the powers of being—represents a certain rendering of the human condition that is available to everyone, Christian or not, "religious" or not, a "public" religion, a rendering of which a positive philosophy is cut to fit. Schelling's philosophical religion is the source of Tillich's notion that religion in the deep sense is the content of culture and culture is the form of religion. The distinction dissolves into the difference between differing mythological revelations and differing revelatory myths, differing cultural forms, where the underlying common feature is that they are all so many different forms of life, differing ways to come to grips with an infinite and incomprehensible power—of being rather than not. They are different, not rank ordered. The mystery, beauty, and power of the world are put on display in multiple ways—in Stonehenge, a Greek temple, a great mosque, a Gothic cathedral. Different, not higher or lower; different with a differential difference, not a binary, dialectical, or hierarchical difference. In each case we are differently moved by the majesty of being, dazzled by the play of dark and light, made to feel the distance between the finite and the infinite, between our short and difficult lives and some endless, nameless cosmic power. In these structures, all the "powers" of a given "world" are gathered, and we are made to feel the grip that being has on us. Dazzled, swept away, gripped—by what? By a power that overpowers us, by the unconditional, for which all our "arts and sciences" seek a name.

These are not (only) "objects" to be scrutinized by historians of art or religion, which reduces them to abstract, diminished, one-sided objectifications. What is really going on in these differing forms of life is an experience of awe and wonder, *tremendum et fascinans*, beautiful and sublime, which is the beginning of the wisdom of philosophy. Indeed, as Tillich, drawing upon Schelling, makes plain, this philosophical religion is not confined to "religion." Our experience of the powers of being is found every bit as much in the work of art, in the extraordinary mysteries of the cosmos brought to light in contemporary physics, in the fight to the death for justice, in the depths of ordinary life. At this elementary level of experience, not only does the distinction between mythology and revelation break down, but the distinction between the "religious" and the "secular" also vanishes. Better still, it is redescribed; no longer a distinction between objects or content, it becomes a distinction between modalities, not of a what but of a how. Not only cathedrals and temples, but Picassos and quantum physics. Even the most "secular" thing can be the occasion of an experience of the ground of being, of the depth dimension in things, of the deep and impenetrable mystery of the fact that there is being at all, rather than not. We do not need to book a trip to Stonehenge. The mystery of being is everywhere. In inadvertently coming upon the old, beat-up hat of someone we loved long ago more dearly than words can say, the abyss of being opens up before our gaze. We are brought up short before that in which we live and move and have our being, which are, we should recall, not Paul's words but the words of the "pagan" poet he was citing.[28]

EIGHT

HEGEL AND SCHELLING
The Critique and the Scarecrow

WE NEED TO BE CLEAR about how Schelling and Hegel differ, and about how to assess Schelling's critique of Hegel, in order to see what progress we have made on the road from an edifying to a radical apophatic theology.

THE ONTOLOGICAL ARGUMENT

Schelling's case against Hegel is not that Hegel practices a strictly negative philosophy and never gets to positive philosophy.[1] It is that Hegel promiscuously passes back and forth between the two, mixing the sphere of pure logic with the sphere of existence.[2] Hegel, he complains, effects the transition from the *Logic* to the *Philosophy of Nature* by waving a metaphysical wand where the Idea begins magically emitting existence, "releasing itself" from the Idea—this from the philosopher who says that the pure *Ur-grund* "decides" to "divide itself."[3] It is as if Hegel's Concept were a living personal being, capable of deciding to quit the sphere of thinking and enter the sphere of being. Schelling thinks that at the end of day, Hegel has deceptively insinuated back into post-Kantian thought the illusionary logic of the "ontological argument," which attempts to derive existence from essence. That, I think, is a distortion of Hegel and encouraged the caricatures of Hegel by Kierkegaard's pseudonyms, what Žižek calls the "scarecrow Hegel." As we have seen, Hegel is engaged in a speculative hermeneutics that aptly describes both Hegel and Schelling, and seeing this point allows us to sort out the scarecrow from the critique—what is going wrong in Schelling's critique of Hegel from what Schelling is getting right.[4]

The operative distinction in Hegel is not between essence and existence. That is how Schelling framed Hegel after coming in contact with Catholic scholasticism in Bavaria.[5] The operative distinction in Hegel obtains between essence and manifestation, inner essence and outer manifestation, inner force and its outer expression, implicit logic and explicit being, inner content and outer form. Hegel does not think of the *Logic* as an exploration of the sphere of *essentia* in such a way that it stands in need of some external kick start to shift it into actualization and bring it over to the order of existence. He takes himself to be giving a metaphysical analysis of being as an auto-telic dynamic procession (*entelecheia*) that has, much like Schelling himself, an inner potency and an outer actualization where the two are ontologically bound to each other by a kind of ontological valence, comparable to the "jointure of being," the *Band* invoked by Schelling in the *Freedom* essay. The *Logic* is a study of *Wesen*, of the substantial core of Being, but *Wesen* is not *essentia* in Schelling's sense. What Schelling calls essence, *das "Was,"* is, for Hegel, a one-sided, abstract product of *Verstand*. *Wesen* is the first moment in the unitary unfolding of an organic whole, which can only by grasped by a more ample *Vernunft*.

Hegel's paradigm is an organic process composed of moments, not a flat quiddity in need of a "that." To begin with, Hegel's model (like Schelling) is the Trinity, which is a *process* not a triangle, where the processions form a system of *internal relations*, each moment of which is defined in terms of the other and is absolutely inseparable from the rest, as inseparable as the inside (*an sich*) and outside (*für sich*) of the same substantial reality. Furthermore, Hegel analyzes these processions in organic Aristotelian terms—again, more like Schelling's own *Weltalter* manuscripts—not formal mathematical Platonic terms. In Aristotle, there is no distinction between essence and existence, a point explored earlier (chapter 2) in dealing with the difference between Aristotle and Aquinas. Aristotle distinguished between *ousia* and its accidental properties, or between first *ousia* and second, but *ousia* is not *essentia* as opposed to existence. *Ousia* is substance, *substantia*, *die Sache*, the concrete substantial thing (primary substance, let us say, Socrates) that can always be represented in its abstract universality (secondary substance, being-human). It is substantial content taking a variety of forms. By distinguishing negative and positive philosophy in terms of essence and existence, Schelling invokes an innovation of medieval Christian Aristotelians like Thomas Aquinas in search of an explanation of *creatio ex nihilo*. Like them, the later Schelling criticizes Hegel for lacking this idea of creation as a divine activity freely effecting the transition from possibility (essence) to actuality (existence).[6] For Aristotle, this distinction solves a problem that never arises. For Hegel, a superbeing who freely creates the world out of love is piety, not philosophy. It does not respond to a philosophical question but to the needs of prayer. It is an edifying religious *Vorstellung*, but philosophically it is a personification, like representing the sun or thunder as a god, allowing piety to picture the dependence of the world on God or the Heavenly Father.

CIRCULARITY AND LINEARITY

Schelling also charged Hegel with circularity, loading up the idea of God in the *Logic* and then deriving it again at the end, giving us the same God whose idea he had at the beginning, so that nothing was gained by the effort. Schelling claimed his own thought, by contrast, made linear progress from an innocent and untested beginning to the fully developed thing. This is only half true. While Schelling's dialectical method, as Edward Beach shows, does follow a logic of productivity, not of *Aufhebung*, it is no less circular. It moves in an organic teleological circle, the unfolding development of being and God from alpha to omega, where the origin and the telos are different stages of development of the same thing, so that nothing is at risk. The primordial *Lauterkeit* is an innocent unity that can only become itself by being put to the test of the contest, of the strife. In perfect conformity to the Neoplatonic schema of *exitus* and *reditus*, it moves from implicit, undeveloped *actus purus* to an explicit and fully actualized one. The Trinitarian schema of the ages of the world overrides a *genuinely linear* movement forward, one in which we could come to the *end* of the line and God or the world could run out of rope, never complete the circuit, a possibility imagined only by the radical Schelling. To be absolutely serious about freedom and God's quest for self-revelation in the expanse of nature and the pages of history, God's life would have to be on the line so that God may reach the end of the line. Circles go on forever, but on a linear model, the universe could all end in oblivion, complete destruction, driving off the road. History could be a one-way street with no return. Instead of a *pleroma*, a *kenosis*. If Hegel travels in a circle of *Vernunft*, Schelling travels in a circle of love and will. The two represent intellectualist and voluntarist versions of Christian providence. In a bolder theory of linearity, any talk of providence would have to be a contingent retrospective construction made at the end of history. It may all end in ashes, which is precisely the outcome predicted by contemporary physics, a point we return to later (chapter 14).

PERSONAL GOD

For Hegel, Schelling's fiat is a religious *Vorstellung*, an exercise of pious personification, as if being itself were an agent cause, somebody doing something; it is like imagining the big bang as a big somebody with a big heart expanding out of sheer love for the stars and galaxies to come. That is what Heidegger calls metaphysical *Subjektität*, the propensity of metaphysics to model being itself on some ontic feature of human subjectivity. As Tillich points out, Schelling tries to position himself between a narrowly theistic view of God as a separately subsistent being, removed from creation, like Aristotle's *noesis noeseos*, and a pantheistic God who is dissolved without remainder into creation. His God has features of both views, tilting to the side of panentheism in the early work and to the theistic side in the later work. His God is the essential being of beings, but this being is "not suspended in mid-air"[7] because God is also subsistent as an individual substance—*das was das Seiende ist*, that which *is* what is, or the one who is that which being is. This is an ontico-ontological formula that invites comparison to Aquinas's notion that God is *ipsum esse per se subsistens*, meaning both being itself and individually subsistent. This individual being is God's selfhood or egoism, which contracts the divine being to itself like a centripetal force, as opposed to God's personal being as love, which is expansive, centrifugal, communicative of being, and world creating.[8]

The personal God is the edifying Schelling taking a step back from the brink of the radical Schelling. I think, with Žižek and Habermas, that the elderly Schelling, called to Berlin (after living many years in Catholic Bavaria) by royal appointment to put down a rising tide of young atheists, tempered his most radical views from the *Weltalter* fragments and inched himself much closer to orthodoxy. Schelling contains the threat of evil by confiding the history of the world to the loving care of divine providence—just where facticity demands that any such divine foresight remains to be seen. At this point, as Habermas says, Schelling took out an "insurance policy" against the very threat he better than anyone else dared to expose,[9] and he ended with the same result as Hegel: that the way of the Spirit is inwardly guided by God and assured of final success. The radical implication of the *factical* question of

God is to say that the existence of God is the "kingdom of God" and that the kingdom of God has been entrusted to *us*, where there are no guarantees. As Walter Benjamin says, *we* are the messianic age.[10] *We* are ones God has been waiting for to make the kingdom of God come true! And that was one risky move for God to make! That is why both Žižek and Habermas think the later positive philosophy is "flat," which explains the empty seats in the auditorium at the University of Berlin. The radicals in his audience expected to hear more than that.

On the question of the personal God, Hegel is the more radical thinker, the more radical panentheist. For Hegel—as for Tillich—God is not a being, not even the highest being, but the ground of being, being itself, and not a "personal" being, although that is the way God is imagined in prayer and piety. There is, however, no "entity" that is what-is. The name of God is the name of the underlying being of beings, not less than the personal but the ground of the personal. Any given being is finite, and the name of God is the name of the infinite substantial reality from which beings arise and into which they return. On this point, Hegel and Tillich adopt the "bold" position and Schelling the "timid" one, because Schelling wants to keep one foot not in the concept but in the *ens supremum*, the *ens realissimum*, the Supreme Being. His personal God could, were he so minded, remain in eternal isolation. When it comes to making the ontological reduction, Schelling stops short.

INTELLECTUALISM AND VOLUNTARISM

What Schelling is getting right is Hegel's *intellectualism*. When Hegel says the real is the rational and the rational is the real, he is not being an *essentialist* in the sense that Schelling had in mind, but he is being an *intellectualist*, which Schelling calls his "panlogism." Hegel is not saying essence magically exudes existence, but he is saying that the really existing world is thoroughly penetrated by *Vernunft*. What Hegel does with reason, Schelling does with will, which is to *read* the real world *as* the work of Spirit (speculative hermeneutics). What Victor Nuovo says of Schelling, that "positive philosophy is the hermeneutics of historical events and traditions viewed as moments in a process that culminates in revelation,"[11] I think can also be said of Hegel. Hegel and Schelling offer variant versions of a speculative hermeneutics of the history of the Spirit. So, the difference between Schelling and Hegel must lie elsewhere. What really divides Schelling from Hegel is not a clandestine use of the ontological argument but the voluntarism of Schelling—running from its roots in Augustine and medieval Franciscan thought through German mysticism and Luther up to Schelling—which is at odds with the intellectualism of Hegel, which goes back to Aristotle and the *noesis noeseos* and the medieval Dominicans.[12]

Hegel held that the world is through and through a work of law, of transparent intelligibility. The philosophical task is to put our finger on that law, which is the office of philosophy. The philosophers—this is the *Phenomenology of Spirit*—report what they observe as Being unfolds into thought and thought enfolds being. *That*, I think, is where Hegel was rightly and decisively criticized by Schelling, for his *intellectualism*, while Schelling never lost sight of our inner demons, the underside of our nature and even, especially, of God's. That is the Hegel who came under fire in the wake of the carnage of the twentieth century, of which it almost seems Schelling had a premonition. The catastrophic destruction of Europe after World War II, the evils of twentieth-century "totalitarianism" systems of the left and the right—what is that other than the "barbarian principle" that Schelling had presciently identified? A Hegelian would be forced to say that slavery, the trench warfare of World War I, the Holocaust, and the various genocides of the twentieth century belong to a deep, long-term logic (the cunning of Reason), to God writing straight with crooked lines. On this point, Schelling is the more radical thinker. He describes an anarchic unruly ground in the heart of being and of God, which blocks the progress of ontology by casting the shadow of unprethinkable being across its path. He was worried that freedom is deprived of oxygen by Hegel's intellectualism, that being is deprived of depth by Hegel's *Begriff*, that Hegel was too quick to give divine legitimacy to the present order[13] and too willing to write off the cost of human suffering to advance the cause of the Spirit in the world. Schelling said that while Christ had defeated Satan, Satan was a wily one who could reinvent himself as often as circumstances required and continue to cause death and destruction.[14] Freedom *meant* the possibility of evildoing, and while he thought freedom was worth the risk, he thought the risk was terrible. That is why Schelling did not propose, as Hegel did, that everything comes to a head in *philosophy* but rather in what philosophy is the philosophy *of*—life, real and concrete life. At first, he thought that art is the instrument on which being plays its tune and later that religion is the hymn in which being sings its song, while Hegel treated art and religion as inferior forms of thought. That is where Shelling differs from Hegel and why Schelling more than Hegel advances the cause of a radical apophaticism.

Schelling's breakthrough, forever dividing him from Hegel, was to insist upon the irreducibility of facticity—meaning temporality, contingency and an open future, the limits of intelligibility and rationalization, the concealment that inheres in the intelligible light, the diachrony of the prius that preempts any possible synchrony, the unconscious that disturbs consciousness, the lack that awakens every desire, the natural and the affective, the work of art—in short, the unprethinkable. Schelling's own limit was to think that his remarkable phenomenological analyses of the irreducible sphere of factical life needed to be grounded upon a metaphysical voluntarism in which God and humankind seek *Seligkeit*. Schelling grounds an undebatable factical experience— that as soon as I awake in the world, being is always already there—upon an obscure, highly debatable body of edifying speculation bordering on theosophy. Factical life can speak for itself, thank you very much, and it stands there, as big as life, without Schelling's *Wollen* to shore it up by flooding it with love and without Hegel's absolute *Geist* to flood it with the light of Reason.

In short, in Hegel radical theology finds a panentheism and in Schelling an apophaticism. What is needed next is to see how these belong together, which is what we find in Tillich (chapter 9).

FROM SCHELLING TO RADICAL APOPHATICS

I do not think that being is love or being is reason or being is Somebody. If I had to say anything at all, I would say that being is the concealed ground, the unlit core, the hidden depths, which is to say that I do not know what being is, and I have learned from Kant to stop talking like that. Whatever being is, it is at best the ground of love and reason and persons and who knows what else, maybe of its own self-destruction. Why not that? Being is at best a groundless ground because love and reason never arrive without their "dark companions,"[15] which is what I am calling the mystical and what draws me to Schelling. So the laurel goes to Schelling, the *radical* Schelling, as the philosopher par excellence of the apophatic imagination. His "philosophical religion" provides a crucial opening to radical theology, which I summarize here as a deep or radical *hermeneutics of facticity*, and this on three registers, in each of which the concealed groundless ground proves inescapable.

First is the *facticity of Being*, the simple but imponderable and unprethinkable fact that there is something rather than not. *Es gibt. Il y a.* There is being. The addendum, the "rather than not," delivers the punch. Being happens like an extraordinary event, like a Derridean gift in which no one can identify a giver giving and the recipients are not put in a permanent debt, for who or what is to be thanked? We know *that* things are, but, if asked to say anything more ultimate than that about the *that*, we have to confess that we do not know *what* is *what*. That, the ultimate *that*, is what Kant called the abyss of reason. If we knew *that*, we would know everything. On the level of the unprethinkable, we are all in the same boat, all equally at sea. *Quaestio mihi magna factus sum*, Augustine famously said. I am not trying to maintain a position but to sustain the suspense, the ontological *epochē*, the elemental wonder, the wonder of all wonders, *that* there is anything at all, *rather than not*. "It"—the *that*—has us before we have it. We do not get it (*id*, *Ça*); it has got us. It has (*il a*) us there (*y*), as in the "anonymous rumbling of *il y a*" in Levinas. We are thus led up to the point of a certain *religion*, not the fully equipped religion of rites and righteousness, clergy and candles, exorcisms and excommunications, but a kind of weak, spare, naked crucified religion, divested of the long robes and trappings of the traditional religion, a kind of *Ur*-religion, or protoreligion, a religion without religion, the religion of the ultimate *that*. If we are not religious in the sense of the protoreligion of the unprethinkable that Schelling is getting at, we are condemned to lead trivial lives in which we let the mystery of things pass us by, completely unnoticed, in favor of managing our stock portfolio. We fail to make ourselves worthy of what is happening to us.

Second is the *facticity of God*. Given the fact of unprethinkable being, the name of God is an afterthought, a posteriori. Given the irreducible *that*, the name of God is the name of a *what*, of a contingent predicate we come up with, after the fact, for what is without predicates, for an unprethinkable subject, one of many names for the unnamable. The predicate, the predication, is meant as the praise we are prompted to heap on unprethinkable being under the name of *divinity*. The name of God is the highest praise we can think of, God as the *ens laudabilissimum*, even while admitting that what is what with God is an open question. We will see *what* that turns out to be. Does God exist? The radical Schelling's remarkable answer is that we cannot tell yet. History is not over until it is over. God may exist but then again may not. Perhaps. Or perhaps the name of God will prove to be, as it does time and again, our best alibi for murder. In radical theology, God *is* this very *perhaps*, God's *être* is *peut-être*. God does not exist, not yet, but God *insists*. In Schelling's terms, it remains to be seen whether the *Dass* has a heart, because God, to quote a famous atheist, Karl Marx (Engels was in the audience in Berlin), is the heart of a heartless world. Perhaps there will have been a God. Perhaps not. We will not know until the history of humankind is written, when no one will be around to read or write it. By their fruits you shall not only determine whether people are merely paying lip service to the name of God but also whether *God exists*, for on this accounting the very meaning and the being of God, what is going in and under the name of "God," lies in these fruits.

Finally is the *facticity of the future*. The future is always open. We cannot know what is coming. Even for God, especially for God, the very heart of the to-come is an *event*. If the to-come needed a metaphysician to shore it up (which it does not), Schelling would get the call. The to-come is a nonnegotiable for him because the contingency of the future is what he means by freedom, and freedom is what he means by the Spirit, as opposed to the necessitarianism of nature in Spinoza and the panlogism of the Spirit in Hegel. To the unprethinkability of the *prius* we add the unforeseeability of the *posterius*, of the future, which is what Derrida calls the "absolute future," the one that takes us by surprise, for which no one holds the hermeneutic key, not even God.

Today this philosophy of the future, of the coming age of the world, faces other challenges, and it is put to other tests unimaginable to Schelling, who had quite an imagination. Today, what is coming for us human beings—in both a descriptive and spectral sense, what is coming to get us—is the posthuman. Imagine that! Furthermore, according to the view of what is to-come presently prevailing in physics, the universe is consuming its own energy and heading—*linearly, not in an ontological circle*—for entropic oblivion, which puts both God and the future at *maximal risk*. God cannot be all in all if there is nothing at all. In an updated view of the "ages of the world," we presently live in the "stellaferous" age (birth of the stars), to be followed by the "degenerate" age (death of the stars) and finally by the "dark era." Then the *dark ground* will be all in all, the part of God where God is not being God! At that endpoint, "The universe is dark, randomized, silent. And it will remain so forever."[16] Is the ultimate upshot of the *Potenzlehre* that all the *dynamis* and *energeia* of the universe will someday be spent and things will subside in an eerie cosmic *requeiscat in pace*, a *Gelassenheit* stiller than death? Pure act will be reduced to pure inactivity. And that will be that, that is what will come of the *that*. Then the question would be—were there anyone around to ask or answer it—Why is there nothing *rather than something*? Does the renegade principle B win out in the end? Maybe the battle between Satan—the prince of death—and Jesus—the way, the truth, and the life—is the battle between entropy and life. Maybe it will turn out that Jesus really did make a deal with the devil. That is the devilish proposal I address later (chapters 14–15).

―∞―

In sum, in my own view of the matter, in German idealism there has been both a breakthrough and a misunderstanding. The breakthrough is the post-theism—that God has abdicated the heavenly throne to dwell among us as Spirit in the world—and the apophatics of the hidden ground. The misunderstanding is that the Spirit is precisely *not* a matter of ontology but of hauntology, not of a *Geist* but of a ghost, not of a Spirit but a specter. The name of God is the name of a call, a provocation, a disturbance, a lure, a solicitation, a summons to make the existence of God *come true*. In radical apophatics, idealist ontology submits to an *epochē* in which it is dialed down to a phenomenology; the *Potenzlehre* submits to a reduction resulting in a theopoetics of the perhaps. We move beyond strong theology to *weak*; beyond theology to theo*poetics*; beyond omnipotence to the omnipotential; beyond essence and existence to *insistence*. Faced with the unprethinkable character of being, with the dead end with which thinking is confronted in asking why, the ultimate religious moment, coming face to face with the facelessness of the unprethinkable ground, lies in living "without why."

And therein lies the apophatic.

PART TWO

THE HAUNTOLOGICAL IMAGINARY

NINE

THEISM TRANSCENDED
The Post-Theism of Paul Tillich

FOR PAUL TILLICH (1887–1965), THE challenge theology must meet is to answer the question put to it by a world steeped in anxiety, doubt, and meaninglessness with something other than a timeless, immobile, and distant deity served up by a church grown rigid in doctrine and authoritarianism. Shaped first by his experience as a chaplain in World War I—he served at Verdun—which was the turning point in his life,[1] and then by the horror of National Socialism, which cost him his job, he saw in the expressionist artists of the Weimar Republic a more profound response than anything coming from the German theologians. The expressionists were saying, in their own idiom, something deeply theological, addressing matters of "unconditional concern," which is, he concluded, what "religion" is all about. For this he drew upon the work of Schelling, who had seen better than anyone that evil is an active power, a positive force, rooted in being-itself[2] and not the pale "privation" put forth by traditional philosophy and theology. Schelling had taken the "principalities and powers" of this world seriously in which he saw, *as a philosopher*, a symbol of unparalleled import. Tillich found in Schelling the philosopher of the demonic forces with which divine forces—the two sides of the "Holy"—must contend, a philosopher who indeed located these contending forces in the very being of God whose fate was inextricably bound up with the world. The Schelling who did not hesitate to treat some very exotic and, for many, toxic material—Boehme, mythology, theosophy, the underside of God, the barbarian principle, the irrational—is the Schelling who interested Tillich and provided him with a vocabulary to address the deep irrationalities of the twentieth century. Schelling was deeply influential on any number of creative geniuses,[3] and among the theologians none was more important than Tillich, for whom Schelling was an ever-present muse. In Tillich, Schelling's critique of Hegel came home to roost in theology.

WHAT DOES TRANSCENDING THEISM MEAN?

While Schelling tried to distance himself from classical theism and even described his own position as pantheism, it was Tillich who struck the more boldly post-theistic position by declaring the need to "transcend theism" and the "personal" God, who meets the needs of piety but philosophically and theologically is a symbol. With Tillich, a genuinely post-theistic theology is in place, combining the panentheism of Hegel and the apophaticism of Schelling. In Tillich, in tandem with A. N. Whitehead, Dietrich Bonhoeffer, and Rudolf Bultmann, the project of radical theology in the twentieth century was launched, one with an ear for the concealed depths unearthed by Schelling. It hit the streets with the popular success of John Robinson's *Honest to God*.[4] "Theism transcended"[5] does not mean a world without God but a world without theism. Tillich does not mean a world without theology but a theology without the God of classical theology. He does not mean to turn away from God but to approach God in terms that are otherwise than theism. If God is taken to mean the God of theism, then Tillich is interested in the "God beyond God"— the God who appears when the God of theism disappears.[6] Tillich's post-theism does not mean beyond God; it means the God beyond God. The God beyond God does not mean a still more exalted God found beyond time and finitude, as in classical theology, but a God still more deeply embedded in time and finitude than theism allows and even than Schelling allows. Theism is transcended because the post-theist God is posttranscendent. Transcending theism does not represent a rationalistic critique of theology, an antitheology, but a theological critique of theology resulting in a new post-theistic theology. When Jesus cried out on the cross, "My God, my God, why have you forsaken me?" that was Jesus crying to the God beyond God, beyond the God who was supposed to comfort him and come to his aid but instead left him hanging on the cross, dying, disconsolate, and in doubt.[7]

The God beyond God is not a Neoplatonic trope referring to an absolute One beyond time and change but importantly, a God more deeply embedded in the world than can be accessed by any cultural and symbolic construction—like the theist "God." The God beyond God is inaccessible not because it is too exalted, too high, but because it is the encompassing and hence unencompassable depths of being-itself. Like the unprethinkable in Schelling, thinking cannot reach back that far in being. Being is always prior to thought. The God beyond God is a symbol of the incommensurability and the unencompassability of being by thought. In Schelling and Tillich, "religion," beyond a body of confessional statements, is a way of resonating with powers of being too deep for thought to reach.

The God of theism is the Supreme Being, a supereminent but identifiable and discrete entity whose existence or nonexistence is open to debate. In theism, faith means believing such a being exists, calling upon faith to fill in where the evidence is lacking to unaided reason. An atheist agrees with the theist description of God but denies there is any such entity. A post-theist like Tillich agrees with the atheists that such a God should be rejected, but with a difference. The atheist thinks that the debate is finished and theology has been sent packing. The post-theist thinks that theology is just getting started. Atheism is not the end of theology but the beginning of a new post-theistic theology. For the post-theist, an obstacle to theology has been cleared away and now theological work can begin anew. The end of the theology of the God of theism is the beginning of a radical theology of the God after this God, the God of post-theism.

In Schelling, God as discrete, personal, and individuated being does exist, as the first and primordial being, but, unlike classical theism, without the world this God remains incomplete. In Tillich, any talk of the discrete existence of this being as an existing being is the way piety speaks. In philosophy and theology, atheism about the God of theism is better than theism and closer to the truly divine God. This atheistic moment, a version of which is also found in all the great mystics going back to Eckhart's *Gottheit*, is mandatory because theism's God, Tillich says, is "half-blasphemous and mythological."[8] That is strong language and requires an explanation.

Mythological: The mythological gesture is found in the hypostasization or personification of *moral* powers or forces. As we learned from Schelling, in the mythological world, a great cosmic battle is waged between demonic and divine forces, which are the forces of good and evil portrayed as magical, half-subhuman and half-superhuman personalities playing out their roles through their mythic masks. The demonic powers are decisively defeated by the God of Israel, the Just One, the universal power of powers, who becomes the God of biblical religion, someone to whom we are personally related in faith and prayer and rite. We search for meaning, and God gives our life purpose and meaning. If we are lonely, God will be our companion. If we are disconsolate, God will console us. If we are lost, God will save us. By portraying God as a superperson with whom we can converse, whom we please or offend at our peril, theism *mythologizes* the *moral* dimension of the divine power (of the Holy).

Half-blasphemous: Theism is "half-blasphemous" because it betrays the *ontological* dimension of the Holy.[9] By treating God as the Supreme Being, it compromises the infinite, ultimate, unconditional, and inexhaustible depth of being-itself. The God of theism is a discrete being rather than being-itself, a definite object for us as subjects, not the absolute that is prior to and encompasses both subjects and objects. As such, we may doubt and debate whether this discrete being exists. These arguments were first cultivated in the Middle Ages, within a horizon saturated with religious piety, *fides quaerens intellectum*, but when they turn up in the Enlightenment, God is called before the court of reason convened to pass judgment on this being, to assess the evidence, to judge whether its credentials are valid. Once this box is opened, it cannot be closed. Once the question of "the existence of God" is put on the table, the God beyond God has disappeared and the modern atheistic outcome is all but assured. Once the ontological cord that binds us to God has been cut, it cannot be repaired by producing a "proof" for the existence of God. Once theology attempts to prove God's existence, it has been corrupted and the truly divine God has fled.

Theism is both a mythological portrayal of the moral and religious side of the Holy (what ought to be) and a blasphemous betrayal of its ontological and philosophical side (what is). To this God, the right *religious* and *theological* response is atheism.[10] Atheism about this God is better than theism because to deny the existence of such a being removes an impediment to authentic theology; to affirm its existence is to betray theology and consign it to magic and superstition.[11] Theology is capable of doing more damage to itself than any scientific or philosophical critique.[12]

THE ONTOLOGICAL WAY

Tillich famously formulated the difference between the God of theism and the God beyond God of post-theism in terms of two different ways of approaching God, "the way of overcoming estrangement and the way of meeting a stranger": "In the first way, man discovers *himself* when he discovers God; he discovers something that is identical with himself, although it transcends him infinitely, something from which he is estranged, but from which he never has been and never can be separated."[13] Tillich's point is captured nicely in our go-to text in Acts, when Paul says the pagans already know God but do not know what they know, even "though indeed he is not far from each one of us. For 'in him we live and move and have our being'" (Acts 17:28).

God is something we know even when God is unknown, something we know implicitly but have not made explicit. But it is there as surely as we are there, for it is *in* us, and it *is* us, and we are *it*. We are constituted by it, and if we did not have it, we would not exist at all. *Nolite ire foras*, Augustine said. Do not go out and about looking for God, for God is here. God is in us because we are in God, always and already. So in not knowing God, we do not know ourselves; we do not know what is going on within our own restless heart, and we do not understand our own restlessness. We are alienated from ourselves because we are alienated from God. In coming to know God, we come to know what we have always known but did not know we knew. We do not come to know something *else*; we come to know *ourselves*. We do not come upon an alien being whom we never met before; we overcome our alienation from ourselves and from God in whom we have our being.

God is not a being or an object seen *by* or *in* the light of reason or faith. God is the *light itself*. God is power—not one of the powers, not even *the highest* power, but the very power of being-itself. God is not something other which we seek; God is the power of the seeking. God is not an object for a subject but the depth of every object and every subject. From God, from out of the depths of God, *ex profundis*—not *ex nihilo*—emerge all living and moving, all thinking and being. God is the all-encompassing reality within which all things come to be and pass away. God is not something or somebody but the ground of everything and everybody. God is not a being but being-itself, the ground of being, the power of being, the truth of being. Even to deny God, or to doubt God, is to do so in the search for truth, but God is truth, which is the very element of affirmation and denial, of certainty and doubt. As soon as I open my mouth, I assume the truth. If I deny God with ultimate seriousness, my seriousness reflects my love of truth, which is God. God is the presupposition of God.[14]

Invoking the language of Schelling, his lifelong muse, Tillich says that God is the *prius*, the absolutely unconditionally *prior*. This is not because "he" or "she" or "it"—here language has its revenge on us, forcing us to choose one of these falsifying constrictions—is the First Being or First Cause but because God is the primordial reality of each and every him or her or it. Although Tillich's language is not gender neutral, this God is neither masculine nor feminine, but neither is God impersonal, lower than the personal, because God is the primordial depth of the personal of which particular persons are expressions. The symbol of a personal God is necessary for piety, rather the way we personify a favorite tree or treasured family keepsake, but it must not be given literal ontological status.[15] God is the absolutely first presupposition of every position and everything that is posited in the order of things. God is the *prius* because God is the absolute, unconditional source and origin of everything. The *prius* is not first numerically, as the first cause uncaused in a series of caused causes or the highest being in a great chain of beings, because God is not any point *in the series*, not as the head of the series, not as the culminating end of the series, and not even as the sum total of the series. The series is *in God*. God is not *ontically first*, the highest or supreme being, but *ontologically prior*, the primordial element in which all beings come to be and pass away. Here we can see the unprethinkable in Tillich: as soon as thinking comes to be, God is already there. Thinking always arrives too late. It will never be able to catch up to the *prius*, to "comprehend" it. God is unconditionally "older" than anything we think or say or do, that than which nothing more ultimate can be thought, prior to any distinction between theism and atheism.

Tillich calls this approach the "ontological" way because it has to do with establishing our mooring in being-itself, the very element or ground of our being, proceeding a priori, starting out from the *prius* itself. The ontological way is the Augustinian way, pursued in the High Middle Ages by Franciscans like Bonaventure. It is ultimately an Augustinian adaptation of the Platonic notion of *anamnesis*, of knowing as the recollecting of something already known and deeply planted in the soul but forgotten on the occasion of the soul's arrival in the sensible world. The ontological *argument* is a corruption of the ontological way, which is an existential, phenomenological, and hermeneutic experience. As soon as an "argument" is in place, God has fled.

THE COSMOLOGICAL WAY

Unhappily, Tillich thinks, the ontological way was eclipsed by the rise of the scholastic masters who drew their inspiration from Aristotle, who said that the soul is a blank tablet—there is no innate inscription on the soul—upon which experience writes. This tradition, as seen prior (chapter 2), which laid the foundation of the modern universities, was carried on in the High Middle Ages by the Dominican order, whose most eminent representative was Thomas Aquinas. Tillich calls this the "cosmological" way, meaning that the soul, a blank slate, starts out from worldly experience, proceeding a posteriori, from the empirical world of sensible things, in search of God. Of this way Tillich writes: "In the second way man meets a *stranger* when he meets God. The meeting is accidental. Essentially they do not belong to each other. They may become friends on a tentative and conjectural basis. But there is no certainty about the stranger man has met. He may disappear, and only *probable* statements can be made about his nature."[16]

That is a caricature of Thomas Aquinas, unrecognizable to any student of Aquinas, of which I have taken some pains (chapter

2) to disabuse us. Aquinas's relationship with Augustine and Neoplatonism is much more complicated than Tillich realizes. Aquinas took exquisite care to analyze how God could be at one and the same time *both* a subsistent being, *per se subsistens*, and being-itself, *ipsum esse*, which means that finite beings have their being *in God* and God is *in finite* beings, a presence of which they have a *scientia connaturalis*, for which he had recourse to a Platonic model of "participation." That is why God is ultimately incomprehensible in Aquinas and why negative theology is central to Aquinas. Tillich was either ignorant of this avalanche of Thomistic scholarship going on all around him at the time or chose to simply ignore it. If anything, Schelling in his Berlin lectures, in dialogue with Catholic theologians, came very close to holding the same position. Schelling was grappling with the same problem because he wanted to maintain *both* that there is nothing outside God, as in the pantheism of his middle writings, *and* that God is a distinct personal being who freely created the world out of love and whose being does not depend upon the world. That is the very position that Tillich—and Hegel—says is a "symbol" that meets the demands of piety, but it is not the position of philosophy.

That being said, Tillich clearly defends a different position than Aquinas (and the late Schelling), and so there is an underlying point to what he is arguing here. In saying that God is a "stranger," Tillich means that God is a *discretely subsistent being*, and it is true that in the cosmological way, God is indeed the First Cause, the Supreme Being, independently subsistent, and the soul comes to know God by following the chain of causes and effects, of caused causes, in the empirical world, all the way back, or up, to the First Cause uncaused, the invisible supersensible being that "everyone calls God." Calling God a stranger also means that, while it is true that, in the cosmological way, God is immanently present in and to creatures, this takes place as a cause is present to its effects, not as the inner substance of creatures. In the ontological way, the to-be of God is to-be-the-ground of creatures, and God only *is* by being related to and unfolding in the unfolding course of the world; that is what panentheism means. But in the cosmological way, which is the way of theism, the uncaused cause is pure act, so quarantined from change and motion that Aquinas could say that while we are related to God, God is not related to us, an Aristotelian point that is a scandal to biblical ears. When Tillich says that God and world do not belong to each other "essentially," he would not deny that the causal power of the First Cause is *essential* to its effects. What Tillich means is that on this approach God is not our *inner essence* or substance. God and humankind belong together in the second way as an effect belongs to its cause, but the cause and the effect are separate or discrete beings that have their own act of existence (a point that is not clear in Eckhart). God is the cause of beings in theism but not the ground of being in Tillich's sense.

In the cosmological way, God's own being is incommunicably God's own, and if God's sustaining power were withdrawn, the world would instantly vanish while God would remain standing, which is also a position that Schelling took in the Berlin lectures (although God would be "lonely").[17] The ontological way is *post*-theistic: God is being-itself, a process of continually passing over into the world, what Hegel called the "transition" from the infinite into the finite and vice versa. The being of the *world* is the coming to be *of God* in the world and the being of *God* is the coming to be *in the world*, and they cannot possibly, in principle, be separated. Separation would mean death, the instantaneous and simultaneous annihilation of everything, because each is a function of the other. In theism, the cosmological way, God's relation to the world is linear, forming a cause-and-effect chain, and unidirectional. In post-theism, it is circular, God in the world and the world in God. In the cosmological way, God is Somebody who is doing something, an agent who is producing the world as an effect, and, were God so minded, for some mysterious reason, God could withdraw the creative action (or even could have chosen not to initiate it). God's being is self-subsistent (*a se*), not in and through the world (*in alio*). As the First Being (*primum ens*), God would always be the last being standing. In the first way, the ontological way, God is a ground, not an agent. The emergence of the world from God is not God's *doing* but God's *being*, not something God *does*, which is piety's symbolic way of imagining it, but something God *is*, which is the properly ontological way to think. On this point, Tillich stands with Hegel and breaks with Schelling and advances to a genuinely radical theology.[18]

The basis upon which we make our way back to God from the world in the cosmological way is that the visible world analogically resembles the invisible God the way an effect resembles a cause. When we say a painting is a "Picasso" we mean it has the mark of his hand. But the world is not the very embodiment and incarnation of God, just as the painting is not the man himself. The painting is "a Picasso," not Picasso. If the painting were destroyed, the painter would still be standing. This is fundamentally different from the ontological way, where the world *is* the embodiment of God and the soul does not have to launch an analogical study of sensible things in search of God. We already have God within us. Not found as a result of a search, God is the light that guides the search, even the light that drives the doubt that God exists. God is not something to be reached, God is already in the reaching, in the searching, in the desiring.[19]

In the first way, God is an inner certainty, as certain as our very being, as certain as being-itself, but in the second way, God is only a probability, the outcome of conjectural reasoning—of arguments and proofs that can be debated, which is the "weakness" of the human intellect Rousselot seizes upon (chapter 2)— but ultimately in need of a booster shot from faith. The first way is the way of wisdom, *sapientia*, savoring (*sapor*) the element of truth in which we abide. The second is that of *scientia*; it constructs a discursive argument. God's being is self-evident in itself, but not for us, Aquinas says, which for Tillich cuts the nerve of the ontological way in theology.[20] In the first way, even when we doubt God, the very energy and earnestness and depth of our doubting are testimony to the power of God within us. Indeed, when passions flare among "atheistic" scientists debating a point in quantum theory or the history of evolution, that is God's light aglow. We can debate and have doubts about what is showing up under the light of our investigations, but we cannot doubt the light itself. God is the light and the source of our trust in truth. God is given as much in our doubts as in the certainties, and maybe even more so. Doubts about the Supreme Being weaken the faith of a theist. But doubting the Supreme Being steels a deeper "absolute" faith in the God beyond God.[21] The very earnestness of the doubting taps into the inner ground and depth of our being. Tillich admired atheistic existentialists like Camus whose earnest doubts and denials of the Supreme Being and search for justice brought them into touch with the ground of being. Doubting removes the mythology and blasphemy, the superstition and the supernaturalism, that obscure the work of a deeper theology of the God beyond God. Tillich's famous book entitled the *Dynamics of Faith* could just as easily have been entitled the *Dynamics of Doubt*. Both enjoy the primordial certainty of the God beyond God of theism.[22]

BEING-ITSELF IS NOT GOD

Like Schelling, Tillich says that God is absolute but the absolute is not God. God is the unconditional, but the unconditional is not God. God is being-itself, but being-itself is not God.[23] These propositions are not logically convertible because "God" is a historical *symbol*, which means it is historically constituted, culturally inherited, and embedded in a concrete community; if we were born elsewhere, in a different time, we might never have heard of it.[24] This position derives from Schelling's *Philosophy of Mythology*, but Tillich is taking it further than Schelling. "God" is a symbol for God, for the God beyond God, for the absolute, so we could always deny "God," this symbol, but not being-itself,[25] that of which it is a symbol. Being-itself is necessary, and the symbol "God" can do service as necessary being, but the question is whether necessary being needs necessarily to bear the name of God or, alternately, whether the name of God can sustain the weight and depth of absolute being.

But even were we to deny the validity of the symbol "God," that would be done in the name of the God beyond "God," of which it is the symbol. The absolute is not accessed directly but always in and through particular beings, traditions, and cultural symbols, in which we must put our faith—otherwise we would be floating about in empty space—which is always a risk, for there are multiple symbols.[26] The real question is whether a given symbol of the unconditional is *worthy* of unconditional affirmation or whether it is an idol. Is the symbol of such depth and power that it can sustain and communicate the power of being-itself? Love is such a symbol, but nation is not. Justice is such a symbol, but law is not. Even so, nothing is safe; no symbol is insulated from abuse. We know how much hate parades around as love, how much injustice and revenge call themselves justice. We put our faith and trust not exactly in the symbol but in the power of the symbol to carry us through to that of which it is the symbol. As a Christian theologian, Tillich puts his faith in the power of "the tremendous word God"[27] and the symbol of the cross to sustain his faith. The cross in particular, Tillich says, carries with it the power to crucify any symbol unworthy of the name; it is a symbol of the self-effacing of the symbol in favor of what is being symbolized.[28] In that sense, the cross is a symbol of a symbol. That is what Derrida would call the "auto-deconstructibility" of the symbol.[29]

This is the dynamics of our "absolute" faith in being-itself, an ontological faith that is sustained despite every ontic doubt and the frailty of every symbol. This is the "courage to be"—not an ontic courage in the face of this or that fearsome thing but an ontological courage in the face of the forces of nonbeing. This amounts to a faith and courage to *interpret* the primacy of being prevailing over nonbeing, to *affirm* a hope prevailing over despair. To reject the God beyond God would mean to reject hope and faith in their deepest ontological sense. Again, this is Schelling; it all comes down to our freedom, to *choosing* the sort of being we want to be. Despair is always an available choice, but to choose the path of despair is to fall into the sickness unto death, into a kind of ontological free fall. It is to reject the dynamics of life and being-itself, to reject the element in which we live and move and have our being. If we lose this faith, we reject our *conatus essendi*,[30] our very *joie de vivre*. Of course, we cannot absolutely lose the *conatus essendi* or we would cease to be altogether. As long as we exist, the power of being is available, circulating through our ontological veins and arteries. Our being may be alienated from God, but God is not an alien being. We are always accepted by being, even if we are not acceptable, which is Tillich's adaptation of Luther, which Tillich first heard from his teacher Martin Kähler, which Tillich describes as a breakthrough moment for him.[31]

THE ONTOLOGICAL ARGUMENT

In distinguishing the ontological and cosmological approaches, which he calls the "two types of the philosophy of religion," Tillich is positioning himself in the element of the ontological, but not in the discursive space of an argument, ontological or cosmological.[32] As soon as the question of the proofs for the existence of God is on the table, the God beyond God has fled the scene. Nonetheless, like Hegel and Schelling, Tillich does attach a special *significance* to the ontological argument, which, he thinks, was distorted by Anselm and deservedly refuted by Aquinas and Kant. Misled by his rational and scholastic frame of mind, Anselm took what was in fact a deep Augustinian and ontological truth and distorted it into a theistic argument. Under his hand an ontological experience of being-itself (*sapientia*) becomes a proof for the existence of a Supreme Being (*scientia*)—this from the same theologian who, faced with the mystery of the Incarnation, came up with an argument explaining "why the God Man," which has given us ever since the "satisfaction" theory of the cross. Anselm is arguably the most influential theologian in history because he has made two enormously influential mistakes! Still, as logically suspicious as Anselm's argument is, it has long exerted an irresistible attraction. Logically suspect, it commands ontological respect. It is fetching, and the reason is that it draws upon ancient ontological depths, that than which there is nothing more ultimate, Parmenides's "being is," Schelling's *prius*, inexhaustible and incomprehensible, unprethinkable and unconditional, that than which we cannot think anything deeper or greater, anything prior or more ultimate. It is the same experience that emerges in Leibniz's "Why is there something rather than not?" But instead of *meditating* this experience in a kind of sapiential savoring of the insuperable, instead of treating it as the very element of our lives, Anselm mistreats it: he makes this element into an entity. Instead of seeing that this is being-itself, he makes it into the greatest being. Instead of seeing that this is the very light by which we see, the very power by which we exist, that in which we live and move and have our being, he concludes that this is the Highest Being. Hegel, Schelling, and Tillich all think the ontological argument holds a deeper truth and can be fruitfully *re*described—as Paul did in the Areopagus—and so has a deeper truth. Indeed, if we put this argument back in its historical context, even in Anselm himself it is less what modern philosophers call an argument than faith trying to clear its head (*fides quaerens intellectum*).

THE MYSTICAL ELEMENT

The fetching quality of the ontological argument derives from its location "on the boundary"—an expression that was life defining for Tillich[33]—between a metaphysical argument and a mystical experience, a dual sensibility that Tillich shares with Schelling. That line is crossed when the ontological approach is submitted to the forces of rationalization, not to a deep "ecstatic" reason,[34] which concedes that it is breached by the primacy of being over thought, but to a calculative reason that abides no breaches. The God of theism is fair game for a calculative rationality, for argumentation and debate, for conjecture and probability, for logicians and theo-logicians. But the God beyond the God of theism is a matter of an undebatable elemental experience. What the ontological argument reveals is not a particular being with extraordinary gifts and powers but the extraordinary gift and power of being-itself. The revelation is not the result of an argument but of an experience, or what Tillich calls an "awareness,"[35] meaning a kind of awakening to what is going on within us, a nondiscursive, meditative, or phenomenological realization of the absolute within and all around us. It is clarified by way of a radical hermeneutic rendering, not a calculative-rational argument, drawing upon an experience of the *prius* that precedes every proposition and proof, every subject and every object, not unlike Maritain's intuition of being or Heidegger's "understanding of Being."[36] Post-theism in Tillich is ante-theism or pre-theism, prior to theism and atheism, recovering a sphere where the debate between theism and atheism has not yet broken out, not completely unlike the protomonotheism that Schelling postulated in the first era of mythological consciousness.

Post-theism for Tillich takes place in the mystical element. Mysticism, the mystical element of our lives, is the very essence of religion for Tillich.[37] Without this mystical sense, our lives are soulless, devoid of inner meaning, cut off from everything of substance, severed from the deepest mystery of being. Without it, our lives are flat. We are absorbed by the mediocre means-end rationality of middle-of-the-road utilitarian bourgeois life, which puts safety before truth,[38] of which Tillich was a lifelong critic.[39] The mystical sense is a matter of being seized in the depths of our own being by the power of being-itself, which, with some precautions, can be compared to the way "ground of the soul" is touched by the "ground of God" in Meister Eckhart. This is what Tillich calls "theonomy," taking our lead not purely from our own egological interests (autonomy) or allowing ourselves to be led by the authority of the other (church, state, a Supreme Being) (heteronomy) but drawing upon the inner depths of being. In his theology of culture, Tillich argued that this deep mystical sense of life is found in religion, where it has, or at least should have, a privileged home, but that it is not confined to religion in the narrow sense. It can be found whenever and wherever human life touches upon the depths, whenever and wherever we are brought up short by the sheer mystery of the that-it-is-rather-than-not. It is to be found in the life-saving work of physicians and nurses who put themselves in harm's way to heal others, in radical political action, in laboratories and in the streets, in the arts and sciences, whenever and wherever we engage life unconditionally. Religion, he famously said, means being seized by a matter of ultimate concern. If this awareness were to become general, there would be no need at all for religion in the narrow sense, which would be heavenly, metaphorically and in the most literal sense—in the heavenly Jerusalem there is no religion (no temples).[40] What we call religion is at best an "emergency" measure, "plan B," made necessary only because the mystical sense of life is so regularly "covered by the dust of our daily life and the noise of our secular work."[41]

By mysticism, Tillich, like Meister Eckhart, did not mean exotic out-of-body experiences. But, unlike Meister Eckhart, neither did he mean an *immediate* union with God, absolutely "pure" and "detached" from all creatures—that is blocked by our finitude and alienation, which in theology is thought under the symbol of the "Fall." He was, after all, a Lutheran theologian, *justus et peccator*, united with God but also separated as a sinner, or rather, united *as* a sinner, saved by our doubt as much as by our faith, accepted while not acceptable.[42] We are not, and we cannot be, rejected by being-itself. Our union with God is always already *interrupted* by our alienation from God, but it cannot be completely *severed*. Overcoming alienation is carried out not by rejecting beings and turning to being-itself, which does not exist, but by acquiring the eyes to see God *in* all things. It is achieved in an awareness of the depth of things, of the *prius*, of the primordial ground of being, which makes its presence felt if we are open and attentive, if we learn to read it by a kind of ontotheological hermeneutics.

So any such unity with God as is possible would be a *mediated* unity, which Tillich bases upon the "principle of identity" in Schelling as "belonging together." He denies the possibility of any pure and simple identification of the infinite with the finite, of the eternal with the temporal, of necessity with freedom, which was the unitative ideal of the classical Christian Neoplatonic mystics, which would result in an annihilation of the self, entirely losing the self.[43] The dyadic scheme of *exitus/reditus* allows the reduction of time and multiplicity; in dialectics, time and multiplicity are irreducible mediators, serving the purpose of conduction and not subject to reduction. That also explains the *danger* of mediation, the possible confusion of the mediator with the substance of what it is mediating. Mediation means that the unity is the belonging-together of the infinite *and* the finite, which results from the fact that the infinite and eternal come to expression *in* the finite and temporal and the finite and temporary come to be as the expression *of* the infinite and eternal.[44] The *relation* is a *circu*lation, indeed a hermeneutic circularity, that requires the ability to *read* the infinite in the finite. The conjunctive *and* is explained by the prepositional *in* and *of*. On the one side, *we* meet God, not face to face (in an intellectual intuition or exceptional experience) but *in* the finite things of the world in which God is expressed, not only in church on Sunday but in sunflowers, not only in "religious" things but in any and everything regarded in its depth. And on the other side, *God's* side, God does not *exist* as a separate being that could be met face to face. Immediate unity, fusion, transcending doubt and uncertainty, is the nostalgic ideal of theism, where discrete individuals ("strangers") long to restore their lost unity and melt into each other, like the Platonic myth of the original androgynous unity. But in post-theism, God and the world are neither separated strangers nor beings fused back together in unbroken unity. Rather, they always already "belong to each other," in a mutual circulation, each to the other, God in the world, the world in God. We always and already live and move and have our being in God, and our vocation is not only to make ourselves aware of this depth of being but to make ourselves *worthy* of it.

PANENTHEISM

It is because of this notion of mediated unity that Tillich's post-theistic position can be described as pan*en*theism, as distinguished from pantheism, meaning not the immediacy of God *is* all but the mediated relation of God *in* all and all *in* God. Tillich did not use either term. "What I dislike," he said, "is the easy way in which these phrases are used: theism is so wonderful and pantheism so horrible. This makes the understanding of the whole history of theology impossible."[45] This point, as we saw prior, was also made by Mary-Jane Rubenstein, who speaks of the *"panic"* at *"pantheism."*[46] As a way to criticize the dualism and the thinly veiled Docetism of classical theism, as a way to waken theology from its dogmatic-theistic slumbers, one can do no better than the language of pantheism. The reason pantheism is "so horrible" to theism is that, for theism, it is either atheism (for it denies that there is an existent called God) or blasphemy (it makes the most abject things divine). Either way, Tillich would agree with Rubenstein that theism deserves the shock delivered by pantheism. For Tillich himself, pantheism is a "much-abused term" since it is mistaken to mean that God is the sum total of everything that exists, a position he thinks no so-called pantheist has ever actually held. The critics of pantheism do not understand what they are criticizing. If God is not an entity, not even the highest one, then God could not be the sum total of all entities. There is a divide—or, as Heidegger would say, an ontological difference—between the being of God and entitative beings.

For Tillich, God is the creative ground from which entities emerge and to which they return. If that is what is meant by pantheism, then one might call his post-theism pantheism, but given how misleading the term is, Tillich avoids it, and we would be better served by distinguishing pantheism from pan*en*theism. Whatever term is used, we would like to affirm, on the one hand, that all things are holy and that the world is theophanic while, on the other hand, we want to still be able to distinguish the unconditional from the conditional, the divine from the demonic, the icon from the idol.[47] Tillich's position goes back to Schelling, where not everything in the divine being is divine, where there is a struggle going on in the divine being between the forces of expansion (generosity) and contraction (egoism), where what is *conquest* in the divine being is still *contest* in us.[48] In God, the forces of being and light are victorious over the forces of nonbeing, but in us, there is a continual contest with no surety of success. So we would need to find some way to avoid implying the simple and unmediated unity of the infinite and finite, of the unconditional and the conditional, for which calling it panentheism seems more appropriate, and Tillich seems to agree. "If you call it panentheism," he says, "that would be all right, because that means everything is in God."[49]

Tillich's post-theism is distinctively pan*en*theistic.[50] That is Tillich's argument, if not his vocabulary. In Tillich's own vocabulary, the critique of blasphemy and idolatry requires a *critical distance* be maintained between the unconditional and the conditional, the infinite and the finite, constantly submitting the latter to the judgment of the former. That is what Tillich calls the "Protestant principle,"[51] taken from Schelling's philosophy of revelation, by which he does not mean denominational Protestantism but a universal ontological-theological principle in virtue of which we can differentiate between a symbol and what it is a symbol of. Without this critical distance, we are left exposed to the danger of a symbol that is unworthy of the name, of something conditional that is undeserving of our unconditional faith. For Tillich, being is an autodeconstructive process whose symbol is the cross, which crucifies anything conditional that purports to be unconditional—like money or power, like a book (the Bible) or an institution (the Roman Catholic Church).

THE COSMOLOGICAL WAY RECONSIDERED

Just as the ontological argument is a corruption of a genuine ontological way, so the cosmological argument is a corruption of a genuine cosmological way, just so long as it has been given an ontological orientation. The ontological way has not turned us away *from* the world *acosmically* but *to* the world *ontologically*. The ontological way is a priori, uncovering our deepest suppositions and presuppositions, which is being-itself as the unprethinkable *prius*. The cosmological way is a posteriori, discovering God not by staying at home but by venturing out into the world of experience, of particular things. But this time it has its onto-cosmological bearings, knowing that God is already there, everywhere to be found, in the depths of everything, just as Paul said to the Athenians entities or like St. Francis's *Laudato si*, which is a hymn to God's creation. This renewed cosmological approach is vintage Schelling, the philosophy of nature, which turns on the axiom that nature is visible Spirit and Spirit invisible nature. Dig deeply enough into either one and you will hit the other. The reoriented cosmological way allows for both a theology of *culture*, of the historical products of human creativity probed in their unconditional depth, and a theology of *nature*, where the natural world is thought on the model of being-itself, as an all-encompassing matrix in which we live and move and have our being, not as a causally connected concatenation of inert chunks of lifeless stuff in motion. For the natural world and the cultural world are alike the *expression* and *manifestation* of being-itself and not discrete *effects* of a supreme causal agent. In principle, one could begin with nature and find the spirit within or begin with spirit and follow its expression in nature. So there can be a theology of culture that is not secularist and a theology of nature that is not naturalistic or mechanistic. Nature is approached not in terms of causal links but of expressive exchanges of energy all leading up—in an unapologetically anthropocentric way—to *homo sapiens*, in whom nature and spirit are thought to be harmoniously united. Robert Corrington has described this position as an "ecstatic naturalism"[52]—namely, as a nonreductionistic naturalism that understands the way that nature opens up to spirit in the world. Spirit is the fluorescence of nature, nature the seed of spirit.

On this ontologically oriented approach to nature, the mystical sense is palpable. The inexhaustible depth of being takes the form of our immersion in an infinite universe, a sense of the oceanic or the encompassing expanse of the heavens. Being is nature, *natura naturans* birthing *natura naturata*. If this insight was already variously available to Scotus Eriugena in the ninth century, to Cusa in the fifteenth century, to Spinoza in the seventeenth century, and to Schelling in the nineteenth century, it has become still more pressingly evident in the age of Einstein and quantum physics. This invites a tantalizing comparison. The difference between the two approaches to God—the two types of philosophy of religion, post-theist and theist—is the difference between a principle of *expressivity* and a principle of *linear causality*. The one employs the model of an inner power expressing itself—potentialization, emergent power[53]—and the other of a discrete but supreme entity producing an effect on another discrete but dependent entity. The expressive model lends itself to metaphors of womb and birth, the causal model to a powerful patriarchal sovereign. In the first way, the "created" world is an expression, an actualization, a materialization of an underlying ground or power of being, of an inner energy or force, and in the second way, creation is an effect produced by a discrete causal agent.

This bears a provocative resemblance to the distinction between the linear causality that held sway in classical physics and quantum excitations in contemporary physics. The rule of linear causality was described by Hume as requiring the contiguity of cause and effect and the temporal priority of the cause to the effect. This differs in a fundamental way from the excitation of a quantum field, which follows a principle of expression, actualization, or materialization. In other words, the difference between the two philosophies of religion resembles the difference between Newtonian and post-Newtonian physics! The post-theistic, ontological approach to God, which identifies a ground of being, bears a striking resemblance to a quantum field whereas the classical theist model, which turns on linear causality, resembles classical physics and in fact gave us deism. *Being-itself*, the ground of being, is well conceived as a *field* and particular *beings* as *excitations* of the field; a particular being is not a substantial thing but an *event*. The well-known paradox of "quantum entanglement"—where discrete objects, having been separated in space, continue to act in tandem—completely confounds the model of linear causality—the "theistic" model—so much so that Einstein, who was a great admirer of Hume, rejected it. God does not play dice. Which God? The God of classical theism! But the God of quantum fields—the post-theist God—is playing a different, probabilistic, and, let us say, theonomous game, and there the same underlying field may be actualized at the same time in different places. The two discrete objects communicate not through spatial contiguity but through the commonality of their field, of which they are simultaneous but noncontiguous excitations.

This point was neither observed nor pursued by Tillich, who held a famous conversation with Einstein about physics and theology.[54] But quantum physics was central to Whitehead's metaphysics, and it provides a suggestive opening for process theology, offering a felicitous congruity between panentheism and quantum physics. It has been taken up by contemporary post-theists, including Philip Clayton, Catherine Keller, and Mary-Jane Rubenstein, and it has been explored in a theologically suggestive way by Karen Barad. Furthermore, that the Heideggerian model of Being/beings is closer to quantum field theory than is Humean empiricism can be counted as further Heideggerian revenge on the scorn Carnap heaped on Heidegger in the name of logical empiricism.

POLITICAL THEOLOGY

The "powers" and "principalities" are the forces of the "world"—in the New Testament they meant the *imperium Romanum*—and as such they are political forces. Because Tillich, like Schelling, understood that being-itself was marked by the demonic, which may be mastered but never eliminated, theology is always political theology—always a contest between the forces of being and nonbeing, good and evil—and history always has a tragic quality. The symbol of the cross is politically important not only because the crucifixion was a political act but also because it flags the confusion of the unconditional with any given conditional expression of the unconditional, not only the Bible or the Roman Catholic Church—but also a nation or party. That is the danger Tillich first encountered in the political idolatry of National Socialism in his native Germany and in the failure of the German church to denounce it. His criticism of the Nazis in *The Socialist Decision*, a 1933 book on religious or prophetic socialism, which he opposed to both (soulless) Soviet and (pagan) national socialism, cost him his livelihood in Germany, and had he stayed around long enough, it could have cost him his life, as it did Bonhoeffer.[55] Tillich's post-theism was from the start a *political* theology, which seizes the moment (the *kairos*) and brings the message of the cross to bear upon the concrete political situation. This brings us to a problematic side of Tillich that cannot be ignored.

If Tillich's theology was set in motion politically by the critique of the "extreme nationalisms" of our time in the name of the "God of justice,"[56] his prophetic-political voice was more muted after the war, less attentive to the *kairos* by which he was confronted in his later life in the United States. How could he fail to single out and condemn the idols of the day—of race and gender—and the evils of racism and sexism? Martin Luther King Jr. wrote his doctoral dissertation on Tillich and briefly corresponded with him, and Tillich was also a major resource for James H. Cone's black theology of liberation, but Tillich did not address the civil rights movement going on all around him.[57] Tillich was also unresponsive to the feminist alarms that were being set off in the last years of his life, as Mary Daly points out. De Beauvoir's *The Second Sex* was published in 1949, long before Tillich died in 1965, but Tillich routinely speaks of God in the patriarchal masculine and refers not to human beings but to man. This insensitivity, taken in conjunction with the publication of Hannah Tillich's memoir, *From Time to Time* (1973),[58] which exposed a personal life of philandering, poses a serious problem today. There can be no ontotheological "new being" without social and political emancipation. There is no salvation outside liberation—if we may update a notorious ancient axiom to formulate a motto for political theology.

So what are we to do with Tillich today? Mary Daly is an instructive case in point. She attended Tillich's lectures at Harvard Divinity School and mounted a sharp and uncompromising feminist critique of Tillich. But she went on to "pirate" his work to her own feminist ends, extending the implications of the "God beyond God" to *Beyond God the Father*. There she remobilized the "courage to be" as the courage to be a woman in the face of the sexist and patriarchal forces of nonbeing in the church and the world at large. She saw in it a way to encourage the "I am" of women and to redeploy the courage to be as a "courage to see" hitherto invisible women.[59] She did not reject the courage to be; she just thought Tillich was not radical enough about it. He did not carry the courage to be into the vision to see it all the way through, down into the concrete being of gender and race. Just so, James Cone redeployed the courage to be in terms of the power to be black, the courage of black power, against the racist powers of nonbeing and the "white Christ." The notions of God as male or white, American or European, fall before the critical power of the Protestant principle.[60] Any such blasphemous distortion of God is a function of the mythological personification of God in theism. As the title of Daly's book makes clear, theism transcended also implies patriarchy transcended. Post-theism belongs to a more emancipatory, bottom-up imaginary. To call God a "sovereign," which is a basic theistic trope, is to employ a dangerous—and contingent—historical symbol with disastrous social and political consequences. Theism regularly invokes the top-down patriarchal image of the Father Almighty—*Credo in unum Deum, Patrem omnipotentem*—which has licensed a patriarchal world to cloak itself with divine authority. Tillich's post-theism, by contrast, and panentheism generally, invites an image of God as a matrix or an encompassing womb and of creation as the birthing process of the *natura naturans*, in a manner suggestive of Irigaray on the natural elements. It suggests a sense of being enveloped and surrounded in an oceanic element in which we live and move have our being, which leads us back to the cosmological way, but this time with a radically new orientation. After all, the new being, Saint Paul said, would transform not just human history but all creation (2 Cor. 5:17–19). So the courage to be requires the courage to be political, a point examined more closely in the next chapter.

In sum, Tillich's project of transcending theism—along with Whitehead, Bonhoeffer, Bultmann, and the 1960s "death of God" theologians—is a major twentieth-century fountainhead of post-theistic theology. It follows Schelling in breaking with the rationalism of Hegel and pushes past the remnants of theism still clinging to Schelling. Tillich's theology of symbols carries out the theopoetic reduction, and his critique of theism carries out the ontological reduction (chapter 1), and his interest in the demonic moves him in the direction of a radical apophatics. His post-theism is both theism transcended and atheism transcended. Post-theism is also anticipated in the "transformational criticism" of the young Hegelians, especially Marx and Feuerbach, who helped purify theology of its superstition and supernaturalism. It includes Freud's analysis of the unconscious and Nietzsche's analysis of the death of God and the pathology of the religious soul, both of whom also worked in the wake of Schelling. While post-theism *includes* every earnest and searching atheism, it is not *concluded* by any of them. It goes on to locate in that earnestness the wellsprings of our being and our link with the God beyond theism's God, to think a God coming after the death of God.[61] The *post-* in post-theism is not a postmortem; it does not announce a death but a new arrival. The *post-* does not mean done and over with but, having passed through theism, coming out on the other end, steeled by the passage in a theology of a radical and nonorthodox kind. Rather than an assault on theology, it protects theology from itself, from its "mythological and half-blasphemous" side. Post-theism offers itself to the wider world beyond theology as radical thinking, as a genuinely thoughtful and nondogmatic inventory of the depth of the human condition, as a thinking not afraid to hit theological ground and a theology not afraid to hit radical ground. In a world consumed by selfishness, greed, animosity, and dissemblance, of which Donald

Trump is both the symbol and the substance,[62] it dares to raise the most elemental questions of our being, exposing our common mortal condition. Post-theism reminds us that we are, all of us, contending with the "powers" and "principalities," all siblings of the same nocturnal womb, grounded in a groundless ground, in search of the courage to be.

TEN

VIOLENCE AND THE UNCONDITIONAL
The Politics of the Apophatic

AS I SAID AT THE outset, my premise is that the concealed ground of apophaticism is everywhere, in everything, for better *and* for worse. It is the best of us, it is the worst of us, and it explains why we can be so benevolent and so violent. It gives war its fury, hatred its rage, and self-seeking its passion, and it can make politics the continuation of war by other means. That is why theology is not true to itself unless it is radical theology, and theology is not radical if it is not also radical political theology.[1] When Hegel said that religion is a *Vorstellung*, more conceptual than art and more sensuous than philosophy, and when Schelling analyzed the unconscious powers at work in mythology, they were telling us that the conceptual content of religion is embedded in our bowels. Its sensuousness seizes our imaginary, its images stir our soul, its ideas and ideals touch our heart. Situated between art and philosophy, saturating the culture at large, religion is uniquely suited to mediate the unconditional and the conditional. Everything is political, but religion is pointedly so, and it always has been. The story of Exodus and the execution of Jesus are thoroughly political matters. Theorizing God and the unconditional is not a matter of strictly theoretical interest. Nothing matters more than matters of ultimate and unconditional concern in the conduct of conditional, proximate, and practical affairs. Politics is the art of the possible because it is the impossible, the unconditional, that is at stake. Politics is the art of the possibility of the impossible.

The reason "religion is the most glorious and the most cruel part of man's history," Tillich says, is that "religion is not a matter of wishful thinking, but a matter of the powers of being which men encounter."[2] That is the ambiguity, the undecidability, the paradox of the unconditional, that I want to address here. The unconditional is unconditionally important in politics, which means it inspires the unconditional pursuit of justice—except when it inspires unconditional violence. That is the ambiguity of the Holy, its divine and demonic bipolarity, the better and the worse angels of our nature. The creative powers of being are the very same powers that produce the greatest evils. Without the "barbarian principle," civilization would never emerge. This is a function of the *ambiguity* of a *mediating* term: the unconditional is never present except under concrete conditions, by which it is mediated and with which it is prone to be confused. The unconditional is *risky* business, and the risk it runs, always, structurally, is that it tempts us to invest unconditional worth in something of merely conditional value. If God is all in all, then it is possible to confuse God with anything, that is, to invest anything with divine worth—to make money God or to make a political movement God—whether it is worthy of it or not. The ambiguity that besets thinking the unconditional requires discretion, insight, discernment, what Aristotle called *phronesis*, practical wisdom, which is the beating heart of hermeneutics.

THE RELIGIOUS AND THE SECULAR

In religious violence, the nocturnal powers of being break out under the very name of God. The distinction between religion and the secular order, one of the underpinnings of the modern world, protects us from theocracy but it also provides the occasion for a conflict between religion and the secular order that gets worse with every day. Pitched in lethal combat, each one misunderstands itself and misunderstands the other. Religion, thinking itself authorized by supernatural voices, requires the suspension of the *supernatural signified*. Secular reason, mistaking itself for a pure, overarching ahistorical rationality, requires the suspension of the *transcendental signified*. The one misunderstands its own faith, the other misunderstands its own reason, and with these misunderstandings firmly in place, each one attacks the other. This has profoundly distorted both religion and politics today. It has handed religion over to the violent, reactionary forces of the religious Right, who think that Jesus was a white supremacist, and leads the secular Left to hand over the tremendous power of religion to the fundamentalists, who reared their ugliest head on January 6, 2021, instead of enlisting that power, like Martin Luther King Jr., in a prophetic call for justice.

Relying methodologically upon the model of Tillich's theology of culture, I seek here to weaken, displace, and redescribe the distinction between the religious and the secular by distinguishing instead between the unconditional and the conditional elements of the culture, between a *matter of ultimate concern* and the *material culture*. Crossing over the religious/secular distinction allows us to frame things differently. The unconditional circulates throughout the length and breadth of the material culture without being confined to a special region called "religion" where it is kept separate from the secular. Religion in this radical sense trades in matters of unconditional import, while in the material culture, theists and atheists trade insults. There are no atheists in the trenches of the unconditional.

The conditional element, the material culture, refers to the concrete constructions, the historically particular beliefs and practices of a given culture—its identifiable ethical and religious beliefs, political parties and social movements, and artistic and scientific achievements. The material culture is the complex of concrete inherited conditions under which matters of unconditional import are expressed, without which the unconditional is a free-floating abstraction and the culture is reduced to an amusement or a contractual arrangement. The relationship between the two is not oppositional but circular. The unconditional element surfaces in the conditional one, and the conditional culture draws upon the resources of the unconditional; neither one can be without the other. The unconditional is recessed in the concrete conditions; the concrete conditions provide access to the unconditional. The unconditional content emerges in multiple, unpredictable, and contradictory forms in the multiple structures of a given culture—in the multiple cultures, in the plural. As Tillich himself points out, we cannot deduce the form things take in the material culture; they do not unfold necessarily from the ground as conclusions flow from premises.[3]

It is striking that Tillich, my favorite official theologian, and Derrida, my favorite unofficial slightly atheistic a/theologian, both have recourse to the word *unconditional* to explain what matters most to them. Tillich does so under the figure of being and Derrida of what is without being. Tillich has in mind the underlying depth and power of the ground of being, in which matters of ultimate concern are invested, which allows us to mount the courage to be in the faces of the powers of nonbeing. Derrida has in mind the "weak force" of may-being that spooks being with the possibility of what can be otherwise. The unconditional is "without sovereignty," neither a being nor the ground of being but a call to which we are called upon to respond, a solicitation, even a promise or a hope. So, for Derrida, the university is "without conditions"—that is, it has the unconditional right to ask any question—but in the real world, the university is expected to do useful research that will promote the interests of its benefactors, its sponsoring church, or the supporting state. Tillich thinks of culture as high culture, which he thinks has an underlying unity, while Derrida has a far more pluralistic conception of culture, and so he shies away from figures like ground or depth and prefers the terms of multiplicity, dissemination, and drift in which the unconditional must find its way (chapter 12).

I further differentiate what Tillich and Derrida mean by the unconditional in the next chapter, but at present, in addressing the question of violence, I want to focus on what Tillich's "theology of culture" and Derrida's "unconditional without sovereignty" have in common. In both cases, the unconditional element—a matter of ultimate concern (Tillich), the undeconstructible or the impossible (Derrida)—is what is *affirmed unconditionally*. For both, the unconditional is, let us say, a matter for which we are willing to put ourselves in harm's way (without putting others in harm's way), and it can be found anywhere in the culture. Artists, journalists, and activists who suffer imprisonment or death for their work are martyrs of the unconditional, with or without "religion" in the narrow sense, as are thinkers, scientists, or humanists who are persecuted for what they say or write by the state or church. So what Tillich and Derrida are saying about the unconditional is risky business. For both, it is a question of keeping the future open rather than arming ourselves against it—that is what Tillich calls the prophetic and Derrida calls the messianic—but the future may be a disaster, and a promise is never far from a threat. For Tillich, that is the divine/demonic ambiguity of the Holy, and for Derrida, that is the *pharmakon*, the poison/cure, the ghost of undecidability.

ON THE VERGE OF VIOLENCE

The ambiguous power of the unconditional shows up unmistakably in religious violence. To put my hypothesis as pointedly as possible, *religion is not accidentally violent*; religion is violent in virtue of *something essential to* religion. We sometimes hear it said that religious violence is not true religion but false religion, not good religion but bad religion, as if the violence were an *external perversion* that befalls religion from without, as if a pure religion had been contaminated by a foreign substance. Beyond being a facile simplification, that is a misunderstanding, like saying that there are two kinds of fire, bad fire that burns us and good fire that keeps us warm and cooks our food. That is just playing around with religion, and religion is not playing around. Or better still, religion is *really* playing with fire. God is a raging fire (Deut. 4:24–26), as Schelling liked to say, and religion is playing with the *real fire* of the concealed depths, of the unconditional, of the impossible, of the undeconstructible. Religion is the best way to save the world, but it is also the best way to burn it down. It is both of these things just in virtue of the same property.

To say that *religion is violent in virtue of something essential to religion* is to say that the violence arises from forces that are constitutive of religion, within religion, not from without, without which religion would not be religion at all and we would have no use for it. As we learn from the magnificent mimicry of Christendom by Kierkegaard's pseudonyms, religion is not for those who play by the rules, who make themselves commensurable with the universal. It is not for the timid bourgeoisie who are neither hot nor cold; it is not for those who are content with the shelter afforded by "ethics." In *Fear and Trembling*, Kierkegaard stages his archetypal religious act, his leap of faith, in a scene of terrible transgression—a father with his knife drawn to slay his son. The very structure of the religious act, for him, lies in a divine violence, a divinely authorized transgression of the universal that reduced Abraham to silence and anxiety, leaving him alone with the voice he was obeying as he slowly made his way up the side of Mount Moriah. This haunting scene Kierkegaard opposed to the garrulous and mediocre masses who stay safely within the normalizing lanes of modern Christian Europe, who go to church on Sunday and to work on Monday with the greatest of ease, without the least suspicion of deeper trouble, in an age in which, as Johannes Climacus muses, everything is being made easy.[4]

This is *not* to say that *religion is structurally violent*, always and necessarily violent. As we have seen in Schelling and Tillich, the Holy is structurally *ambiguous*, fluctuating between the divine and the demonic, both of which are distrusted by ethics.[5] We are forced to act in a twilight, marked by what Derrida calls "undecidability," a *pharmakon*, a poison/cure, a drug that will cure us unless it kills us first. That is because the ground of being in Tillich is also groundless, a tossing sea of competing *potentialities*. It is not a formal essence dictating the course of existence (Leibniz) or an implicit essence to be made explicit in the material culture (German idealism). We are in the grips of something ambiguous, undecidable, and we must not simply respond ("just follow orders," "heteronomy") but must *assume responsibility* for our *response*. The material culture does not "instantiate" a deep essence as a particular case that falls under a universal essence; it actualizes indeterminate potencies that are astir in the culture but without being predetermined by them. The concrete culture is neither controlled from above by a Platonic *eidos*, an overseeing divine providence, an intervening divine omnipotence, nor steered about from below by some invisible law at its base. If it emerges from below, it does so as from a churning sea of unpredictable potencies, from an unforeseeable omnipotentiality.[6] The unconditional precedes and exceeds the material culture, leaving the latter in a structurally unstable and restless condition—for better or for worse. As Schelling says, if we are too tepid in forming these potencies, the result will be a drunken riot, and if too enthusiastic, we will crush them, so we have to find a way to be both sober and drunk at the same time, both Apollonian and Dionysian.[7] That is its ambiguity.

Religion is risky business because it crosses over the borders into a terra incognita, what Luther called the *Deus absconditus*, the backside or underside of God; it engages with forces which, like Lacan's real, elude both imaginative figuration and conceptual articulation. Religion is not structurally violent, but it is structurally *dangerous,* risky, on the verge of violence. It is just this danger that interests me here, its *whipsaw* effect, its capacity for violent swings back and forth between the *extremes* of the most *radical violence* and the most radical *nonviolence,* between martyrdom and murder, between terrible wars and the most profound peace, between the greatest works of mercy and the worst, most merciless violence. Religious people serve the wretched of the earth, the poor, the homeless, and the victims of war and natural disasters even as it is people with religion on their mind who bomb abortion clinics in the name of life, oppress women, kill one another for Christ, were responsible for September 11, 2001, and fueled the violent insurrection of January 6, 2021. Since 2017, some seven hundred thousand Muslims—the Rohingya—have been mercilessly persecuted and driven into deplorable refugee camps in the name of the Buddha, even as in Buddhism everything turns on the suspension of self and desire and demands the "great compassion."[8]

This whipsaw is endemic to the scriptures themselves. In the New Testament, the Jesus of the synoptics is a pacific teacher, exorcist, and healer who counsels us to put down our sword and love our enemies; he even forgives his own executioners instead of calling down divine wrath upon them. In the terrifying Book of Revelation, by contrast, Jesus returns with apocalyptic fury riding on a white horse with a sword in his mouth (Rev. 19:11–21). The fourth gospel, the "gospel of love," did not show much love for "the Jews" and—without knowing what it was doing—laid the theological foundation for a bloody history of anti-Semitism. In the Jewish scriptures, the God of Genesis and Exodus is a fierce tribal warlord, bloodthirsty and genocidal, whose violence is not fit reading for Sunday School classes. As Jack Miles said, "God is no saint."[9] From beginning to end, from Genesis to Revelation, the Bible is rife with violence. Even so, the God of the prophets stands on the side the poor and oppressed, and the prophets call for justice to flow like water over the land. The Bible is not one book but an anthology, and it speaks not with unanimity but with an apophatic ambiguity issuing from its concealed depths. It did not drop from the sky but was constructed under human conditions by poets and storytellers dreaming of the impossible and contending with forces greater than themselves.[10]

THE PROFUNDITY OF FUNDAMENTALISM

Religious violence has only a contingent, sometimes even occasional, relationship to *particular theological beliefs*. Theological disagreements, whether interconfessional or intraconfessional, are often just a symptom of an underlying division or even a pure façade for something else, like patriarchy, nationalism, or ethnic hatred. The widespread violence endemic to the various fundamentalisms, particularly among the religions of the Book—Christian, Jewish, and Islamic—has next to nothing to do with a difference in hermeneutic theory about how to read a book. In the case of biblical literalism, being able to understand the literal meaning of a text, say of a poem, is a basic place to begin the work of interpretation. With an ancient text like the Bible, this is far from easy; it requires a knowledge of several ancient languages and the original historical context. But if this is an indispensable *first* reading, it is *not normative*. The original context is formative, not normative, and the argument that it is normative, literal*ism*, is insupportable.

While the arguments against literalism are decisive, they are also irrelevant. They fall on deaf ears. Like the arguments against deniers of anthropogenic climate change, reasoned argument here is tilting at windmills. That is because something of more elemental import is at stake, and the failure to recognize this is a source of the Left's underestimation and misunderstanding of religion, not to mention its missed opportunity.

As a conceptual matter, literal*ism* is a simple and obvious mistake. In Derrida's terms, it refuses to concede that once a text is constructed in a given context, it is endlessly recontextualizable (deconstructible); in Tillich's terms, it conflates something conditional (a historical book) with the unconditional (God). We have learned from Tillich and Schelling to take myths seriously, but fundamentalists do not live in a mythic world the way indigenous *premodern* people did, with a serious but innocent simplicity (Tillich's "unbroken" myth); they live in it in a reactionary and *anti*-modern way, having seen the myth broken by science. So the *conceptual* debate is over almost before it begins. Furthermore, literalism faces a practical problem. There are over thirty thousand verses in the scriptures, composed over many centuries, by multiple sources, and they say many different and conflicting things. Taking everything they say literally would be impossible; even trying it would produce very traumatizing results. But the *real* debate involves much more than that because the unconditional is a great deal more than a conceptual matter; it is embedded in our bowels.

To be sure, literalism is an easy target. Not every conservative Christian is an evangelical, and not every evangelical is a fundamentalist or literalist.[11] On the contrary, today Evangelicalism in the US has fractured. On the one hand there are those who want to save Evangelicalism from itself, who still think that it is by love that you shall know they are Christian. On the other hand, there are the militant right-wing culture warriors, unapologetic about their sexism and racism, who support Donald Trump. It is no surprise that Evangelicalism's numbers are in decline; it is bleeding young people who are sick of the nastiness, the hypocrisy, and corruption of their elders.[12] But literalism is a symptom of a more widespread frame of mind in Christian Right culture, of an anxiety that has thrown it into a panic and led it—some 70 percent—to embrace Trump as an (admittedly imperfect) chosen one, as an instrument of the Lord to make America great again. By this they mean make it a white Christian nation again on the misguided assumption that it was founded as a Christian nation in the first place and that Jesus was a white Christian nationalist who supported the right to bear arms; this Jesus looks like John Wayne.[13]

The menacing groundswell of Christian nationalism reached its peak in the insurrection against the Capitol on January 6, 2021, which was the Christian white supremacist version of Matthew 11:12, "the kingdom of God has suffered violence, and the violent take it by force." This attack was launched by a motley bag of angry anarchists, white militias, and conspiracy theorists, but unmistakable in the mix were multiple Christian symbols—crosses, the Christian flag, "Jesus, 2020" (election poster), and prayer groups—right there alongside swastikas and "Camp Auschwitz" shirts.[14] The Christians involved in this attack were inspired by a falsehood perpetrated by a pathological liar who uses churches for photo opportunities, not prayer, brags of grabbing female genitalia, and is involved in several lawsuits over buying the silence of prostitutes. What is the goal of these Christians? Not simply to be left free to live a Christian life (as they see it) and privately repent of their sins (as if anyone were stopping them), but a tribalist, theocratic power grab. They think God has authorized them to violently impose on everyone else their distorted version of Christianity as a "prosperity gospel," in which birth control is a more serious offense against God than poverty and racial discrimination. Or as a patriarchy modeled after one Father in heaven: a Strong Man to lead the nation and a strong father on earth to maintain order and discipline in the family, all in America as a country especially favored by God, founded by white evangelical Christians (they were mostly deists!) whose mission was to maintain white Christian supremacy. Make America great again by destroying constitutional democracy itself. *Pro Deo et Patria* gone mad. Christianity is all about "sex, power, race, and nation."[15] The culture war becomes civil war. This is written all over the "hot button" issues that ignite their passions:

- First among them are issues surrounding sexuality, like gender identity, same-sex love and marriage, birth control, and abortion. For people who are committed to adhering to what the New Testament says, they seem not to have noticed how little it has to say about sexual matters—it is actually remarkable on this point—while its concerns with the poor, the hungry, the imprisoned, the outcast, the blind, the lepers, and the lame leap off every page.

- "Family values" fare even more poorly in the New Testament, as almost every mention made of the family seems to involve the obstacles the family throws up against the coming of the kingdom of God.
- No less striking is the glaring contradiction between the antipathy Christian nationalists display against immigrants—people of color—and the prophetic motif of welcoming "the widow, the orphan, and the stranger." What alarms Christian nationalists in the United States, like the nationalist movements of western Europe, is the "invasion" of white Euro-American Christian culture by third-world peoples.[16] They fear that the days of white supremacy are numbered and white people will end up as a minority, leaving the "sons of Ham" in charge. Of course, the Bible is full of things like that—"the sons of Ham"—to support their animosity, but that inconsistency does not authorize this animosity. It just points to the need for a better theory of biblical hermeneutics, one in which we assume responsibility for how we interpret what we read.
- Finally, they join a love of guns with their love of Jesus, which is truly remarkable given that Jesus's own advice to the disciple in the garden is to put down his sword and the example of Jesus on the cross is to forgive his executioners.

In general, if there are good arguments for a strict code of sexual ethics, family values, hostility to immigrants, and the currently prevailing interpretation of the Second Amendment, they are not to be found in the New Testament, especially not if one's (misguided) guiding principle is *sola scriptura*.

What do all these issues have in common? Their *profundity*—in the strictest physical sense of the word. They are deeply *visceral* issues, instinctual, primitive, rooted in neither moral theology nor a theory of biblical hermeneutics but in what Schelling and Tillich call the dark forces of being. They are gut issues, rooted not in the Book but in the bowels, in our felt being-in-the-world, physiologically rooted in an ancient passion to protect one's own family, clan, and way of life. They show that religion is not to be found merely in a set of "beliefs," which are located in the material culture, but in an underlying form of life (Wittgenstein), a mode of being-in-the-world (Heidegger), of embodied and impassioned being (Merleau-Ponty). The world of the Christian Right is a "life-world" (Husserl), a constellation of bodily passions and material practices, anchored in our corporeality and materiality. While we live *on* the plane of beings, *in* the material culture, we live *from* the ground of being, of our felt being-in-the-world (*ex profundis*), on a level where matters of ultimate concern make themselves felt.

Religion reflects what Heidegger calls a *Grundstimmung*, a fundamental mode of attunement to the world. This means not only the way we are tuned to the world but also the tune the world is playing on us, on our bodies, long before reflective thought arrives on the scene to try to sort things out. Going along with its traditional and edifying if dubious etymology, religion has served as the way we are "bound back" to being, to the ground of being. That is why religion comes accompanied by song and dance, by bodies completely possessed by deeper rhythms, be they divine or demonic, cosmic or theo-cosmic —*Deus sive natura*. Religion is capable of everything from the elegant and luxuriant liturgies of the Greek Orthodox Church to speaking in tongues and snake handling, from the "blues" to the song and dance of indigenous religion, everything from "In the Sweet By and By" to "We Shall Overcome" to Brahms's *Requiem*, like so many sparks flaring up from a volcano against a midnight sky.

So the reaction of the religious Right to the contemporary world is not a *superficial* phenomenon; it is quite profound, and the secular order shows no sign of understanding this. The reactionary slogans on the billboards and bumper stickers in rural America give words to a theology that is naïve and reactionary but not superficial, to a literally *primitive* theology that touches upon the *prius*, reflecting the *primal resonance* of their embodied being-in-the-world with the world around them—but a theology deeply *dissonant* with the pluralistic and postmodern world, which seems to them like Sodom and Gomorrah and by which they are viscerally repulsed. This attunement—this attachment to the nearby, the close, this sense of rootedness—reaches back into a time immemorial in our evolution, when to wander far from our clan, to fall in among people who do not look like us, meant we stood a good chance of being clubbed to death. That explains the force of the familiar, the power of the local place, the kindness with which we regard the kindred, and our natural inclination to nativism, to favor the natal and native born. This rootedness explains our resistance to being uprooted; it helps us understand our wariness of the alien, the foreign, the different, the other, as well as our innate resistance to sweeping change. I am *describing* rather than *endorsing* these effects. Even when we want to resist these impulses, we do so because we have them. As we learn from Schelling, they belong to our unconscious, to a murky mythology that is in need of the light of a philosophical revelation.

The repulsion the Christian Right experiences to the pluralism of the postmodern world is rather more a matter of biosociopolitical and cultural passion than theological beliefs. How else to explain the unrepentant hypocrisy with which they winced but then looked the other way in the matter of the personal corruption of Donald Trump while an African American president who embodied everything they said they believed about family values and personal integrity leaves them seething with anger and they refuse to believe a devout Irish Catholic could have legitimately been elected. For them, the vitality of the Good News has degenerated into the vitriol of Fox News, where our ties to being turn into lies. This has left in tatters the moral authority with which they once loudly, proudly, and publicly anointed themselves, against the advice of Jesus to pray in private! "Character matters"—except when it does not. They have heard these criticisms—hypocrisy, a deal with the devil—but none matter to them because they fear something bigger, something apocalyptic. They feel the ground trembling beneath their feet. They fear an existential threat—that something is happening to their whole world, to their jobs, to their youth, to their families, to their farms and coal mines, to their factory towns and local communities, and, of course, about that part they are right.[17] The information age favors those who work with their heads, not their hands; the global economy has shipped blue-collar manufacturing jobs overseas; concern with climate change is relentlessly eroding the fossil fuel industries; the evolving demographics of white and nonwhite is not in their favor. This has filled them with fear and visceral resentment against the "elite"—the urban and educated—and has encouraged the spread of conspiracy theories and distrust of scientific expertise, even in the face of a lethal pandemic.[18] The *real* question is how they are to cope with these changes and transition to a new future for which they are profoundly ill-prepared and ill-equipped and that they deeply resent.

While I disdain and deplore what they think, and while I certainly do not condone the violence that they think their plight justifies, I do not doubt the profundity of their concerns. They bear out the point I am making about the ambiguity of the unconditional and the nocturnal powers of being. Traditionally, it has fallen to religion to give paradigmatic voice to our bond with being—to articulate it, narrate it, and perform it. But as the religious Right makes religion today more and more unbelievable and reactionary to democratic pluralism, that role is being passed on to art and science. The secular Left, in turn, needs to understand this as well as how religion can be turned—or rather returned—to a prophetic purpose. What the future holds for religion, not merely the postmodern but the posthuman future, is an open question I address in the following (chapters 13–15).

RADICAL CORRELATIONALISM

I subscribe to a "correlational" theology, not only between a given confessional theology and the rest of the culture (the "religious" and the "secular"), both of which belong to the material culture, but still more fundamentally between the material culture at large and the unconditional—that is, between the unconditional that lays claim to us and the concrete conditional constructions in which we respond to this claim. His German language allowed Novalis to put this correlation thus, "Everywhere we search for the unconditioned (*Unbedingte*) but only ever find things (*Dinge*)." [19] Between these two, I hold, there is a double law of correlation, of circularity and incommensurability.

- *Circularity*: In Heideggerian terms, Being (the unconditional) is never to be found except as the *Being of* beings, and beings (conditioned factual entities) are never to be found except *in their Being*. Being belongs to beings and beings belong to Being in the circulation of their mutual belonging-together (*Zusammengehören*).
- *Incommensurability*: But in their circularity, they remain mutually incommensurable. The conditional (beings, concrete cultural constructions) can never capture, equal, exhaust, or adequately express the unconditional (the undeconstructible, the matter of ultimate concern), even as the matter of ultimate concern would be destroyed as such were it ever contracted to a particular state, condition, or entity

in the material culture. The (transcendental) conditions that make it possible for the unconditional to be expressed also make it impossible to express the unconditional adequately (quasi-transcendental).

Together this circularity and incommensurability result in structural instability, a mobile process—ongoing, revisable, reformable, reinventable, and deconstructible—that leaves the ground of being always equally groundless. This double law is expressed in Heidegger as the ontico-ontological difference; it is expressed in Tillich under the name of the "Protestant principle," which refers not to denominational Protestantism but to the structural inadequacy of every conditional religious expression of the unconditional. It is signified in Derrida appositionally, by the ever-present qualifier *s'il y en a*: the undeconstructible, the impossible, the unconditional, *if there is such a thing*. In the Bible, it is simply known as the critique of idols.

Religion in the narrow sense is, as such, a conditioned, constructed, contingent response to the unconditional, by which it is seized or addressed and to which it is never adequate. Religion is structurally deconstructible just because it is inwardly disturbed by the undeconstructible. Religion is a matter of being claimed *by* something unconditional, which means it should have the good sense not to lay claim *to* it. We should never trust anything that has not passed through that *apophasis*. What we *say and name*, what we claim to *know and believe*, what we *make or do*, the many claims we advance, the many constructions we produce—all that bounces off the wall of what lays claim to us in advance, just the way thought cannot get there in time to lay down the conditions under which being happens. Naming, claiming, and choosing are all structurally too late (a posteriori); they come in response—to the unconditional, to the recessed mystery of the unconditional, which comes first (a priori, the *prius*), the "unprethinkable" (*das Unvordenkliche*).

The unconditional resides in the recess, in the deep ground, which precedes, exceeds, and recedes from the reach of the material, the conditional, the construction, even as it depends upon the conditional to come into view. Existence precedes essence; *that* it is precedes *what* it is. Every concrete, determinate, and conditioned experience contains something—implicitly, preconceptually, prereflectively—that it cannot contain, that escapes its determinations and conditions, by which it is made inwardly restless and unstable. While this is also true of religion in the narrow sense, which deals with the matter of ultimate concern in an explicit way under the name of God, it is not restricted to confessional religion.

- It is also true of the work of *art*—today more than ever when more and more people find religious beliefs unbelievable. Art is every bit as capable as religion—art and religion have overlapping concerns—in bringing us face-to-face with the mystery of our lives.
- It is true of *science*, especially in the remarkable explorations of contemporary quantum science and astrophysics, on the one hand, and neurobiology on the other hand.
- The unconditioned shows up in *ethics*, which reflects our hope for the future long before it is contracted into a code of conduct or assembled as a set of practices shaped by a community, local or national.
- It is never absent from *politics*, where the vitriolic polarized politics of tribal and party warfare and personal destruction everywhere around us today obscures an ancient and more radical sense of the polis as the matrix in which lives are shaped (Aristotle). Before politics, beneath politics, within politics, there stirs an excess, an archipolitical event, where politics makes contact with the unconditional, an excess by which any particular political schematism is inwardly disturbed. Everything is political, but politics is not everything.

So we may speak of an archiaesthetic, archiethical, an archipolitical event, which is why these practices can never be formalized or programmed and why they can be practiced only by an archi-*phronesis*. The true correlation is between Being and beings, the *prius* and the *posterius*, the call and the response, the simmering potencies and their actualizations—maybe even, who knows, between the quantum field and its excitations.

IS THE UNCONDITIONAL POISON?

We gain some insight into the unconditional by examining a misguided way of addressing religious violence proposed by the (not so very) "new atheists." For Christopher Hitchens, "religion poisons everything."[20] They propose to treat religion the way we treat any toxic substance. If, in a democratic society, we cannot ban it outright, at least we can put a warning on the label. Treat poison with poison, the poisonous weed of religious violence with the herbicide of the toxic Islamophobic polemics of the new atheists. Treat violence with more violence—polemical violence against Muslims or whatever religious beliefs are under attack. Counter terrorism with their own discursive form of terrorism. In doing so, they reproduce the structure of religious violence: the justification for burning heretics that is given by the church is that heresy is worse than murder: murders kills the body, but heresy poisons the soul. The difference between the old Inquisition and the new atheists is which one is holding the torch to ignite the other.

The new atheists are playing a game of intellectual whack-a-mole on the surface of the material culture. If unconditional desire is suppressed here, it will pop up there. If it is repressed here, it will return as the repressed elsewhere. The unconditional transgresses the conditions in which it finds itself. and it is encouraged by every prohibition. The unconditional is there—in the material culture—whether we like it or not. It is there, for better *and* for worse. That is why, even if we could somehow ban the unconditional, and I am not sure what that would even mean, what form of totalitarian terror that would require, it would not be a good idea. Eliminating the unconditional would eliminate everything exceptional, creative, novel, revolutionary, surprising, and unforeseeable. We learn this from Luther and Schelling, both of whom thought Satan ultimately is playing a constructive role as a devilish advocate of advancing life beyond the sedimented status quo by exposing it to the dangerous perhaps. The unconditional is the excess in any given order or discipline, epoch or episteme, set or category, which keeps it open to the future. It is not a totality and is nothing totalitarian. Close down the unconditional and the computers will run everything. It will be robots all the way down.

Truth to tell, the new atheists are *half right*, which is why they are dangerous. The unconditional is not poison, but it is an ambiguous divine/demonic, as in Tillich and Schelling, a *pharmakon* in Derrida's sense, a poison/cure, an *undecidable*, a promise/threat, capable of whipsawing between violence and works of mercy. So, rather than the ham-fisted denunciation of the unconditional as poison, we would do better to approach it with discernment, with interpretive care and caution, which is Rambach's venerable definition of hermeneutics (*subtilitas intelligendi*). Habermas rightly criticizes "unconditional validity claims," propositional *claims* that pretend to be free of the conditions under which they are constructed in the first place, constructions that pretend to be undeconstructible. That is my own criticism of the *strong* version of the modernist distinction between the religious and the secular and why I call for an *epochē*. The religious makes *supernaturalist* claims, which would require supernatural beings whispering in our natural ears, as if the evangelists, theirs ears cocked heavenward, were taking dictation from a hovering angel. The secular makes *transcendental* claims, which would depend upon an angelicism of another sort, a disembodied, ahistorical consciousness capable of neutralizing the concrete conditions under which making a claim is possible in the first place. Supernaturalism and transcendentalism are alternate angelicisms, which delude themselves into thinking that they stand free of the bonds of material being.

For Derrida, Tillich, and Schelling, the unconditional belongs on the side of the *prius*, while we belong to the other side, that of *being-claimed*, so that the claims *we make* are always made in response, a posteriori, tethered to the conditions under which it is possible to make claims to begin with. The unconditional always already lays claim to us before we open our mouth. The way Derrida puts this point is to say that whenever *I decide*, that is the decision *of the other in me*. Every claim or decision we make comes in response to something that addressed us first, without seeking our permission or a by-your-leave. When I say yes, that is the second yes, the first one having always already embraced me. We are, as Levinas liked to put it, always in the accusative, *me voici* (*hinneni*), never in the nominative, always responding, never in the driver's seat. By the unconditional they mean what lays claim to us unconditionally, to which *we* are to be the response, our lives, our works and days. We are the ones the dead are waiting for, and we are the messianic age, as Benjamin says.[21] If you *are* not in your *life* this truth of which I *speak*, Meister Eckhart says, you do not know what I am saying.[22]

In reducing religion to a poison and handing it over to the Right, the secular Left gets it wrong, not only on the conceptual grounds I am advancing here but also as a purely practical strategy. It does not understand what everyone in the civil rights movement—from Robert Kennedy and Martin Luther King Jr. a half century ago to Desmond Tutu and John Lewis in our own time—understands, that religion, a certain religion, creatively empowers peace and justice. Politically, it is not enough to hold a merely dispassionate, rational-liberal view that, as a matter of public policy, supports the welfare state apparatus while having nothing to say about personal life, as if that were a private concern, better left to weekends and after-hours during the workweek. Even as the Left has forgotten the role the black Baptist church played in the civil rights movement, it neglects the Catholic social encyclicals, which are more suspicious of the destructive greed that lurks in capitalism than most of what passes for the Left in the United States. Today, Pope Francis has tried to redirect the church away from its blinding preoccupation with sexual and reproductive matters and toward the cause of poverty and environmental destruction, even as Joseph Biden is the most religiously observant US president since Jimmy Carter. Using the powers of government to assist the poor and persecuted, who were the defining focus of the ministry of Jesus—instead of crossing our fingers and hoping private wealth comes to their rescue—reflects Catholic social teaching, centered on the obligation to serve the common good (*bonum commune*). Welcoming immigrants and refugees to our shores reflects the teachings of the prophets. The Left neglects all this to its peril as religiously affiliated people increasingly embrace angry, reactionary, conspiratorial, and mendacious fabrications that lead to violence.

By contrast, the cruelty of the policies of the Right—apart from their hypocrisy (Donald Trump) and their selfishness in refusing to wear a mask to help bring an end to a pandemic—punish lower- and middle-class working people, starving their children of food programs, their public schools of needed resources, their hospitals of much-needed federal support, and their cities of adequate public transportation; depriving the unemployed and underemployed of medical insurance; cutting programs to comfort the afflicted in order to further comfort the already comfortable and further afflict the afflicted; condoning racist, sexist, and xenophobic policies—all that flatly contradicts the Sermon on the Mount and the message of the prophets. Sneering leftist intellectuals do not understand that religion is a very material matter. The Bible is all about land and children; the "promised land" means real estate, not a heavenly estate. They do not appreciate that the religious Right feels instinctually, existentially threatened by the postmodern world. The Left does not grasp that there is a religious remainder—what Derrida calls an "unavowed theologeme"[23]—an excess in the political order, in the passion of the political, that contrary to the received maxim is not the art of the possible but a passion to make the impossible possible. The Left is too much in love with Enlightenment reason to appreciate Schelling's ecstatic reason.

Religion radically conceived arises, on the one hand, from what Derrida would call mourning and Schelling and Tillich would call the immemorial roots sunk deep in the groundless ground of being and, on the other hand, from hopes lodged in the depths of our heart for what Schelling and Tillich call the new being, Paul calls the "new creation," and Derrida calls the to-come, the possibility of being otherwise. Such religion is dreaming of a world that would be (in the subjunctive) ruled by God, by the events (like mercy, hospitality) that are promised in the name (of) "God." That dream is precisely what drives it to excess, what sends it into overdrive, what gives it a certain unlimited or "infinite" force, reaching all the way back, *ad infinitum*, into the groundless ground of being (Schelling, Tillich), and all the way forward, infinitively, *ad infinitivum*, to what is to-come (Derrida). Both the generosity of religious works of mercy and the merciless violence of religion are triggered by a passage to the limits, a *dangerous* passage (*gredi, gressus*), a transgression.

IS THE UNCONDITIONAL LOVE?

If we ought not to say the unconditional is poison, perhaps we should say that the unconditional is *love*. Love is certainly unconditional. Love is an expenditure made without the expectation of a return, a gift given without demanding reciprocity, professed without conditions. Loving those who love us in return makes perfect sense. Loving those who return our love with ingratitude or unfaithfulness is a bigger challenge. Loving one's outright enemies, like forgiving those who have persecuted us, by contrast, is impossible, *the* impossible, both in the biblical sense (with God, nothing is impossible) and in Derrida's sense of an excessive, horizon-shattering *event*. Conditional love—loving under conditions we set down in advance so as to minimize our risk and exposure, loving others when there is something in it for us—is a sensible deal, a way to get things done, not unlike honor among thieves. Conditional love looks like love, but real love is unconditional.

Love is certainly unconditional, but we cannot conclude that the unconditional is love, in just the way violence is unconditional but the unconditional is not violence. We cannot give love a pass. Love is not safe. We cannot excuse it from the ghost of undecidability, from the twilight of the infinite and unconditional. I do not exempt its excess from the play of transgression. I do not fetishize this word or treat it as an elixir. The worst things are done in the name of love. *Corruptio optimi pessima*: the worse things result from corrupting the best. In invoking the unconditionality of love, I am not denying that love can lead to the worst violence. I am not abandoning my constant warning that the unconditional is something that lays claim to us, not something to which we can lay claim. Love, like anything else, like any *name* we invoke, like "God" or "country" (*pro Deo et Patria*)—the more prestigious, the more dangerous—is an inherently ambiguous and risky business, on the verge of violence. The structure of love as a name for the unconditional, its ability to draw upon infinite depths, means it is prone to excess, to an expenditure without return—for better or for worse. *What would we not do for love?* In that question is concentrated all the ambiguity of love, all the courage and depth, the selfless generosity of the martyr—but no less the violence of the suicide bomber. What would we not do for love—bomb abortion clinics, persecute gays and lesbians, lynch the "sons of

Ham," drive the "infidels" from their home, deprive little girls and grown women of their human rights, slam an airliner into the side of a tall building, attack the Capitol building as Congress carries out its constitutional duties? But how could the love of Jesus go wrong? It could lead you to support a man like Donald Trump, who separated little children from their parents and encouraged a violent insurrection against his country, and to do so in the name of the gospel of Jesus.

The pragmatic marker of love, the rule of action to follow, is that love must always be located in being willing to put oneself in harm's way on behalf of whom or what we love without putting others in harm's way. To fundamentalist violence, we oppose a fundamental nonviolence. The great example of this in US political history is the practice of nonviolent resistance in the civil rights movement, which turned on a willingness to die—to be killed but not to kill. We see the unconditional in act in the life and death of Gandhi, of Martin Luther King Jr., and in John Lewis on Bloody Sunday, 1965, attacked by state troopers as he led a civil rights march across the Edmund Pettus Bridge in Selma, Alabama. The march was a concrete strategic action, but a strategy will not get you across that bridge because the passage across the bridge was a "passage to the limits" (*passage aux frontières*) in which they put their lives at risk, driven by a deep, even unfathomable affirmation of something more important than their lives. The unconditional is not a remote speculative object; it is found on ordinary bridges—or on buses. When Rosa Parks refused to sit in the back of a bus, that bus became a scene of the unconditional, an iconic moment in US history. The ecstatic quality is not some private paranormal state but exposing oneself to lethal danger when the next breath you take could be your last.

Love is mad, good for nothing (else), a divine, sublime "waste," like a brilliant lawyer working as an underpaid, overworked public defender; a brilliant physician serving the poorest of the poor; dedicated schoolteachers and social workers who could certainly have earned a better salary doing something else; people who give all to safeguard the environment, or animals, or the artifacts of antiquity. It is found whenever an occupation is not just a job but a calling, a vocation, in people who have been touched by something beyond themselves, wounded by the unconditional, unhorsed, which is the way the Renaissance painters portrayed Paul on the road to Damascus.

Love is not a good investment, a strategy, a means to an end. Unconditional love is not given on the condition that it "works," that it will achieve our goals, that is more effective than taking up arms, that it will stay the hand of the oppressor, that it will reform the world. It may or may not. Love is given *unconditionally*, win or lose, come what may, without the expectation of a return, *without why*. It is *that* unconditionality, which loves because it loves, whose cause I advance. An elemental power stirs obscurely but incessantly in names like "love" and "God" and even, if you can still hear it, in what we call today in Christian Latin "religion"—a religion *without* religion, as Derrida says, without a good deal of what passes itself off as religion today, or, we might say, a religion *before* religion, an archireligion or protoreligion prior to confessional religion, a religion of the *prius*. I am not sure if the word *religion* can be saved, not only from its detractors but especially from its own defenders these days, or even if it is worth saving, or if we would not be better off dropping it altogether and speaking otherwise. But if it can be saved, that is what a religion worthy of the name would mean.

ETHICS AND THE UNCONDITIONAL

The ambiguity of the unconditional, which is the excess in politics, also shows up as the excess of any particular ethical order (for better or for worse). When Tillich says that both the divine and the demonic alike are distrusted by ethics, he is pointing to the exceptionality of the unconditional, which cannot be contracted into a code of conduct or regulated practices in the material culture. That is because the material culture, which is constituted by its inherited beliefs and practices, is inwardly disturbed by *matters of ultimate concern* stirring within it. The unconditional has to do with something more ultimate than "values," which is a distinctly modernist notion that is constituted by its distinction from "facts" and belongs, part and parcel, to the subject/object distinction. In a theory of values, we evaluate actions by a measure we set forth, but the unconditional is what takes our measure.

The unconditional has to do with a deeper and wider embrace of the world than any ethical judgment. Ethics is too tidy for the unconditional. The unconditional elicits an abiding affirmation, yes, yes, *oui, oui*, yes, I said yes, a sweeping *Amen* that saturates, underlies, precedes, permeates, and pervades the particular positions we take. Schelling saw this, but he mystified it with his metaphysics into an eternal decision made in the noumenal world. Using a Kierkegaardian analogy, the unconditional is the concern of a religion—without the dogmas or the long robes—released by the suspension of ethics, where ethics (the comfort of the universal, the normalizing) is the temptation. Ethics loves rules; the unconditional lets love rule. Ethics is prudent; the unconditional is folly. Ethics prizes the mean state, staying in the lane, and it holds suspect everything singular, excessive, and exceptional, which is why the unconditional is capable of being the best of us or the worst, reflecting the better angels of our nature or the worst.

This distrust of ethics shows up in both Tillich and Derrida. Tillich distinguishes the moral virtue of courage, the strength to face a particular and identifiable danger—let us say, an ontic courage—from an ontological courage, the courage to be itself, to affirm the forces of being over nonbeing, the lack of which would result not in a particular failure but in an erosive, enervating sickness unto death. Such courage is the underlying energy of life, the *conatus essendi*, the power that stands firm in the face of the to-be-or-not-to-be crises of life.[24] The courage to be goes hand in hand with an *absolute faith*, which he distinguished from the impoverished idea of faith as assenting to a proposition lacking in evidence. Particular hopes and beliefs are weakened by doubt and despair, whereas doubt and despair fire the steel of absolute faith and are taken up into them. Faith is faith in the unconditional worth of life itself no matter what, *win or lose*.[25] Indeed, in doubt and uncertainty *about* the meaning of life, we *experience* the meaning of life. There is something positive in their negativity, because even in doubt and despair, we are reeling and restless, which is the stirring of a faith and hope in life even if, especially if, life seems meaningless. We see this faith in the life and work of Albert Camus, who, in voicing his philosophy of the absurd, gives testimony to the earnestness of his search for meaning, thereby enacting his faith in life.[26]

Derrida, in turn, speaks of the "ethicity of ethics,"[27] beyond ethical duty, which is expressed in terms of his Jewish messianic imaginary, which dreams of the possibility of "the impossible."[28] Ethics evades real responsibility by allowing us to say we were only following the rules. A real responsibility makes itself responsible for the rules it follows and makes itself ready for what exceeds the rules or takes them by surprise. Derrida signifies the excess messianically, infinit*ively*, affirming not any given, positive system of laws belonging to the material culture but the justice-*to-come*, or the democracy-*to-come*, where justice and democracy are calls calling unconditionally but without sovereignty. Events, which belong to the promise of the world, send the ethicians back to the drawing board looking for ways to make sense of what just happened.

Tillich and Derrida each mark out the open space of an unconditional life, which precedes any attempt to formalize or regulate our lives, and they both harbor a suspicion of the confined space, the measured conformism of ethics. They expose the snake oil, the sales pitch of "religion," the theological terrorism of the economy of eternal rewards and punishments. They reject the illusion of a deep underlying ontotheological warranty that all will be well, and they understand the risk that, like Levinas, they both could call the "beautiful risk" of life.

ELEVEN

HAUNTING TILLICH
Spectralizing the Ground of Being

IN THE PREVIOUS CHAPTER, I prescinded from the difference between Tillich's and Derrida's notion of the unconditional, which I must now clarify because the movement from a classical to a radical apophatic imagination depends upon it. Tillich is the border figure, but our idea is to cross that border. With Tillich we encounter a radical apophatic theology in a recognizable form, one in which the post-theism of Hegel and the apophaticism of Schelling converge. In the terms I set out at the beginning, Tillich's theology of the symbol carries out a theopoetic reduction, and his post-theism carries out an ontological reduction. But to establish radical apophaticism in the sense that I intend here, as a discourse that does no injury to the mystical or apophatic sense of life, we need to carry out what I have been calling the hauntological reduction, which requires "spectralizing" Tillich. In terms of our guiding trope, to angels and demons we now add spooks and specters. Spectralization demands that we move past an ontological ground of being to an hauntological groundlessness in an effort to remain *unconditionally loyal to the unconditional*.

RADICALIZING TILLICH

My thesis is not only that the unconditional is possible "without sovereignty" but that it is *only possible* without sovereignty, which means without being. Derrida's "unconditional without sovereignty" is the unconditional in a still more unconditional form. The "undeconstructible" is a more radically unprotected unconditional than both the ontic Supreme Being and the ontological ground of being and so steers clear of the semi-blasphemous and mythological in a still more searching way. For Derrida, the unconditional is at best, at most, lodged within in a haunting call or solicitation without ever setting foot on the ground of being. The unconditional is left to speak for itself, crucified and abandoned by its Father, be it ontological or theological, its only recourse being the powerless power of its call, of what it is calling for, of what we are called upon to do—without the support of the sovereign power of a Supreme Being (theism) or the deep power of the ground of being (post-theism). That is what is behind the constellation of spectral tropes in Derrida, in which the *Geist* becomes a ghost, the Spirit but a specter, ontology a hauntology. Theism confines the unconditional to a personified hyperbeing, to a sovereign Other; panentheism avoids all that, but panentheism conflates the unconditional with the ground of being. Both are looking to underwrite the unconditional with an ontological insurance policy, which avoids thve risk of radical groundlessness.

I do not want to turn this into a bidding war in which Derrida outbids Tillich and Tillich is forced to fold. This is not a modernist "critique" of Tillich but a radicalization of Tillich. Just as with Schelling, we situate ourselves within Tillich's standpoint and release or "retrieve" a "radical Tillich,"[1] reading against and in between the lines of a more traditional one by making use of deconstruction. I seek to release the radical Tillich from the familiar figures of Tillich's theology, here repeated in a more radical form.[2] Deconstruction is not a competitor position. It is not a position at all but a deposition, an imposition, not a position but an underlying affirmation. Left to itself deconstruction is nothing at all. Deconstruction is always the deconstruction *of* something—of hermeneutics, theology, metaphysics, ethics, politics, *anything*—which effects its radicalization. Furthermore, it is not something someone is doing to something else; it is going on in the thing itself. So if you ask me where I got all this, I would say from Tillich. On the accounting I am tendering here, all the characteristic Tillichian motifs are transformed:

- The *ground of being* gives way to the inconceivable, unprogrammable *event*.
- The event elicits a more radical *hope* in a future we also hope will not be a disaster, requiring a more radical *dynamics of faith* in the future that is inhabited by a considerable postmodern incredulity (*doubt*) about saying anything more.
- The *ontological* yields to the *eschatological* and the eschatological to a pure *messianicity*, without any ontotheological buttressing.
- Theopoetics is a more *radically symbolic* discourse, where religion is a song we sing to what lays claim to us unconditionally.
- A hermeneutics where nobody has the key, the code, the legendum, makes even more demands on us to summon the *courage to be*.
- A *culture* is more radically conceived or reconstrued as a *construction*, at a far remove from *Geist*, a way to negotiate with the underlying eventiveness of life.
- Any possible *systematic theology* is redescribed as a tangled, entangled *network* of interwoven but open-ended connections.
- The dynamics of the *depth of being*, of which the culture is the "expression," yields to a *differential play* and the disseminative effects produced by the play.

- The genuine *correlation* is not between our questions and theology's answers but between the claim made by the unconditional and our response.
- The *Protestant principle* is here given a slightly *Jewish* twist.

In exposing the radical side of Tillich, we also see the religious side of deconstruction. We do both at once, without having to choose between them. Radical apophatic theology is structured like a deconstruction of the conditional in the name of the unconditional. Deconstruction is structured like a religion, a faith, a hope, a prayer for the unconditional, not a confessional religion but a religion resonating with the unconditional.

By rethinking the unconditional as the undeconstructible, deconstruction does singular service to a radical theology in the tradition launched by Tillich. But Tillich, in turn, predicts the appearance of Derrida. That Derrida "quite rightly passes for an atheist,"[3] not a theologian, is telling from the point of view of Tillich, who predicts that the unconditional is so elementary a notion that it should show up everywhere—in the depth dimension of anything and everything. *Tout autre est tout autre*, Derrida says. So, sure enough, there it is—the unconditional—as big as life, right in the core of a so-called secular and atheistic philosophy like deconstruction. For both Tillich and Derrida, two famous trespassers and border crossers, in the best traditions of Hermes, the much-vaunted distinctions between theology and philosophy—the religious and the secular, faith and reason, theism and atheism—are all so many futile attempts made in modernity to draw conditional lines in the sands of the unconditional.

WHAT IS A CULTURE?

Like Tillich, Derrida was working on a theory of culture, but unlike Tillich, he did not treat culture as the expression of a deeper ground of being. Derrida's view is antiessentialist—in classical terms it would be described as "nominalist"—since for Derrida "culture," in the singular, would always be used in scare quotes.[4] *Of Grammatology* is an inquiry into the tendency that goes back to Rousseau to romanticize "nature" as innocent and treat "culture" as corrupt. Derrida's argument is not to show that nature is also corrupt but that both "nature" and "culture" are constructions, that we are always dealing with constructions, substitutes, stand-ins, and delegates and have no access to any pure "nature," no more than we do to a pure culture, if there even are any such things. Culture is a construction; it is neither a corruption, as Rousseau thought, nor, as the German idealists thought, some underlying substantial unity, a *Geist*, and the same thing is true of nature.

Culture is rather an assemblage of contingent beliefs and practices and of institutional structures, an ongoing—nowadays—multicultural, polyglot, and polymorphic collection, a historically constituted and shaky configuration of disparate elements that work together, for better or for worse, and usually both. A culture may have an identity, like French or American, but it is not identical with itself;[5] it is a multivocal multiplex, a complicated complex of different forces. But if cultures have been constructed, then they are deconstructible. Historical constructions have a tendency to sediment, to calcify, to fall into patterns of normalization, which creates the illusion that they have fallen from the sky. As a result, the more irregular, incommensurate, disruptive, marginal, odd-(wo)man-out elements tend to drop out of view or get pushed aside and the whole thing settles into regular order, into hierarchical, top-down, binary patterns. Things begins to look like they are "self-evident," the "natural" order, the way it always was and should be. This is what Derrida, citing Pascal, calls its "mystical force,"[6] which means magical, not classical mysticism, something like those cartoon characters who walk off a cliff but do not fall until they look down and realize that nothing is holding them up. Deconstruction, in these terms, looks down. It is a theory of desedimentation and demarginalization, which is not to be confused with simple destruction; it is a way of stirring up the mix, of desedimenting, of remixing, of releasing the elements that have dropped to the bottom or have been marginalized, opening up the received order to hitherto occluded or excluded possibilities, exposing the contingency of the arrangements that have settled into place and acquired mystical authority, thereby opening things up to their future.

If we have reasons for clinging to the language of "being"—and deconstruction has not come into the world to abolish words like *being* or *presence* but to show their endless recontextualizability—then the idea would be to keep being as fluid and as "plastic"[7] as possible and to keep being in flux, as Shelling insisted. Much of the fluidity in culture for which Derrida presses—a concern shared by Tillich—is accomplished in German idealism by the historicality of the *Geist* that is obeying a law of essence, unfolding its implicit powers in time and history—not a mystical force but a metaphysical-spiritual one. If I resist the language of being, it is not because I favor nonbeing, and it is not because I do not think that being is good (Gen. 1:31). My reservation is that, as a strategic matter, "being" has a way of settling in place and meaning immutable presence, and God is framed as some sort of *Deus erectus*, stiff, unbending, and patriarchal, static and unchanging. I put a strategic emphasis on nonbeing, on the not-yet, on the openness of the to-come. My emphasis is less on being than on becoming, less on form than on transforming, less on the present than on reinventing the past and inventing the future, less on being than on the temporality of being. I am not against "being" so long as we all agree that being is spooked by time, in which case the most felicitous choice of all is not the language of being but the language of "event," which is not exactly being but far from nothing.

Deconstruction is the opposite of the Neoplatonic view that diversity and multiplicity are always derivative, that the many flows from the One and is meant to flow back into the One (*exitus* and *reditus*). This is the complaint I lodged with Schelling on the *Urgrund*. On the contrary, in deconstruction, unities are the effect of multiplicity, of the repetition and reiteration—the way a word acquires sense by being repeated, by catching on and building up a repertoire of usages, which is another way of saying that in deconstruction, things do not have an essence; they have a history. Accordingly, a *culture is a cluster of contingent effects, not an outer expression of an inner depth or essence*. As a cluster, everything is connected, part of a network, entangled—which does service for any possible "system." Deconstruction breaks not only with the dualist metaphysics of temporal immanence and eternal transcendence (theism) but also with the antidualist metaphysics of inner essence and outer manifestation (panentheism). The ingredients of a culture—languages and meanings, beliefs and practices, institutions and traditions—are effects of the systems that produce them. They are effects, neither temporal copies of eternal exemplars nor outer expressions of inner essences. They are not surface expressions of a depth dimension but disseminative effects. These effects link and concatenate, forming loose chains that we call "traditions" and "cultures," forming "networks" instead of metaphysical "systems." If we say they unfold, this does not mean they make explicit an implicit essence. It means they unfold laterally across the surface, not vertically from the deep. Even—and especially—the name of "God" has a history, not an essence. This name, like any name, does not get hold of a deeply lodged essence; it holds together as a series of historical links across time. To pronounce the "meaning" of something is to give a progress report on the current state of usage, not to have an intuition of an essence. The idea behind deconstruction is to keep that in mind, especially with highly prestigious and self-important names, and in that way keep the future open. To announce a final meaning or essence is to announce the time of death. It belongs in a coroner's report or a eulogy to the late lamented.

The role of deconstruction is not to *make* events happen in the culture but to *let* them happen, to take the emphasis off self and subjectivity, to dethrone the famous "liberal individual" or "autonomous subject" of modernity and redirect it to the systems (networks) that produce effects, but with the proviso that these systems are open, not closed, whence the *post-* in post-structuralist. The systems themselves are internally unstable, contingent clusters that left to themselves are given to shifts—sometimes small course corrections and sometimes large seismic shifts, like Kuhn's idea of paradigm shifts or Heidegger's *Grundbegriffe*. This is what Derrida calls "auto-deconstruction," meaning that he is not doing this, just reporting it, that the quasi-systems we inhabit are inherently unstable, which means only relatively stable. The aim is to reduce the pressures that prevent the event and release the pressures that let events happen, to maintain a certain optimal cultural disequilibrium, since too much pressure in either direction spells death—from chaos, on the one hand, or stagnation, on the other. The life of a culture is not conserved by being conservative; it is stifled. Traditions survive by autocorrecting. The conservative impulse to keep things safe is just what puts them in danger. Too much conservation spells death to the institution or tradition, death by rigidification or calcification. Too much event-ing also spells death—madness, trauma, and chaos, death by dissipation. James Joyce described the way around too much order (cosmos) and too little (chaos) with the magnificent locution *chaosmos*, which is a felicitous formulation of optimal disequilibrium.

THE UNCONDITIONAL AND THE UNDECONSTRUCTIBLE

Then is there anything to which deconstruction is prepared to swear an oath of allegiance? Any authority it recognizes? Anything it affirms? To what is it responsible? Can it be loyal to anything? These are important questions the answer to which reveals a side of Derrida's work that was not clear in the beginning and became clear only when Derrida first spoke of the "undeconstructible" in the famous lecture at Cardozo Law School in which he defended the deconstructibility of the law and the undeconstructibility of justice. This lecture proved unnerving to the secular-minded deconstructors because it sounded a bit religious, a bit messianic, and with good reason—it was! Justice is the affirmation, the desire, we could even say the love, that drives the law, produces the law, constructs the law, and, in so doing, assures that the law is deconstructible, given that whatever has been constructed can be deconstructed. But justice is "undeconstructible," justice in itself, if there is such a thing.[8] This underlying affirmation goes beyond any particular "position" we might adopt. The undeconstructible is not a Platonic *eidos* or metaphysical essence, which is why Derrida always adds "if there is such a thing" (*s'il y en a*), and, of course, there is not. Justice does not exist. Justice insists; it calls, is called for, and calls upon us, demanding a response, putting us in the accusative. Wherever there is a construction—and where is there not, if culture itself is a construction?—something undeconstructible *calls*, is called for, is getting itself called. Justice is not an eternal ideal to be approximated asymptotically in empirical time, not an essence, but a call, a hope, a desire, an affirmation—and why not say it, a prayer—over and beyond, or inhabiting from within, any particular affirmation. It would not fit into Schelling's "negative" philosophy because it is not an essence, and it would not fit into the positive philosophy because it does not exist. Then what is it? For starters, it is neither a *what* nor an *is*.

The pressure put by the undeconstructible on any given cultural construction is twofold. On the one hand, as a construction, a culture is inherently autodeconstructible, destabilized from within. But on the other hand, a culture is a tradition, which means it gives or hands over (*traditio* derives from *trans* + *dare*) a legacy, a complex of promises and aspirations and desires—in paradigmatic words like *justice, freedom,* and *democracy*—that make the present order restless with desire for what is coming. So the present is made restless by a past that promises a future, by an always unfulfilled promise, by a memory and a hope, which calls upon *us* to make this promise come true. That is where we do have a role to play. That means there is (1) a deconstructibility that is inherent to the process, which is not our doing, and (2) a deconstructibility to which we lend the weight of our desire, let us say a deconstructibility from within and a deconstructibility from without, which is where we come in.

In any given or existing democracy, for example, there is the memory of what democracy was meant to be but never was (hence "mourning") and the dream of the democracy to come (hence messianic, always a "to-come"), and living a democratic life means negotiating the difference between the two. The conditions under which democracy exists must be negotiated in the light of the unconditional dream of democracy. The conditions are real, powerful (like the "law"), but the unconditional call to which the law is a response is—like justice—a wisp of a thing, without force, without sovereign power.[9] The unconditional is not a Supreme Being, not the Being of beings, not a Neoplatonic beyond-being, but a call. There is a *correlation* between the undeconstructible, which is an unconditional call, and our being called upon to respond, in the accusative, as to the authority to which we are responsible. The temporality of the call is the call of temporality, of a past and a future, a memory and a promise. It has no deeper "ground" than that. The unconditional is a function of its temporal links; what is called the "ground of being" is ultimately the structure of temporality.

So Derrida does not try to "ground" things in "being" but to meticulously analyze a history. A history is coconstituted by a memory, which is always haunted by the memory of death and persecution, of justice denied, a matter of "mourning," and by a promise, a call that stirs in words of elemental promise, a matter of hope not unmixed with fear. We have not been consulted in advance about our inheritance; we were never asked to sign off before being born. Language and culture and the world were already up and running when we arrived on the scene. We have inherited unkept promises, calls that "spook" us in the night, calling upon us to finish the unfinished business of the dead, coming back to haunt us, *les revenants* "shaking the foundations" of the present order, calling for something that eye has not seen, something coming, *les arrivants*. Events belong not to the *ontological* order but the *hauntological* order,[10] a bit of wit in which Derrida's difference from Hegel, Schelling, and Tillich is condensed. If language is, as Heidegger said, the "house of Being," Derrida is insisting it is a haunted house!

DECONSTRUCTION AND THE PROTESTANT PRINCIPLE

Their differences notwithstanding, the convergence of Derrida and Tillich around this notion of the unconditional shows up in an interesting way in what Tillich calls "the Protestant principle," which he adapted from Schelling's history of the church (chapter 6), which is, in brief, that nothing conditional is ever up to the demands of the unconditional.[11] No concrete set of conditions ever exhausts what the unconditional demands of us. But whatever the conditions are—a work of art, science, or political action—we know that they are inwardly disturbed by something unconditional, by the desire and the affirmation of the unconditional by which they have been seized. That establishes a principle of criticism, which *protests* whenever we are tempted to confuse the unconditional with something conditioned, like a belief or a book, a person or an institution. The principle demands unrelenting vigilance about idolatry, blasphemy, and mythologization. It demands that we never confuse the symbol with what is being symbolized.

By the same token, in Derrida, the undeconstructible functions like a white light that exposes the blemishes of any given construction. "O my fellow democrats," he says (improvising upon a text from Montaigne, who is citing Aristotle), "there are no democrats."[12] That is to say, any existing democracy is to some extent and in some measure undemocratic, which means that in the word *democracy* there is the memory of something that never existed and the promise of something that never will exist, something that is to-come, something of which we are dreaming, even praying. This temporality is, I am claiming, the cash value of Schelling's ages of the world, of a time immemorial and an absolute future, but this time without all the distress and excess of his metaphysical fabulation and fabrication. These structures belong neither to empirical history nor to metaphysical history but to the *messianic*. The messianic figure is at work in anything from the university, a poem, or a scientific theory to political action in the streets, where we hold up traffic on behalf of the unconditional. The messianic figure is the figure of something that never actually shows up, not as long as we live in time, and when else would we live? Tillich's Protestant principle and Derrida's pure messianic share a common genealogy in the biblical critique of idolatry, where anything we say about God must be held suspect for its structural tendency to become an idol.

So, when Marx says that the critique of religion is the paradigm for all critique because of its mystifications, which can then be extended to the mystification of the commodity, he has it exactly backward. It is the religious critique of idolatry—the Protestant principle, the Jewish-deconstructive principle—that is the paradigm of what Marx calls critique, which shows up in Marx's own adaptation of the messianic, his dream of the economic order to come in which the invidious and unjust war of the classes gives way to a (messianic) age of justice without classes, which is what Tillich called the irreducible promise of the prophetic in *The Socialist Decision*.[13] That is why Marx begins *The Communist Manifesto* by saying, to loosely paraphrase him, that the specter of a justice-to-come is spooking all Europe.[14]

WEAKENING THE BEING OF GOD

Tillich remains comfortable with the classical language of ground and being, which is ultimately the language of *ousia, substantia,* and *Geist,* which is condensed by Derrida into the concept of "presence." But in order to think the unconditional in still more unconditional terms, we set out to weaken this ontological language into a hauntological discourse, one that is no longer attached to the language of strong thinking, of a metaphysics of being, *all this in order to be more loyal to the unconditional as such, without a backup in being*—that is my claim. We think in terms of a memory and a hope that is forged at the level of cultural formations, in language and institutional structures, that speaks for itself and from its own resources and is not taken to be the *expression* of some metaphysical *Wesen.*

We think in term of cultural constructions giving off of sparks of hope and finding traces of memory, which are historical forces, not directions being voiced for us from God above or the *Geist* within. On this level, historical matters are up for grabs, very much in the spirit of the "strife" described by Schelling but this time taken strictly as a phenomenology of historical life. These events of hope and memory are instead messages that are "harbored" within inherited histories, institutions, and structures, which means both hidden and kept safe, distorted, contorted, and re*invent*ed in the very process of cultural transmission. This keeps the system open, but it does not guarantee anything. God is not the ground of being in this account, but the name (of) "God" is one of the most evocative effects of the quasi-system. To be loyal to the unconditional in this account means to "crucify" not only the Supreme Being but also the ground of being—as well as the God beyond being of mystical theology. If God is not the depths of being (*ousia*), neither is God the height of the *hyperousios.* The movement of classical apophatic theology is directed toward safeguarding the eminence of the God beyond being, inscribing a zone of absolute respect around the God beyond God, and the silence it observes about God is the silence of praise for God in the highest (edifying apophatics).

But in deconstruction the name (of) "God" is a word of elemental suggestiveness and promise, which cannot be protected from posing a maximum threat (anxious apophatics). God is love but also one of our best alibis for murder. God is not a transcendental signified residing beyond the constructions of culture but an effect issuing from its complex networks, which expose the culture to an unforeseeable future. That is why Derrida describes several voices, several tropics of nonknowing, including a nonknowing that is not praising anything, which is a genuine confession of *really not knowing* what is what, something that he compares not to *ta agathon*, the Good, the God beyond being, but to the *khora*, the elemental spacing in which things are inscribed.[15]

A THEOLOGY OF PERHAPS

What then can we say about God? The name of God is the name of the unconditional, although the unconditional cannot be confined to God. Then what is the unconditional? Not a *what* and not something that *is* at all, not the being of what is, not the beyond-being of the God without being—but something that *calls*, like justice in itself, *if there is such a thing*, which of course there is not, since whatever *is* exists under determinate conditions in space and time. Justice is not deconstructible not because it is an eternal being but because it *calls* for being, calls for justice to be done. Justice does not enjoy being (*être*) but trembles in the winds of may-being (*peut-être*) because justice may or may not be done. The worst things, the most awful revenge, are done in the name of justice, or God, or democracy, or even, God help us, peace and love. That is the way the name of God, of any undeconstructible, works in deconstruction; it is an opening, a possibility, not a garden-variety possibility but the possibility of the impossible. What we learn from Schelling's analysis of Satan is that Satan is not somebody, which is piety's way of representing him, but the principle of the possible, of the vertigo of possibility (Kierkegaard), like Sartre's example of someone who has led a life of exemplary virtue contemplating how easy it would be to commit the worst evil. What really preserves the unconditionality of God is to keep God free of being, not because there is anything wrong with being, not because being is not good, but because the name of God calls being to becoming better even as it exposes us to the risk that we will make things worse. In deconstruction we avoid the blasphemy and the mythology, just as Tillich demands, but we also avoid the ontology, which is where Derrida parts ways with Tillich.

God insists, but God does not exist.[16] As soon as God is installed in being as the Supreme Being, a person who knows and wills, whose honor and glory can be offended, an economy of rewards and punishments is likewise installed and the unconditional is compromised. But if the unconditional cannot be contained by theism, neither can it be contained by panentheism, which I think is a lovely story, as far as it goes, but one that must yield to a still larger one, at which point theopoetics expands into cosmo-theopoetics.[17] I love the story of *natura naturans* naturing into *natura naturata*, the splendid effulgence of the natural world around us from the ground of the divine being into the glory of the world. Far be it from me to deny seeing God in a sunflower. But I think we need to add to this story the permanent possibility of *natura de-naturata*, the completely denatured world. That is what would result if, as a good many scientists think today, the universe, having begun in a point of infinite concentration, is expanding at an increasingly rapid rate of acceleration into entropic dissipation—oblivion and nonbeing. That, of course, is not an immediate *problem*, but it is ingredient in a cosmic *mystery*, to which I return later (chapters 14–15).

By depriving the unconditional of the power of being, we reduce it to its powers of persuasion. Without power, without sovereignty, its voice ever soft and low, it comes gently soliciting, on the wings of angels, luring, calling for a response. It offers no assurances, cannot guarantee a thing, cannot promise a reward. It speaks in dulcet tones of something coming, something of a messianic nature, something we hope and pray for but cannot quite say or foresee. For Hegel, Schelling, and even Tillich, the "death of God" in any radical ontological sense makes no sense. Death comes to individual beings, removing them from the scene of history as easily as their birth has escorted them onto it, but death never touches the absolute Spirit or Being itself. But in deconstruction, everything, including being, God, and spirit, is exposed to death. God is mortal, but mortals are very much alive, and in a theology of the perhaps, the task is to make the insistence of God come true, to make God happen in the world, to be the body of the life of God, world with or without end.

In this theology of the unconditional, the *courage to be* falls on me, in the accusative, *me voici*, and on us, in the collective. The ground of courage, like the ground of faith and hope and love, is a groundless one, not the ground of being but the open-ended structure of temporality—that the future is always better, not because it *is* but because that is our hope and faith. If the temporality of our lives does not give us courage ontologically, it at least encourages us to have courage messianically, encourages us to hope and have faith, encourages us to be rather than not. So it is a hope against hope, a hope in the impossible, an affirmation of the possibility of the impossible, which I submit is the purest affirmation of the unconditional of which we are capable. The more *grounds* we have for faith and hope, the less faith and hope are *required* and the more they look like reasonable expectations. It takes courage, and faith and hope and love, to call for the coming of what we cannot see coming, to answer a call we have hardly heard, to expose the present to a future that risks turning into a disaster.

TILLICH KNOWS ALL THIS

I am not trying to mount a critique of Tillich but to open, or rather reopen, Tillich to something I think Tillich already knows, almost. A deconstruction is not a drive-by shooting but a close reading, one that finds the text at certain points at odds with itself or finds it no longer remembers or has suppressed what it once knew. That is why, before I conclude, I have to point out that Derrida has nothing on Tillich, that he has not said something that Tillich has not already said and already knew, at least once before, at least in his own way, even if, later on, after arriving in New York City, it was to a certain extent occluded. We must be wary of self-congratulation about our own conduct today—about the environment, for example, and the racism and sexism all around us today—when we criticize Tillich, as we should, for being blind to the racism and sexism of the United States he found upon his arrival. Without discounting that criticism, it is interesting to see that while his American period was marked by the language of ontology, his most politically sensitive work in Germany, at the advent of the Third Reich, adopted the language of eschatology, as George Pattison argued.[18]

I refer to *The Socialist Decision*, in which the language of *being* is held suspect, cast as conservative, preoccupied with the past—make America/*Deutschland* great *again*—and this in contrast with the language of *expectation*, the prophetic language of the Bible, which is turned to the future, which does not exist ("there are no democrats"). So the highly eschatological terms of Tillich's work written in the shadow of National Socialism stand in contrast to the ontological terms in which his later writings are cast. In *The Socialist Decision*, being is linked with *Blut und Boden* and longing to return to the primeval, to the lost origin.

In his critique of "Romantic conservativism," Tillich, who knew nothing of the turn the later Heidegger was taking at that very moment, almost perfectly identifies the way Heidegger would outfit his *Seinsdenken* to accommodate what he notoriously called the inner truth and greatness of National Socialism. If, in the later writings, the unconditional takes the form of the ground of being, in the early writings, it takes an eschatological form as the unconditional demand for justice. The God of the prophets is the God of history, and history is directed at the future, at the promise, not the primitive origin.

The idea there is not to get back in touch with the ground of Being (by "overcoming estrangement") but to make ready for the coming of something very strange, not to discover oneself but to open oneself to something quite undiscovered, quite other. In other words, if we "distinguish two ways of approaching God: the way of overcoming estrangement and the way of meeting a stranger," in *The Socialist Decision*, he held a position that was the perfect opposite of the famous opening sentence of the "Two Types of Philosophy of Religion."[19] In eschatology, all things are made new and history is opened to the future, which Tillich describes as a discontinuous break with the present, an inbreaking of something that eye has not seen nor ear heard. Socialism, left to itself as a work of reason, without the prophets, is insufficient to the task. In a remarkable text, Tillich writes: "Insofar as expectation has a prophetic character, it transcends the known, the calculable, the manipulable aspects of being. It points to a new creation, something 'wholly other.' Insofar as expectation has a rational character, it remains within the dimensions of the knowable. Here, too, it looks for something 'other,' but not 'wholly other,' since that which is coming stands in direct continuity with what is present now. Prophetic expectation is transcendent; rational expectation is immanent."[20]

This position is strikingly similar to Derrida's messianic hope, or desire beyond desire, which distinguishes between the coming of the possible—of the calculable and foreseeable, which Derrida calls the future present—and the messianic affirmation of the impossible—of the incalculable and unforeseeable, which he calls the absolute future and the wholly other. Tillich's eschatological advent sounds a very great deal like Derrida's messianic event, where God brings about a radically new being. The kingdom of God is not behind us, already possessed in an ancient origin from which we have become estranged, but up ahead, a radical *novum*, a stranger, *tout autre*, in a prophetic time, futural and unanticipatable. The past—is Tillich thinking of Verdun?—is not renewed but wiped away, and all things are made new. "Behold I am doing a new thing" (Isa 43:19). The new wine bursts the old skins. The emphasis falls not on the eternal and the ontological ground, on the always already (*immer schon*), but on the futural and eschatological.

Was the influence of Schelling attenuated over the years of his life in the United States? His early position is closer to the abyss that disturbs and precedes the life of God in Schelling and Boehme, where being is exposed to nonbeing, engaged in a strife with the powers of the abyss, than to the later view, in which God has taken this nothingness into himself and submitted nonbeing to Being, which sounds more like Hegel. Radicalizing Tillich means rereading Tillich in terms of Schelling, where the abyss precedes God, exposing God to an underside that God has to keep in check. Tillich has incorporated the unruly ground in Schelling and Boehme that looks the "problem of evil" in the eye by taking it all the way back to God and finding not only a backside in God, as Luther did, but an underside in the depths of the divine being. But if we are to take this strife seriously, as Schelling insisted about the temptations of Jesus by Satan, we must stay open to the risk—this was Habermas's point—that things will not end well, that the unruly forces will rule, which might not be far from what the physicists are currently predicting about history of the universe.

Tillich knows all this, in his own way. The position, I think, needs only to be repositioned. To be absolutely loyal to the unconditional, not only must the ontological become eschatological, but the eschatological must become hauntological. The ground of being becomes an event. That is the sum of my argument. The unconditional is not the ground of the promise; it *is* the promise, a "perhaps," a hope against hope.

ON BEING UNCONDITIONALLY LOYAL TO THE UNCONDITIONAL: THE PARADOX OF MATTHEW 25

The final turn of the screw in my argument is to show that the unconditional is not only *possible* without such sovereignty but *only possible* without such sovereignty. The unconditional is without sovereignty—*or it is not unconditional at all!* Leading an unconditional life is only possible under the condition that the call is deprived of being and reduced to the call for being. For the call, to be is to call for being. The call does not have being and does not rest on the ground of being; being is what is called for. For the call to be unconditional, it cannot be empowered or enforced by existence; it belongs to the order of insistence, of the call for existence.

The unconditionality of the call is annulled if it is taken as the work of an Unconditional Being, a Supreme Being, handing out rewards and punishments, a terrifying Judge in the Sky appearing in the end times to sort out the sheep from the goats. The paradox of Matthew 25 is the merciless setting within which the works of mercy are framed there. The powerless power of the core story is abolished by the framing of the story—maybe the work of some unknown redactor reworking a core story—within the overwhelming power of the coming Son of man, into which Yeshua the healer and exorcist who was crucified for his troubles was transformed by the authors of the gospels. Living an unconditional life means that we are always in the situation of the righteous, asking, "Lord, when was it that we saw you hungry and gave you food, or thirsty and gave you something to drink? And when was it that we saw you a stranger and welcomed you, or naked and gave you clothing? And when was it that we saw you sick or in prison and visited you?" (Matt. 25:37–39). This is a *structural* situation, a structural unknowability (apophatics), by which I mean that the unknowability is the condition of possibility of the works and that this unknowability goes all the way down. It is not like a secret that somebody knows and can then reveal to us at a later time. It is not only that *we did not know* the king's reply, "Truly I tell you, just as you did it to one of the least of these who are members of my family, you did it to me" (25:40), but *if we did*, then the whole thing would be annulled. For that would mean that we had struck gold, that our mercifulness merits us untold rewards—and now, having read this text, we know that, and we cannot unring that bell.

The point is that the "kingdom of God" does not come as a *reward* for the works of mercy; the kingdom of God *is* the works of mercy. The mark of God, the mark of the "kingdom of God," of the event that takes place in and under the name (of) "God," is upon the face of the hungry and the thirsty, the imprisoned, the naked, and the stranger, from whose very bodies the call is called, *without further ado*. That is what God does—or better, what gets done in the name (of) "God." The spectrality of God means that the name of God is the name of a call *before* being, a call *for* being, of an insistence, a solicitation, an invitation—to feed the hungry, to greet the stranger, tout court, without condition, without why, *unconditionally*. The unconditional itself, if there is a thing, does not reign or rule with the power of terrestrial or celestial royalties who belong to the order of being but with an insistence that intervenes in the world and calls for mercy. This is a kingdom without a king, ruled by a sovereign without sovereignty, without power or authority, a kingdom that overturns, inverts, or subverts the kind of kingdom we expect of kings, a kingdom found in messianic space and time.²¹ The kingdom of God is the name of an *unconditional insistence* for which *we* are expected to supply the *existence*. *We* are the messianic generation, Walter Benjamin says, the ones the dead have been waiting for. We are asked to accept an unconditional *respons*ibility, we who must have the courage to be, to provide for the existence of what insists. The real *correlation* is between the unconditional call without sovereignty and the unconditional response made without something up our sleeve.

It is necessary to preserve the call from the conditions of existence, which have the coercive force of law. Atheism about the God who is subjected to the *conditions of existence* is not the end of theology but the beginning of another and *more unconditional* theology of what Heidegger calls, in that famous text, the "truly divine God" (*der göttliche Gott*),²² a theopoetics of the unconditional call that goes under the name (of) "God." The call calls; it gets itself called, *in the middle voice*, without guarantees, without a superbeing coming on a cloud or the ground of being emerging from below to hold it up. What get itself called, feed the hungry, comes without the least assurance that we will later on enjoy a heavenly banquet. The call calls without promises, without threats.

The call calls without assurances that there is anything in it for us, without why or warranty, without being or sovereign power, without conditions, unconditionally. Period! Enough said. That is the radical apophasis of a radical theology, the cross on which theology is crucified, stripped of the garments of being, girded with nothing but itself, a radical *theologia crucis*.²³

TWELVE

THE DEVIL IS IN THE DISSEMINATION

IN THIS PROJECT OF RETHINKING the apophatic imagination, I have called upon Derrida to serve as a devilish knight of faith, a radical *advocatus diaboli*, whose appointed task is to relieve the apophatic of any suggestion of esoteric knowledge, metaphysical foundationalism, theo-anthropocentrism, or religious edification that might be suggested by speaking of the "dark ground" or "concealed depths."

DISSEMINATION AND APPROPRIATION

What distinguishes Derrida from everything that has gone before him in the story I am telling is that here we first come face-to-face with the facelessness of the *posthuman*. I have, in the past, spent no little time and trouble rebutting the notion that Derrida is a relativist or an irrationalist, but I also want to avoid domesticating Derrida and making *différance* and dissemination fit for polite seminar/seminary society. Derrida's differences with the classical metaphysical tradition start with *différance*, his (in)famous notation signifying linguistic difference, which takes its point of departure from de Saussure on the differential spacing and timing that are productive of linguistic effects. Ring/king/

sing, *moi/roi/loi, der/die/das* are significant just in virtue of the discernible differences, phonic or graphic, internal to their respective linguistic systems. *Différance* is central to his critique of "humanism," which shocks traditional ears because it displaces the purely *human* speaker by introducing an *impersonal*, anonymous structure. Instead of an inner self outwardly expressing inner thoughts, Derrida posits an "it," an anonymous, differential, machinelike operation. In contrast, Tillich's "ground of being" is still quite traditional. Tillich's theonomy is meant to displace human autonomy but not to displace the human itself. On the contrary, it locates the true place of the human in the ground of being as its *pre*personal foundation (potency, power). When Tillich says God is not an alien being but we are alienated from God, that is a logic of the appropriation and alienation of our genuine humanity. Just where *différance* bedevils humanism, the ground of being grounds the human in the divine.

Différance is not a mediating moment in an economy of unity, not a stage through which unity passes on the way to returning to itself enriched and diversified by difference. *Différance* is not aimed at some later reconciliation or higher unification. Unity is an effect of *différance*, the way a unity of meaning is produced by the repetition of signifiers. *Différance* is not the ground of being or of language; it is an impersonal, nonliving, even machinelike or technological medium, an anonymous field in which "meaning"—along with "unity," "truth," "being," "presence," and so forth—is constituted as an *effect*. Presence is a differential effect produced by repetition, by representation. Representation is the production, not the *re*production of presence. Repetition repeats forward, producing what it repeats.[1] So there is a kind of death (technological machine) at the heart of life (culture). Schelling broke down the binary opposition of spirit and nature, but Derrida goes a step further and takes on any binary opposition—of living and nonliving, human and nonhuman, life and death, nature and machine—because every opposition, binary or not, is a function of differential difference. I hasten to add that Derrida is not engaged in a modernist, reductionistic *critique* but a deconstructive *dissemination* of assured, clear-cut, hard-and-fast distinctions, which displaces and spooks them. His love of "margins" gives Tillich's favorite metaphor of "borders" even more bite.

Derrida describes dissemination by distinguishing it from "polysemy," a term used by Paul Ricoeur to account for the "excess" or plurality of meanings.[2] In polysemy, every new metaphoric use or innovation on a word can be appropriated as an extension into an enlarged meaning, becoming part of its ever-expanding range. Polysemy diversifies but never destroys the unity of meaning, working in a way that is comparable to analogy in Aquinas, dialectics in German idealism, and symbol in Tillich. The excess of dissemination, by contrast, is an excess *outside* the order of meaning, in virtue of an *epochē* of meaning itself, which allows for the unregulated play of *textual* effects, both phonic and graphic, like spacings, rhythms, diacritical markings, textual corruptions, interruptions, copyist errors, caesuras, palimpsests, puns even multilingual puns, hyphenations, homonyms, acronyms, chance convergences, and collisions. The effects of dissemination cannot be gathered together by analogy, dialectics, metaphorics, or symbolics—by any principle of unification. They are not attributed to the creative imagination of the author but are functions of the impersonal structure of *textuality*. As they are not produced by the conscious life of the authors, they do not arise from their unconscious; they are not explained by the public life of the authors or by their secret life, all of which are matters of meaning and life, of psychology and biography.

Both the analogy of being in Aquinas (theism) and the Spirit in Hegel, Schelling, and Tillich (panentheism) belong to the order of polysemy, of *unity-in-difference*. Panentheism, God in all and all in God, is modeled on the circulatory order of organic life and creative imagination marking both human and divine being. What is going on in Aquinas, Hegel, Schelling, and Tillich belongs to the sphere of meaning and life, being and truth—to the lifeworld, phenomenality. Deconstruction, by contrast, if I may be a bit hyperbolic, deals in *death*, a structural death, not only with the death of the author but a prior systemic (or quasi-systemic) play (or network) of lifeless traces emblematized by the coinage *différance*, a technical system for producing the differential effects, an eerie or spooky nonword for how we do things with words.

The hermeneutic demand is to put our own presuppositions in question by exposing them to the risk of an intersubjective conversation in which somebody says something about something to someone else. In deconstruction the subject is exposed not to other subjects but to a presubjective, impersonal, anonymous, quasi-transcendental field. In hermeneutics, somebody is having a conversation; in deconstruction, *différance* is not a somebody. The *personal* and the *interpersonal* are *effects* of *impersonal* forces—one might even say of cold dead forces, of a machine for making meaning—making for a cold hermeneutics and a phenomenology not of the lifeworld but of the world shadowed forth by the nonliving trace. That also explains Derrida's interest in animals, where the play of traces, of meaning-like and conversation-like phenomena, are found in a *nonhuman* sphere. Dissemination delimits meaning by way of exposing it to a spooky randomness, errancy, and chance. *Différance* is why a chimpanzee working at a keyboard long enough could eventually hit upon something sensible, true, funny, or even "clever," where nothing depended upon the intention of the author. Polysemy is the plurality of meaning, but dissemination does not *mean*; dissemination spooks meaning.

The pivotal term is *appropriation*, which means to own it, to make it one's own. Polysemy is distinguished from dissemination as the appropriable from the inappropriable. The history of the Spirit in German idealism and Gadamer's "history of effects" forged by a "classic" are alike the history of the appropriation—that is, the endless (but ultimately unitary) interpretation and application of a text, an artwork, a law, a tradition. That is polysemy. Dissemination, by contrast, concerns the *inappropriable as such*—random play, errancy, chance effects that cannot *in principle* be appropriated, a *loss* that cannot be made to make a contribution to the cause, a randomness that cannot be gathered into a unity of meaning, either dialectical, analogical, or symbolic unity. I say "in principle" because, in fact, some disseminative effects can be appropriated. A random typo can sometimes be turned into a brilliant pun if we are lucky, and psychoanalysts earn a good living on Freudian slips.

BARBARIAN HERMENEUTICS, *DESTINERRANCE*, AND THE LOGIC OF RUINS

Dissemination is a transgression. It would be rejected by Aquinas's theory of analogy as equivocacy and by Hegel's *Vernunft* as irrational, and it would offend Schelling's vitalism and panpsychism. Nonetheless, this transgression shows up in the playful way that Eckhart could take up the parables and especially when he plays with the vagaries of his German language,[3] and it also appears in Schelling's notion of a breached, ruptured, and ecstatic reason—of the "barbarian" principle, which cannot be appropriated by reason, cannot be civilized. Here reason loses the good manners of a seminar or seminary conversation and things get irreducibly unruly and resist being *productive*, enlisted in the economy of reason. In no case is the idea to reduce everything to chaos, of course, but to introduce an element of *irreducible unruliness* into every rule, which leaves things open ended and at risk. In no case, too, I should add, does speaking of the "barbarian" principle mean to condone barbaric cruelty; it does not mean to pass over Auschwitz lightly. Just so, Schelling's interest in Satan as philosophical principle has nothing to do with encouraging

Satanic cults or diabolical cruelty. So we should not be too casual in using this language.

For the conservative side of Schelling, dialectics is an economy. The second potency is productive: it advances the cause of the first potency, putting it to a test that draws it out of its self-centeredness, trying to be both drunk and sober at the same time. Edward Beach nicely contrasts the dialectical logic of reconciling *Aufhebung* in Hegel with the dialectic of productivity in Schelling, but to both of these we would contrast the differential play of dissemination, which is neither an *Aufhebung* nor productive work.[4] It is not a logic unless we want to count *ruinology* as a logic. Dissemination implies loss, debris, detritus, *ruins*. Dissemination concerns the *structurally* inappropriable, a limit to meaning, not the incorporation of new meanings, as with polysemy. The "absolute secret" in Derrida is in principle inappropriable, structurally inoperative, useless; it is not somebody hiding something from us. Dissemination is not a dispersal contained within the unity of understanding or the occasion of a new understanding but the dispersal of understanding; it is structurally uncivil. Dissemination is a barbarian principle that cannot be civilized by the laws of analogy, dialectics, symbolics, or polysemy. We can distinguish two infinities here, the infinity of inexhaustible meaning and truth (appropriation) and what we might call in Derrida the infinity of endless drift (dissemination). The drift built into dissemination is Derrida's version of principle B, the principle of the stray, of what Derrida himself calls errancy (*errance*). Errancy is not just an error or a mistake but a *structural* error, not an error someone commits but the *rule* of errancy. Derrida is translating what Heidegger called *die Irre* or *Irrtum*, the kingdom of error, the reign or rule of error, like the rule of "sin" in Paul's letters, the structural feature or principle of going astray, which for Heidegger is rooted in the *lethe* lying at the heart of the *aletheia*-process, which inevitably skews the result.[5]

Once again, to be clear, Derrida is *not* saying that everything inevitably falls into error and confusion, no more than Schelling said the principle B, or the philosophical meaning of Satan, is evil itself. They both describe a *structural feature*, meaning built right in, a principle or possibility or tendency to drift, to destabilize, to deflect or distort things, to overflow their boundaries. This drift is sometimes productive and sometimes not, which comes down to taking the notion of chance in earnest. Not everything can be saved, recuperated, appropriated, or put to good use. Sometimes God just writes with crooked lines, period! In contrast to a teleological or eschatological concept of history, to a history guided toward its destiny by the hidden hand of the Creator or the Concept, of the Revolution or the Market, Derrida would of speak of *destinerrance*, the lack of assured destination, the structural tendency that history will go astray, that history may not end well, that the event may eventuate in catastrophe, that nobody is at the wheel.[6]

To his credit, Tillich, a witness to the atrocities of Verdun, put some light between himself and German idealism on this point. Unlike Hegel, who thought that Reason was making its cunning way to consummation in history, Tillich has a weaker theory of providence, guided by his rejection of supernaturalism as some supervening power intervening upon nature and history to make things right.[7] On this point, Tillich was being more faithful to Schelling than Schelling was to himself, because Schelling should have said that if history is the history of real freedom in contest with the powers of the abyss, who knows what will happen next, which is pretty much what he thought in the *Freedom* essay. But in the 1840s, he backed off from this and held, with perfect piety and royal approval, that history is marching ahead into the age of the Spirit where God will be all in all (instead of saying what is coming looks very spooky). Tillich, by contrast, said that providence is a "paradox" because we maintain this faith "in spite of" its contradiction in reality, where evil and distress are everywhere. Christ has redeemed all creation, but the rich keep getting richer and the ecology is going to hell. So providence is basically a figure of *faith* in the vision that being will prevail over the forces of nonbeing, of *hope* that the inextinguishable power of being and God prevails over the powers of darkness, which give us the courage to be. But unlike philosophical teleologists like Hegel and Marx, and unlike Christian eschatologists, nothing is guaranteed. There is no place where we can buy "insurance" for the ground of being against the victory of evil and insure a good outcome, which is Habermas's critique of Schelling.

Die Irre, destinerrance, the paradox, the barbarian principle, dissemination, all of this scandalous language points us back to a new revised but definitely not standard version of Paul's letters, where we do not know the outcome of Christ's battle with the powers and principalities, a battle scene that at the least illustrates, if it is not actually the source of, Schelling's notion of the principle B, the dark powers that actively strive against the light. This power, Schelling says, is not evil itself, which is Manicheanism, but the *possibility* of evil, which is the condition of freedom, the possibility of what ought not to be. This represents an uncertainty, an indeterminism, an undecidability, a "maybe" or "perhaps" that Nietzsche called the "dangerous perhaps." But this threat is *also* the possibility of novelty and innovation, of creation and production, of a creative destruction that Derrida would call the incoming of the event. The promise and the threat are the same thing viewed from different sides. That is why Schelling and Tillich spoke of the "ambiguity" of the demonic and why Derrida speaks of its undecidability.[8] To deconstruct something is not to destroy it but to expose it to its future, which can turn out for the better unless it is for the worse. Either way, creation and innovation are possible only under the very conditions that expose them to corruption and destruction, which is something of an axiom in deconstruction, if not its definition, if it had one. In Schelling, in Tillich, in radical apophatic theology, the totality of these competing possibilities is clustered under and concentrated in the name of "God," like a metonym, and the radicality of the apophatic imagination is to do no injury to this contest with some kind of supernatural guarantee that in the end, all things work unto good.

What interests me is the radical side of Schelling and Tillich, which is the side that allows the transgression, the anarchy of dissemination into the sanctuary of the divine being—where the Son may choose not to hand over the world to his Father, where the unruly powers of the ground may rule, the "barbarian" side may overrun the rule of Rome, and the gathering *legein* of the Logos may be overtaken by dispersal. For Derrida, dissemination is something of a *diabolos,* its forces throwing obstacles (*dia* + *ballein*) in the way of unity, providing for a devilish hermeneutics, with no guarantees. Dissemination belongs to the underside of the Holy, the demonic side, where it threatens us with chaos and destruction. The border between classical theology and radical apophatics is whether and to what extent things are at risk. In Luther, and this is picked up by Schelling, Satan is a figure of God, who wants to put our obedience to the test. The test of radial apophatic theology is the degree to which God, too, is put to the test, is genuinely put at risk.

My idea is to dislodge the apophatic imagination from the piety of its classical logic and bedevil it with a devilish hermeneutics, whence my regular recourse to Derrida's quip, the devil in his eye, that what he offers is not ontology but hauntology—the sort of thing for which he (like Kierkegaard) was sometimes caricaturized as a joker. My idea is to extricate the figure of depth, which I love, from the axiomatics of supernaturalism and metaphysics. If I were a Platonist, I would say I never met anyone who managed to escape the cave, who does not see things darkly as in a mirror. When Schelling distinguished empirical history from deep history, he meant reading history as the unfolding of the Absolute Spirit, whereas if I speak of a deep history, I mean *the* meaning of history, *s'il y en a*, is over my head. I do not know what is going to happen next. I do not oppose the deep and stand with the superficial, except rhetorically—in deconstruction, this is called a "strategic reversal"—when it serves the purpose of mocking the pretense of those who claim to know what is going on. This is the course adopted by Kierkegaard's pseudonyms, whose humor is their way of being deadly serious about the transcendence of God over all things, especially over oversized Hegelian heads. I am like Johannes Climacus saying he has no gigantic head for world history. My idea is to displace the metaphysics of the deep with a poetics of the deep, which means I do not know in any deep way who I am or what being means, although I have invested a lifetime of study in the search. I love the unnerving ruminations of Luther on the *Deus absconditus* but not the Augustinian dualism in which it is ensconced. I love the explorations of the concealed depths, the barbarian principle in Schelling and the ground of being in Tillich, but not the German idealist metaphysics of the *Geist* with which they are entangled. I love *Gelassenheit*, which is the mystical sense of life in Meister Eckhart, but not the Neoplatonic metaphysics of the One with which he melded it.

Instead of equipping the apophatic with a Neoplatonic logic, I submit it to an inverse, perverse, or reverse logic, a contrarian logic, as in Luther's theology of the cross, which operates *sub contraria specie*, under the opposite look. The theologians of glory, he says, call a good thing—insecurity and risk—bad and a bad thing—like ease and foundations—good.[9] My model is Johannes Climacus musing in Frederiksberg Garden: since everyone is making things easy, my task is to make them difficult.

PART THREE

THE POSTHUMAN IMAGINARY

THIRTEEN

ANGELOLOGY—POSTHUMAN STYLE

Would You Rather Be a Cyborg, a Posthuman, or an Angel?

WELCOME TO THE POSTHUMAN IMAGINARY

In what follows (part 3), we encounter the unfolding of the apophatic imagination in its eeriest form, in the era of the posthuman, to which Derrida was our first introduction. Instead of inner self or soul expressing itself outwardly in words, which is the classical humanist model of language, Derrida invoked *différance*, a system of coded sign making. Instead of Aristotle's "rational animal," Derrida identifies an impersonal, nonliving, *machinelike technology* at the heart of reason. Today we know that impersonal information systems are not confined to the "rational" in Aristotle's definition but also belong to the "animal," the living body, which is written in the language of DNA and rDNA code. Information is ubiquitous; it goes all the way down. It extends across the divide between human and nonhuman, living and nonliving, matter and spirit, the universe *itself* being a vast information system (ecosystems, planetary systems, etc.). When the ground beneath these distinctions begins to tremble, we know we have entered a spooky posthuman zone.

In this chapter I take my point of departure from the curious and telling link between the present age of unnerving advances in the information technologies and medieval angelology, which makes for an uncanny *angelology* posthuman style. In the next chapter, I take up a cosmic spectrality, the haunting prospect that the universe may be headed for oblivion, meaning that cosmology might indeed be a *ruinology*, which dramatically reframes the apophatic sense of life in cosmic terms. The final step is to demonstrate that the upshot of this ruinology is not nihilism or despair but what I describe as a radical *axiology*, where what matters is not how it ends, since it might all end in ruins, and not whether what we are doing is "worth it," since it may not pay a return. What matters is whether it is worthy of us and whether we are making ourselves worthy of what is happening to us, whether or not it all ends well, since it might not.

WOULD YOU RATHER BE A CYBORG OR A POSTHUMAN?

Derrida's hypothesis some forty years ago—that, in virtue of the new technologies, the future will belong to ghosts—proved prescient. Today more than ever, accelerated by the COVID-19 pandemic, we live in a world of virtual reality, of simulations that look and sound real, spectral effects extending even to the "physical sciences." When Einstein criticized the counterintuitive results of quantum science, he called them "spooky." These contemporary ghostly apparitions are not premodern superstitions but the product of advanced information technologies and the mind-bending results in current physics. They force us to rethink everything. The old materialism is taking a beating. Today, if you want to be a materialist, it has to be a "new materialism," in which the settled distinctions between matter and the immaterial are unsettled. But if theology (like everything else) must be rethought when everything around it resets, then these specters are also the specters of theology. The world in which theology must make its way is haunted by uncanny creatures—electronic machines that converse with us, cyborgs, and posthumans—none of whom were born of Adam and Eve or need to be saved by Jesus. If posthumans are making humans obsolete, what remains of theology?

To see what is going on today under the unsettling name of posthumanism,[1] I adopt the strategy of theologian Jennifer Thweatt-Bates in *Cyborg Selves* of sorting out the difference between the "cyborg" and the "upload," which are, as she argues, two figures of the posthuman around which most of the other possibilities cluster.[2]

CYBORGS

In 1985, Donna Haraway published a watershed paper entitled "A Manifesto for Cyborgs," whose very title sent humanists running for cover.[3] Haraway describes three boundary breakdowns: between the human and the nonhuman, the organism and the machine, and physical and nonphysical. The cyborg, short for cybernetic organism, is a hybrid of the two orders, the natural and the artificial, the biological and the technological, where the borders between the two are broken down and the two become permeable and mutually interactive. Haraway's cyborg is a new, ironic, and blasphemous "myth," an impious and defiant symbol that contests the pious myth of origins that ties women to a natural and pristine order that men are free to transcend and also flouts an ancient taboo against exposing the natural order to impurity and contamination. Her cyborg breaks the mold of essentialism (second-wave feminism); it is a satiric but serious play of deconstructing and reconstructing, which is of political, anthropological, and ontological import. The cyborg is an emblem of the polymorphic, the gender bender, the shape-shifter, the boundary breaker, of nontotalization, of an "infidel heteroglossia" that seeks to "keep ecofeminism and technoscience joined in the flesh." Rejecting human exceptionalism, it embraces kinship with our "companion species," other animals, stressing both our own animality and what is human about them, flagging the harm human animals cause other animals and the planet. The cyborg was not born in the garden of Eden and is not part of the history of salvation. Far from demonizing technology, the cyborg also embraces its "cybernetic" side, interfacing, intersecting with the technological, breaking down human exceptionalism from the side of the nonliving. Taking the human/divine as still another hybridity, the cyborg and the goddess are kin, paired together in a "spiral dance," but even so, as Haraway says in the famous last line, she "would rather be a cyborg than a goddess"—that is, she would rather be a shape-shifting and provisional construction than an ice queen, frozen into a divine and essentialized Woman.

This final sentence is telling and reflects the central thrust of her work in animal rights and ecology. Haraway does not want to become a disembodied angel (a goddess, a pure spirit); her cyborg is irreducibly embodied carnal life. But she also does not want to become the *original* cyborg, which was *not* supposed to be a myth—a cultural and political symbol for postmodernism, postcolonialism, and socialist ecofeminism—but hard science. As Haraway points out, the word was coined in 1960 by scientists working with the United States Air Force to describe technohumans equipped to live in outer space. So Haraway would rather be *her* cyborg not *that* one, a postterrestrial, technologically enhanced macho warrior transcending biological limitations. That *for her* is a myth, an old myth, Irigaray's patriarchal myth of men shaking off their watery origins in the womb and becoming autonomous liberal individuals. The question raised later (chapter 15) is whether Haraway and the theologians who follow her are selling the scientific cyborg short and whether it is in theology's interests to reconsider this position—and this without minimizing the risks, the menace of a Frankensteinian outcome, the utopian/dystopian threat this all poses.

For the hard-line posthumanists, Haraway's cyborg is a half step, satisfied with hybridity with the cybernetic but not invested in following where cybernetics is leading—into advanced techno-human states that tend toward and, at their endpoint, would *transcend biology* itself.[4] For them, transhumanism is not hybridity; it is *enhancement*. It is not ecofeminism; it is set on transcending gender and sexual reproduction. It is not merely postmodern polymorphism; it is posthuman, or at least that is its desire. Viewed thus, posthumanism is the *replacement* of religion. Religion merely fantasizes about "healing" the sick, "exorcizing" evil spirits, and "immortal life," whereas for the transhumanists, a life free of physical and mental illness and even death itself is a matter of hard science and technology. We should not fail to notice the techno-optimism in hard-line posthumanism. Dinosaurs were not replaced with bigger and better dinosaurs. Just so, humans may find ourselves replaced by insects, which preceded us and may very well succeed us in ruling the earth if we are not careful.

Unlike the hard-line posthumanists, theologian Ilia Delio, who sides with the embodied feminist cyborg of Haraway, does not seek a war between posthumanism and religion but a collaboration. AI extends the reach of religion; it does not replace it. Religion does not reject posthumanism; it gives it purpose and direction.[5] For Delio, religion's fate is tied to the sacramental character of the material world and the body signified by the Incarnation. Interestingly, Haraway would agree with this, crediting the Irish Catholicism of her youth with giving her a sense of the "sacramental."[6] So the question of religion and transhumanism comes down to a debate about transcending the biological. We might say the theological cyborg is a cybORG, while the purely scientific one is a CYBorg. Hard-line transhumanists seek ultimately to transcend the biological (upload), whereas cyborg theology remains loyal to the body and the earth and finds transcendence in another way. In this view, the theologians are the materialists and the (hard-line) materialists want to transcend matter. The theologians would rather be cyborgs; the materialists want to live like the angels.

On Delio's view, AI is not the problem and religion is not the solution. It is only the failure of religion *as it presently exists* that tempts us to turn to technology to realize transcendence and only the *misuse* of AI that opposes it to religion. So the two "must find each other for the good of the whole earth."[7] In her view, AI expands religion into something planetary, pushing it beyond its provincialism and individualism, extending the borders of the human community beyond its previous geographical limits. AI enables the religious aspiration for a global community, not simply as a pious figure of speech but based upon advanced electronics. Just so, religion, which she characterizes in the Tillichian terms of matters of ultimate meaning and concern, gives the posthuman project point, purpose, and direction, saving it from its worst and most rationalistic instincts. Religion steers AI away from the radical postbiological aims of the uploaders by respecting the sanctity of the material world and bodily life. If AI is focused on the mind and superintelligence, religion supplies the heart and body.

Delio's project of "re-enchanting of the earth" in the midst of an ecological crisis is inspired by the work of Pierre Teilhard de Chardin, the visionary scientist-theologian-maybe-even-mystic who spoke of a new "religion of the earth." In Teilhard's view, God is immersed in matter as its "inner energy," which is the energy of love driving evolution forward toward planetary convergence. While this sounds like panentheism or maybe panpsychism, Delio holds that it represents dual-aspect monism (mind and matter as different but complementary sides of the same process). Evolution is religion in formation; religion is evolution in its inner formative energy. If advanced technology is itself the latest stage in the history of human evolution, then, Delio holds, AI is quite natural, not really "artificial"; it is quite simply evolution become conscious of itself. While, for hard-line transhumanists, the cyborg model is halfhearted, keeping one foot in the body, so to speak, for Delio, hard-line transhumanists represent a "shallow AI," confined to the technological enhancement and ultimately the transcendence of biological functions, which she opposes to "deep AI," a holistic view of human personhood and sociality that Teilhard calls the "ultrahuman."[8]

Delio's complaint with classical theology centers on its provenance in what she, following Karl Jaspers, called the Axial Age (200 BCE–600 CE), a time when the great philosophical systems and world religions were born as humanity emerged from tribal life into a new sense of self-consciousness and critical rationality, individuality, and autonomy. This encouraged a distinction between human being and the natural world, ultimately leading to the Cartesian polarity of subjectivity and objectivity. But today, religion must rise to the challenge of a *new* axial period, the age of information. Today, we are witness to a growing sense of a collective—AI-assisted, networked, hyperconnected, relational—mind or consciousness that Teilhard called the "noosphere," a divine (and electronic) milieu, envisaged by him as a cosmic person, a global Christ consciousness, a universal humanity united in love and justice. For the hard-line posthumanists, however, it is not Christ who is evolving but Watson, a global superintelligence.[9] In the *new* axial period, religion must reconfigure and acquire a new sensibility, and that means it must shed its ancient metaphysics and its hostility to science and technology, let go of its preoccupation with otherworldly personal salvation and its institutional-doctrinal tribalism, and allow the several world religious and national traditions to converge in a new collective consciousness. AI, in turn, needs to hear the demands of community, love, and justice.

UPLOADING

The difference between the cyborg and the hard-line posthumanists turns on the ultimate status of *biological* life. A lot of older people walking around today are low-grade starter cyborgs—with titanium joint replacements, silicone lenses in their eyes, and porcelain teeth. These artificial replacement parts are not just "mine"; they are, so to speak, *me*. The "so to speak" signals a Haraway border breakdown. But these enhancements are becoming increasingly sophisticated, which is nicely illustrated by avant-garde theorist Mark C. Taylor.[10] Taylor, who suffers from type 1 diabetes, tells of being kept alive by what is, in effect, an artificial pancreas. This is a wearable device affixed to his belt "whose brain interacts *on its own* with continuously updated data transmitted to it by a glucose monitor with implanted sensors" where data are "uploaded to the cloud where they can be seen by my doctor, the pump and monitor manufacturers, and I don't know who else." Taylor describes "a technological revolution that raises profound questions about what was once known as human being. Where does my body begin? Where does it end? What is natural? What is artificial? Who owns my pancreas and its data?" He posits an internet of "smart things," interlinked electronic devices like smartphones and global positioning and home security systems, and an internet of "smart bodies," which we see in his AI-controlled insulin pump and comparable devices like implanted pacemakers and brain chips linked to the internet. These technologically "extended bodies and extended minds" make up what he calls "intervolution," a surrounding network of "superorganisms"—bodies melded with prostheses and implants communicating with other living bodies through the cloud—all part of a network of AI systems that can and in many ways already do outsmart us. Taylor says he has become "a node in this network of networks," an "expression of an intelligence that is neither simply natural nor merely artificial ... that will shape everything and everyone for a long, long while to come."

The radical transhumanist urges us to *imagine*—this is an imaginary, a dream, a *desire*—just how far this can go. What *limit* is there *in principle* to the development of artificial joints and organs and their integration with AI? Indeed, with the new CRISPR technology, science can "edit" the genetic composition of the body so that, in principle, we might never develop cataracts or arthritic limbs or diseased teeth and organs to begin with. At that point, the biology and the technology are pretty much identical because when *we* are *recoding* the *biology*, biology is recoding itself. Why, *in principle*, can we not engineer out sickness and disease, including the breakdown in telomeres that seems to be the basis of aging itself? For transhumanists, "aging is a disease" to be cured,[11] making use of advanced nanotechnology, genetic engineering, psychopharmacology, neural interfaces, wearable computers, and cognitive techniques.[12] For the cyborg theologians, mortality is part of the human condition, not a curable disease. That is the (organic) heart of the difference between the Haraway cyborg and posthumanism. *Her* cyborg is a subversive trope, a figure for living with contradictions, with a nature/culture mix, which *embraces mortality* as the *condition of life* and even allows an *opening for religion*.[13]

But there is one organ that gives everyone pause. Can AI science produce a machine that emulates or reproduces the human brain (mind, us!)? Today, we are "joined at the hip," if I may say so, to our electronic devices, but imagine implanting miniaturized chips that interface with the brain so that the entire internet would be at our disposal simply by directing our attention to it. We might also find a way to genetically engineer the brain, not only to correct or eliminate organic defects and brain disease but also to produce superintelligent beings. The *ultimate* step is this. Instead of implanting a link to the internet in the brain, transplant the brain to the internet—that is, "upload" the brain to a computer, where it *can live like the angels*, on the "cloud." This project is most prominently associated with Hans Moravec and Ray Kurzweil, who call it "strong AI," as opposed to the cyborg, which by comparison is an antecedent and, as it were, a half-hearted figure. They think that at some point—they estimate the 2040s—called the "Singularity," the technology will be available to carry this out.[14] (That is about the same time that the really punishing effects of climate change will set in. Remember the dinosaurs.) Life on the cloud is economical, relieved of the cost of food, shelter, and clothing. Travel is fast and efficient, visiting anywhere on the World Wide Web as swiftly as our electrons could carry us. While virtual experience would be vastly enhanced, we could occasionally "rent" a robot body ("downloading") to move about in physical space. We will not need to sleep, will not be tormented by an unconscious, and will have no racial or ethnic identity or gender to fight over. Overcoming death would then be mostly a matter of having the prudence to store backup copies of ourselves, like the "resurrection ships" in *Battlestar Galactica*. The *scientific cyborg* technologically enhances our biological bodies to enable extraterrestrial life and space travel. The *transhumanists* continue this technological enhancement as far as possible in *transition* to an entirely *posthuman* life, perhaps at some point no longer recognizably human, which in the strongest sense is *postbiological*.

To say the least, the upload is a controversial suggestion. It assumes consciousness to be a neurological pattern, a purely formal information system, in which the material substrate is replaceable, rather the way the rules of chess hold whether the pieces are made of wood, ivory, or pixels. Instead of "thinking meat"—the organic brain—is a substrate of silicon or perhaps some even more suitable medium still in the planning stages. Apart from the immense technological challenges (there are about a hundred billion neurons), there are ethical and political ones. Who would have access to these advancements? How might intervening upon the random distribution of genetic materials go wrong? Remember the dinosaurs. Remember Mary Shelley's *Frankenstein*. Apart from all these problems, there are conceptual ones. What guarantees that the uploaded information system would be *self-conscious*? If it is, does the "upload" represent a *"cut* and paste," where the original brain is destroyed? That would make it easier to understand, because if it is a *"copy* and paste," then which version is *me*? The biological me would still be stuck in my biological body and would consider the upload a failure while the disembodied me would be body-free and would consider the upload a success. Are these the same me? Who am I? *Quaestio mihi magna factus sum*—Have I ever!

"AN INTELLIGENCE NEITHER SIMPLY NATURAL NOR MERELY ARTIFICIAL"

I am, like Derrida and Haraway, an antiessentialist. Accordingly, I do not think that organic and cybernetic are stable categories to begin with. The concept of hybridity is caught up in the paradox of presupposing and feeding off the binary it sets out to deconstruct. But as Haraway herself points out, in the scientific cyborg project, the body and the machine are treated as *communication systems* in *symbiosis*, not as opposites. The communication sciences and modern biology are translating the world into a problem of *coding*, which maximizes control, in which everything turns on determining the rate, direction, and probability of a flow of information. Biology becomes a reading technology, organisms become information processors, and the mind becomes an artificial intelligence system. Haraway is not saying that technology is destiny, but she is arguing that we need a "fresh analysis."[15] As the problems just noted indicate, we should take responsibility for what we are doing to and with ourselves, our companion species, and our planet. But the point stands that the more we have learned (since 1985) about the biological organism, the more the distinction between the organic and the cybernetic becomes a distinction between two different kinds of informational systems. "Information" is ubiquitous. Today, texts, codes, and programs lie at the heart of the material and biological world. Today, if we think there is an opposition between the "lived body" and information systems, programs, writing, and texts, we are living in the nineteenth century. Our biological bodies are *written* in the code of DNA and rDNA, and the new

CRISPR technology is giving us the means to put out ever-new "editions" of our organic body. The meaning of life is not forty-two; it is the alphabet.

Still more generally, as Delio is arguing, I also do not think the "natural" and the "artificial" are stable categories to begin with. Exactly what is "artificial" about artificial intelligence? Is it not simply the latest stage of human *evolution*? When Aristotle defined human nature as a "rational animal," he was only reporting the state of the art of human beings at the time. He was describing upright biped sentient animals with a capacity for articulate speech and thinking. Two hundred thousand years earlier, no one was around who could answer to that description. With the discovery of the theory of evolution by Darwin, who was *himself* a product of the history of evolution, evolution became *conscious of itself*. Today, evolution is not only conscious of itself but also taking over the controls—for better or for worse. Now, as I have been insisting, there are a number of good reasons to be exceedingly cautious about altering our genetic makeup, but to object that *we* should not interfere with *nature* is not one of them. It makes no sense since we *are* nature in its present stage of evolution. *We* are not "interfering with nature," as if we are alien beings fallen from the sky. We are human nature *naturing*, being human nature. The distinction between nature (*physis, natura*) and art (*techne, ars*) boils down to the distinction between *inherited* nature at any given stage of its development and nature naturing into *new* forms (for better or for worse).

What I called nature naturing, Mark C. Taylor calls an "*intelligence that is neither simply natural nor merely artificial*," which signals the breakdown of this distinction.[16] Natural intelligence is inwardly inhabited by impersonal artifices and artifacts, and artificial intelligence makes use of processes found in nature. That is why, with each passing day, AI is getting unnervingly lifelike. Human thinking is plastic but formalizable up to a point, and artificial intelligence is mechanical but is more and more approaching the plasticity and the flexibility of human intelligence. IBM's Watson is an "expert system," loaded with information that it searches with blinding speed, but "neural networks" are self-correcting systems that detect patterns and learn as they go, just like us![17] Add to that the possibilities that will open up with "quantum" computing and the defenders of "human" intelligence begin more and more to look like the theologians of the "God of the gaps," constantly retrenching, coming up with something that computers *still* can't do—until they can. Given the fragility of this distinction, we could say *either* that there is no such thing as "artificial" intelligence *or* that intelligence has *always* been artificial and we have *never* been purely human.

If the debate between natural and artificial is obsolete and a red herring, the important debate is between open and closed systems. It is not exactly the German idealist "System," so demonized by Kierkegaard, that is the problem, but the *closure*. All things are entangled and interconnected in systems, in systems of systems—but in an *open-ended* way. One of the central arguments of Derrida's *Of Grammatology* (1967), describing the "dangerous supplement" of *writing*, is to defeat the "structuralist" position on the *formalizability* of the programs, or the *programmability* of the systems, which run not just our language but our culture and, as we realize today, our bodies, our minds, and nature itself. The classical debates about freedom and creativity, then, are really debates about *open and closed systems*, about total formalizability, which is what Derrida is contesting. Today, writing a program to deal with what is *unprogrammable* has become a goal for AI, not a contradiction. What Derrida called an "ultra-" or "quasi-transcendental"[18] is the exception or excess of the system, which is the "event" the system cannot *predict or prevent*. So Derrida was making a Gödel-like argument for the "formal undecidability" of these systems (which goes along with the "plasticity" of the brain, the paradoxes of quantum science, and the cut the unconscious makes in consciousness, all so many "spectral" effects that keep their systems *open*).

The tendency of what Taylor is calling "intervolution" is the ever-increasing integration of our minds and body into a network of AI technology and the gradual reduction of their dependence upon biology, which, were it to continue to its logical conclusion—assuming we do not destroy ourselves in the meantime—would make us humans today the biological ancestors of entirely postbiological beings. With indefinitely extended life spans, the beings formerly known as human would be fit for decades-long space travel or living elsewhere in the solar system, an eerie idea. The "upload" is the most extreme case imaginable of the uncanny, of not-at-homeness—*Unheimlichkeit*—of what is no longer even human, where we are "alienated" to the point that we become "aliens" to ourselves. But that does not mean that it, or something like it, will not someday come true.[19] I add "or something like it" because I think the upload is a limit case; it may be impossible, it may even be incoherent, and it may be a terrible idea. But it remains standing as the de facto tendency of the work, a siren song, an all-but-irresistible regulative ideal being asymptotically approached, whether or not it is possible or even desirable. The great question Augustine was to himself is an even bigger one for us. We are increasingly unable to say exactly what the difference really is between us and these highly advanced technologies. Is it the case that humans are being reduced to machines, which is what worried the Romantics and Heidegger, or that the machines are replacing humans in the workforce, which is what worries the working class, or that humans *never were human* in the first place, which no one ever worried about before?

QUANTUM HAUNTOLOGY

Heidegger once distinguished the stone, which is worldless (no life or sentience), and the animal, which is "world-poor" (sentient but no self-reflective knowledge), from Dasein, which is genuinely being-in-the-world.[20] However radical Heidegger can otherwise be, this is exactly the completely classical metaphysical and humanistic axiomatic that "A Manifesto for Cyborgs" intended to shred. Haraway liked to point out that nature is not a dumb inert thing, purely *vorhanden* in Heidegger's sense, but itself a bit of a trickster, a coyote, a kind of agent, that is capable of confusing and outsmarting us.

This point is brought out in a striking way by the work of Karen Barad, which, we might say, is focused on Haraway's third boundary breakdown, between the physical and the nonphysical. A trained quantum physicist, Barad has taken up Derrida's notion of the specter under the title of a "quantum hauntology" to describe the eerie things that go on in the quantum realm, like the "spooky action at a distance" of quantum entanglement, which Einstein complained about in the very language of spectrality.[21] There things happen at a distance and do not abide by Hume's billiard ball laws of causality, which require continuity and contiguity. (Einstein, unfortunately, was something of a fan of Hume.) There material things are not *vorhanden*—not stone-cold, solid, stable, actual, and determinate objects but potential and indeterminate ones—and they are not so much things knocking into one another as interacting events taking place in a field. Material things are materializations, excitations—what Barad calls "spacetimemattering"—occurring in quantum fields, depending on the interaction of quanta with one another, which includes their interaction with observers, meaning us! So they are anything but "worldless," as they exist only in virtue of the networks in which they are entangled. Barad describes this as "agential realism"—so neither realist nor anti-realist—meaning that things (*res*) are real in virtue of being realized in and by their interactions. That reminds us of Latour's notion of a "network" of "actants" and of Serres's description of supposedly inert objects as "quasi-subjects." As Terence Blake points out, it is extremely misleading of Graham Harman to redescribe Latour's theory as "object-oriented-ontology" when the whole idea is to deconstruct the complex of freestanding objects and opposing subjects.[22] It is unhelpful to describe Schrödinger's cat as an object; it is in superposition between life and death, which is at least as spooky as Einstein's complaint about quantum entanglement (and even spookier than Derrida's cat).

Far better than "realism" and "materialism," Barad says, is the language of spectrology, of eerie events and happenings. While classical physics describes an ontology of presence, of inert self-identical things, contemporary physics explores a hauntology of indeterminate, uncertain, and undecidable potencies whose actualization is a function of probability. To such a world, Barad is suggesting, the imaginary, the intellectual framework, the frame of mind of deconstruction is more congenial—shall I say they are kindred specters?—than is classical substance metaphysics, which makes a more comfortable fit with hard-rock classical or Newtonian physics. In the world of quantum mechanics, the word *materialism* does less and less work, whereas to speak of the quantum realm as a "ghost dance" is actually a scientifically suggestive figure. According to the holographic theory, for example, the entire universe is a two-dimensional object that only *looks* three dimensional; three-dimensional things are apparitions. All the information needed for the appearance of a three-dimensional object is stored on a two-dimensional one.

PLUS DE L'ÊTRE = +

Spookier still, we have actually begun to wonder whether we are living in a virtual world, not merely as a cultural metaphor, but really, whether the world which we call real is in reality a virtual world, where our being-in-the-world is really being-in-a-virtual-world. Up to now, virtual reality has largely meant audio and two-dimensional video images, which no one has been tempted to confuse with the real thing. But there is a great deal of virtuosity in virtual reality today, which has begun to expand into interactive three-dimensional simulations, like many popular video games, that are far more realistic and lifelike. At some point, it is projected, virtual reality will include all five senses and offer total immersion simulations. But wait. Is that not what we call "reality"? How would we tell the difference? Enter *The Matrix*, only this time with an added twist. Now we ask whether the red pill might have pulled Neo out of the real world, landing him in a virtual one, and—here is the point—how could we or Neo tell the difference?

Long before the Wachowski sisters (they have transgendered), Plato wondered if our lives are not spent in a cave guessing at shadowy likenesses of a real world up above, and Descartes asked how we can be sure the real world is not a dream or a grand illusion produced by—what else?—an evil spirit bent on deceiving us. A century later, Bishop Berkeley (1685–1753) advanced a more angelic or heavenly hypothesis that *esse est percipi*, to-be is to-be-perceived, where God is the Prime Simulator Unsimulated and what we call the real (material) world is a well-ordered simulation God produces in our souls. So much for the materialists, the good bishop thought. Berkeley was serious but Descartes's doubts were strictly methodological. Descartes did not actually doubt the existence of the world; he was just looking for a good proof that there is one. Thus far this has all been mostly good material for an introductory course in philosophy, but ever since Nick Bostrom proposed the "simulation hypothesis" as a scientifically possible postulate, we have started really wondering about this.[23] In *Reality+*, a book which has turned into a best-seller, philosopher David Chalmers (who famously called consciousness the "hard problem") explores this argument in detail. It is possible—we cannot prove that it is not the case—that we ourselves, our entire world, are simulations, where all the blood, sweat, and tears of the lives we lead are perfectly bloody, sweaty, tearful simulations conjured up by an unknown simulator, maybe an advanced civilization somewhere else in the universe.[24] Who am I? A sim.

Cogito, ergo sim. The *ego sum* is a sim. *Quaestio mihi factus sum* (sim). Imagine that! Just try!

When neuroscientists and physicists today become uneasy about their own results, it is because they are worried that these phenomena are too spooky to be science!

I cannot resist adding that, for readers of Derrida, this is all extremely ironic. Derrida's early and very vocal critics accused him of "textualism," favoring "words" over the real material world (of which they appointed themselves the guardian angels)! Of course by texts he meant coded systems. Today, these critics could "text" their criticism of textualism to everyone or tweet it! Today, texts and traces, codes and programs lie at the heart of the real material world. Today, we wonder whether the world is made of coded bits, whether we are made of coded bits. Today, the train has left the station on the opposition between "real matter" and information systems, programs, writing, and texts. Today, any possible "materialism" turns on a grammatology and an attendant hauntology! Speaking and writing were pretty much the world's first system of virtual reality, and what Derrida early on called *archi-écriture*, the coded use of signifiers in *any* medium whatsoever, spoken or written, cultural or natural, physical or digital, is pretty much what the "age of information" is all about. The "+" in "Humanity+" and "Reality+" is what Derrida called the "dangerous supplement," where the plus cannot be insulated from the minus. *Plus de l'être* = +. More being, more than just being, no longer being. Maybe it is information all the way down.

In short, the classical binary of bodily matter and immaterial spirit, upon which everything in religion and theology up to now has turned, has become an undecidable—that is, pretty much collapsed. When Schelling said nature is visible spirit and spirit is invisible nature, he described *avant la lettre* the space that quantum physics and neuroscience occupies today.

Es spukt in der ganzen Welt. The whole world is spooked.[25]

WOULD YOU RATHER BE A TRANSHUMAN OR AN ANGEL?

The curious thing is that *today* the theologians would rather be cyborgs while the uploaders would rather be angels, like the theologians of *yesterday*. I say this only half in jest. To be sure, one of the problems with the posthumanist project is that it springs from dualist-Cartesian and rationalist-Enlightenment origins, which disdain our carnal-material limitations but disdain theology even more. The upload is the absolutization of the autonomous liberal individual criticized by postmodern feminists like Hayles.[26] Still, the uploaders share the same desire with *classical* theology. "O death, where is your victory? O death where is your sting?" serves pretty well as the epigraph for both Kurzweil—*The Singularity Is Near: When Humans Transcend Biology*—and the apocalyptic preaching of Paul. The text of 1 Corinthians 15 is a comparatively articulate theological rendering of something that bears an interesting comparison to uploading. For the uploaders, the last and greatest "disease" is death; for Paul, the last "enemy" is death. For the uploaders, our biological-based minds will be lifted up into electronic ones. For Paul, the wet-earthy corruptible body (*soma psychikon*, animate, biological) we slog around with in mortal life will be raised up (transcended) into a fiery-airy, incorruptible, heavenly, spiritual body (*soma pneumatikon*)—shall we say a body+? Either way, we all end up on a cloud. When? At the time of the Second Coming (Singularity), which both Kurzweil and Paul are sure is "near." The difference is that one vision is utopian and scientific (which does not mean it is confirmed) and the other is mythological and prescientific (which does not mean it is rubbish).

The upload and the risen body have a lot in common. They are both in search of the "+," an enhanced or transcendent life without death. They represent different but comparable desires to *live like the angels*, a desire I myself have confessed to sharing in my pious Catholic youth. In *La legende des anges,* Michel Serres works out the analogy between angelology and information technology.[27] The French *legende* means both a mythical tale and a *legendum*—that is, a hermeneutic key to reading the various kinds of angels as antecedents of contemporary technologies. This analogy is also an ontology, not simply a curiosity, for Serres, who, like Gilles Deleuze, thinks of history not in sequential periods but in terms of what Deleuze calls events. This refers to certain powers or *potencies* (Schelling), certain *desires* (Deleuze) that are getting themselves actualized repeatedly across time so that episodes distant in time can "touch" one another like the opposite ends of a scarf that have been folded together (*complicatio*). Contemporary AI, then, is a new iteration of medieval AI (angelic intelligence), the way an underlying potency is getting reactivated, the way a seventeenth-century drama could be replayed as a Broadway musical. *What was going on* in medieval angelology is *now* going on, is being *repeated*, is being *replayed*, today, in the age of advanced information technology.

And what is that? *The desire to live like the angels!*

The angelic analogy is extensive. Angels (*angelos* means "messenger") are history's first "instant message" systems, called upon whenever the Most High had something urgent and important to say down below.[28] As intermediates between God and the world, they have the power of *flight* "at the speed of thought," the premodern antecedent of the speed of light. Serres provides images on opposing pages of Renaissance paintings of angels and pictures of contemporary jet planes spreading their "wings" in fetchingly similar postures. Angels are *superintelligent*, like Watson, equipped with an instant intellectual intuition, and they are *immortal*, which Kurzweil and Moravec are still working on. They think with surpassing speed, simply sharing their thoughts with each other immediately, communicating instantly like computers on the same network, while storing enormous amounts of *information* in a microspace smaller than the head of a pin. They live quite economically, without need of food, shelter, or clothing. They are famous as guides and *guardians* (global positioning systems). Angels are also warriors who come in "heavenly hosts" (armies) like super cyborg warriors or *smart bombs* streaking across the skies to slay enemies on the other side of the world with devastating accuracy by remote control, like a video game. That reminds us that there are also malicious spirits, bad angels, demons. The news they deliver is not all good. Satan is *dy*sangelic—the prince of lies, *fake news*, and *dis*information, of devious *hackers* stealing money, identities, and good information and spreading *misinformation* and destructive con*spir*acy theories. Finally, as to what angels are made of, ontologically, which explains their intelligence and immortality, recall the medieval debate. While Aquinas held they were pure forms, purely immaterial substances, the Franciscans argued the angels were made of ethereal incorruptible "celestial matter," like Paul's risen body and more like the electronic realm we call virtual reality. If the theologians want to update their theology of the resurrection, maybe they should listen to what the uploaders have to say.

In sum, angels are an antecedent form of what the uploaders *desire*—to *live like the angels*, as Jesus promised. Superintelligence, immortality, instant travel and communication, all maintenance free! What's not to envy? Would you rather be a transhuman or an angel?

A COMING SPECIES OF THEOLOGIANS OF THE POSTHUMAN

Whether we call it a Kuhnian paradigm switch, a new axial age, a Foucauldian episteme, or a Heideggerian epoch of Being, we are witness now to a seismic shift in the apophatic imagination. Posthumanism is a particularly eerie condition. Exposed to a humanity-to-come, the very meaning of "human" has been destabilized. By not even intending or pretending to be human, we today are left to wonder what "they"—these posthuman beings—will call themselves. Even if the radical posthumanists are a *repetition* in the Serresian or Deleuzian sense of classical angelology, we should not be deceived. Their intent is that theology is to be *replaced* by the techno-science of the posthuman age, which *transcends biology* not merely magically and imaginatively (religion) but really, fulfilling the desires of classical theology to gain immortal life as the fruit not of the Crucifixion but of computer engineering. By transcending biology, they mean to transcend theology.

When Haraway said she would rather be a cyborg than a goddess, the theologians were quick to agree. That is the biologically conservative position. Their response to the posthumanist challenge has been to invoke the *Haraway* cyborg, the feminist postmodern mythic cyborg, the embodied organic being that interfaces with the cybernetic. Up to now the theologians have taken their stand with the body; for them, theology and biology are joined at the hip. But what if—ethico-political, philosophical, theological, climatological, scientific, and technological problems aside—the uploaders were to succeed in the total transcendence of biology? Is there a posthumanist theology *beyond the biological*? Would transcending biology also result in transcending religion and theology? Would the cyborg theologians then concede that God, theology, and religion along with humanity have all simply become obsolete, part of the ancient "human" prehistory of a future even the futurists struggle to imagine? Would beings such as these posthumans ever write their *Confessions,* or does that Augustinian scene require having a corruptible body of flesh that is reduced to prayers and tears by its mortality? Does the *theos* of theology require the *humus* of our humanity? Is theology tethered to biology?

Of what value is the Incarnation to a species that has twisted free from its carnality? Will not the mission of the earthly life of

Jesus—to give good news to the poor and sight to the blind, to feed the hungry and heal the lame—and the "salvific" action of the celestial Christ diminish to the point of obsolescence as the posthuman project progressively becomes postcarnal? Will the "year of Jubilee" Jesus announced turn out to be the "Singularity," of which Ray Kurzweil would be the prophet? Might the true meaning of the "Incarnation," of the "God/Man," be that these two are "companion species," to adapt Haraway's language about our fellowship with animals, and hence that they will suffer a common fate? Is the answer to the question *Cur deus homo*? that we cannot have one without the other, which is pretty much what Schelling's Adam Kadmon means? God would be immortally "lonely" without us, Schelling said, and we mortals would be helpless without God. That means that when one disappears, so does the other.

The religions of the Book turn on a person-to-person narrative, a personalist imaginary; they cannot tolerate the thought that, at bottom, being is impersonal, that there is not "somebody" who loves us behind all this. Theism is not only theocentric; it is in that very same gesture also anthropocentric. That means it is elliptical, with two centers, theo-anthropocentric, where God and human beings are companions, confidantes, intimates, soul mates, intrinsically correlational, and the history of salvation is a drama whose protagonists are a couple. Like Father, like Son. So much self, so much God; so much God, so much self (Kierkegaard). My ground and God's ground are the same (Eckhart). What would thou be, O great sun, without us to shine upon? (Nietzsche's Zarathustra). The less *mortal* and *human* we become, the more our divine partner will fade away.

Would that be the end of theology?

I think that the biblical imaginary, both Jewish and Christian, as we know it, which is all about land and children and wounded bodies, would need to be radically rethought in such an eventuality (as would everything else, including ethics and politics), which is why theologians are wary of posthumanism. For example, when Derrida discusses the "pure messianic," the very idea of the "to-come" (*l'à-venir*), the coming of what we cannot see coming, he is taking his point of departure from a biblical figure but reinventing it. Derrida describes a Messiah who never shows up, who is always *structurally promised*, an *arrivant* who will never actually be present. Approached thus, the apophatic includes the mystery of the coming species of these posthumans whom we cannot see coming *and no less* the possibility of *a coming species of theologians of the posthuman* and even of the "coming God." In the expression "the x to come," the "to come" is more important than the x.[29] Thinking radically is always a matter of thinking at the limit, and the apophatic is always positioned on the limit, at the liminal point at which knowledge bounces off the wall of the unknowable, of the unprethinkable and unforeseeable, which leaves us wondering what is going on. Who are we, we who are so confounded? This sharpens the edges of the riddle posed by Augustine, the *quaestio mihi magna factus sum*, lending it a force no one, including Augustine, could have imagined.

Let us recall that, as Haraway points out, the original cyborg was not a myth. It was a piece of military hardware, designed by the United States Air Force for space travel, to equip astronauts to explore the *new* "new world" of outer space, so the emphasis fell on a postterrestrial, technologically enhanced *cyber*-body, never far from "Star Wars." From this the theologians take flight, taking it to be more hostile to their *organic*-bodily and peaceful purposes. But the scientific cyborg is no less interesting; indeed, it may be *far more interesting to the theologians to come*, the coming species of posthuman theologians, *s'il y en a*. In my view, the universe may well turn out to be what the theologians, thinking of God, call the power and the ground of being, the *mysterium tremendum et fascinans*. We are on every front being drawn into a strange and unfamiliar world—of artificial intelligence, of virtual reality, of quantum reality, of an unencompassable cosmic mystery—

advancing, adventuring into an incomparable, *unheimlich* expanse. This exploration is the repetition, the reinvention today of the ancient Greek "wonder," which was also directed at the stars, which they called *philosophia*. The apophatic imagination today is *reconfiguring* in terms of another apophatic sphere, of something deeper and vaster than both the human and the posthuman—God, the world, *Deus sive natura*—however we are able to describe that in which we live and move and have our being. The horizon is shifting to the mystery of the future of the species, the planet, and the "last frontier" and "galaxies far, far away." Today the silent call by which we are always already addressed, meaning both the spirit that inspires us and the specters that unnerve us, which hitherto traveled under various incognitos, like God, the Spirit, the unconditional, the Absolute, is turning out to be the call of the *universe itself*, traces of whose ancient particles are stirring at this very moment within our bodies.

It may be that the present biological human race will be the last stage in the evolution of new beings whom we cannot imagine, unless we succeed in annihilating ourselves first. Our short mortal lives may become the stuff of the museums of the posthuman future, where visitors will look back on us as upon a primitive civilization whose lives will seem to them Hobbesian, "solitary, poor, nasty, brutish, and short."[30] They will mark the emergence of the age of information in the last quarter of the twentieth century as the beginning of the end of the biological and earthbound human stage of intelligent life, when it began to detach itself from its biological moorings and escape the grip of planet earth, the way we mark our ancestral beginning in the migration from Africa. Perhaps. Were that to eventuate, I am proposing, it will not be the end of the *mysterium tremendum et fascinans* but the beginning of another stage in its unfolding, the next hermeneutic setting in which the apophatic finds itself. Consciousness is the hard problem, as Chalmers says. Harder still is the problem of the unprethinkable, the radical priority of what there is, the *Sein* in

Bewusstsein, as Heidegger said, which has always been older than thought, and harder to think than thinking thinks it is. Today, thinking is being stretched to the limits, to its limits, to the unprethinkable, unencompassable, unconditional. Talk about hard!

Traditionally, theology and philosophy are where humanity does its most radical thinking; once radical thinking gets its bearings on something, it outsources its results to the sciences, where they can be worked on in a more methodic way. But today, theology and philosophy are faced with specters of a hitherto unimagined kind, and they are in danger of being replaced by art and science. They cannot continue functioning with the assured distinctions upon which they have always relied—between spirit and matter, soul and body, eternity and time, heaven and earth, natural and historical/artificial/supernatural, revelation and reason, God and the world—or now it seems even human and nonhuman! This throws the name of God and everything we hold holy into deep confusion—maybe sheer chaos, but maybe a sacred anarchy. If theology ignores these specters, it does so at the cost of its own credibility. The *mystical* is more and more lining itself up with *science*; traditional *religion* is increasingly lining itself up with *superstition*. The *mysterium tremendum et fascinans* is beginning to detach itself from the hold of classical theology and Greek philosophy, even as a more radical apophatic thinking is inching closer to cosmology, to the mystery of the universe, maybe of multiple universes. That is one of religion's problems today, and the failure to appreciate that is of a piece with its reactionary politics.

God as the constitutive exception and human exceptionalism go hand in hand—like Father, like Son. Theism is dominated by a personalistic, theocentric-anthropocentric, geocentric imaginary. Consequently, the decentering of the *theos* of theism goes along with the decentering of the *homo* in humanism. Post-theism and posthumanism have something to offer each other.

Do post-theism and post-humanism provide a favorable opening for pan*en*theism, where (unlike biblical religions) being, nature, the universe itself, is taken to be a great divine milieu, a matrix or cosmic womb from which we emerge and to which we and all other things will return? Having transcended the notion of a personal Supreme Being, is not panentheism the theology of choice, the theology to come? Is it not a better fit for a cosmos filled with cyborgs and cosmonauts traversing the vast and sweeping body of the universe, of *Deus sive natura*?

That is a devilishly tempting hypothesis, but panentheism too faces an interesting challenge, to which we now turn.

FOURTEEN

RUINOLOGY

Why Will There Be Nothing at All Rather Than Something?

FROM THE POSTHUMAN TO THE INHUMAN

You would be forgiven had you concluded that the parade of specters has finally passed by, that the riddle of our posthuman future is all quite enough, that now, at last, the ghost dance is over. But I have saved for last something that may turn out to be the spookiest specter of all, a kind of *ens spectralissimum*.

Even if everything the transhumanists and posthumanists contemplate was possible, which is far from clear and far from being clearly desirable, that would only be, cosmically speaking, a short-term solution, if it is a solution at all. The desire for immortality—which, we should recall, Genesis tried to discourage—faces a serious renewable energy problem. The sun is consuming its own fuel, destined to flare up, reduce the planetary system to toast, and collapse upon itself, ending up eventually a black dwarf. Alas, another mortal. When the ancients looked up at the night sky, they saw gods—immortal, incorruptible celestial bodies—fully unaware that some of those starry gods were already long dead.

But wait, it gets worse. As Philip Plait says, "The universe is trying to kill you. It's nothing personal. It's trying to kill me too.

It's trying to kill everybody."[1] Cosmically speaking, according to the most widely received theory today, there is no long-term solution. In the long run, as they say, we are all dead. Our solar system, the whole galaxy, the entire cosmos is expanding at an increasing rate of acceleration, to the point of cosmic oblivion, at which point nothing, living or nonliving, will survive. In an up-to-date version of Schelling's "ages of the world," his fanciful exercise of dialectical-Trinitarian imagination, the present age is that of the birth of the stars ("stelliferous"), to be followed by the age of the death of the stars ("degenerate," Genesis in reverse), which culminates in the "dark era," when, instead of God being "all in all," there will be nothing at all, and instead of Spirit, just cold, dark, randomized, silent, dissipated energy.[2] In the dark era, the dark ground triumphs. Lyotard calls this age not the posthuman but the "inhuman," meaning there will be no one, human or posthuman, to tell the story of the end of the cosmos and no one to tell it to, just mute, eternal darkness. In addition to an unprethinkable beginning before thought is an unthinkable end after thought, post-thought, post-everything.[3]

If the *mysterium tremendum et fascinans* is beginning to distance itself from theology and inch its way to cosmology, that would seem to provide an opening for the *Deus sive natura* of panentheism. But what if the *logos* of the *cosmos* turns out to be an eerie, inescapable a logic of ruins, if cosmology is a ruinology? The entire universe, we are told, is an expenditure without return, an investment that suffers an irrecuperable loss. The end of creation is cosmic dissemination, cessation, a termination, pure and simple. All the eschatologies and teleologies come crashing down in ruins. Imagine that. There is hardly an eerier thought, hardly a thought as unthinkable as that.

Is *that* the apophatic?

Is *that* the *Deus absconditus*, the hidden God of whom we know nothing? Is *that* what Eckhart and Luther knew without knowing?

Is *that* sunyata, the groundless ground, the void, *der dunkle Grund*?

Is *that* the Nothing that nothings (*das Nichts nichtet*)? Does Heidegger get the last word, not Carnap?

Or Derrida? In the end *dissemination* will have its way, or so we are told.

Or Satan? Maybe Jesus cut a deal with Satan after all. In exchange for the year of Jubilee back here on earth, the unruly, ruinous cosmic powers could have their way, but it would have to be deferred for another and distant day when no one will be around to notice.

WHY WILL THERE BE NOTHING AT ALL RATHER THAN SOMETHING?

Of course, if no one will be there to worry about it, there is a limit to just how spooked we should be. We have more immediate problems, like the ongoing destruction of the ecosystem, not to mention the ancient prophetic lament that the wicked continue to prosper while the righteous go under. A prospect so far removed in time from the present is really not a problem. Still, we, today, while we are still here, in the meantime, cannot avoid asking what to make of such a spectral prospect. In a slightly downbeat updating of Leibniz's famous question, we today can ask, "Why will there be nothing at all rather than something?"

We are talking about a future at such an immense and unimaginable distance that it strains our numerical system just to formulate it. So we can agree that cosmic destruction is not a *problem*—that is, something that threatens us that we can address, like famines, pandemics, nuclear war, or climate change. The Anthropocene is a problem; the "dark era" is not. But the "dark era" is a *mystery*, something that brings us up short and provokes important questions about ends, about ultimates, about the meaning of things, about philosophical teleology, theological eschatology, and divine providence.[4] It brushes against the grain of teleological interpretation in the philosophy of history, against the eschatological grain of a theology of history and even Saint Paul. He wrote that nature itself had fallen into disarray as a result of the fall of Adam and Eve and that Christ's obedience unto death not only reconciled humankind to God but reconciled *all creation*. But the idea of cosmic destruction does not seem very reconciling.

Of course, the present scientific consensus on this theory (which is not universal) could change. I have no horse in that race. It is enough for my argument that if it is scientifically *possible*, then there is no *necessity* in its opposite, a necessary superbeing like God (theism) or the inexhaustible depth and power of being-itself (panentheism), both of which are challenged by this prospect. To be sure, theists, having recourse to an eternal omnibeing, have more options. Because the idea of such a being is unfalsifiable—as is belief in alien abductions, so unfalsifiability is not a compliment—theists can always come up with something (a characteristic feature of Kant's "antinomies"). An ex nihilo creator could simply do a "new creation." But then again, why not create the new creation in the first place, without a principle of entropy?[5]

That is one reason I welcome the displacement of the classical theistic view of God by a *panentheistic* view, which I am calling the ontological reduction: from God as Supreme Being to God as Spirit-in-the-world. But panentheism has a problem of its own and fewer options because it has bound the fortunes of God to the cosmos (*Deus sive natura*). The destruction of the universe leaves panentheism holding the bag of a world headed for oblivion; the end of the world will take Spirit-in-the-world down with it. As seen in the case of Hegel (chapter 3), by reinterpreting God in terms of immanence rather than transcendence, panentheism remains in alliance with the God of classical theology. Thus, God's infinity and eternity are not destroyed but relocated in the inexhaustible depth of being-itself; particular beings come and go but being-itself is imperishable. Unless it is not. Unless the Spirit is expiring, unless being-in-time is running out of time and burning out its being. Theists can at least say that the destruction of the cosmos leaves God still standing (although Schelling says God would be lonely and unfulfilled), but panentheists, having invested everything in the world of space and time, are left holding a stock whose price is in free fall. Panentheism must keep its fingers crossed, hoping that the weight of the evidence will someday shift to the current minority view of endless universes.[6] Panentheism definitely does have a horse in that race.

So theism falls into speculative antinomies and panentheism is a suggestive but also speculative metaphysics, ultimately incapable of experimental confirmation. Whether the current view of the universe holds up will depend upon neither theistic magic nor panentheistic speculation but upon the mathematics and experimental evidence. Neither theists nor panentheists "know" something about the material world—namely, that it is sustained by inexhaustible being-itself—that is withheld from the physicists and misleading them. Physics is all the hard-rock metaphysics we are going to get—if by metaphysics we mean how things are when we are not around to say how we would like them to be. While we applaud the "ontological reduction," from beings to being-itself, we require another reduction—of ontology, of purely speculative claims about being-itself. We require the reduction of ontology to hauntology, of cosmology to cosmopoetics. So the expanding universe represents a blow to theological eschatology, both theistic and panentheistic, and to philosophical teleology, to all the contemporary variants on Joachim of Fiore and to the German idealist dialectics of the Absolute Spirit and, for that matter, to a metaphysical materialism that invested all its funds in the eternity and necessity of "matter."

To describe this outcome as the death of the universe, is to raise the question of *death*. It is clear enough in Genesis 3:22–24 that death is not a punishment. In fact, the opposite is the case: the punishment resulted from the desire to avoid death, to eat of the tree of life and be like the gods. In the Genesis myths, death is the natural order. The difference between the gods and us is that the gods are immortal and we are not, and the trouble starts when we try to disturb that order. For the transhumanists, death is a disease to be cured. For Saint Paul, death is an enemy to be defeated by Christ. But death is neither. Death is part of the rhythm of our life, how life is passed on from generation to generation. Life and death are two sides of the same coin, so intimately interwoven that Derrida simply speaks of "life/death."[7]

To this point, contemporary physicists and cosmologists add the big picture: the cycle of life and death is a transient *negentropic* episode, the local and temporary resistance life throws up to entropy, which is what is all in all. So the entire universe is mortal, an *exitus* without *reditus*, expansion without return, an expenditure without reserve, ending in ruins, an irrecuperable loss, irreversible dissipation, a pure loss. The evolution of the universe, the "ages of the world," is not a history of being or God, of salvation or the Spirit, but a history of dissemination, a history of ruins. Our destiny is *destinerrance*. Cosmology is ruinology.

Or so we are told. So what do we do now?

COSMOPOETICS, OR THE POETICS OF THE WORLD

This entropic destiny radicalizes the reduction. We leave the *theists* hoping that the superbeing has something up the sleeve of divine omnipotence and the panentheists hoping that there are multiple universes (although, even if there are, this is the only one, by definition, that we are going to know).[8] For those of us for whom theology has become theopoetics, this all means that cosmology must include a cosmopoetics, that theopoetics must include cosmo-theopoetics. In cosmopoetics we are prepared to admit that dissemination is part of the whole, that coming to an end is not an objection to things, but the way things are. When we say the universe is "all there is," we are not dismayed or being dismissive, not complaining that this is all that is left after we lost eternal life. Quite the opposite, we affirm that all there is, is a staggering and glorious mystery, the glory being to have been offered a part in its cosmic play. The task of cosmopoetics is not—like the pope telling Galileo what he was allowed to see when he looked through his telescope—to instruct the physicists about the physical universe. That is a misunderstanding. The task is not to explain the being of the world but to interpret our *place* in the world based upon what we know about the world at the time, which is what is what the authors of the scriptures were doing and why we have to start all over again in every new age. The subject matter of a poetics is not being-in-itself but our being-in-the-world, our interface with being and world, which is why everything depends upon the theopoetic reduction.

Even saying that is a bit misleading, inasmuch as it imagines that we and the world, our being and being-itself, are different, which is a distinction that Heidegger tried to collapse with locutions like being-in-the-world and Dasein, meaning the place in being where being puts itself in question. We humans are one bit (perhaps one of many) of the world where the world has begun to worry about itself, that bit of evolution where evolution becomes conscious of itself and tries to take over the steering wheel. This is the cosmopoetic correction of the phenomenon of reflexivity, of self-reflection, which preoccupied the German idealists, which was not destroyed but delimited by what Schelling called the unprethinkable. By the time reflection arrives on the scene, being is already there. Reflection is always aimed at where the rabbit was. Reflection is, as William James put it, the futile attempt to turn on the lights quickly enough to see the dark. Heidegger reproduced Schelling's move on Hegel when he contested the purity of what Husserl called the transcendental reduction, which is the failed attempt to "neutralize" the grip that factical being has upon us so that we can see purely and without some inherited interpretive lens. Merleau-Ponty put it nicely. The most that transcendental reflection can do is loosen the grips of the bonds of being just long enough to get a quick look, like a whale coming up for oxygen.[9] Heidegger said we cannot bring the world as a totality into view, but we can give an account of our *being-in*-the-world *as* a totality, in moments in which our sense of being-in is lit up as a whole, say in anxiety when all the world wavers in meaninglessness, or in joy, when the weight of all the world is lifted.

The task of cosmopoetics is to describe our *encounter* with the world, to make sense of our *relationship* to the world—in short, to *interpret* our *experience* in the world, which is the work of hermeneutics, not "speculative hermeneutics," in which we purport to read the mind of God or being itself unfolding in history, but the hermeneutics of our *factical* life in the world. Whatever else we may *say* we are doing, that is what we always end up *really doing* anyway. That aim is explicit in the humanities, but the "hard" sciences, too, have a hermeneutics, a history, a poetic, an elegance, an imaginary of their own, not to mention the uncanny link between consciousness and matter suggested by quantum physics. The difference between the two lies not in the *what* but the *how*. In the humanities, we are looking for words in which to express the *non*mathematical features of the world, not its controlled experimental but its free experiential features, the sorts of things that are expressed in a constellation of narratives and poems, parables and paintings, striking sayings and imaginative figures. But both undertakings, each in its own order, end up at a limit, confounded by the abyss that is opened up, whether by the open-ended experience or by the controlled experiment. That is why Schelling and Plato agree that at the limit point, philosophy must cut the lines of concepts and adopt the language of the poets, of theopoetics.

Every attempt to assess our place in the world is working within a given conception of the world, within hermeneutic horizons and frontiers that are continually being tested. The prospect that our cosmos is expanding into oblivion is part of the current state of knowledge of the physical world. That is rather different than the stories that eventually got canonized in what we call the New Testament, which, as Bultmann showed, assume a pre-Copernican universe and a world full of demons and angels. Paul wanted to spread the word about Messiah Yeshua to the very end of the world, by which he meant Spain. Today we now know the cosmos is of staggering proportions, of which our planet is a miniscule part, and even our life on this planet is an extremely recent development. What we have learned about evolution and genetics, about the neurological basis of our intelligence, about the expansion of the universe, is all part of our expanded knowledge of *what* the world is, and we cannot even imagine how positively primitive this worldview will look in another thousand years. What Schelling called "negative philosophy" is not, as he thought, an *ideal* world of *essential* relationships but the *factical* state of knowledge of *what* the world is, the present state of the art, the latest let-the-chips-fall-where-they-may conceptual repertoire available, which keeps making the mystery *that* such a world *is* all the more mysterious. What he called the negative philosophy describes the *hermeneutic context* (the conceptual framework available at the time) for the positive, for the *affirmation* of the world, the *oui, oui,* yes, I said yes, which arises in response to the hermeneutic shock, the event of all events, *that* the world is at all, which is the mystical. Contrary to Schelling, unprethinkable facticity encompasses both sides, the what and the that.

So it goes without saying that the only way for philosophy and theology to make sense today is to do so in collaboration with the natural sciences, as do thinkers like Bruno Latour and Catherine Malabou and as Whitehead did a century ago. The best way to make themselves even more irrelevant than they presently are is to ignore or otherwise marginalize contemporary science—which is, at present, stealing both their wonder and their thunder.

Worst of all is to claim that they know something about biological evolution or the history of the universe that science does not because a Super-Somebody passed along a "special revelation" of it to them, and the next worst is to claim that they can access it on the basis of metaphysical intuitions not subject to empirical-experimental confirmation. The more philosophers delude themselves with transcendental illusions of pure ahistorical reason and theologians with the illusion of "supernatural" revelations, the more they will accelerate the turn to art that the contemporary world has *rightly* made—just the way Tillich thought the expressionists had more to say than the German theologians—in order to find (nonmathematical) meaning. We are turning away from philosophy and theology today because they have lost their way.

Accordingly, in the theopoetic and cosmo-theopoetic view I am advancing, the prospect of cosmic oblivion proves to be not an objection or an obstacle but a still more radical *hermeneutical setting* for the apophatic imagination. It provides the radical hermeneutic *what* that sets the stage for the radical mystical *that*. The apophatic imagination is a matter of lived experience, but it cannot be now and has never been in the past without a cosmological setting. In classical mysticism this setting was supplied by an unholy wedding of pre-Copernican cosmology with Neoplatonism, a great chain of being going out (*exitus*) from eternal unity into multiplicity and returning back again (*reditus*), a satisfying rhetorical trope, an onto-poetics, not to be mistaken for a reliable metaphysics. This schema, from the one to the many and back again, was still in full force in the Rhineland mystics and even in breakthrough Renaissance thinkers like Cusa, who, as Richard Kearney and Catherine Keller have shown, is a fascinating bridge to modernity. It returned radicalized and dialecticized in German idealism, where it was amplified into a triadic schema but not overturned.

Today, we contemplate rather the opposite, an *exitus* without *reditus*, an expansion without return, a dissemination that cannot be captured by polysemy. But if the apophatic imagination is marked by its sense of the limit, the concealed depths, the hidden core, what darkness is deeper than the prospect of an eternity of cold, dark nothing? The apophatic imagination is not defeated by this prospect but deepened. The darker the night, the brighter the star.

Far be it from me to absolutize the mathematical-natural sciences. Their success can and has led to a naturalistic-reductionistic view of the world among many intellectuals, who would describe themselves as agnostics or atheists. They are the "cultured despisers" of our day, who look upon religion the way one views an infectious disease. In this they are aided and abetted by the religious Right, which has done its best to make itself a plague, rightly deserving of rebuke. The venerable definition of hermeneutics is *subtilitas explicandi*, unfolding (ex-plicating) things with a light and delicate touch, knowing how to "read" things—and not just books!—with sensitivity, insight, and discernment, with an appreciation that, just as there are many ways to be, there are many ways to think and understand. That is why there is today a growing witness to a rather different and more sensitive and discerning rendering of the aesthetic and apophatic dimension of science itself, of the sort we see in Carlo Rovelli,[10] and why Einstein himself could not resist making several tantalizing references to exploring the mind of God. We are also reminded of the lovely, lyrical reflections of Carl Sagan on the "pale blue dot" called earth, a "mote of dust suspended in a sunbeam," he said. "There is perhaps no better demonstration of the folly of human conceits than this distant image of our tiny world. To me, it underscores our responsibility to deal more kindly with one another, and to preserve and cherish the pale blue dot, the only home we've ever known."[11] The more discerning reading of the religious dimension of our lives is to wrest it free from the hubris and hypocrisy of religious authorities, the delusions of the long robes, and from the god they try to trap inside their self-proclaimed infallible doctrines, inerrant books, and divine revelations, in order to expose it to its apophatic core, to submit it to apophatic discipline (*ascesis*). Whether such a project can be accommodated by a word as seriously damaged as *religion* remains to be seen. Hegel placed religion in the middle, between art and knowledge, and the threat to religion is whether it whether it will become the excluded middle, eliminated by its own obstinacy and folly, all its purposes served by art and science.

WHY HAS A WORLD DESTINED TO DESTRUCTION CREATED GOD?

In theopoetics, where limits play a productive rather than destructive role, the way a sculptor chips away the stone, we do not ask, theistically or panentheistically, why God would create a world that is destined to destruction or why the ground of being would go to ground like that. That is to get the whole thing backward. We ask instead, *Why has a world that is destined to destruction created God?* Thus would I rewire Schelling's reformulation of the question of God, whether world history will prove the divine existence, this time without the metaphysics.

In the theopoetic version, the question is, What sense are we to make of the fact that the universe, in the course of its evolution from the big bang to cosmic destruction, has in the meantime generated living, knowing, questioning, and mortal beings such as us (and for all we know many others elsewhere in the universe)? More to the point, how is it that these troubled and trouble-making creatures consistently express their troubles and concerns in the language—and it is more than a language, it is a profound and transforming *form of life*—of what I am calling the apophatic imagination, which is the heart of what, for lack of a better word, and depending on what day you ask me, I might still be willing to call religion? Why has one of the most recurrent and profound ways of asking what is going on in their lives been to speak and act in terms like "God" and the "coming" of God's "kingdom"? The "new creation" is to be taken not as cosmothe*ological* speculation—as representational propositions about the facts of the matter—but as a poetics, a form of faith in life and hope for life and love of life. The "year of Jubilee" does not belong to the calendar time of history or to the deep time of the metaphysics of history or to the cosmological time of physics but to *theopoetic time.*

If the question is then asked, Why has a given form of life articulated itself in terms like "God"? the answer is, broadly speaking, because it *is* a form of life. That is to say, this name provides a *resource for* that form of life, nourishing a body of beliefs and practices that collect around this name and resonate with the powers of being. The name (of) "God" is neither a capricious fantasy nor a term of art devised in an academic seminar but a name forged in the blood, sweat, and tears of tears of historical experience to give words and image to something that has us before we have it. The name (of) "God," which does not pick out an empirical object or a metaphysical entity, has work to do, which is to effect a *passage to the limits.* It pushes the form of life toward its limits, puts pressure on its horizons, and tests its frontiers, straining toward what Derrida calls the possibility of the impossible. That means it gives form to a given culture's deepest hopes and aspirations, reminding it of a time immemorial and opening it to its unforeseeable future. It is the seat, the focal object, in which its faith and hope are invested and in which it names what is to be loved *for itself.* It is not the name of a being or of the ground of being but of a way of being-in-the-world. It is not the name of an entity but an experience, not a thing but a relationship, not merely a thought but a deed, in which everything that is sacred and holy is concentrated. It is the deepest source of the vitality of the form of life, the least bad way it has of naming the *mysterium tremendum et fascinans,* which sustains the apophatic imagination. To be sure, this holds only so long as the name (of) "God" is approached under the apophatic imperative, within the mystical and apophatic sense of life. Otherwise, the name of God can represent the worst terror, the most terrible dogma, one of our best alibis for murder, in which case the form of life it organizes is nothing but a form of living death.

A name like this cannot be disproven by an argument, but it can become moribund, lose its vitality, and die off by losing contact with the apophatic imagination, which is the genuine sense of the death of God, and when that happens, no argument can save it. If "God" dies, the living symbol, all is not lost, but the form of life needs to reconfigure in a new way or it itself will die, as there is a theology, or rather a theopoetics, in every culture.[12] The name of God is but *one* way, one historically contingent symbol, particular to this form of life, one that turns on a classical name, a venerable paleonym. I am clearly *not* saying there are no other names or other forms of life in which the passage to the limits is carried out. I am not saying that this one is *privileged*, not denying that it is time bound and destined to go under like all things great and small. As Schelling and Tillich say, God is the unconditional but the unconditional is not God. The challenge to this name today, after Neoplatonism has run its course, is how and whether it can reconfigure in the face of a death not only human but cosmic. How can God be reimagined today?

FIFTEEN

AXIOLOGY
A Mortal God, A World without Why

A MORTAL GOD

For Hegel (chapter 3), the "death of God" is a "vanishing moment" in the larger life of God, where only finite beings die but death cannot reach the infinite Spirit, which is the ontological matrix of finite beings. But the evident heat death of the universe means that the ground of being also goes to ground, which spells the end of panentheism. Unless it does not, unless it is possible to tell a different story about God and hence about panentheism, an alternative I have saved for last. This possibility is raised by Derrida, who wrote that "wherever the name of God would allow us to think something else, for example a vulnerable nonsovereignty, one that suffers and is divisible, one that is mortal even... it would be a completely different story, perhaps even the story of a God who deconstructs himself in his ipseity."[1] This suggests a panentheism of a *mortal God*—and, by the same token, the *mortality* of *being* and *ground*. Then the mortality that besets all things would not be an objection to the being of God but constitutive of it, making for a completely different God, suffering and nonsovereign, a living God whose life, like every life—like the universe itself—is mortal. In this panentheism, the "body of God"—a venerable panentheistic figure of the universe—is also perishable. Death is ingredient in all life, darkness in all light, nonbeing in all being, up to and including God, who is all in all. In just the way we came to learn that the celestial bodies above, whom we once trusted to be there forever, were subject to the same mortal constraints as terrestrial bodies below, so too with God. To be sure, panentheism of any sort is only possible as theopoetics, as cosmo-theopoetics, as a way we name *our relationship* to the cosmos. Cosmopoetics is a matter neither of mathematical physics nor speculative metaphysics but of apophatic hermeneutics, not proving a predicate of being-in-itself but describing a modality of our being-in-the-world, not of being but of may-being.

AXIOLOGY NOT ONTOLOGY

The theopoetic attitude (chapter 1) demands that, instead of thinking the divine (*theios*) in terms of being, substance, essence, and cause, of permanence, omniperfection, and imperishability, all summed up in the *ens realissimum*, which are the *ontological* terms set by classical Hellenistic metaphysics, we reimagine God in strictly *axiological* terms. I have in mind the root meaning of the Greek word *axioma*, not a first principle in a deductive system but what is held in the highest regard and prized for its own intrinsic *worth*. The name of God is indeed the name of something *unconditional*, but the *unconditional* must be conceived axiologically, not ontologically. God is taken not as unconditional being, perfect and imperishable, but as the unconditional *worth* of being, not the *realissimum* but the *dignissimum*, what is *worthy* of being *unconditionally affirmed*, not in spite of its mortality but precisely in virtue of it. For mortality does not destroy the worth of a life but makes it all the more precious. Death's finality is defining, etching the edges of life so that life stands out all the more saliently, like a bright star against a clear, dark sky. What is affirmed unconditionally is affirmed for itself, up to and including its limits, which do not compromise its unconditional worth but constitute it. To affirm something unconditionally is to affirm it unto death, like the vows that lovers make, where the mortality is constitutive. The unconditional does not mean inexhaustible being, immune from all limiting conditions, but *unconditional worth*. Ontological finitude is the condition of axiological worth. It falls on us, for our part, to *make ourselves worthy* of what is of unconditional worth, to make ourselves worthy of the events that happen to us, an endeavor galvanized by the event harbored in the name of God. To elaborate this point, let us go back to Meister Eckhart, with whom we began (chapter 2).

THE GROUND OF THE SOUL

Meister Eckhart speaks—in a theopoetic discourse his Inquisitors could not comprehend—of a "little spark in the soul" or "ground of the soul" as a way to describe an element in our mind that links us up with what Schelling and Tillich would regard as the unprethinkable ground and power of being, which Eckhart calls, in the language available to him, the "ground of God." He depicts what Nicolas of Cusa would later call a coincidence of opposites, where the ground of the soul, an infinitesimally fine point in the soul, like the tip of a triangle, makes contact with the fine tip of the infinite God. The contact occurs in a spaceless point and a timeless "now," when the flow of time is intersected by the shock of eternity. This is a zone of absolute suspension, stillness, silence, and timelessness, which is entered by giving up my "I" and letting (*lassen*) God be God in me. Using the language of scholastic metaphysics, Eckhart says this unity with God takes place below the level of the "faculties" of the soul (intellect and will), which are concerned with creatures. It is effected *in* me but not *by* me, in the "substance" of the soul—the ground, basis, or source of the faculties where there is no knowing or doing. Here the finite has vanished in order to let the infinite happen. "I" am not *doing* something, but rather something else, something deep within me, something we might even call "it," is doing it in and through me. I am trying to get out of the way and *let it be* in me.

What Meister Eckhart describes in the vocabulary of medieval metaphysics is not confined to that vocabulary. In Tillichian terms, the self is neither autonomous nor heteronomous but theonomous, driven and sustained by the ground of God within and overflowing into the world. It is remarkably similar to what we read in the Zen masters, who never heard of medieval or Western metaphysics. In Zen archery, the art is to become completely artless, the effort to be completely effortless, the aim aimless. The training is complete when the master is satisfied that it is no longer the student who aims and directs the arrow at the target but "it" which shoots. At that point, the archer releasing the arrow has let go of self and entered into a state of "awareness" of what, in Zen, is called *sunyata*—the void, emptiness.[2] The theopoetic (experiential) structure that Eckhart calls the "ground of the soul" can take multiple forms, where the "it" is not "God" or *sunyata* but the depth and power and immensity of the *universe* itself. Indeed, one of the things that accounts for the enduring success of *Star Wars* in the popular culture is the mythic and mystical element with which it was suffused by George Lucas (a friend of Joseph Campbell), characters robed like monks with mysterious names, even including its own version of the art of Zen swordsmanship. When it is not the skill of the Jedi warrior but the "Force" that guides his lightsaber, he—or rather "it"—can anticipate his opponent's moves. It all comes down to letting go of the self.

That is why—without underestimating the threats it poses—I think the relentless and unnerving advance of the transhuman and posthuman project is not the sworn enemy of the mystical and apophatic element. I recall here the advice of Ilia Delio (chapter 14) that religion should not seek a war with posthumanism but a collaboration. As already noted, the original cyborg—the one of which the theologians are wary—was designed by the United

States Air Force for space travel, for the exploration of the universe. In my view, the *cosmic* mystery is fast becoming our candidate for the *mysterium tremendum et fascinans*, the mystery, dark and unencompassable, the sublimity, simultaneously attracting and repelling. The scientific cyborg, too, has apophatic and religious significance and is the stuff of new and no longer earth-bound mysticism. The scary, scarcely human, techno-human look of Darth Vader (the dark ground) as well as of the American and Russian astronauts, equipping them to explore the new "new world" of outer space, are the icons for a posthuman version of the apophatic imaginary, where mysticism and mathematics mix. To be sure, for most of Western history, we have described this point in the finite mind that opens itself to infinite mystery in terms of "God and the soul," which is an imaginative fiction. But the value of the name of God is *precisely that*. It is an *imaginative* fiction, a work of creative imagination, of *poetics*, of theopoetics, of the apophatic imagination. It is a figure, an image, a story, a parable, an epic poem, a mythic tale of the contact established between human beings and some great excess—God or the world, *Deus sive natura*, being or nothingness, the power of being, the ground of being, sunyata, the groundless ground or void—the several ways we describe that "in which we live and move and have our being" (Acts 17:28).

THE MYSTICAL ROSE, A WORLD WITHOUT WHY

The vast, ever increasingly expanding and for that very reason also *mortal* cosmos is the setting in which we today *reimagine* the mystery, the occasion for the apophatic imagination to *reconfigure*, the framework in which we revisit the world in *axiological* terms. The logos or *alogos* of this axiology is formulated with poetic precision in the famous couplet from Angelus Silesius on the mystical rose, upon which Heidegger made a memorable commentary:[3]

> The rose is without why; it blossoms because it blossoms;
> It cares not for itself, asks not if it's seen.

The mystical rose is an axiological figure par excellence. By "releasing" (*lassen*) the rose—God, the world, love, life—from the demand of reason to know why, the poet allows the rose to be *for itself*, cherished for its own worth. Reason's mandate that things give an account of themselves (*rationem reddere*) to justify their existence represents the height of irreverence, of *impiety*, toward the rose. Reason refuses the rose the right to stand in itself, without being made to answer to some higher authority. The mystical poet, by contrast, ponders over (*denken*) the self-standing of the rose, devotedly holding it in sacred memory (*andenken*). That leads Heidegger to speak of *die Frömmigkeit des Denkens*, a piety that has nothing to do with incense, clergy, and candles. He means a meditative openness, another piety that, having been released from the clutches of calculation (*rechnen*) and the clergy, inscribes a zone of *unconditional respect* around the world.

We might even dare to say, without fear of long robes, churchiness, or religiosity, that the mystical rose is the occasion of a great theopoetic *prayer*, not a petitionary prayer for power, wealth, health, or success but the highest or the deepest, the greatest and the most humble sentiment of prayer—Amen, *oui, oui*, yes, I said yes, let it be—addressed to the rose, to God, to the cosmos, to life, to life/death. When I say *prayer*, when I speak of the "prayers and tears of Jacques Derrida," that is not a trope, a riff, a clever mime of "real" religion. I am being perfectly—gravely—serious. I think we here make contact with the depths of prayer and, in so doing, put to rest the objection that "radical theology" is a strictly academic enterprise of no interest to people who are interested in "real" religion, meaning the traditional confessional religious bodies. On the contrary, this represents an archireligion, an archispirituality, one that can, should, and must be lived, breathed, and, yes, prayed.[4]

The point of the mystical poet's verse, Heidegger says, is not that we human beings, who ask why, are superior to the rose, which is unable to think, but quite the opposite. We are being invited by the mystical poet to model our lives after the rose, to live "without why."[5] That means to say yes to life's cyclic rhythms, to life/death, to mortal life, to affirm its trials and its joys, to feel the sheer upsurge of the world like the wind in our face and the cold breath of death, to embrace the flow of life *for itself*. Otherwise, life is shrunk down to a trial or a transaction, a test or a contest, an economic exchange, getting through this life in order to win an afterlife, whereas in truth there is nothing for which life can be exchanged. The blossoming of the rose is a general figure of both the *unconditional glory* of the world, which blossoms because it blossoms, and of our relationship to the world, which is without why, an *unconditional affirmation* of the world, not subject to conditions hidden in the small print. Living without why allows the world to stand (*stehen*) free as world, standing in itself, not as an object (*Gegen-stand*) in need of being justified to a subject. It releases what Heidegger called the "the worlding of the world," its coming-to-presence of itself, without conditions being laid down in advance by reason (or, let us add, by revelation), addressing us on its own terms without being spoken for by ontotheology.[6] The world worlds (*die Welt weltet*) of itself, in the open, as an open region. The worlding of the world is the *prius* that is *prior* to the principle of sufficient reason, prior to the seeking and rendering of reasons, prior to the distinction between reason and the irrational—and, we might add, prior to pretentious supernatural revelations pretending to supervene upon it. Then we are free because our love is free—that is, not made to serve some other purpose. Just so life itself.

By speaking of a *piety* of thinking and even of its *prayer*, we enter the apophatic space of the rose. This piety confirms the inherent *undecidability* of the two apophatics with which we began: the mutual permeability of piety and anxiety, the edifying abyss of loving praise and the abyss pure and simple. Undecidability means every piety is inwardly disturbed by anxiety (mortality), even as anxiety (mortality) implies a certain piety. This convergence comes to pass in the *mystical rose*, which is an abyss, without why, not without rhyme but without a reason beyond or outside itself. But unlike the mystical rose, the more austere piety of affirming the *cosmic rose* does not mean making contact with *eternal life*, entering into the *eternal now* of the Neoplatonic metaphysics saturating late medieval mysticism, but embracing the *temporality* and *mortality* of the world—*come what may, win or lose*. Living without why is not about winning. If it is, then, we lose. In the long run, we are all dead, which is the impious answer to Paul's question, "O death, where is your victory?" (1 Cor 15:55). Paul mistakenly assumes that death is an enemy either victor or vanquished. On the axiological accounting, death is neither. It is simply a limit, a *finis* that defines life, the way the life is passed on, part of life/death, part of the *Weltspiel*, of the way the world "worlds," of the "whiling" of the world, of the play of the world for the while that it plays, which plays because (*weil*) it plays—a play the poet invites us to join.

THE AXIOLOGY OF JOY

The expression "without why" in the mystical poetry of Angelus Silesius goes back to the sermons of Eckhart,[7] who we now believe picked it up from Marguerite Porete.[8] Porete was an aristocratic woman who made the fatal mistake of learning to read and write and then to author a beautiful book in which she criticized a rigid, powerful, and patriarchal church, which she mockingly called the "little church." That book earned her a burning at the stake, condemned by twenty-one male theologians of the little church. Unlike Socrates, she refused to recognize the authority of her executioners, and rightly so. In the realm of the rose, the region of being without why, which she called the "big church," there are no authorities (neither reason nor revelation, neither church nor state). Marguerite antagonized the little church by even speaking "against ethics,"[9] or at least against the virtues, when she wrote, "Virtues, I take my leave of you forever."[10] By this she meant not to recommend something lower, a life of vice, but something higher, which for her was love. Virtues are Aristotelian qualities teleologically aimed at happiness (*beatitudo*), but love is without why, a-teleological, cherished for itself, *come what may* (axiological). As David Kangas shows, what is beyond virtue and any teleology is what Marguerite calls *joy* (*joie, gaudium*), the "sea of joy," which is not inconsistent with suffering and death, like the *unhappy* fate visited upon Marguerite herself, which from all accounts she met with unshaken joy.[11] Joy is not a reward we get afterward in return for enduring suffering. Joy emerges *in* the suffering; it is a quality *of* the suffering. Marguerite made herself worthy of what was happening to her. She did not call a good thing bad. In that lies the joy, the exultation. Her idea, which became general throughout the Rhineland mystical tradition, was to purify love of self-love (the "simple soul"), to detach the self from self-interest. While a virtuous will is better than self-will, Eckhart said, best of all is no will at all, meaning not absolute indifference or diffidence but living solely by God's will.[12] The simple soul abandons its creaturely self-will, living in pure releasement (*Gelassenheit*) and detachment (*Abgeschiedenheit*) from its self-interests.

This creates an interesting dilemma: the love of God earns us an "eternal reward," but love is not in it for the rewards. Some people love God, Meister Eckhart complained, the way they love their cow, for its milk.[13] Eckhart says that were we to ask life, were that possible, "Why do you live?" life would answer, "I live because I live." Life is its own reward; there is nothing for which it could be exchanged.[14] That leads Eckhart to pose a paradoxical mystical limit case (drawing upon Rom. 9:3) called the *resignatio ad infernum*: were God to will my eternal separation from God, then, since my will would be God's will, I would prefer the pains of hell to the happiness of heaven.[15] In Porete's terms, in letting go of heavenly happiness (*beatitudo*), there is an unshakeable joy (*gaudium*) in God, even in the pains of hell. Eckhart was speaking *emphatice*. His hypothesis, letting go of unity with God for the sake of God,[16] was posed per impossibile, with some degree of confidence—as a scholastic magister at Paris in the Dominican intellectualist tradition—that it would be a square circle for a just and loving God to commit a just person to hell. Posing that hypothesis as a *real possibility* had to wait for one of a darker disposition, a moody and guilt-ridden Augustinian in the voluntarist tradition. I refer to the *Deus absconditus* proposed by Luther in response to Erasmus's claim that God would never condemn a just person (chapter 2).

This hypothetical limit case shears love free from the economy of rewards and punishment. In the effort to separate love from anything external to the love, the mystics imagine the grimmest of possibilities, the darkest of grounds, which in the piety of their apophatic imagination takes the demonic form of *eternal damnation*, an imaginative figure we might consider a placeholder for the notion of planetary, stellar, and indeed *cosmic death*, which belongs to our imaginary. Where they saw everlasting punishment, we foresee eternal cosmic oblivion.

THE AXIOLOGICAL SUSPENSION OF THE TELEOLOGICAL

For Derrida, the logic of the mystical "without why," the suspension of the teleological, takes the form of the "pure" gift (like Marguerite's "simple" soul), which he distinguishes from the "economy" of the gift exchange. A pure gift is given without an ulterior end, without the expectation of a return, so pure indeed that it is not even visible as a gift (lest it set off a chain of debt and gratitude), like the rose that blossoms unseen.[17] Derrida's point is brought home by the paradox of Matthew 25:31–46 discussed earlier (chapter 11). The moment *we read* this story, the *economic* operation of the gift is made *visible*, and with that the gift is annulled. From now on we *know* that if you love God, you will be rewarded forever, and if not, you will be punished forever. Whatever that is, it is not love. If it were a marriage, it would be called spousal abuse.

In axiology, love is gratuitously given, given "for *nothing*," for nothing *else*, nothing outside, beyond or beside itself, constituting a certain nihilism of grace, because anything *else* would annul the gift, undo the love. Sometimes we hear "religious" people ask, If there is no heaven and hell, why not indulge every immoral impulse? In axiology, that would be the real nihilism, a real devaluation of life, a craven cynicism that takes life to be a nightmare unless we get rewarded, unless it is "worth it" to us. Why feed the hungry if there is no heavenly banquet in store for us? That is *unworthy* of us. The "kingdom of God" is not given as a *reward* for performing works of mercy; the works of mercy *are* the kingdom of God. The mercenary view of mercy aided and abetted by teleology becomes a perfect ontotheological storm when it is backed up with the Neoplatonic metaphysics that was deeply planted in Christianity by Augustine and the church fathers and has never lost its grip. Unless something lasts forever, it cannot be truly valued. Only the *eternal* can be loved *unconditionally*. Use the temporal as a means to an eternal reward (*uti*), but to enjoy it for itself (*frui*) is sinful. But in axiology, what makes something precious is precisely its *perishability*, like the beauty of the rose, like the beauty of the vow of love "until death do us part," like the beauty of a slowly disappearing sunset, like youth and health, like life itself, like the worlding of the world itself, like the small blue dot (Carl Sagan) that will eventually dissipate over cosmic eons.

In axiology, we are released from the heterology of the puffed-up powers that be, the booming imperial voices of the princes and *principia*—a Divine Command, a Categorical Imperative, a Natural Law, the Economy of Salvation, a Supernatural Revelation. The joy arises from embracing a call that comes without an identifiable caller—is it the world or God, *Deus sive natura*? The call comes without a warrant, without principles or proper authorization, without grounds, completely *sans papiers*, a weak force, where there is no divine flamethrower waiting in the wings to torch the offenders with eternal fire or reward the obedient with the spoils of Egypt, as a duty without debt, where we ought not to say ought.[18] The only way the call is known at all is in our response, so when we answer it, we look foolish, like dancers dancing to music no one else hears. An axiology is not verified but testified. Joy makes its way without any deep underlying ontotheological ground, without any ontoteleological warranty that all will be well in the end, without assurance that the purposes of divine providence or reason in history, of evolutionary survival or utilitarian advantage, will be served. Joy affirms the rose—the worlding of the world, the play of the world—for what it is, because it is, without why, come what may, *quoi qu'il arrive*. [19] Instead of a thunderous command, we are visited by a quiet question; instead of a terrifying inquisition, a gentle query, which, if we listen, should rattle us to the bone. It does not shout "thou shalt." It does not ask "What do you want to get out of all this?" but "Who are you? Who do you want to be?" It does not ask "Of what worth are these things to you?" but "How can you make yourself worthy of them?"

In an axiology, what mystics like Porete and Eckhart are saying about the rose as a theopoetic figure of the love of God applies, *mutatis mutandis*, to the cosmos, the cosmopoetic body of a mortal God, which is likewise without why, blossoming because and for the while (*weil*) that it blossoms. The axiology releases the world from all the teleological and eschatological schemes that the philosophers and theologians have devised in order to "save" it. The axiology disarms the triadic mythological-soteriological schemata—of origin/fall/salvation or creator/redeemer/sanctifier—running in the background of classical theology and dialectics. Axiological letting-be represents an affirmation of the world without trying to "save" the world because *the world was never lost.* Accordingly, the cold, dark, mute oblivion the physicists forecast does no harm to axiological joy, even as axiological joy does not annul the groundless ground of the apophatic. On the contrary, cosmic oblivion throws the call of the world back on its own resources, providing the occasion of an absolute and *unconditional affirmation of what there is*, of what is because it is, for the while that it is, without demanding *ontological assurance* or promising *eternal compensation* for our trouble. Axiology extricates us from a childlike economy of rewards and punishments, of ontotheological sticks and carrots, producing a postmodern expansion of Kant's narrowly modernist and rationalistic affect-free version of the maturity of humankind. Far from undermining the affirmation of the world, the prospect of oblivion incites a humble gratitude for life. *Finitude is the sadness of every ending that is constitutive of the beauty of every love story*. It leads us to count our lucky stars, in the most literal sense, that we are born of stardust and unto stardust will return, our birth and death being a function of theirs. We are all star stuff.

That the cosmos will end up as nothing (*nihil*) at all is not nihilism, or rather, since it almost literally is, it is a nihilism *of grace*, where the response to the question of why there is something rather than nothing is enacted in the *without why*. The power of the without why is to experience its powerlessness before the unprethinkable power of being and its unforethinkable end. The cosmological limit is the condition of an unconditional axiology, of an affirmation of life lived within these conditions and embraced precisely as such. Axiology is freedom. We are free because life and love are freed from servitude to some goal external to themselves.

THE MYSTICAL ROSE AND THE COSMIC ROSE

What, then, is the difference between the mystical rose and the cosmic rose, between the releasement (*Gelassenheit*) of the Rhineland mystics and what is possible for us today? To answer that question, I go back to a passage in *Being and Time* where Heidegger is discussing the fundamental moods that Dasein experiences in its anticipatory projection upon death. Here he speaks not simply of *Angst* but of a *nüchterne Angst*, an anxiety that is not disabling or pathological but calm, clearheaded, and sober—we might even say a dispassionate passion (or mood)—such that it is not only reason that demands calm but also anxiety. This, he says, is accompanied by a *gerüstete Freude*, a joy that is strong and unshakeable, firm and fortified,[20] a joy in life that stands clearheaded before death, like Porete before her executioners. The affirmation of life is not defeated by death but intensified, drawing its strength, its clarity, its resolve about life from opening itself to death. This joy is a gift of death, a gift born of death, which sounds a bit eerie and uncanny, an effect I do not deny or dismiss.

In *Being and Time*, being-toward-death is famously described in heroic-individualist terms, each of us alone before death, like Augustine alone before God (*coram deo*). I propose a larger, gentler, and more communal structure applied, *mutatis mutandis*, to our collective death, not just mine, not just our species, not just terrestrial or solar, but cosmic death. Accordingly, we take unshakeable joy in the world itself arising from a calm, clear understanding of the limits of all things great and small. This joy does not nullify or reverse, sublate or supersede the nullity of the end, and it is not crushed by it. On the contrary, the joy is made possible *by* the very prospect of the end. Here, in an austere piety—a sober anxiety, an eerie and uncanny calm, a firm joy—we can see the mutual communication of the two apophaticisms, as well as the inner communication of the theopoetic suspension of the supernatural signified and axiological suspension of teleology. The world worlds, having been released from the grip of supernaturalist soteriology and philosophical teleology. Letting-be liberates the glory embedded in the darkness, releases the joy embedded in the anxiety. It does not call a good thing bad. The expanding universe itself is an expenditure without return, a pure gift without an identifiable giver, a gift of death. Death—personal, planetary, solar, and cosmic—is an intrinsic and constitutive part of the pattern of life/death, which makes the light of life all the more intense and bright.

Here (*da*), in a remote corner of a galaxy, for a fleeting cosmic Camelot moment, the cosmos *rejoices, celebrates itself,* affirms itself, confirms itself, says yes to itself, in a kind of cosmic *guadium*, without why. This gives a cosmological dimension to Heidegger's existential notion of the "*da*" of *Sein* as a place of cosmic disclosure, where, for a transient moment, a cosmic *Augenblick*, a cosmological *kairos*, the universe catches sight of itself and says yes, *oui, oui,* come, *gaudete*. At the end, the lights dim and go out, the curtain closes, while the world, for its part, cares not for itself, asks not if it is seen. The dark ground is all in all. That is the uncanny part, the spectrality of it all. Instead of the machoism of Dasein's heroic combat with an abyss, the *Kampf* (*polemos*) that Heidegger loved, I follow the advice of thinkers like Catherine Keller, Luce Irigaray, and Hannah Arendt to see the world in terms of a matrix, the darkness of the deep (*tehom*), the dark watery womb that has given birth to us, the juxtaposed dynamics of mortality and natality—*natura* and *physis*, after all, having to do with birth, and birth having to do ultimately with death.

The mystical rose differs from the cosmic rose as the mystics' more innocent angelic imaginary differs from our more austere one. In their pious and edifying apophatics, the dark ground is ultimately annulled and flooded with light, while we are clear about the irreducibility of the abyss. In Porete and Eckhart, the thematic of living and loving without why is a way to let God be God, and *Gelassenheit* means a perfect trust in an eternally unfailing Light, in whom there is nothing to fear, a source of divine consolation, of everlasting life in an eternal now. Theirs is the blindness of excessive light, where the blindness is a temporary condition—"and then face to face," when we will be like the angels. But the cosmic rose is a figure of a mortal God, and living and loving without why involves a steely joy, armed and fortified (*gerüstete*) for temporality, finitude, and death. Releasement does not mean trust in an eternal benevolence and everlasting life but a sober calm that affirms the chiaroscuro of life and death. Death and finitude are not a mythic curse, not a punishment or test, not the issue of a mythic "fall," but the order of things, which is, they tell us, not an order of unity and everlasting peace but an order of increasing disorder, an irreversible arrow aimed straight at oblivion, being's own oblivion. To release the cosmos from the grip of teleology is to free the world to be the world, whatever it may be, come what may, including the eerie outcome physicists presently foresee,[21] to affirm it unconditionally—*oui, oui*, yes, I said yes—in a cosmo-doxology, world without why, Amen.

The cosmic rose blossoms because it blossoms, for the while that it blossoms, until at the end, fully expanded and expended, its petals fall and it ceases to blossom, caring not for itself, asking not if it is seen. Thus does the apophatic imagination make its way:

> *Imagine* a kind of cosmic Good Friday with no one at the foot of the cross to witness it, whose *consummatum est* bears witness without witness to the glory of a world now long gone, the glory having been resurrection enough.
> *Imagine* a galaxy far, far away, where a star now long dead once nourished a planet with beings who laughed and wept,

lived and died—who were wise and foolish, heroes and cowards—only to disappear without a trace.

Imagine now that eerie story is ours.

The dark depth of the ground intensifies the brightness of the light. That is the law of the apophatic imagination. The cosmic night intensifies the glory of the cosmos like a brilliant shower of meteors against a pitch-black sky. The brightness of the body of God is magnified by the part of God where God is not being God. The abyss dispels the angelic innocence and illusion of "eternal life" and "eternal light" where there are no contrasts, just a blinding white, a white-on-white mythology. After all, it is not as if the big bang set out in search of multiplicity in order to return to itself at the end in a higher unity. It is not as if a Super-Somebody has staged the whole thing as a trial such that, if we behave ourselves and keep all the rules, we will be rewarded with a "new creation," in which we are promised there will be neither trials nor temptation, neither toothaches nor entropy. Surely we have had enough of Neoplatonism.

CONCLUSION

The Name (of) "God"

THE VALUE OF A VARIABLE

In speaking of God axiologically, theopoetically, cosmopoetically, and hauntologically, it is obvious that I do not take God to be someone who does things (or fails to) when we are in need of divine intervention to get us through the day. Nevertheless, we do speak to God—thanking God, sometimes complaining bitterly at how badly things are going, and variously calling upon God, *de profundis*, from our deepest recesses, abyss to abyss. In general, we cannot resist behaving as if "someone" is "there." That I treat as a desire to personify but not as something to be dismissed because personification springs from sources deep in our imaginary, representing the desire, the need to tell a story (*mythos*), to narrate what is happening to us, to converse with the powers of being. That is what Schelling meant by a myth, Hegel by a *Vorstellung*, Tillich by a symbol, and what I call a poetics (and what for me has become of what Aquinas called analogy). In a poetics, something has taken hold of our innermost bodily forces, something with which they resonate, and the question, as Deleuze would say, is not "What does it mean?" but, "How do I play it? How do we stage it, script it, sing and dance it?"

In a poetics, we freely converse with things, with anything, whatever it is, anonymous as it may be; we personify it, proffer our love for it, or express our anger. That is the way we talk to the land or sky or sea, a language fluently spoken by indigenous peoples. It is the way we speak to animals; our favorite tree; the old house we grew up in, now in disrepair; or an old hat worn by a parent now long dead. It is how we talk to the stars when we thank our lucky stars. All of this is modeled after the way we talk to someone we love. But when we try to convert this imagery into a concept, we hit a limit. In a poetics, we do not go high, because high and mighty concepts are beyond us; we go low, down into the earth, to the ground, into the bowels of being. We grope for words because we are lost for words, for words that resonate with the depths, for images that make our bodies quiver and our minds reel, leaving us trembling with fascination, fear, awe, anxiety, love, joy—all words found in the thesaurus of the apophatic imagination.

If I knew all the languages in the world and were personally acquainted with all the forms of life, here and everywhere else, now and into the distant past, I could make a list of such words and images and include them in a large appendix. If I were an indigenous Hawaiian, for example, I might head my list with lava rock, if an ancient Greek, with a glorious sun. As it is, I know only a few, and I make use of the family of words and images I have inherited in the genealogical line in which I found myself, in which everything turns on the name (of) "God" (in Greco-Judeo-Christian-Latin-Anglo-Saxon). Why have I chosen this word? I just said I did not. It chose me. I chose it because it chose me first. It is far too late to ask me this question. As soon as I opened my eyes in the world, I was greeted by it, my head doused by its waters while my "*god*parents" stood in for me and vowed in my place that this is the word I would have chosen had I been able to speak. This all took place in a time immemorial, at the beginning of the world, at my unprethinkable birth. No one asked for my consent. I was immersed first in a womb, then in a baptismal wash of words and images, songs and rites, a flow of black cassocks and fluttering white surplices, of priests and nuns, in a history and tradition, a culture and church, in which this word held pride of place. I never had a chance. It is all a priori, and I am entirely a posteriori. I have been digging through it ever since. I have repeatedly tried to dig out of it only to find out later I was digging into it all the more deeply.

I gave up trying to escape my unprethinkable point of departure and tried instead, within my limits, to inscape it, as Gerard Manley Hopkins might say, to think what is thinkable in the thick unprethinkable *prius* in which I found myself. That means, be forewarned, there is a coefficient of contingency attached to everything I say, an historical asterisk. Were I born elsewhere and in a different time, where other choices would have been made for me, I would have been given a different story to tell. Every theology is a theology of the culture it inhabits; every culture is inhabited by a theology, by something in which it bares its heart. There are as many theologies as there are forms of life and lifeworlds, languages and cultures, times and traditions, with different and conflicting interpretations of what is going on—all so many configurations of the apophatic imagination, all so many failed attempts to think the unprethinkable. But that very failure constitutes a happy fault, for it is the very thing we all have in common. *Tout autre est tout autre.* We are all siblings of the same dark ground, all compatriots of the same nameless country, the same *unheimlich* home, all companions of the uncanny, called to share (*com*) our bread (*panis*). Asking, as do doctrinaire theists and atheists, which is *the* one true name, the one true story, makes no sense. That question is dense in the hermeneutic sense, no *subtilitas*. It is like asking what is the one true song, or language, or poem, or culture. The question arises from what the philosophers call a category mistake, like calling checkmate in football.

If a poetics can take many different forms, *theo*poetics celebrates the event that is harbored in the name (of) "God," and *cosmo*poetics celebrates the mystery that the world is, the mystery of the *that*. The name (of) "God" is one way among many others to resonate with the "powers of being," as Schelling liked to call them; to "sync up," as they say in the IT world, with what Tillich calls the ground of being; or to affirm the unconditional event coming from a future we cannot see coming, as Derrida put it. It is a limit word, a word we use at the limits, to book our passage to the limits, setting out for a shore we know we cannot reach. It seeks to access what is in recess, necessarily and structurally, to give words to the silent concealed depths. It is the Hegelian *Vorstellung* I inherited—something more conceptual than art but more sensuous than a concept—but, *pace* Hegel, I have no Concept for it because it conceived me before I could conceive it. I am attached to it because it attached itself to me. It is a focal word in which all the lines of force that traverse my body, mind, and heart converge. It is that than which I cannot conceive a more convergent, insurgent, resurgent source of power (*dynamis*) and activity (*energeia*). The words I give to it are the music it has all along been playing on me. I am attuned to it because I am the tune it is playing on me, which is why we resonate, syncopate, synchronize, sympathize.

The name (of) "God" is not the name of a being (theism) or the ground of being (panentheism) but of a way of being-in-the-world. It is not the name of the being beyond being (mystical theology) but the name of a *call* from beyond being, of a may-being without being, of a promise and a memory, neither being nor nonbeing, like a specter or ghost. Those of us who indulge in the dark art of hauntology hear voices, expecting specters everywhere and in everything. We keep our ear close to the breast of the world to hear its heartbeat, to detect what is calling, what is being called for. Unlike other calls, this one is constituted by its nonknowing and nonbeing, from which it draws all its powerless power, like the specter that it is. This is a call of unknown provenance, "God" serving as its incognito. Who or what is calling in the name (of)

"God"? Is it the call of the world, of the cosmos racing by me as it heads straight for oblivion, an adieu the universe utters as it passes by like a meteor? Or is it really God, or maybe my guardian angel, or even a wily spirit bent on deceiving me, Satan tempting me up to the top of the temple? Is it just a noise my body makes when it resonates with the world?[1]

Asking who or what is the caller of the call is like asking who is the author of justice, love, or mercy. These are events embedded in the form of life, neither active nor passive but, to invoke a category of classical grammar, taking place in the middle voice. The call gets itself called in the form of life, undecidably, the way the word *God/god* fluctuates between a proper and a common noun. Whoever participates in the form of life feels its force, is drawn by its pull, less like a powerful wind than the weak force of a solicitation, the soft sway of an insinuation or an invitation, an imperative but without an imperial army to enforce it. The call is a potency in need of actualization, a field inviting an excitation, an implicit force trying to become explicit. What does it call for? It does not say precisely. It is like a specter who wakes me in the middle of the night and then just sits on the side of my bed and stares at me, without saying a word, which is very spooky. It puts me on the spot, leaving me searching myself for what I am being called to do. Of it I do not say it is, but it spooks. The whole world is spooked.

That I have condensed this entire story into the name (of) "God," organized everything around it, is a debatable, locatable, and revisable decision. It is a personal decision that I am wagering is a prism in which others can see themselves, like an autobiography in which others hear their own story. Treat it as a placeholder that can be replaced by other names, as a variable, an X, that has other values, which actually is the case. This is the interpretation I have made—or that has made me from a time out of mind. I cannot remember anything older than the name (of) "God." It belongs to the very meaning of *an* interpretation that there are *other* interpretations, that any interpretation belongs to a conflict of interpretations. There is no such thing as "only one interpretation," which is the definition of the violence of dogma. That, I think, is the hermeneutic nerve of Schelling's decisionistic way of putting the same point; radical hermeneutics means interpretation springing from the roots of our being, where our choices cumulatively define us. Radical thinking, whether it laces itself up in the garments of philosophy or theology, of science or art, situates itself at a certain point, the limit point, where we run up against the limits, the dark center, the concealed depths. There we ask basic questions, limit questions, asking why where there is ultimately no why. There we are forced—by the urgency of life and the shortness of time—to construe the play of shadows in the cave, to form an imaginary, tell a story, to write an epic poem, in which we expose our soul, bare our hearts, show our true colors. In an axiology of the event, the whole idea is to make ourselves worthy of the events that happen to us, to respond to what they call for, to make them welcome and converse with them, however spooky their uninvited visitations. Our true worth and worthiness, the true worth and worthiness of what is going on in the name (of) "God," makes itself visible in what for all the world is foolishness or even defeat, where the dignity rises up from those laid low by the powers of the world, like those who resist evil and forgive their persecutors, which seems impossible.

That explains why I have not yet given up on the word "God." It is the most felicitous way I can imagine—and I am talking about an imaginary and confessing the limits of my imagination—to name the limit, the passage to the limits, which Derrida described as the possibility of *the* impossible, for with God all things are possible, including the impossible. *By* the impossible, the event begins. *The* impossible does not mean a logical contradiction but a phenomenological shock, the event that shatters the horizon of expectation. The possibility of the impossible is the definition of keeping the future open. It is the way to give things their future, to free them from the limits of the possible, to make all things new, constituting the theopoetic content of any "new creation."

THE HARMONY OF THE SPHERES

We can hardly imagine what the posthuman future will be like. For that we depend upon the scientists and the artists and, perhaps, a new species of philosophers and theologians worthy of the name. But one thing I can imagine is that, if and when we would ever surpass our earthly habitat and venture far into the vast and unfathomable cosmos, which is our "new world," our sense of the *mysterium tremendum et fascinans* will remain intact, not destroyed—expanded to cosmic dimensions, not collapsed. As the island of knowledge grows larger, the shorelines of ignorance grow longer.[2] We already see this in the sense of *mystery*, and I choose this word carefully, that descends upon both astrophysicists and the quantum scientists confronting ever "spookier" entanglements and superpositions and multiverses. Maybe even we ourselves, our entire world, are a virtual reality, a simulation conjured up by a computer somewhere in the universe. Imagine that! Just try!

I can imagine that the posthuman will all prove too much for (the word) "God," that the name (of) "God" will be overwhelmed, finished, drained of its mythic, symbolic, dramatic, rhetorical, and poetic power to galvanize a form of life. Perhaps, in the posthuman and transhuman world ahead, they will look back upon this word with smiling condescension, as we do upon the four humors or bloodletting, as an archaic and obsolete feature of the "human" stage in the prehistory of whatever these posthumans will call themselves. It may be, as we saw earlier (chapter 13), that we need a body to use the word *God*, that were we ever to cease to be *biological*, we would also cease to be *theological*, that "God" and "human" beings are companions, one never found without the other.

But even then I cannot imagine that our apophantic imagination will not seek other more high-tech, cosmic, and galactic ways to image, figure, and reconfigure the *mysterium* by which we will be engulfed. "May the Force be with you." Watch and pray that you do not go over to the Dark Side. These figures from the popular culture are not without comparison to the mythic battle with the powers and principalities in the New Testament. I cannot imagine, and this is a basic axiom of the apophantic imagination, that we will not always and everywhere be confronted by the unimaginable. My wager is that the X we have valued as God will be transvalued, transformed in a new cosmo-theopoetics. The mystery and the mysticism will move closer and closer to the mathematics, where the earth is a speck of galactic dust, a mote suspended on a sunbeam, our star but one of many millions in our galaxy, our galaxy but one among many millions of galaxies, and maybe, who knows, our universe but one of innumerable universes.

The apophatic imaginary, left groping for new words and figures, struck by the staggering complexity and resplendence of the heavenly spheres, in awe at the birth and death of the stars, will hearken to the ancient belief in the supersonic "music of the spheres," the celestial bodies having always had, ever since Pythagoras, at least, a mathematical-musical-mystical resonance. What is that music if not the call by which we are summoned, and what is that call if not the mystical element in our lives? Aristotle, never a mystic, ever a man of good common sense, objected that surely we would be able to hear this music if it were really there, to which we reply that theopoetics gives us the ears to hear.

And if to this majestic scene we must add, as we are presently instructed, the spooky thought that all of that may end in naught, that over a spread of time, unimaginable and barely calculable, everything is slowly being torn apart, then what? Is that not to think the end of a beautiful ballad rendered all the more beautiful because it is sad? What is that if not a cosmic hymn to a little bit of stardust on which once, long ago, there were gods and roses, heroes and knaves, mountains and valleys, when Elohim filled the earth and sea and sky with living things and called them all good, very good (while no doubt keeping the divine fingers crossed)? What is that if not the end of a beautiful film flashing playbacks of our favorites scenes as the final credits roll down the screen and then cutting off, leaving us sitting in a dark and silent theater dabbing at our tears? What is that if not to put a dark apophatic frame around a brilliant streak of light darting across the cosmic skies only to be swallowed up by the dark center, the concealed depths in which we live and move and have our being, which are nearer to us than we are to ourselves?

The spectrality of God means that the name (of) "God" will have then turned out to be a cosmic rumble, a transient effect produced by the harmony of the spheres, a haunting hymn to the mystery I have all along been trying to summon up, a psalm to the *prius* with which we are never able to catch up, to the event of which we are trying to make ourselves worthy. The spectrality of God means the mysterious cosmic music playing in the background that for a while breaks the ancient silence of the elements in the opening scene of Genesis. The music plays because it plays and cares not whether it is heard, while we, having overheard it, are applauding, discerning in it a great doxology:

> Glory be to the world,
> whatever it was in the beginning and whatever it will be at the end,
> world without why, Amen.

NOTES

INTRODUCTION

1. Benoît Peeters, *Derrida: A Biography*, trans. Andrew Brown (Cambridge: Polity, 2013), 345–46.

CHAPTER 1

1. For the grammar of weakness I employ, see John D. Caputo, *The Weakness of God: A Theology of the Event* (Bloomington: Indiana University Press, 2006).
2. Jean Grondin, *Introduction to Philosophical Hermeneutics*, trans. Joel Weinsheimer (New Haven, CT: Yale University Press, 1994), 60–62 explains Gadamer's adaptation of Rambach's idea of hermeneutics.
3. On the distinction between insistence and existence, see John D. Caputo, *The Insistence of God: A Theology of Perhaps* (Bloomington: Indiana University Press, 2013).
4. See my interpretation of Matthew 25 in John D. Caputo, *The Folly of God: A Theology of the Unconditional* (Salem, OR: Polebridge, 2016), 111–28.
5. See Gilles Deleuze, *The Logic of Sense*, trans. Mark Lester with Charles Stivale, ed. Constantin V. Boundas (New York: Columbia University Press, 1969), 149.
6. Ernst Kantorowicz, *The King's Two Bodies: A Study in Medieval Political Theology* (Princeton, NJ: Princeton University Press, 1957).
7. In chapter 13, I consider whether resurrection and ascension might, in fact, be reconceived as "uploading."

8. J. Denny Weaver, "Violence in Christian Theology," in *Cross Examinations: Readings on the Meaning of the Cross Today*, ed. Marit Trelstad (Minneapolis, MN: Augsburg Fortress, 2006), 235.

9. Johann Baptist Metz, *Faith in History and Society*, trans. D. Smith (New York: Crossroads, 1980), 109–15.

10. See Christophe Chalamet and Hans-Christoph Askani, eds., *The Wisdom and Foolishness of God: First Corinthians 1–2 in Theological Exploration* (Minneapolis, MN: Fortress, 2015).

11. See David L. Miller, "Theopoetry or Theopoetics," *Cross Currents* 60, no. 1 (March 2010): 6–23.

12. Heidegger sets out his differences with Husserl most clearly in *History of the Concept of Time: Prolegomena*, trans. Theodore Kisiel (Bloomington: Indiana University Press, 1985).

13. It first appeared in print in Martin Heidegger, "On the Essence of Ground" (1928), in *Martin Heidegger: Pathmarks*, ed. William McNeill (Cambridge: Cambridge University Press, 1998), 105; it was first announced in a 1927 lecture course, Martin Heidegger, *The Basic Problems of Phenomenology*, trans. Albert Hofstadter (Bloomington: Indiana University Press, 1978), 227–30. Both texts were projected versions of the original "Time and Being."

14. Martin Heidegger, "What Is Metaphysics," trans. David Farrell Krell, in *Pathmarks*, ed. William McNeil (Cambridge: Cambridge University Press, 1998), 82–96.

15. Martin Heidegger, *Being and Time*, trans. John Macquarrie and Edward Robinson (New York: Harper & Row, 1962), 28–31 (§3).

16. Max Müller, *Existenzphilosophie im Geistigen Leben der Gegenwart* (Heidelberg, Germany: Kerle Verlag, 1964), 67.

17. Martin Heidegger, "The Ontological Difference," in *Nietzsche*, vol. 4, *Nihilism*, trans. David Krell (New York: Harper & Row, 1993), 150–59, and "The Onto-theo-logical Constitution of Metaphysics," in *Identity and Difference*, trans. Joan Stambaugh (New York: Harper & Row, 1969), 42–76.

18. Martin Heidegger, "Der Spruch des Anaximander," in *Gesamtausgabe*, vol. 5, *Holzwege*, ed. F.-W. von Herrmann (Frankfurt, Germany: Klosterman, 1977), 364 note (d).

19. Heidegger, "The Ontological Difference," 155.

20. Heidegger, "The Onto-theo-logical Constitution of Metaphysics," 72.

21. Paul Tillich, *Theology of Culture* (Oxford: Oxford University Press, 1959), 25.

22. Martin Heidegger, "Phenomenology and Theology," in *Martin Heidegger: Pathmarks*, ed. William McNeill (Cambridge: Cambridge University Press, 1998), 43–45.
23. Tillich, *Theology of Culture*, 3–9.
24. In Jacques Derrida, "Geschlecht I: Sexual Difference, Ontological Difference," trans. Ruben Berezdivin, *Research in Phenomenology* 13, no. 1 (1983): 65–83, Derrida showed the difficulty Heidegger had in maintaining the sexual neutrality of the ontological difference. A purely differential relationship displaces the primacy of binary relations and allows for more complex and multiplex relationships.
25. Jacques Derrida, "Différance," in *Margins of Philosophy*, trans. Alan Bass (Chicago: University of Chicago Press, 1982), 1–27.
26. See John D. Caputo, *Radical Hermeneutics: Repetition, Deconstruction, and the Hermeneutic Project* (Bloomington: Indiana University Press, 1987), 120–23.
27. It would be "foolish" to criticize Heidegger's ontological difference, Derrida says; the higher task is to return to "its power to provoke." Derrida, "Différance," 23.
28. Walter Benjamin, "The Concept of History," IX, in *Walter Benjamin: Selected Writings*, vol. 4, *1938–40*, ed. Michael Jennings (Cambridge, MA: Belknap Press of Harvard University Press, 2003), 389–400.

CHAPTER 2

1. See Bernard McGinn, *The Mystical Thought of Meister Eckhart: The Man from Whom God Hid Nothing* (New York: Crossroad, 2003). The expression is based upon a saying attributed to Eckhart found in *Meister Eckhart*, vol. 1, ed. Franz Pfeiffer, trans. C. de B. Evans (London: Watkins, 1956), 417.
2. To be sure, demons and the occult arts also flourished in the wider culture; the one implies the other. See Richard Kieckhefer, *Magic in the Middle Ages*, Canto edition (Cambridge: Cambridge University Press, 2000).
3. Martin Heidegger, *Frühe Schriften*, ed. F.-W. von Herrmann (Frankfurt: Klostermann, 1978), 149.
4. Derrida distinguishes "two tropics of negativity" in "How to Avoid Speaking: Denials," in *Derrida and Negative Theology*, ed. Howard Coward and Toby Foshay (Albany: State University of New York Press, 1992), 100–108; see also, "Post-Scriptum: Aporias, Ways and Voices," 283–323.

5. Aquinas, *Summa Theologica*, pt. I, question 13, art. 12, ad 1, and *Summa Contra Gentiles*, bk. III, chap. 49.

6. He might actually have suffered a cerebral hemorrhage. See Edmund Colledge, *Friar Thomas d'Aquino: His Life, Thoughts, and Work* (Garden City, NJ: Doubleday, 1974), 321, and his "The Legend of St. Thomas Aquinas," in *Thomas Aquinas: 1274–1974*, ed. Armand Maurer (Toronto: Pontifical University of Medieval Studies, 1974), 126.

7. Aquinas, *Summa Theologica*, pt. I, question 50, art. 1.

8. Nick Bostrom, *Superintelligence: Paths, Dangers, Strategies* (Oxford: Oxford University Press, 2014).

9. Thomas Aquinas, "On Being and Essence," in *Selected Writings of St. Thomas Aquinas*, ed. and trans. Robert P. Goodwin (Indianapolis, IN: Bobbs-Merrill, 1965), 33–67.

10. See the classic study by W. Norris Clarke, "The Limitation of Act by Potency: Aristotelianism or Neoplatonism," *The New Scholasticism* 26 (1952): 167–94.

11. William Carlo, *The Ultimate Reducibility of Essence to Existence in Existential Metaphysics* (The Hague, Netherlands: Martinus Nijhoff, 1966).

12. "Heidegger's Dif-ference and the *esse/ens* Distinction in Aquinas," in *The Essential Caputo: Selected Writings*, ed. B. Keith Putt (Bloomington: Indiana University Press, 2018), 93–108.

13. Jacques Maritain, *Existence and the Existent*, trans. Lewis Galantier and Gerald B. Phelan (Garden City, NJ: Doubleday, Image Books, 1956), 31. Mary Daly wrote her doctoral dissertation on Maritain and shared my enthusiasm for his "intuition of being."

14. Maritain, *Existence and the Existent*, 45, 51.

15. The notion of *creatio ex nihilo* is a second-century CE innovation; see Gerhard May, *Creatio ex Nihilo: The Doctrine of "Creation Out of Nothing" in Early Christian Thought*, trans. A. S. Worrall (Edinburgh: T & T Clark, 1994).

16. Cornelio Fabro, *Participation et causalité selon saint Thomas d'Aquin* (Louvain: Publications Universitaires de Louvain; Paris, Editions Beatrice-Lauwelaerts, 1961).

17. Aquinas, *Summa Theologica*, pt. I, question 13.

18. Thomas Aquinas, *Quaestiones disputatae de Potentia*, question 7, art. 3.

19. Aquinas, *Summa Theologica*, pt. I, question 33, art. 1; question 13, art. 11.

20. Aquinas, *Summa Theologica*, pt. I, question 58, art. 3; and even a "defect," *Summa Contra Gentiles*, part I, chap. 8.

21. Pierre Rousselot, *L'Intellectualisme de Saint Thomas* (Paris: Alcan, 1908). I am citing the new translation, *Intelligence: Sense of Being, Faculty of God*, trans. Andrew Tallon (Milwaukee, WI: Marquette University Press, 1999), 8, which contains the French pagination in square brackets, which I prefer to the older translation: *The Intellectualism of St. Thomas*, trans. James Mahoney (New York: Sheed and Ward, 1935). "Intellectualism" is the wrong word. For more on Rousselot, see Hans Boersma, *Nouvelle Théologie and Sacramental Ontology: A Return to Mystery* (Oxford: Oxford University Press, 2009), 67–83; see my *Heidegger and Aquinas: An Essay on Overcoming Metaphysics* (New York: Fordham University Press, 1982), 260–79.

22. Rousselot, *Intelligence: Sense of Being, Faculty of God*, 55.

23. Rousselot, *Intelligence: Sense of Being, Faculty of God*, 98.

24. Rousselot, *Intelligence: Sense of Being, Faculty of God*, 124, 130.

25. Rousselot, *Intelligence: Sense of Being, Faculty of God*, 13. Beings without knowledge are "contracted" to themselves, while knowledge expands the knower "intentionally" into the world.

26. Rousselot, *Intelligence: Sense of Being, Faculty of God*, 26.

27. Rousselot, *Intelligence: Sense of Being, Faculty of God*, 11, 42–43.

28. Rousselot, *Intelligence: Sense of Being, Faculty of God*, 15–16.

29. Rousselot, *Intelligence: Sense of Being, Faculty of God*, 35.

30. Rousselot belongs to the prehistory of the *nouvelle théologie* controversy that swirled around Henri de Lubac, SJ, who criticized, on both historical and systematic grounds, the idea of a state of "pure nature" over which the supernatural is laid like the second floor of a building. One might say that, for Rousselot, as intellectual beings, we have a natural dynamism toward a supernatural end, which profoundly destabilizes the distinction between natural and supernatural, particularly as it gets systematized in modern scholastic theologians like Suarez and Cajetan. Tillich's critique of supernaturalism also destabilizes this distinction, but differently. Tillich says that the unconditional ought not to be mystified as something supernatural, located in some higher sphere outside the natural world we live in. On either account, the distinction is a mystification. See Paul Tillich, *The Protestant Era*, abridged ed., trans. John Luther Adams (1948; repr., Chicago: University of Chicago Press, Phoenix Books, 1957), 82.

31. Rousselot, *Intelligence: Sense of Being, Faculty of God*, 158.

32. Rousselot, *Intelligence: Sense of Being, Faculty of God*, 181–84 concludes with a series of regrettable decisions—we should have a mystical disdain of reason, the senses block our vision of spiritual reality, the

dogmas of the Catholic Church trump everything—that reflect an "angelicism" that can be avoided by sticking with the theopoetic reduction he himself identified.

33. The leading interpreter of Eckhart in English is Bernard McGinn; see his *The Mystical Work of Meister Eckhart*; for my approach to Eckhart, see John D. Caputo, *The Mystical Element in Heidegger's Thought* (Athens: Ohio University Press, 1978; repr.: New York: Fordham University Press, 1986); "The Nothingness of the Intellect in Eckhart's *Parisian Questions*," *The Thomist* 39 (1975): 85–115; "Fundamental Themes in Eckhart's Mysticism," *The Thomist* 42 (1978): 197–225; "Poverty of Thought: Heidegger and Eckhart," in *Heidegger: The Man and the Thinker*, ed. Thomas Sheehan (Chicago: Precedent, 1981), 209–16; "Mysticism and Transgression: Derrida and Meister Eckhart," *Continental Philosophy* 2 (1989): 24–39.

34. For a detailed presentation, see Caputo, "The Nothingness of the Intellect in Eckhart's *Parisian Questions*."

35. Aristotle, *On the Soul*, trans. Hugh Lawson-Tancred (London: Penguin Books, 1987), Book III, chapter 4, 429a15–25.

36. Meister Eckhart, *Parisian Questions and Prologues*, trans. Armand Maurer (Toronto: Pontifical Institute of Medieval Studies, 1974), 51.

37. Eckhart, *Parisian Questions*, 45.

38. Eckhart, *Parisian Questions*, 85.

39. See Armand Maurer, introduction to Eckhart, *Parisian Questions*, 37.

40. Eckhart, *Parisian Questions*, 50.

41. See Maurer, introduction, 38; Bernard McGinn, "Meister Eckhart on God as Absolute Unity," in *Neoplatonism and Christian Thought*, ed. Dominic O'Meara (Albany: State University of New York Press, 1982), 128–39.

42. See John D. Caputo, "Mysticism and Transgression: Derrida and Meister Eckhart," in *Derrida and Deconstruction*, ed. H. J. Silverman (New York: Routledge, 1989), 24–39.

43. Meister Eckhart, *Meister Eckhart: The Essential Sermons, Commentaries, Treatises and Defense*, trans. Edmund Colledge and Bernard McGinn (New York: Paulist, 1981), 203.

44. Meister Eckhart, "Édition critique des pièces relatives au procès d'Eckhart," ed. Gabriel Théry, *Archives d'histoire doctrinale et littéraire du moyen âge* 1 (1926): 241–42.

45. Eckhart, *Meister Eckhart: The Essential Sermons*, 200.

46. Interestingly, both *divinitas* and *Gottheit* are feminine nouns.

47. See the Latin Sermon XXIX, "Deus unus est," in Meister Eckhart, *Meister Eckhart: Selected Writings*, ed. and trans. Oliver Davies (London: Penguin Classics, 1994), 258–62; McGinn, "Meister Eckhart on God as Absolute Unity."

48. Maurer, introduction, 40n89.

49. Meister Eckhart, *The Complete Mystical Works of Meister Eckhart*, trans. and ed. Maurice O'C. Walshe (New York: Crossroad, 2009), 420–26. I return to this issue in chapter 15.

50. See Caputo, *The Mystical Element in Heidegger's Thought*, 113–18.

51. See Meister Eckhart, "On Detachment," in *Meister Eckhart: The Essential Sermons*, 285–94.

52. Eckhart, *Complete Mystical Works*, 110.

53. Caputo, *The Mystical Element in Heidegger's Thought*, 132–34; "Fundamental Themes," 217–25.

54. For a detailed explanation of the "patchwork theory" in English, see Robert Paul Wolff, *Kant's Theory of Mental Activity* (Cambridge, MA: Harvard University Press, 1963).

55. Søren Kierkegaard, *Kierkegaard's Writings*, 12.1, *Concluding Unscientific Postscript to "Philosophical Fragments*,*"* trans. and ed. Howard Hong and Edna Hong (Princeton, NJ: Princeton University Press, 1992), 118.

56. Meister Eckhart, "The Talks of Instruction," in *Complete Mystical Works*, 521–22.

57. Eckhart, *Complete Mystical Works*, 524–56. This, I have argued, is the difference between the place of *Gelassenheit* in Heidegger and in Eckhart, in Caputo, *The Mystical Element in Heidegger's Thought*, 245–54. For an impressively detailed study of Heidegger and Eckhart, see Ian Alexander Moore, *Eckhart, Heidegger, and the Imperative of Releasement* (Albany: State University of New York Press, 2019) and a review of this book by Donald Duclos in *Medieval Mystical Theology* 29, no. 1 (2020): 54–57. See also Bret W. Davis, *Heidegger and the Will: On the Way to Gelassenheit* (Evanston, IL: Northwestern University Press, 2007).

58. See the 1329 Bull of Pope John XXII, "In agro dominico," in Eckhart, *Meister Eckhart: The Essential Sermons*, 77–81.

59. See Martin Heidegger, *The Principle of Reason*, trans. Reginald Lilly (Bloomington: Indiana University Press, 1991) and the Heideggerian rendering of Eckhart in Reiner Schürmann, *Wandering Joy: Meister Eckhart's Mystical Philosophy*, trans. David Appelbaum (Great Barrington, MA: Lindisfarne Books, 2001); see also the approaches to Eckhart in terms of absolute immanence, like Michel Henry, *The Essence of Manifestation*,

trans. Girard Etzkorn (The Hague, Netherlands: Martinus Nijhoff, 1973) and more recently in terms of Francoise Laruelle, in Alex Dubilet, *The Self-Emptying Subject: Kenosis and Immanence, Medieval to Modern* (New York: Fordham University Press, 2018). The more *transcendent* God is, the more *immanent* God is—that is, the more thoroughly the creature is penetrated by (because dependent upon) God. John Milbank deploys an argument like that, but in the direction of orthodoxy, in Slavoj Žižek and John Milbank, *The Monstrosity of Christ: Paradox or Dialectic*, ed. Creston Davis (Cambridge, MA: MIT Press, 2009).

60. Meister Eckhart, *Die Lateinische Werke*, ed. Konrad Weiss, vol. 1 (Stuttgart: Kohlhammer, 1965), 95–96 (numbers 298–300).

61. On the link between Eckhart and Luther, see the work of Steven Ozment, "Eckhart and Luther: German Mysticism and Protestantism," *The Thomist* 42 (1978): 271–72.

62. Martin Luther, *The Bondage of the Will*, trans. J. I. Packer and O. R. Johnston (London: Clarke, 1957) 169–70; Alastair McGrath, *Luther's Theology of the Cross* (Oxford: Blackwell, 1985), 164–68.

63. Vítor Westhelle, *The Scandalous God: The Use and Abuse of the Cross* (Minneapolis, MN: Fortress, 2006), 55–59.

64. McGrath, *Luther's Theology of the Cross*, 166; Luther, *The Bondage of the Will*, 176.

65. This was a favorite theme of Thomas J. J. Altizer, *The New Gospel of Christian Atheism* (Aurora, CO: Davies Group, 2002), 89–96. This is a revised edition of *The Gospel of Christian Atheism* (Philadelphia, PA: Westminster, 1966).

66. John D. Caputo, *Cross and Cosmos: A Theology of Difficult Glory* (Bloomington: Indiana University Press, 2019), 142–57.

67. Friedrich Nietzsche, *Beyond Good and Evil*, trans. R. J. Hollingdale (London: Penguin, 1973), Number 39, p. 50.

68. See Heiko A. Oberman, *Luther: Man between God and the Devil* (New Haven, CT: Yale University Press, 1989).

69. Caputo, *Cross and Cosmos*, 167–80.

70. Nietzsche, *Beyond Good and Evil*, Number 39, p. 50.

71. Edmund Husserl, *Ideas for a Pure Phenomenology and Phenomenological Philosophy: First Book: General Introduction to Pure Phenomenology*, trans. Daniel O. Dahlstrom (Indianapolis, IN: Hackett, 2014), 88–90 (§49).

72. Emmanuel Levinas, *Otherwise than Being or Beyond Essence*, trans. Alphonso Lingis (The Hague, Netherlands: Martinus Nijhoff, 1981), 176.

73. John D. Caputo, "To the Point of a Possible Confusion: God and *il y a*," in *Levinas: The Face of the Other* (Pittsburgh, PA: Simon Silverman

Center, Duquesne University, 1998), 1–36; reprinted in *John D. Caputo: Collected Philosophical and Theological Papers*, vol. 3, *1997–2000: The Return of Religion*, ed. Eric Weislogel (John D. Caputo Archives, 2021), 93–131.

74. Emmanuel Levinas, *Totality and Infinity: Essay on Exteriority*, trans. Alphonso Lingis (Pittsburgh, PA: Duquesne University Press, 1969), 191.

75. Jacques Derrida, "Khora," in *On the Name*, ed. Thomas Dutoit (Stanford, CA: Stanford University Press, 1995), 87–127; see *Deconstruction in a Nutshell: A Conversation with Jacques Derrida*, ed. John D. Caputo, with a new introduction (New York: Fordham University Press, 1997, 2020), 82–92.

CHAPTER 3

1. The most well-known book to emerge from this movement is Thomas J. J. Altizer, *The Gospel of Christian Atheism* (Philadelphia, PA: Westminster, 1966); see also Thomas J. J. Altizer and William Hamilton, *The Death of God* (Indianapolis, IN: Bobbs-Merrill, 1966) and their helpful bibliography of the antecedents of the movement. In addition to Altizer and Hamilton, the broader movement includes the works of Gabriel Vahanian, Paul Van Buren, and Richard Rubenstein. It would also reinvent itself as a form of deconstruction; see Thomas J. J. Altizer et al., eds., *Deconstruction and Theology* (New York: Crossroad, 1982).

2. I adopt this expression from Catherine Malabou, *The Future of Hegel: Plasticity, Temporality and Dialectic*, trans. Lisabeth During (New York: Routledge, 2005), 167–69; I discussed Malabou's analysis in John D. Caputo, *The Insistence of God: A Theology of Perhaps* (Bloomington: Indiana University Press, 2013), 117–35.

3. G.W.F. Hegel, *Lectures on the Philosophy of Religion*, one-volume edition, *The Lectures of 1827*, ed. Peter Hodgson (Berkeley: University of California Press, 1988), 488n265.

4. Hegel, *Lectures*, 180, 123.

5. As God is not an entity but a process, the true idea of God in Hegel's *speculative* logic depicts a process of concepts mutating into other concepts. This movement is not real but ideal, like a hologram or like the movement of a pantomime who simulates walking while remaining in place. Hegel's *Logic* corresponds to the "immanent" Trinity, which he calls the "play of love"—the internal processions of Father, Son, and Holy Spirit—as opposed to the economic Trinity, which externalizes itself in the real world.

6. See Caputo, *The Insistence of God*.

7. G.W.F. Hegel, *Hegel's Phenomenology of Spirit*, trans. A. V. Miller (Oxford: Clarendon, 1977), 493.

8. Luther translated Paul's *kenosis* as *Entäusserung*, parting with or divesting oneself of something, hence alienating itself (*Entfremdung*).

9. Hegel, *Lectures*, 171.

10. Hegel, *Lectures*, 163n111.

11. John D. Caputo, *Cross and Cosmos: A Theology of Difficult Glory* (Bloomington: Indiana University Press, 2019), 126–41.

12. Hegel, *Lectures*, 167.

13. Hegel, *Lectures*, 165.

14. Hegel, *Lectures*, 169.

15. Hegel, *Lectures*, 168.

16. Hegel, *Lectures*, 172.

17. Hegel, *Lectures*, 172–73.

18. Hegel, *Lectures*, 181.

19. Meister Eckhart, *The Complete Mystical Works of Meister Eckhart*, trans. and ed. Maurice O'C. Walshe (New York: Crossroad, 2009), 298.

20. Hegel, *Lectures*, 84–85.

21. Hegel, *Lectures*, 82.

22. Hegel, *Lectures*, 402.

23. Hegel, *Lectures*, 467–69.

24. Hegel, *Lectures*, 422.

25. Hegel, *Lectures*, 525–27.

26. Hegel, *Lectures*, 403.

27. Hegel, *Lectures*, 75–77.

28. I refer to Lyotard's famous "incredulity to meta-narratives," his definition of postmodernism in Jean-François Lyotard, *The Postmodern Condition: A Report on Knowledge*, trans. Geoff Bennington and Brian Massumi (Minneapolis: University of Minnesota Press, 1984), xxiii–xxiv.

29. Martin Heidegger, "What Is Metaphysics," trans. David Farrell Krell, in *Pathmarks*, ed. William McNeil (Cambridge: Cambridge University Press, 1998), 86–87.

30. Hegel, *Lectures*, 468.

31. Hegel, *Lectures*, 464–69.

32. G.W.F. Hegel, *Faith and Knowledge*, trans. Walter Cerf and H. S. Harris (Albany: State University of New York Press, 1988), 191, where Hegel says philosophy replaces the historic Good Friday with the speculative one. In the final paragraph of the *Phenomenology of the Spirit*, 493, he refers to the "Calvary of absolute Spirit."

33. Caputo, *The Insistence of God*, 92–97.
34. Jean-François Lyotard, *The Différend: Phrases in Dispute*, trans. Georges Van Den Abeele (Minneapolis: University of Minnesota Press, 1988), 86–106.

CHAPTER 4

1. Schelling says that he fears that modern culture is losing contact with a "darkness and force, or (why not use the right word?) with the barbarian principle that, conquered and not abolished, is the actual foundation of everything that is great." F.W.J. Schelling, *The Ages of the World (1811)*, trans. Joseph P. Lawrence (Albany: State University of New York Press, 2019), 111.
2. F.W.J. von Schelling, *Sämmtliche Werke*, ed. Kurt F. A. Schelling, Bd XIV, *Philosophie der Offenbarung* (Stuttgart: Cotta'scher Verlag, 1858), 328. Available online at https://play.google.com/books/reader?id=Fc2FqJA LccgC&hl=en&pg=GBS.PR2. For a helpful commentary and numerous translated passages, see Victor C. Hayes, *Schelling's Philosophy of Mythology and Revelation: Three of Seven Books Translated and Reduced* (Armidale, Australia: Australian Association for the Study of Religion, 1995).
3. Jacques Lacan, *The Triumph of Religion Preceded by Discourse to Catholics*, trans. Bruce Fink (Cambridge, UK: Polity, 2013), 64. Lacan's project of coming to grips with the concealed "Real" (the *Dass, das Ding, id, Ça*) in and through the way it is imagined and symbolically revealed is not at odds with "religion" in the radical sense; it is an introduction to it. See Slavoj Žižek, "The Abyss of Freedom," in *The Abyss of Freedom and the Ages of the World*, trans. Judith Norman (Ann Arbor: University of Michigan Press, 1997). For Žižek, the three potencies in *Die Weltalter* are to be read as blind, unconscious Freudian drives whose conflict is resolved in conscious desire, allegorized for him in the essay as the production of the Son, of the Logos—that is, of the symbolic order. For Žižek, compared to the topsy-turvy of the rotary movements of the potencies, the late "positive philosophy" is "flat," a judgment he shares with Habermas, meaning that Schelling ended up with a Christocentric affirmation of revelation and divine providence.
4. Edward Allen Beach, *The Potencies of God: Schelling's Philosophy of Mythology* (Albany: State University of New York Press, 1994), 158–62. I find Beach among the clearest of the Anglophone commentators.

5. F.W.J. Schelling, *Philosophy of Revelation (1841–42) and Related Texts*, ed. and trans. Klaus Ottmann (Putnam, CT: Spring, 2020), 138.

6. Schelling, *The Ages of the World (1811)*, 190.

7. While Schelling regularly speaks of God in the masculine, his panentheistic idea of God is more a maternal matrix moved by love than the macho paternal power of theism. As Joseph Lawrence points out, he has numerous maternal metaphors at his disposal, especially in *The Ages of the World*. See Schelling, *The Ages of the World*, 64n16, 112n40, 168n1.

8. When Schelling speaks of the creation of Adam, he has in mind the Adam Kadmon of the Kabbala and Jacob Boehme, meaning the entire created spiritual realm. Adam, the individual named in the book of Genesis, is only a particular mythic embodiment of Adam Kadmon. See Robert F. Brown, *The Later Philosophy of Schelling: The Influence of Boehme on the Works of 1809–1815* (Plainsborough, NJ: Associated University Presses, 1977); Louis Ginzberg, "Adam Kadmon," in *The Jewish Encyclopedia*, https://www.jewishencyclopedia.com/articles/761-adam-kadmon (accessed January 20, 2022).

9. F.W.J. Schelling, *Philosophical Investigations into the Essence of Human Freedom and Related Matters*, trans. Priscilla Hayden-Roy, in *The Philosophy of German Idealism*, ed. Ernst Behler (New York: Continuum, 1987), 230.

10. See Mary-Jane Rubenstein on "pan(icked) theology" in "The Matter with Pantheism," in *Entangled Worlds: Religion, Science and the New Materialism*, ed. Catherine Keller and Mary-Jane Rubenstein (New York: Fordham University Press, 2017), 159–66.

11. The expression appears to have been coined by a contemporary of the German idealists, Karl C. F. Krause (1781–1832).

12. F.W.J. Schelling, *On the History of Modern Philosophy: Munich Lectures 1833–34*, trans. Andrew Bowie (Cambridge: Cambridge University Press, 1984), 55.

13. Each thing has a soul, however imperfect, undeveloped, and nascent it may be, that unifies its inner forces, and the world as a whole has a soul, which constitutes the natural world as an organic unity.

14 Jürgen Habermas, "Dialectical Idealism in Transition to Materialism: Schelling's Idea of a Contraction of God and Its Consequences for the Philosophy of History," in *The New Schelling*, ed. Judith Norman and Alistair Welchman (New York: Continuum, 2004), 43–90.

15. Robert Corrington, *Ecstatic Naturalism: Signs of the World* (Bloomington: Indiana University Press, 1994); Iain Hamilton Grant, *Philosophies of Nature after Schelling* (New York: Continuum, 2006).

16. Schelling had recently lost his wife, Caroline, which might account for the cloud of melancholy over this work, and his analysis is as audacious as it gets: the root of the problem is God.

17. Schelling, *Philosophical Investigations into the Essence of Human Freedom*, 236–40.

18. Martin Heidegger, *Schelling's Treatise on the Essence of Human Freedom*, trans. Joan Stambaugh (Athens: Ohio University Press, 1985), 106–12.

19. Schelling, *Philosophical Investigations into the Essence of Human Freedom*, 238.

20. Schelling, *Philosophical Investigations into the Essence of Human Freedom*, 237.

21. Put in strictly philosophical terms: God's being is becoming (*actio*), not pure or immobile act (*actus*), because God is living, and life is a process or an activity. God's being is not purely simple but a composite of two principles because life is a process of overcoming the forces that mitigate against life; otherwise, God's being would be inert. To say the ground is found *within* God is to say that God does not have a *separate* potency that needs to be actualized, while creatures do (they would not exist if God did not actualize their ground). These possibilities are God's, *of* God but not God; they are beyond (*praeter*) God but not outside (*extra*) God, which God wills to actualize (creation). That is his "pantheism," that nothing is outside of God, that God's being is expanded into the world, rather like Eckhart saying the act-of-being of creatures is "lent" to them. The principle of existence compares more to the classical idea of God as *ipsum esse*, but the principle of ground compares more to Cusa's idea of God as *ipsum posse*, the absolute plenitude of power and possibility, or to Leibniz's possible worlds God, or to Scotus Eriugena.

22. The (Trinitarian) generation of the Son, the creation of the world and the human race, and the possibility of good and evil emerging in the Fall are *isomorphic*. They all invoke the same model and are barely distinguishable, for they are all the *self-assertion of the ground in God*, where the part of God where God is not being God takes on a life of its own. Like Father, like Son.

23. Schelling, *The Ages of the World (1811)*, 242.

24. Schelling, *Philosophical Investigations into the Essence of Human Freedom*, 242 (emphasis added).

25. Schelling, *Philosophical Investigations into the Essence of Human Freedom*, 241–43.

26. Manfred Frank, "Schelling and Sartre on Being and Nothingness," in *The New Schelling*, ed. Judith Norman and Alistair Welchman (New York: Continuum, 2004), 151–66.

27. Heidegger, *Schelling's Treatise*, 143.

28. Schelling, *Philosophical Investigations into the Essence of Human Freedom*, 241; Heidegger, *Schelling's Treatise*, 140.

29. Schelling, *Philosophical Investigations into the Essence of Human Freedom*, 241–42. The classical tradition affirms an *incomprehensible* depth in God, but that is *quoad nos*, relative to us, a limitation of our knowledge, not one inherent in the divine being, *quoad se*. Schelling proposes a radically different notion of being and God that is marked by an internal strife of order and disorder, conscious and unconscious.

30. The "Fall of Adam," the Genesis myth, was the subject of Schelling's master's degree dissertation.

31. Schelling's theory is anthropomorphic—not by mistake, but by a methodological decision founded on a metaphysics of human being as a microcosm of being in general, as the focal being for understanding being at large. "Human" does not refer (only) to a biological species but to the being in whom all the forces of being itself collide! We are the very center of being as the unity of nature and spirit—what God is absolutely but still ideally (God's existence is absolute, but God's nature is still ideal), we are dependently but really (our nature is real), occupying the intermediate being between the most minimal forms of life in nature and the highest life of God as Spirit. All the lines of force of being pass through us; we are being's prism. If that is a grand illusion, what is not illusion, as I argue in the following, is that the *radical* Schelling is actually engaged in hermeneutic phenomenology *avant la lettre*. While Schelling himself is modeling being after human being, what he is actually delivering is a picture of human being in its point of contact with the world, its being-in-the-world, not us as the real center of the world but us as lodged squarely in the world. Furthermore, if Schelling is anthropomorphizing being, that goes along with ontologizing *anthropos*. The disorder of evil is not merely a "human" matter; it is also a cosmic disorder; all of nature is disordered by human disobedience (shades of Adam Kadmon, not to mention Saint Paul).

32. Habermas, "Dialectical Idealism," 57–61, 66–70.

33. Gianni Vattimo, *After Christianity*, trans. Luca D'Isanto (New York: Columbia University Press, 2002), 25–40

34. Schelling, *Philosophical Investigations into the Essence of Human Freedom*, 270–71.

CHAPTER 5

1. This material on Satan, which Schelling omitted from the 1841–42 lecture course, is found in F.W.J. von Schelling, *Sämmtliche Werke*, ed. Kurt F. A. Schelling, Bd XIV, *Philosophie der Offenbarung* (Stuttgart: Cotta'scher Verlag, 1858), 241–94 (hereafter SW 14) and includes the last half of lecture 33 and lectures 34–35. For a commentary, see Victor C. Hayes, *Schelling's Philosophy of Mythology and Revelation: Three of Seven Books Translated and Reduced* (Armidale, Australia: Australian Association for the Study of Religion, 1995), 299–319.
2. SW 14, 241–47.
3. SW 14, 248.
4. SW 14, 49–50; F.W.J. Schelling, *Philosophy of Revelation (1841–42) and Related Texts*, ed. and trans. Klaus Ottmann (Putnam, CT: Spring, 2020), 252–53.
5. SW 14, 241–43.
6. Schelling, *Philosophy of Revelation*, 262–70; SW 14, 104–5.
7. Schelling, *Philosophy of Revelation*, 296–300.
8. SW 14, 251–52.
9. SW 14, 271.
10. SW 14, 258–59.
11. Søren Kierkegaard, *Kierkegaard's Writings*, VIII, *The Concept of Anxiety*, trans. Reidar Thomte and Albert B. Anderson (Princeton, NJ: Princeton University Press, 1980), 61.
12. SW 14, 279–93 (lecture 35).
13. SW 14, 275.
14. SW 14, 269–70.
15. Schelling, *Philosophy of Revelation*, 315–27; SW 14, 324–33.
16. Jürgen Habermas, "Dialectical Idealism in Transition to Materialism: Schelling's Idea of a Contraction of God and Its Consequences for the Philosophy of History," in *The New Schelling*, ed. Judith Norman and Alistair Welchman (New York: Continuum, 2004), 69.
17. F.W.J. Schelling, *Philosophical Investigations into the Essence of Human Freedom and Related Matters*, trans. Priscilla Hayden-Roy, in *The Philosophy of German Idealism*, ed. Ernst Behler (New York: Continuum, 1987), 270; Martin Heidegger, *Schelling's Treatise on the Essence of Human Freedom*, trans. Joan Stambaugh (Athens: Ohio University Press, 1985), 161. See Kierkegaard, *Kierkegaard's Writings*, XII.1, *Concluding Unscientific Postscript to "Philosophical Fragments,"* trans. and ed. Howard and Edna Hong (Princeton,

NJ: Princeton University Press, 1992), 118, for a closely related sentiment. Kierkegaard's "unscientific" postscript poses the possibility of a logical system against the impossibility of a system of existence (*Postscript*, 106–25).

18. Speaking of *love* here serves the interests of piety. Why should an unruly, concealed, self-contracting, and unconscious power respond to love? A stronger force overcoming a weaker one, perhaps, but not love. Love here is a cover for power, omnipotence, sovereignty. Moreover, why would the ground "long" to be actualized, want to become light and order? Why not simply "want" to exist perversely, contracting into itself all the more tightly at the approach of light and love? Why does it not behave like a black hole and consume any approaching light?

19. Catherine Keller, *Cloud of the Impossible: Negative Theology and Planetary Entanglement* (New York: Columbia University Press, 2015); Bruno Latour, *Reassembling the Social: An Introduction to Actor-Network-Theory* (Oxford: Oxford University Press, 2007).

20. Schelling, *Human Freedom*, 276.

21. Joseph P. Lawrence, "Schelling's Metaphysics of Evil," in *The New Schelling*, ed. Judith Norman and Alistair Welchman (New York: Continuum, 2004), 180.

22. Schelling, *Philosophical Investigations into the Essence of Human Freedom*, 282.

23. See my earlier discussion (chapter 2) of Levinas; see also John D. Caputo, *Cross and Cosmos: A Theology of Difficult Glory* (Bloomington: Indiana University Press, 2019), 167–80.

24. See John D. Caputo, "Proclaiming the Year of the Jubilee: Thoughts on a Spectral Life," in *In Search of Radical Theology: Expositions, Explorations, Exhortations* (New York: Fordham University Press, 2020), 45–76.

25. See Emilio Carlo Corriero, "The Necessity of Contingency in the Late Philosophies of Schelling and Heidegger," in *Nature and Realism in Schelling's Philosophy*, ed. Emilio Carlo Corriero and Andrea Dez (Turin, Italy: Accademia University Press, 2013), 55–86.

CHAPTER 6

1. Søren Kierkegaard, *Kierkegaard's Writings*, XXV, *Letters and Documents*, trans. and ed. Henrik Rosenmeier (Princeton, NJ: Princeton University Press, 1978), 127.

2. Paul Tillich, *Systematic Theology*, vol. 2, *Existence and the Christ* (Chicago: University of Chicago Press, 1957), 24–25.

3. Martin Heidegger, *Being and Time*, trans. John Macquarrie and Edward Robinson (New York: Harper & Row, 1962), 173 (§29).

4. Søren Kierkegaard, *Kierkegaard's Journals and Notebooks*, vol. 3, *Notebooks 1–15*, ed. Niels Jørgen Cappelørn et al. (Princeton, NJ: Princeton University Press, 2010), 229. Kierkegaard's notes are found in *Kierkegaard's Writings*, II, *The Concept of Irony, with Constant Reference to Socrates*, together with *Notes of Schelling's Berlin Lectures*, trans and ed. Howard and Edna Hong (Princeton, NJ: Princeton University Press, 1989).

5. F.W.J. Schelling, *The Grounding of Positive Philosophy: The Berlin Lectures*, trans. Bruce Matthews (Albany: State University of New York, 2008), 203.

6. The best accounts of the unprethinkable in English translation are Schelling, *The Grounding of Positive Philosophy*, 193–212; *Philosophy of Revelation (1841–42) and Related Texts*, ed. and trans. Klaus Ottmann (Putnam, CT: Spring, 2020), 124–45; *On the History of Modern Philosophy: Munich Lectures 1833–34*, trans. Andrew Bowie (Cambridge: Cambridge University Press, 1984). A selection from the *Philosophy of Revelation* lectures (chapter 10, "The Transition to Positive Philosophy") was published in *The Search for Being: Essays from Kierkegaard to Sartre on the Problem of Existence*, ed. and trans. Jean T. Wilde and William Kimmel (New York: Noonday, 1962), 29–48.

7. See the account of the difference between Schelling and Hegel in Andrew Bowie, introduction to Schelling, *On the History of Modern Philosophy*, 23–35.

8. Schelling, *On the History of Modern Philosophy*, 64–65.

9. Levinas's notion of an anarchic, never-present past, the time immemorial of the other, is similar to Schelling's absolute past. See Emmanuel Levinas, *The Time and the Other*, trans. Richard A. Cohen (Pittsburgh, PA: Duquesne University Press, 1987), 101–2, 111–14, 118–20.

10. The prereflective priority of being shows up in Gabriel Marcel, who wrote a dissertation on Coleridge and Schelling. Marcel distinguished a "first reflection," which tries to determine being as an object, from a "secondary reflection," which concedes the failure of first reflection. Reflection can never get back as far as the preobjective world in which we "participate" from the start. See Gabriel Marcel, *The Mystery of Being*, vol. 1, *Reflection and Mystery*, trans. G. S. Fraser (Chicago: Regnery, 1960); Gabriel Marcel, *Being and Having: An Existentialist Diary*, trans. Catherine Farrer (New York: Harper Torchbooks, 1965), 25–27, 100–123; and John D. Caputo, "Marcel and Derrida: Christian Existentialism and the Genesis of Deconstruction," in *Living Existentialism: Essays in Honor of Thomas W. Busch*, ed. Joseph C. Berendzen and Gregory Hoskins (Eugene, OR: Pickwick, 2017), 3–23.

11. Taking Heidegger's hermeneutics of facticity as my point of departure, this is the line of argument I pursue in establishing the notion of a "radical hermeneutics" in *Radical Hermeneutics: Repetition, Deconstruction, and the Hermeneutic Project* (Bloomington: Indiana University Press, 1987).

12. I know of no better presentation of this point than the 1929 text of Martin Heidegger, "What Is Metaphysics?" in trans. David Farrell Krell, in *Pathmarks*, ed. William McNeil (Cambridge: Cambridge University Press, 1998), 82–96. *Basic Writings*, 2nd ed., ed. David F. Krell (New York: Harper & Row, 1993), 89–110.

13. Aristotle, *Eudemian Ethics*, 1248a28.

14. Ed. Gianni Vattimo and Pier Aldo Rovatti, *Weak Thought*, trans. Peter Carravetta (Albany: State University of New York Press, 2013); see Bruce Matthews, introduction to his translation of Schelling, *The Grounding of Positive Philosophy*, 49.

15. Schelling, *Philosophy of Revelation*, 124–25.

16. Schelling, *On the History of Modern Philosophy*, 52–53.

17. Schelling, *Philosophy of Revelation*, 134.

18. Schelling, *Philosophy of Revelation*, 126.

19. Schelling, *Philosophy of Revelation*, 127. In classical metaphysical terms: while blind being does not have a passive potency (it does not pass from potency to act), it does have an active potency, the capacity to move other things from potency to act. To invoke a distinction made by Catherine Keller, its omnipotence implies an omnipotentiality.

20. Schelling, *Philosophy of Revelation*, 127, 137.

21. Schelling, *Philosophy of Revelation*, 129.

22. Schelling, *Philosophy of Revelation*, 19; Kierkegaard, *Kierkegaard's Journals and Notebooks*, 335.

23. Schelling, *Philosophy of Revelation*, 132. See Emmanuel Levinas, *On Escape*, introduced and annotated by Jacques Rolland, trans. Bettina Bergo (Stanford, CA: Stanford University Press, 2003).

24. Schelling, *Philosophy of Revelation*, 138.

25. Schelling, *Philosophy of Revelation*, 137.

26. John D. Caputo, *The Insistence of God: A Theology of Perhaps* (Bloomington: Indiana University Press, 2013), 36–37.

27. Schelling, *Philosophy of Revelation*, 134

28. Gilles Deleuze, *The Logic of Sense*, trans. Mark Lester with Charles Stivale, ed. Constantin V. Boundas (New York: Columbia University Press, 1969), 149.

29. Schelling, *The Grounding of Positive Philosophy*, 208–9.

30. Schelling, *Philosophy of Revelation*, 144.

31. F.W.J. von Schelling, *Sämmtliche Werke*, ed. Kurt F. A. Schelling, Bd XIV, *Philosophie der Offenbarung* (Stuttgart: Cotta'scher Verlag, 1858), 25.

32. See chapter 2 on Eckhart's *Gottheit* and Luther's *Deus absconditus*. I suggest a parallel of Luther with Lacan's distinction between the concealed "Real" (the *Dass, das Ding, id, Ça*) and the way it is imagined and symbolically "revealed" in John D. Caputo, *Cross and Cosmos: A Theology of Difficult Glory* (Bloomington: Indiana University Press, 2019), 142–56. This would complement Žižek's Lacanian appropriation of Schelling.

33. Hans Martensen, *Die Christliche Dogmatik*, 4th ed. (Berlin, 1856), 80, cited by Paul Tillich, *Mysticism and Guilt Consciousness in Schelling's Philosophical Development*, trans. Victor Nuovo (Lewisburg, PA: Bucknell University Press, 1974), 139n12.

34. I pointed out a similar dichotomy between the Neoplatonic and the living God in Meister Eckhart in John D. Caputo, *The Mystical Element in Heidegger's Thought* (Athens: Ohio University Press, 1978; rev. ed, New York: Fordham University Press, 1986), 97–139.

35. In Tillich's theology of culture, religion in the narrow sense occurs *per posterius*, in historical experience, where it is culturally constructed, where the name assigned the *Unvordenkliche*—the ground of being—is "God." But there are other cultural experiences—like art—that also make contact with *das Unvordenkliche*, where the name of God never comes up, and they belong to a primordial religiosity and a mystical sense of life found everywhere in the culture, so long as you dig deep enough.

36. Schelling, *Philosophy of Revelation*, 145–47.

37. Schelling, *Philosophy of Revelation*, 148–49, see note 9. The unprethinkable cannot be sublated in its necessity and eternity, by which it is constituted, but it can be sublated in its "actual" being, put into *further* act, adding new potencies, in which it works to regain its *actus purus*.

38. Schelling, *Philosophy of Revelation*, 155–57.

39. Schelling, *Philosophy of Revelation*, 163.

CHAPTER 7

1. F.W.J. Schelling, *The Grounding of Positive Philosophy: The Berlin Lectures*, trans. Bruce Matthews (Albany: State University of New York Press, 2008), 178–79.

2. Schelling, *The Grounding of Positive Philosophy*, 180.

3. F.W.J. Schelling, *System of Transcendental Idealism*, trans. Peter Heath (Charlottesville: University of Virginia Press, 1978), 211.

4. Schelling, *The Grounding of Positive Philosophy*, 182; Edward Allen Beach, *The Potencies of God: Schelling's Philosophy of Mythology* (Albany: State University of New York Press, 1994), 160.

5. Robert Scharlemann, "Tillich on Schelling and the Principle of Identity," *Journal of Religion* 56, no. 1 (January 1976): 111–12.

6. Schelling, *The Grounding of Positive Philosophy*, 186. In a similar way, Levinas thought the Hebrew scriptures were pointing out something of ethical importance that philosophy could make its own by recasting it in Greek.

7. Schelling, *The Grounding of Positive Philosophy*, 186.

8. Schelling, *The Grounding of Positive Philosophy*, 169.

9. Edmund Husserl, *Cartesian Meditations*, trans. Dorion Cairns (The Hague, Netherlands: Martinus Nijhoff, 1960), 89–151.

10. Medieval empiricism and voluntarism go hand in hand. God's sovereign freedom so transcends our finite intelligence that we can never presume to know a priori anything about the created world; our only recourse is to follow, a posteriori, the choices God made in the world God chose to create.

11. See John D. Caputo, *Hermeneutics: Facts and Interpretation in the Age of Information* (London: Penguin/Pelican, 2018), 112–13.

12. Schelling, *The Grounding of Positive Philosophy*, 182.

13. Just as Hegel is exposed to the objection of "panlogism," the notion that everything is held in the grips of the *Begriff*, Schelling is exposed to a "decisionism," where the measure of being is taken by what we want (*wollen*) and of truth by whether we truly want it.

14. Paul Tillich, *Mysticism and Guilt Consciousness in Schelling's Philosophical Development*, trans. Victor Nuovo (Lewisburg, PA: Bucknell University Press, 1974), 100–101.

15. F.W.J. Schelling, *Philosophy of Revelation (1841–42) and Related Texts*, ed. and trans. Klaus Ottmann (Putnam, CT: Spring, 2020), 172: "it requires heart and courage."

16. Schelling, *The Grounding of Positive Philosophy*, 181.

17. Schelling, *The Grounding of Positive Philosophy*, 185–86.

18. Schelling, *The Grounding of Positive Philosophy*, 190.

19. Søren Kierkegaard, *Kierkegaard's Writings*, VI, *Fear and Trembling and Repetition*, trans. and ed. Howard and Edna Hong (Princeton, NJ: Princeton University Press, 1983), 200.

20. F.W.J. Schelling, *Historical Critical Introduction to the Philosophy of Mythology*, trans. Mason Richey and Markus Zisselberger (Albany: State University of New York Press, 2007); Schelling, *Philosophy of Revelation*, 186–92.

21. Paul Tillich, *A History of Christian Thought* (New York: Simon & Shuster, 1967), 448.

22. Schelling, *Historical Critical Introduction to the Philosophy of Mythology*, 136

23. Tyler Tritten, *Beyond Presence: The Late F.W.J. Schelling's Criticism of Metaphysics* (Boston: De Gruyter, 2012), 274–84.

24. Schelling, *Historical Critical Introduction to the Philosophy of Mythology*, 85–102.

25. Schelling, *Philosophy of Revelation*, 262–70.

26. F.W.J. von Schelling, *Sämmtliche Werke*, ed. Kurt F. A. Schelling, Bd XIV, *Philosophie der Offenbarung* (Stuttgart: Cotta'scher Verlag, 1858), 296.

27. Schelling, *The Grounding of Positive Philosophy*, 175.

28. To which I cannot resist adding that Luke has almost certainly staged the whole scene.

CHAPTER 8

1. His best presentation of the critique of Hegel is F.W.J. Schelling, *On the History of Modern Philosophy: Munich Lectures 1833–34*, trans. Andrew Bowie (Cambridge: Cambridge University Press, 1984), 134–63; he makes substantially the same critique in F.W.J. Schelling, *Philosophy of Revelation (1841–42) and Related Texts*, ed. and trans. Klaus Ottmann (Putnam, CT: Spring, 2020), 70–92.

2. Schelling, *Philosophy of Revelation*, 88.

3. Schelling criticizes Hegel for saying the Idea "resolves" to "release itself" as nature; see Schelling, *On the History of Modern Philosophy*, 154–55. See Bruce Matthews, introduction to F.W.J. Schelling, *The Grounding of Positive Philosophy: The Berlin Lectures*, trans. Bruce Matthews (Albany: State University of New York Press, 2008), 58–60.

4. There are two impressive contemporary attempts to rehabilitate Hegel from the damage done to him by the critique that Schelling spearheaded and Kierkegaard "executed" with exquisite wit. (1) Catherine Malabou, *The Future of Hegel: Plasticity, Temporality and Dialectic*, trans. Lisabeth During (New York: Routledge, 2005), 167–69; for more, see John D.

Caputo, *The Insistence of God: A Theology of Perhaps* (Bloomington: Indiana University Press, 2013), 117–35. Malabou, influenced by Heidegger and Derrida, defends the "plasticity" of the Spirit, which allows for a maximum of contingency, a real future, a genuine "event" in the Derridean sense. I think there is a *limit*: there is no course of events in which the Spirit *fails* to reach its telos. Any given historical occurrence is contingent, but the telos of the Spirit as a whole is absolutely necessary. To pass that limit is to enter the domain of Heidegger and to leave Hegel behind. (2) Slavoj Žižek, "The Fear of Four Words," in Slavoj Žižek and John Milbank, *The Monstrosity of Christ: Paradox or Dialectic?*, ed. Creston Davis (Cambridge: MIT Press, 2009), 26, 60–61; see Caputo, *The Insistence of God*, 136–64. Žižek, influenced by Lacan and Schelling himself, makes it clear that treating the "cunning of reason" as a clever somebody manipulating us results in a "scarecrow Hegel"; the Owl of Minerva is an after-the-fact rationale of the contingent course taken in actuality. For Žižek, the real reconciliation of the dialectic is to realize the impossibility of reconciliation, to reconcile ourselves to the irreconcilable. "Double negation" means no, no, God does not exist, and there never was any plenitude whose loss creates a lack we have to fill. There is no avoiding the void, only its acknowledgment. That is a bridge too far for Hegel.

5. On Schelling's connections with Catholicism, see John Laughland, *Schelling versus Hegel: From German Idealism to Christian Metaphysics* (London: Ashgate, 2007); Thomas O'Meara, *Romantic Idealism and Roman Catholicism: Schelling and the Theologians* (South Bend, IN: Notre Dame University Press, 1982).

6. Schelling, *On the History of Modern Philosophy*, 157–60.

7. Cited by Paul Tillich, *Mysticism and Guilt Consciousness in Schelling's Philosophical Development*, trans. Victor Nuovo (Lewisburg, PA: Bucknell University Press, 1974), 94; Tillich is citing F.W.J. von Schelling, *Sämmtliche Werke*, ed. Kurt F. A. Schelling, Bd VII, *Denkmal der Schrift von den göttlichen Dingen* (Stuttgart: Cotta'scher Verlag, 1858), 438.

8. Tillich, *Mysticism and Guilt*, 93–94.

9. Jürgen Habermas, "Dialectical Idealism in Transition to Materialism: Schelling's Idea of a Contraction of God and Its Consequences for the Philosophy of History," in *The New Schelling*, ed. Judith Norman and Alistair Welchman (New York: Continuum, 2004), 76.

10. Walter Benjamin, "The Concept of History," IX, in *Walter Benjamin: Selected Writings*, vol. 4, *1938–40*, ed. Michael Jennings (Cambridge, MA: Belknap Press of Harvard University Press, 2003), 392.

11. Victor Nuovo, "Translator's Introduction," in Tillich, *Mysticism and Guilt*, 19.

12. Schelling's voluntarism is as extreme as Hegel's intellectualism. Schelling not only defends the superiority of willing over knowing, as in the medieval debate between the Franciscans and the Dominicans, but he goes on to identify willing with being itself (just as Eckhart identified *esse* with *intelligere*). Primordial being is willing (*Wollen ist Ursein*). In one of Tillich's finest essays, "The Two Types of the Philosophy of Religion," in *Theology of Culture*, ed. Robert C Kimball (Oxford: Oxford University Press, 1959), 10–29, Tillich contrasts the tradition of Augustine and the medieval Franciscans, in which the German mystics and Luther stood, with the Dominicans and the medieval Aristotelians, which Luther contested. That is the background of the distinction between Schelling and Hegel.

13. See Habermas, "Dialectical Idealism in Transition," 43–47, for Schelling's evolving conception of the state.

14. F.W.J. von Schelling, *Sämmtliche Werke*, ed. Kurt F. A. Schelling, Bd XIV, *Philosophie der Offenbarung* (Stuttgart: Cotta'scher Verlag, 1858), 269–70.

15. Ramsey Campbell, *Dark Companions* (New York: MacMillan Tor Books, 1985). I have no taste for horror literature or film, but I have a theory about where it is coming from.

16. Philip Plait, *Death from the Skies* (New York: Penguin, 2008), 291.

CHAPTER 9

1. Wilhelm and Marion Pauck, *Paul Tillich: His Life and Thought*, vol. 1, *Life* (London: Collins, 1977), 40–56.

2. I have adopted the convention found in Tillich's works in English of using the hyphenated "being-itself" to signify the ground of being just as the Heidegger translators capitalize "Being" to distinguish it from "beings."

3. Kierkegaard, Freud, Schopenhauer and Nietzsche, Coleridge, late nineteenth-century Catholic theology, Jaspers, Heidegger, and Marcel in the first half of the twentieth century, Habermas in the second half, and Žižek today.

4. John A. T. Robinson, *Honest to God* (Philadelphia, PA: Westminster, 1963).

5. Paul Tillich, *The Courage to Be* (New Haven, CT: Yale University Press, 1952), 182–90.

6. Tillich, *The Courage to Be*, 180.
7. Tillich, *The Courage to Be*, 188.
8. Paul Tillich, *Theology of Culture*, ed. Robert C. Kimball (Oxford: Oxford University Press, 1959), 25.
9. Paul Tillich, *Dynamics of Faith* (New York: HarperCollins, 1957), 64–65.
10. Tillich, *Theology of Culture*, 25.
11. Tillich, *Theology of Culture*, 5.
12. Tillich, *Dynamics of Faith*, 135–47.
13. Tillich, *Theology of Culture*, 10.
14. Tillich, *Theology of Culture*, 12–13.
15. Tillich, *Theology of Culture*, 131–32.
16. Tillich, *Theology of Culture*, 10.
17. F.W.J. Schelling, *Philosophy of Revelation (1841–42) and Related Texts*, ed. and trans. Klaus Ottmann (Putnam, CT: Spring, 2020), 155–57.
18. Tillich's position in his more popular works, of which I am making ample use, is more radical. In his *Systematic Theology*, he is more conservative.
19. Tillich, *The Courage to Be*, 175–76.
20. Tillich, *Theology of Culture*, 17. The point of the work of Pierre Rousselot (chapter 2) is to show it is more complicated than that. The ontological way is found in Aquinas in the notion of a *scientia connaturalis*.
21. Tillich, *The Courage to Be*, 171–78.
22. See Arne Unhjem, *Dynamics of Doubt: A Preface to Tillich* (Philadelphia, PA: Fortress, 1966), for an insightful if now-forgotten introduction to Tillich.
23. Tillich, *Theology of Culture*, 242.
24. Tillich, *Dynamics of Faith*, 136.
25. Tillich, *Dynamics of Faith*, 50–52.
26. Tillich, *Dynamics of Faith*, 115.
27. Tillich, *Theology of Culture*, 5.
28. Tillich, *The Courage to Be*, 18; Tillich, *Dynamics of Faith*, 114.
29. See Derrida's remarks in *Deconstruction in a Nutshell: A Conversation with Jacques Derrida*, edited with a commentary by John D. Caputo (New York: Fordham University Press, 1997; with a new introduction, 2021), 9–10.
30. Tillich, *The Courage to Be*, 20–24.
31. Unhjem, *Dynamics of Doubt*, 13–14.
32. Tillich, *Theology of Culture*, 15.

33. Paul Tillich, *On the Boundary: An Autobiographical Sketch* (New York: Scribner's, 1966).

34. Tillich, *Dynamics of Faith*, 85–88. Ecstatic reason does not reject revelation but sees in its symbols ways to express and expand its horizons. See Tillich, *Dynamics of Faith*, 90–91.

35. Tillich, *Theology of Culture*, 22–23.

36. Tillich, *Theology of Culture*, 14–15.

37. The second of Tillich's two student dissertations on Schelling dealt with the relationship between "mysticism" and "guilt-consciousness," which is arguably—and George Pattison argues it convincingly—his lifelong task. How is our unity with God (mysticism) to be thought in conjunction with our separation from God (guilt)? His answer lies in the Lutheran notion that we are accepted even though we are not acceptable. Paul Tillich, *Mysticism and Guilt Consciousness in Schelling's Philosophical Development*, trans. Victor Nuovo (Lewisburg, PA: Bucknell University Press, 1974). George Pattison, *Paul Tillich's Philosophical Theology: A Fifty-Year Reappraisal* (Basinstoke, UK: Palgrave Macmillan, 2015).

38. Tillich, *The Courage to Be*, 140–41.

39. Tillich, *The Courage to Be*, 103–12. This contempt for bourgeois propriety—"ethics" is uncomfortable with the exceptional—first nurtured by his life in Weimar Republic culture seems not unrelated to his sexual improprieties. Sex and mysticism are not unrelated ecstasies.

40. Tillich, *Theology of Culture*, 8.

41. Tillich, *Theology of Culture*, 9.

42. Tillich, *The Courage to Be*, 163–71.

43. Tillich, *The Courage to Be*, 156–60.

44. Tillich, *Dynamics of Faith*, 64–66.

45. Paul Tillich, *A History of Christian Thought: From Its Judaic and Hellenistic Origins to Existentialism*, edited and with an introduction by Carl E. Braaten (New York: Simon and Shuster, 1967, 1968), 391.

46. See Mary-Jane Rubenstein on "pan(icked) theology" in "The Matter with Pantheism," in *Entangled Worlds: Religion, Science and the New Materialism*, ed. Catherine Keller and Mary-Jane Rubenstein (New York: Fordham University Press, 2017), 159–66.

47. Paul Tillich, *The Interpretation of History*, trans. Elsa L. Talmey (New York: Scribner's Sons, 1936), 77–122.

48. Tillich, *The Courage to Be*, 180.

49. Tillich, *A History of Christian Thought*, 265.

50. Panentheism is one version of post-theism, but post-theism itself comes in many varieties, artfully catalogued and anthologized in *The Palgrave Handbook of Radical Theology*, ed. Christopher D. Rodkey and Jordan E. Miller (Cham, Switzerland: Palgrave Macmillan, 2018); for the broader movement, see the excellent introductory essays in part 1, 3–40.

51. Paul Tillich, *The Protestant Era*, abridged ed., trans. John Luther Adams (1948; repr., Chicago: University of Chicago Press, Phoenix Books, 1957), 161–81.

52. Robert S. Corrington, *Nature and Spirit: An Essay in Ecstatic Naturalism* (New York: Fordham University Press, 1972).

53. Tillich, *The Courage to Be*, 179.

54. Tillich, *Theology of Culture*, 127–32.

55. Paul Tillich, *The Socialist Decision*, trans. Franklin Sherman (New York: Harper & Row, 1977; repr., Eugene, OR: Wipf and Stock, 2012); for more on this book, see chapter 11. See also Tillich, *The Courage to Be*, 96–103; Mark Lewis Taylor, "Socialism's Multitude: Tillich's *The Socialist Decision* and Resisting the US Imperial," in *Retrieving the Radical Tillich*, ed. Russell Re Manning (New York: Palgrave Macmillan, 2015), 137–40.

56. Tillich, *The Courage to Be*, 1–3.

57. In James H. Cone, *A Black Theology of Liberation* (Maryknoll, NY: Orbis Books, 1970, 1986), Cone makes extensive use of Tillich to mount his own argument against the idolatry of race. In *The Cross and the Lynching Tree* (Maryknoll, NY: Orbis Books, 2016), he singles out Reinhold Niebuhr for criticism and lets Tillich off the hook, although he could easily have also taken him to task, given that neither one ever noticed the similarity between the cross and the lynching tree.

58. Hannah Tillich, *From Time to Time* (New York: Stein and Day, 1973).

59. Mary Daly, *Beyond God the Father: Towards a Philosophy of Women's Liberation* (Boston: Beacon, 1973); *Pure Lust: Elemental Feminist Philosophy* (Boston: Beacon, 1984), 155–60. See Mary Ann Stenger, "A Critical Analysis of the Influence of Paul Tillich on Mary Daly's Feminist Theology," *Encounter* 43 (Winter 1982): 219–38; Laurel Schneider, "The Courage to See and to Sin: Mary Daly's Elemental Transformation of Paul Tillich's Ontology," in *Re-Reading the Canon: Feminist Interpretations of Mary Daly*, ed. Marilyn Frye and Sarah Lucia Hoagland (University Park: Pennsylvania State University Press, 2000), 55–72; Christopher Rodkey, "The Nemesis Hex: Mary Daly and Pirated Proto-Patriarchal Paulus," in *Retrieving the Radical Tillich: His Legacy and Contemporary Importance*, ed. Russell Re Manning (Hampshire, UK: Palgrave Macmillan, 2015), 65–80.

60. This does not discount the value of what is called "strategic reversal," like speaking of a "black Christ" or "She Who Is," as a provisional way of countering the force of the hegemonic binary oppositions at work in racist and sexist discourse. Such reversals are necessary on the way to displacement.

61. Hence the "ana-theism" of Richard Kearny, *Anatheism: Returning to God after God* (New York: Columbia University Press, 2011), worked out in the spirit of Paul Ricoeur.

62. For my Tillichian critique of Trump, see "Theology in Trumptime: The Insistence of America," in *In Search of Radical Theology: Expositions, Explorations, Exhortations* (New York: Fordham University Press, 2020), 185–88.

CHAPTER 10

1. See the argument of Calvin D. Ullrich, *Caputo on Radical Political Theology* (Lancashire, UK: William Temple Foundation, 2022) available at https://williamtemplefoundation.org.uk/temple-tracts/temple-continental/ (accessed January 28, 2022).

2. Paul Tillich, *A History of Christian Thought* (New York: Simon & Shuster, 1967), 448.

3. Paul Tillich, *The Interpretation of History*, trans. Elsa L. Talmey (Scribner's Sons: New York, 1936), 83.

4. Søren Kierkegaard, *Kierkegaard's Writings, XII.2, Concluding Unscientific Postscript to "Philosophical Fragments,"* trans. and ed. Howard and Edna Hong (Princeton, NJ: Princeton University Press, 1992), 186.

5. Tillich, *The Interpretation of History*, 77–122.

6. See the felicitous distinction between omnipotence and omnipotential in Catherine Keller, *Cloud of the Impossible: Negative Theology and Planetary Entanglement* (New York: Columbia University Press, 2015), 112, and my discussion of it in *Cross and Cosmos: A Theology of Difficult Glory* (Bloomington: Indiana University Press, 2019), 204–11.

7. F.W.J. von Schelling, *Sämmtliche Werke*, ed. Kurt F. A. Schelling, Bd. XIV, *Philosophie der Offenbarung* (Stuttgart: Cotta'scher Verlag, 1858), 25; *Philosophy of Revelation (1841–42) and Related Texts*, ed. and trans. Klaus Ottmann (Putnam, CT: Spring, 2020), 244.

8. For an impressive collection of case studies in religious violence, see Marc Juergensmeyer, *Terror in the Mind of God: The Global Rise of Religious Violence*, 4th ed. (Oakland: University of California Press, 2017). That

there is no such thing as "pure" religious violence is well argued by William T. Cavanaugh, *The Myth of Religious Violence: Secular Ideology and the Roots of Modern Conflict* (Oxford: Oxford University Press, 2009).

9. Jack Miles, *God: A Biography* (New York: Knopf, 1995), 6. God also ordered the slaughter of the inhabitants of Ai (Josh. 8:24–29). See Regina Schwartz, *The Curse of Cain: The Violent Legacy of Monotheism* (Chicago: University of Chicago Press, 1997).

10. I developed this argument in *On Religion*, 2nd ed. (London: Routledge, 2019), 110–28.

11. The classic history is George M. Mardsen, *Fundamentalism and American Culture*, 2nd ed. (Oxford: Oxford University Press, 2006). On American evangelicalism, see Mark Noll, *The Scandal of the Evangelical Mind* (Grand Rapids, MI: Eerdmans, 1994) and his later assessment of the book in "The Evangelical Mind Today," *First Things*, October 2004, accessed July 2019, https://www.firstthings.com/article/2004/10/the-evangelical-mind-today.

12. David Brooks, "The Dissenters Trying to Save Evangelicalism," *New York Times* (February 6, 2022).

13. See Kristin Kobes Du Mez, *Jesus and John Wayne: How White Evangelicals Corrupted a Faith and Fractured a Nation* (New York: Liveright, 2021); John Fea, *Believe Me: The Evangelical Road to Donald Trump* (Grand Rapids, MI: Eerdmanns, 2018); Robert P. Jones, *The End of White Christian America* (New York: Simon and Schuster, 2016).

14. See Thomas B. Edsall, "The Capitol Insurrection Was as Christian Nationalist as It Gets," *New York Times*, January 28, 2021. For a full account of the movement, see Andrew L. Whitehead and Samuel L. Perry, *Taking America Back for God: Christian Nationalism in the United States* (Cambridge, MA: Oxford University Press, 2020); the authors estimate that about a third of Republicans are Christian nationalists.

15. Du Mez, *Jesus and John Wayne*, 12.

16. Christian nationalism is also symmetric with "Buddhist nationalism" in Myanmar and Sri Lanka, where a nonviolent spiritual tradition became militant and aggressive about a perceived threat from Islam.

17. See J. D. Vance, *Hillbilly Elegy: A Memoir of a Family and Culture in Crisis* (New York: HarperCollins, 2016), for a sympathetic portrait of the present crisis in rural life from within, and David Joy, *The Line That Held Us* (New York: G. P. Putnam's Sons, 2018), for a comparable work of fiction. Vance has since come out as an outspoken right-wing political candidate campaigning on the big lie, that the 2020 election was stolen.

18. See Jonathan Rauch, *The Constitution of Knowledge* (Washington, DC: Brookings Institution, 2021).

19. *Novalis Schriften*, ed. P. Kluckhohn and R. Samuel (Stuttgart: Verlag W. Kohlhammer, 1983), 413, B #1. "Novalis" is the penname of Georg Philipp Friedrich Freiherr von Hardenberg (1772–1801), a German poet.

20. Christopher Hitchens, *God Is Not Great: How Religion Poisons Everything* (New York: Hatchette Book Group, 2007).

21. Walter Benjamin, "The Concept of History," IX, in *Walter Benjamin: Selected Writings*, vol. 4, *1938–40*, ed. Michael Jennings (Cambridge, MA: Belknap Press of Harvard University Press, 2003), 392.

22. Meister Eckhart, *The Complete Mystical Works of Meister Eckhart*, trans. and ed. Maurice O'C. Walshe (New York: Crossroad, 2009), 83–90.

23. Jacques Derrida, *Rogues: Two Essays on Reason*, trans. Pascale-Anne Brault and Michael Naas (Stanford, CA: Stanford University Press, 2005), 110.

24. Paul Tillich, *The Courage to Be* (New Haven, CT: Yale University Press, 1952), 171–81.

25. Tillich's courage to be became the courage to be black in the face of white supremacy, in James Cone, and the courage to be a woman in the face of patriarchy, in Mary Daly, and in Tillich, in 1933, the courage to speak out against National Socialism, which cost him his livelihood in Germany.

26. Tillich denies that absolute faith is the mystical, meaning an absolute unity with God transcending doubt and despair, a classical mysticism suffering from the Neoplatonic illusion of eternal light—but not an apophaticism left shaken and uncertain before the unruly ground I am analyzing under the name of a mystical element.

27. Jacques Derrida, *On the Name*, ed. Thomas Dutoit (Stanford, CA: Stanford University Press, 1995), 132–33n3.

28. John D. Caputo, "The Experience of God and the Axiology of the Impossible," in *The Essential Caputo: Selected Writings*, ed. B. Keith Putt (Bloomington: Indiana University Press, 2018), 321–35.

CHAPTER 11

1. See Russell Re Manning, ed., *Retrieving the Radical Tillich: His Legacy and Contemporary Importance* (Hampshire, UK: Palgrave Macmillan, 2015).

2. For more work like this, see Sigridur Gudmarsdottir, *Tillich and the Abyss: Foundations, Feminism, and Theology of Praxis* (New York: Palgrave Macmillan, 2016).

3. Jacques Derrida, "Circumfession: Fifty-Nine Periods and Periphrases," in Geoffrey Bennington and Jacques Derrida, *Jacques Derrida* (Chicago: University of Chicago Press, 1993), 155.

4. On the difference between the modern conception of culture as a unified and orderly whole and the postmodern culture of contest and plurality, see Kathryn Tanner, *Theories of Culture: A New Agenda for Theology* (Minneapolis, MN: Fortress, 1997), 38–58; David Tracy, *Plurality and Ambiguity: Hermeneutics, Religion and Hope* (San Francisco: Harper & Row, 1987).

5. Jacques Derrida, *The Other Heading: Reflections on Today's Europe*, trans. Pascale-Anne Brault and Michael Naas (Bloomington: Indiana University Press, 1992), 9–11.

6. Jacques Derrida, "Force of Law: 'The Mystical Foundation of Authority,'" trans. Mary Quantaince, in *Acts of Religion*, ed. Gil Anidjar (New York: Routledge, 2002), 228–98.

7. Catherine Malabou, *The Future of Hegel: Plasticity, Temporality, and Dialectic*, trans. Lisabeth During (New York: Routledge, 2005).

8. Derrida, "Force of Law," 242–43.

9. Jacques Derrida, "The University without Conditions," in *Without Alibi*, ed. and trans. Peggy Kamuf (Stanford, CA: Stanford University Press, 2002), 202–37.

10. See John D. Caputo, "Proclaiming the Year of the Jubilee: Thoughts on a Spectral Life," in *In Search of a Radical Theology: Expositions, Explorations, Exhortations* (New York: Fordham University Press, 2020), 45–76.

11. Paul Tillich, "The Protestant Principle and the Proletarian Situation," in *The Protestant Era*, abridged ed., trans. John Luther Adams (1948; repr., Chicago: University of Chicago Press, Phoenix Books, 1957), 161–81.

12. Jacques Derrida, *Politics of Friendship*, trans. George Collins (London: Verso, 1997), 1–2, 172, 306.

13. Paul Tillich, *The Socialist Decision*, trans. Franklin Sherman (New York: Harper & Row, 1977; repr., Eugene, OR: Wipf and Stock, 2012), 102.

14. Jacques Derrida, *Specters of Marx: The State of the Debt, the Work of Mourning, and the New International*, trans. Peggy Kamuf (New York: Routledge, 1994), 174. See John D. Caputo, *The Prayers and Tears of Jacques Derrida: Religion without Religion* (Bloomington: Indiana University Press, 1997), 118–51 for a closer commentary.

15. Jacques Derrida, "How to Avoid Speaking: Denials," in *Derrida and Negative Theology*, ed. Howard Coward and Toby Foshay (Albany: State University of New York Press, 1992), 73–142.

16. This is the thesis of John D. Caputo, *The Insistence of God: A Theology of Perhaps* (Bloomington: Indiana University Press, 2013), 3–23, 259–63. For more on the "perhaps" in this theology, see Derrida, *Politics of Friendship*, 26–48.

17. Caputo, *The Insistence of God*, 167–263.

18. See George Pattison, *Paul Tillich's Philosophical Theology: A Fifty-Year Reappraisal* (Basingstoke, UK: Palgrave Macmillan, 2015).

19. Tillich, *Theology of Culture*, 10.

20. Tillich, *The Socialist Decision*, 110.

21. Jacques Derrida, *Margins of Philosophy*, trans. Alan Bass (Chicago: University of Chicago Press, 1982), 22.

22. Martin Heidegger, *Identity and Difference*, trans. Joan Stambaugh (New York: Harper & Row, 1969), 72.

23. That, in a nutshell, is my argument in *Cross and Cosmos: A Theology of Difficult Glory* (Bloomington: Indiana University Press, 2019).

CHAPTER 12

1. On the role of repetition, see John D. Caputo, *Radical Hermeneutics: Repetition, Deconstruction, and the Hermeneutic Project* (Bloomington: Indiana University Press, 1987).

2. I have worked out this distinction in more detail in "Gadamer and the Postmodern Mind," in *The Gadamerian Mind*, ed. Theodore George and Gert-Jan van der Heidne (London: Routledge, 2021), 435–48.

3. See John D. Caputo, "Mysticism and Transgression: Derrida and Meister Eckhart," in *Derrida and Deconstruction*, ed. Hugh J. Silverman (New York: Routledge, 1989), 24–39.

4. Edward A. Beach, "The Later Schelling's Conception of Dialectical Method, in Contradistinction to Hegel's," *Owl of Minerva* 22, no. 1 (Fall 1990): 35–54; Edward Allen Beach, *The Potencies of God: Schelling's Philosophy of Mythology* (Albany: State University of New York Press, 1994), 84–86.

5. Martin Heidegger, "On the Essence of Truth," in *Martin Heidegger: Pathmarks*, ed. William McNeil (Cambridge: Cambridge University Press, 1998), 150–52. On the limits of using Heidegger here, see my debate with

William Richardson, SJ, in John D. Caputo, "Dark Hearts, Richardson and Evil," in *From Phenomenology to Thought, Errancy, Desire*, ed. Babette Babich (Dordrecht, Netherlands: Kluwer Academic, 1995), 267–75.

6. Jacques Derrida, *Raising the Tone of Philosophy: Late Essays by Immanuel Kant, Transformative Critique by Jacques Derrida*, ed. Peter Fenves (Baltimore: Johns Hopkins University Press, 1993), 162.

7. Paul Tillich, *Systematic Theology*, vol. 1, *Reason and Revelation, Being and God* (Chicago: University of Chicago Press, 1951), 263–70.

8. Paul Tillich, *What Is Religion?*, ed. and trans. John Luther Adams (New York: Harper & Row Torchbooks, 1969), 85–88.

9. For more on this, see John D. Caputo, *Cross and Cosmos: A Theology of Difficult Glory* (Bloomington: Indiana University Press, 2019), 276–78.

CHAPTER 13

1. While there is no settled vocabulary in this field, the most helpful source is https://www.humanityplus.org, the website of Humanity+, Inc., formerly known as the World Transhumanist Association. The best presentation of the transhuman and posthuman problematic is Nick Bostrom, *Superintelligence: Paths, Dangers, Strategies* (Oxford: Oxford University Press, 2014).

2. Jeanine Thweatt-Bates, *Cyborg Selves: A Theological Anthropology of the Posthuman* (London: Routledge, 2012).

3. I am summarizing Donna Haraway, "A Manifesto for Cyborgs: Science, Technology and Socialist Feminism in the 1980s," in *The Haraway Reader* (London: Routledge, 2004), 7–46; see 3, 39 for quotations.

4. See Natasha Vita-More, "The Transhumanist Manifesto," https://natashavita-more.com/transhumanist-manifesto/ (accessed January 23, 2021).

5. Ilia Delio, OSF, *Re-Enchanting the Earth: Why AI Needs Religion* (Maryknoll, NY: Orbis Books, 2020). Delio sides with M. Katherine Hayles, *How We Became Posthuman: Virtual Bodies in Cybernetics, Literature, and Informatics* (Chicago: University of Chicago Press, 1999), who argues, like other feminist posthumanists, that human intelligence requires a human body, as do phenomenologists like Maurice Merleau-Ponty and Hubert Dreyfus.

6. Donna Haraway, "Ecce Homo, Ain't (Ar'n't) I a Woman, and Inappropriate/d Others: The Human in a Post-Humanist Landscape," in

The Haraway Reader, 47–62. There is, she argues, a "humanism" in this posthuman landscape that we would not want to refuse, the prophetic denunciation of *inhumanity* announced (and denounced) in Isaiah's "suffering servant," the just man rejected and despised by men. She portrays Jesus as a trickster figure, something like Luther's idea that in Jesus, God appears under the opposite form. "Ecce homo," Pilate said, behold the man on the margins of humanity, scourged and crowned with thorns but without fault, mockingly adorned in the purple of a king but treated as a criminal and a scapegoat, a (hybrid) God in the form of a servant. Sojourner Truth, born a slave in 1797 in New York (not on a southern plantation), also lives on the margins of the human/inhuman, outside the cultural system of marriage and naming, without legal standing or human status. Just so, she reconstitutes what counts as human, an answer to Pilate's question of what is truth. By asking "But ain't I a woman?" she speaks from a position of excess outside the system, like Jesus, who put the received idea of the human into question. Importantly, the suffering servant is suffering, oppressed, and persecuted *flesh*.

7. Delio, *Re-Enchanting the Earth*, xxv.

8. Teilhard maintained a friendship with Julian Huxley, whose *Religion without Revelation* (New York: Penguin Signet Classics, 1969), first published in 1927, revised edition in 1957, may be the first use of the word *transhumanism*.

9. As early as Asimov's "The Last Question" (1956), speculations about the posthuman future have included a *collective* consciousness, combining the several uploaded individual minds into a superintelligence, which then proceeds to design still more superintelligent collectives. What started out as Descartes's solitary *ego cogito*, and then became the absolute I = I of Fichte and then the *Geist* of Hegel and Schelling, would end up on the internet—or, better, *as* a collective internet. The libertarians and autonomous liberal individuals will never go for this.

10. Mark C. Taylor, "A.I. and I," *New York Times*, December 15, 2020, an op-ed based on Taylor's *Intervolution: Smart Bodies Smart Things* (New York: Columbia University Press, 2020).

11. Vita-More, "Transhumanist Manifesto."

12. "What Is a Posthuman?," Humanity+, https://humanityplus.org/philosophy/transhumanist-faq/.

13. Haraway, 299–301.

14. See "What Is Uploading," Humanity+, https://www.humanityplus.org/transhumanist-faq (accessed January 24, 2022). See also Ray

Kurzweil, *The Singularity Is Near: When Humans Transcend Biology* (New York: Penguin, 2005); Hans Moravec, *Robot: Mere Machine to Transcendent Mind* (Oxford: Oxford University Press, 2000).

15. Haraway, "A Manifesto for Cyborgs," 22–25.

16. Taylor, "A.I. and I."

17. Dennis Overbye, "Could a Computer Devise a Theory of Everything?," *New York Times*, November 24, 2020.

18. Martin Hägglund, arguing for a materialist Derrida, mistakes an ultratranscendental for a dogmatic determination that being is matter! It is almost exactly the opposite. See John D. Caputo, "Unprotected Religion: Radical Theology, Radical Atheism, and the Return of Anti-Religion," in *In Search of Radical Theology: Expositions, Explorations, Exhortations* (New York: Fordham University Press, 2020), 125–50.

19. The Johnny Depp movie *Transcendence* and a cable TV series titled *The Year Million* explore some scenarios of what it would be like.

20. Martin Heidegger, *The Fundamental Concepts of Metaphysics: World, Finitude, Solitude*, trans. William McNeil and Nicholas Walker (Bloomington: Indiana University Press, 2001), 176–77.

21. Karen Barad, "Quantum Entanglements and Hauntological Relations," *Derrida Today* 3 (2010): 244; see Clayton Crockett, *Derrida after the End of Writing: Political Theology and the New Materialism* (New York: Fordham University Press, 2018), 121–38, for a superb commentary.

22. Terence Blake, "Adam S. Miller's *Speculative Grace: Bruno Latour and Object-Oriented Theology*," https://www.academia.edu/4220650/Review_of_Adam_S_Millers_SPECULATIVE_GRACE (accessed January 24, 2022).

23. Nick Bostrom, "Are You Living in a Computer Simulation?," *Philosophical Quarterly*, 53:211 (April 2003): 243–55. doi:10.1111/1467-9213.00309.

24. David Chalmers, *Reality+: Virtual Worlds and the Problems of Philosophy* (New York: W. W. Norton, 2022).

25. Derrida cites this line from Max Stirner in Jacques Derrida, *Specters of Marx: The State of the Debt, the Work of Mourning, and the New International*, trans. Peggy Kamuf (New York: Routledge, 1994), 136.

26. Thweatt-Bates makes a judicious survey and assessment of the several theological debates.

27. Michel Serres, *Angels: A Modern Myth*, trans. Francis Cowper (Paris: Flammarion, 1993). The English title erases the play in the French.

28. As early as "Envois" in *The Post Card: From Socrates to Freud and Beyond*, trans. Alan Bass (Chicago: University of Chicago Press, 1987),

Derrida was interested in the delivery of messages and even made passing reference to angels (43–44).

29. In the expression "democracy to come," the "to come," which is not deconstructible, is more important than the "democracy," which is a historical construction; see Jacques Derrida, *Negotiations: Interventions and Interviews: 1971–2001*, trans. Elizabeth Rottenberg (Stanford, CA: Stanford University Press, 2002), 182.

30. See Nick Bostrom, "Letter from Utopia," https://www.nickbostrom.com/utopia.html (accessed January 24, 2022).

CHAPTER 14

1. Philip Plait, *Death from the Skies* (New York: Penguin, 2008), 1; this work is both informative and engaging.
2. Plait, *Death from the Skies*, 291.
3. Jean-François Lyotard, *The Inhuman*, trans. Geoffrey Bennington and Rachel Bowlby (Stanford, CA: Stanford University Press, 1991), 8–23.
4. I am adapting the distinction between problem and mystery made by Gabriel Marcel, *The Mystery of Being*, vol. 1, *Reflection and Mystery*, trans. G. S. Fraser (Chicago: Regnery, 1960).
5. Theists have several strategies: (1) God would never let such a thing happen—then why create a world like this to begin with? (2) no matter what becomes of matter down here on "earth," everything important is found in "heaven," which you only get to see by dying—unadorned dualism; (3) cosmic destruction is a result of sin—of the bad behavior of a cosmically insignificant species, seriously? (4) questioning God's ways is impertinent—then why create beings who ask impertinent questions? One daring suggestion, which takes the problem seriously, is made by Ned Wisnefske, *Could God Fail?: The Fate of the Universe and the Fate of Christians* (Eugene, OR: Wipf and Stock, Cascade Books, 2020): God tried but *failed* to bring order to the chaos, and the knees of order buckled under the stress of entropy. For more on these theses, see John Polkinghorne and Michael Welker, eds., *The End of the World and the Ends of God* (Harrisburg, PA: Trinity, 2002); John Haught, *Christianity and Science* (Maryknoll, NY: Orbis Books, 2007); Mark W. Worthing, *God, Creation, and Contemporary Physics* (Minneapolis, MN: Augsburg Fortress, 1996).
6. See Paul J. Steinhardt and Neil Turok, *Endless Universe: Beyond the Big Bang—Rewriting Cosmic History* (New York: Broadway, 2007);

Mary-Jane Rubenstein, *Worlds without End: The Many Lives of the Multiverse* (New York: Columbia University Press, 2014).

7. Jacques Derrida, *Life Death*, ed. Pascale-Anne Brault and Peggy Kamuf, trans. Pascale-Anne Brault and Michael Naas (Chicago: University of Chicago Press, 2020).

8. There can be no "continuity" for us if this universe is reduced to oblivion; if there is, then it is the same universe because we are still part of it.

9. Maurice Merleau-Ponty, *The Phenomenology of Perception*, trans. Colin Smith (London: Routledge and Kegan Paul, 1962), xiii.

10. Carlo Rovelli, *Seven Brief Lessons on Physics*, trans. Allen Lane (New York: Riverhead, 2016); *Reality Is Not What It Seems: The Journey to Quantum Gravity*, trans. Simon Carnell and Erica Segre (New York: Riverhead Books, 2018).

11. https://www.youtube.com/watch?v=GO5FwsblpT8 (accessed February 27, 2022).

12. My hypothesis is—another matter for which I lack both the time and the qualifications—that an intercultural or cross-cultural study would reveal analogous forms of life, not a common "essence" of the "mystical," or "religion," but various forms of life bearing certain family resemblances among themselves (Wittgenstein). We can also find family resemblances with our more distant cousins in the nonhuman world, as Jane Goodall assures us; see Donovan O. Schaeffer, *Religious Affects: Animality, Evolution, and Power* (Durham, NC: Duke University Press, 2015).

CHAPTER 15

1. Jacques Derrida, *Rogues: Two Essays on Reason*, trans. Pascale-Anne Brault and Michael Naas (Stanford, CA: Stanford University Press, 2005), 157.

2. Eugen Herrigel, *Zen and the Art of Archery*, trans. R.F.C. Hull (New York: Random House, 1971).

3. Angelus Silesius, *The Cherubinic Wanderer*, trans. Maria Shrady (New York: Paulist, 1986); see Meister Eckhart, "In hoc apparuit caritas dei in nobis," in *The Complete Mystical Works of Meister Eckhart*, trans. and ed. Maurice O'C. Walshe (New York: Crossroad, 2009), 110; Meister Eckhart, *Meister Eckhart: The Essential Sermons, Commentaries, Treatises and Defense*, trans. Edmund Colledge and Bernard McGinn (New York: Paulist, 1981), 184; Martin Heidegger, *The Principle of Reason*, trans. Reginald Lilly (Bloomington: Indiana University Press, 1991), 32–49, 117–29.

4. See John D. Caputo, "Do Radical Theologians Pray? A Spirituality of the Event," *Religions* 12, no. 9 (2021): 679. https://doi.org/10.3390/rel12090679.

5. Heidegger, *The Principle of Reason*, 38.

6. Martin Heidegger, "The Thing," in *Poetry, Language, Thought*, trans. Albert Hofstadter (New York: Harper & Row, 1971), 163–86.

7. Meister Eckhart, Sermon 87 (*"Beati pauperes spiritu"*), in *Complete Mystical Works*, 420–26; *The Essential Sermons*, 199–203.

8. Marguerite Porete, *The Mirror of Simple Souls*, trans. Ellen L. Babinsky (New York: Paulist, 1993), 157, 161, 165, 167, 168, 174, 183, 217, 218.

9. John D. Caputo, *Against Ethics: Contributions to a Poetics of Obligation with Constant Reference to Deconstruction* (Bloomington: Indiana University Press, 1993).

10. Porete, *Mirror*, 84. See John M. Connolly, *Living without Why: Meister Eckhart's Critique of the Medieval Concept of Will* (Oxford: Oxford University Press, 2014).

11. David Kangas, "Dangerous Joy: Marguerite Porete's Good-Bye to the Virtues," *Journal of Religion* 91, no. 3 (2011): 299–319.

12. Meister Eckhart, *The Complete Mystical Works of Meister Eckhart*, 329; *The Essential Sermons*, 186. We are also reminded of the exchange between Madame Guyen and François Fénelon in which Fénelon distinguished self-love (*amour-propre*) from pure love (*amour pur*), in which the self is utterly forgotten.

13. Eckhart, *Complete Mystical Works*, 117.

14. Eckhart, *Complete Mystical Works*, 330; *The Essential Sermons*, 186.

15. Eckhart, *Complete Mystical Works*, 297–98, 363, 530, 540–41. Or, for a more radical twist, to prefer to be in hell in solidarity with those condemned by the little church, see Clark West, "The Deconstruction of Hell: A History of the *Resignatio ad Infernum* Tradition" (PhD diss., Syracuse University, 2013), https://surface.syr.edu/rel_etd/86.

16. "Man's highest and dearest leave-taking is if he takes leave of God for God. St. Paul left God for God: he left everything he could get from God, he left everything that he might receive from God. In leaving these he left God for God." Eckhart, *Complete Mystical Works*, 296.

17. Jacques Derrida, *Given Time*, vol. 1, *Counterfeit Money*, trans. Peggy Kamuf (Chicago: University of Chicago Press, 1991), 6–33. The gift is annulled in direct proportion to the extent that the gift becomes *visible* as a gift. The pure gift would require that no one could know that anyone had given anything to anyone. A *pure* gratitude would be grateful without a debt to pay off, no need to send up sacrificial smoke to please the

temperamental divine nostrils. In debt-free gratitude, where nobody was being generous, we thank our lucky stars.

18. Derrida explores this paradox, constituting the "ethicity of ethics," in *On the Name*, ed. Thomas Dutoit (Stanford, CA: Stanford University Press, 1995), 132–37n3.

19. In addition to joy, we can imagine other axiological effects: (1) to the cosmic modesty of our condition a corresponding *humility*, checking human exceptionalism in theology (*imago dei*) and philosophy (*animal rationale*), which brought us the Anthropocene—see Lynn White Jr., "The Historical Roots of Our Ecological Crisis," *Science* 155 (1967): 1203–7; and (2) a *compassion* for one another, all of us siblings of the same dark ground, all subject to the same cosmic lot, all a bit of common cosmic luck.

20. Martin Heidegger, *Being and Time*, trans. John Macquarrie and Edward Robinson (New York: Harper & Row, 1962), 358 (§62). My thanks to Carson Webb for reminding me of this passage and pointing out the military resonance of the expression. *Rüstung* means a knight's armor.

21. Even on the alternate hypothesis of endless universes, the end of *this* universe would still be the end of *us*, of *our* world.

CONCLUSION

1. For a serious if sometimes-whimsical presentation, not intended for an academic audience, of what the spectrality of God comes down to, see John D. Caputo, "Proclaiming the Year of the Jubilee: Thoughts on a Spectral Life," in *In Search of Radical Theology: Expositions, Explorations, Exhortations* (New York: Fordham University Press, 2020), 45–76.

2. See Marcelo Gleiser, *The Island of Knowledge: The Limits of Science and the Search for Meaning* (New York: Basic Books, 2014).

INDEX

Abelard, Peter, 126
Adam, 128, 279, 307; as Adam Kadmon, 125, 299, 356n8, 358n31
angels, 2–4, 17; angel envy, ix, 13; angelic imaginary 9–10, 15, 16, 333; information technologies and, 2, 13, 53, 277–81; intelligence of, 52–56, 64; Schelling and, 128–29. *See also* Aquinas; artificial intelligence; posthumanism
Angelus Silesius (Johannes Scheffler), 322, 325
anonymous, the, 71, 336; Derrida and, 265, 267; Husserl and, 71–72; Levinas and, 72, 137, 178; Luther and, 63, 70; Schelling and, 137, 150
Anselm, 3, 52, 83–84, 101, 123, 154, 166, 198–99
anxiety, 12, 71, 93, 128, 185, 222; apophatic, 6, 65, 68, 325; Heidegger and, 6, 71, 93, 311, 331; joy and, 331; Kierkegaard and, 128, 218; Luther and, 68–69; sober, 331–32; Tillich and, 12, 185
apophatic, the, x–xiii, 5, 7–8, 37, 143, 212–14, 229, 300, 305, 336
apophatic imagination, the, ix–xiii, 3–5, 8, 14–15, 16–17, 37, 71, 94, 98–99, 105, 138, 242, 264, 272–73, 305, 313–14, 326, 334, 336–37, 342; anti-apophatic in Hegel, 93; cosmo–poetic sense, 301, 313–17, 322, 327, 333–34; edifying versus anxious, 5–7, 41–44, 55–56, 64–72, 104, 255, 272, 324–25, 332–33; personification and, 70, 84, 171, 172–74, 188, 191, 210, 335–36; posthumanism and, 277, 297, 300–302
Aquinas, Thomas, 4, 32–33, 93, 148, 171, 266, 268, 297, 335; analogy of being, 51; angelology, 2, 8–9, 11, 44–56, 104; Aristotle and, 47, 48–50, 171; *esse*, 45–52; God, 49–51; Kant and, 46, 52, 53, 54; negative theology, 51–52, 55; ontological argument, 52, 55; Platonism and, 49–51; *ratio* and *intellectus*, 52–56; Schelling and, 102, 104, 123–24, 147; Tillich and, 50, 51, 191–95, 196. *See also* angels; creation of the world; Eckhart; Tillich, Paul
Arendt, Hannah, 7, 332
Aristotle, 23, 33, 56–57, 61, 171, 175, 192, 214, 230, 253, 277, 288, 342; Hegel and, 75, 79, 84, 97; Schelling and, 111, 142, 145, 147, 151, 171. *See also* Aquinas

artificial intelligence (AI): angels and, 13, 44, 53, 296; distinguished from natural intelligence, 288–89; evolutionary biology and, 284–85, 287–89; religion and, 281–83. *See also* information; posthumanism; transhumanism

atheism: Derrida and, 245; Hegel and, 76, 82; Heidegger and, 31; Schelling and, 109, 110–11; Tillich and, 31–32, 187–89, 191, 200, 203, 211, 245, 263. *See also* panentheism; pantheism; theism

Augustine, 36, 86, 97, 175, 178, 190, 193, 290, 318, 328, 331

Auschwitz, 99, 103, 223, 268

Avicenna (Ibn Sina), 46

axiology, 8, 14–15, 277–78; distinguished from ontology, 319–20; of the event, 340; of joy, 325–32, 333, 336; of love, 326, 328; mortality and, 319; unconditional and, 319, 330

Barad, Karen, 8, 13, 208, 291–92
Barth, Karl, 30, 32–34
Beach, Edward, 172, 269
Beauvoir, Simone de, 209
Benjamin, Walter, 36, 174, 233, 263
Bergson, Henri, 47
Berkeley, George, 293
Biden, Joseph, 234
Blake, Terrence, 291
Blake, William, 68
Boehme, Jacob, 10, 113, 150, 186, 260
Bonaventure, 192
Bonhoeffer, Dietrich, 186, 209, 211
Bostrom, Nick, 45, 53, 293. *See also* superintelligence
boundary breakdowns, 279, 291. *See also* Haraway
Bowie, Andrew, 142
Buddha, 220
Bultmann, Rudolf, 186, 211, 312

call, the: author of, 329, 339; middle voice, 263, 339; response and, 231, 329; temporality and, 251; theopoetics and, 18–19; unconditionality of, 261–63; without being, 261; without ground, 329; of the world, 310, 330, 338–39, 342

Camus, Albert, 6, 196, 240
Carnap, Rudolf, 29, 208, 306
Carter, Jimmy, 234
Chalmers, David, 293, 301
Chardin, Pierre Teilhard de, 282
Christ, 3, 11, 63, 220, 271; celestial, 299; Christ consciousness, 283; death and, 307, 309; Hegel on, 85–86, 95; present in mythology, 164; Schelling on Satan and, 101, 119, 122–26, 129, 149, 164, 166, 176; white, 210; Yeshua, 23–24. *See also* Jesus
Clayton, Phillip, 208
Coleridge, Samuel Taylor, 105
Cone, James, 209–10, 373n25
Corrington, Robert, 111, 206
cosmic rose, 331–34. *See also* mysticism: mystical rose
cosmopoetics, 25, 308, 309–19; existence of God in, 315–17, 318–19; the harmony of the spheres and, 341–43
creation of the world: Aquinas on, 48–49, 123; Hegel on, 171; Levinas on, 72; Schelling on, 114–18, 125, 146–47, 164, 171, 193, 356n8, 357nn21–22; Tillich on, 207, 210
culture: conditional or material, 215–16, 219, 231–32, 239; as a form of life, 166–67, 317, 337; Hegel and, 80; traditional and deconstructive meaning compared, 245–49, 374n4; unconditional elements in, 216. *See also* Tillich, Paul
cyborgs, 13, 279–83; distinguished from uploads, 278–9, 281, 283–87, 290,

295; mortality and, 285; scientific, 280–81, 300, 321–22; theology and, 285. *See also* Delio; Haraway

Daly, Mary, 209–10, 373n25
Damian, Peter, 68
Darth Vader, 126, 322
Darwin, Charles, 288
death: as disease, 309; gift of, 331; mortal God and, 318–19; as punishment, 308–9, 319; of the universe, 308–9, 327. *See also* death of God; Hegel; Schelling
death of God, 74–75, 78, 100, 110, 125, 211, 257, 317, 318, 353n1; Hegel and, 94–98
deconstruction, 35, 42, 66, 243–50; 256, 258, 267, 271, 292; auto-deconstruction, 66, 197, 205, 249–50; barbarian principle and, 268–73; democracy and, 251, 253; *destinerrance*, 13, 268, 270–71, 309; *différance*, 34–36, 135, 277; hermeneutics and, 267; justice and, 250–51; of presence, 264–67; Protestant Principle and, 252–53; undeconstructible, 36, 217–18, 228–29, 232, 243, 245, 249–52, 255. *See also* culture; democracy; Derrida; dissemination; gift
Deleuze, Gilles, 149, 158, 163, 296, 335
Delio, Ilia, 281–83, 288, 321
democracy, 223, 255; to-come, 240, 251–53, 379n29
Derrida, Jacques, 14, 48, 53, 59–60, 72, 141, 179, 197, 216, 242, 254, 278, 287, 289; archi-écriture, 294; culture, 245–47, 316; death, 309; *destinerrance*, 13, 270–71, 309; *différance*, 264–65, 267, 277; gift, 114, 327–28; hauntology, 1–2, 12, 27, 34–36, 243, 252, 272, 291–92; love, 236; the messianic, 250, 259–60,

300; the name of God, 255–58, 318, 338; *pharmakon*, 219, 232; possibility of the impossible, 35–36, 214, 257, 316, 340; prayer, 323; the Protestant Principle, 252–53; "religion without religion," 153, 238; Tillich and, 36–37, 216–17, 221, 233, 255, 239–40, 242–63, 271. *See also* deconstruction; democracy; dissemination; ghost; gift; messianic
Descartes, René, 293
dissemination, 13–14, 217, 244, 248, 264–67, 269–72, 306; cosmic, 305, 306, 309; distinguished from analogy and symbol, 266, 268; distinguished from appropriation, 264–68; distinguished from polysemy, 266–68

Eckhart, Meister: Aquinas and, 56–57, 58–59; birth of the son, 61–63; Derrida and, 59; edifying not anxious, 64–67; *Gelassenheit*, ix–x, xii, 9, 62, 67, 83, 194, 201, 233, 268, 273, 299, 305, 320, 323, 326, 331, 333, 351n57; God, 56–58; Godhead, 59–61, 150; ground of the soul, 320–22; love and, 326–27; Luther's *Deus absconditus* and, 63–70; panentheism, 57–58; Schelling and, 57–58, 120, 151, 188; "without why," 325–27, 329, 333. *See also* Aquinas; mysticism; without why
economy, 265, 268; dialectical, 269; divine, 134–35, 152, 241, 256, 329; global, 141, 227; ontotheological, 138; rewards and punishments, 241, 256, 261, 327–330. *See also* gift
Einstein, Albert, 2, 4, 29, 206–8, 278, 291–92, 314
Enlightenment, 76, 80, 81, 85–86, 88, 159, 189, 235; old versus new, 41; posthumanism and, 295

epochē, 8–9, 16–18, 26, 37, 71, 178, 180, 232, 266. *See also* phenomenology; reduction; transcendental: signified
Erasmus, Desiderius, 67–68, 327
Eriugena, John Scotus, 113, 206
ethics, 12, 23, 224, 244, 299, 326; Deleuze and, 118; Derrida and, 240; Porete and, 326; Schelling and, 101, 156, 159; Tillich and, 218, 219, 369n39; unconditional and, 230, 238–41; violence and 218, 219
Eve, 128, 279, 307
event, the: apophatics and, 143–44; axiology of, 340; facticity of, 12; faith in, 244; Hegel and, 365–66n4; the impossible and, 236, 340; name of God and, 9, 16–17, 24, 179, 262, 320, 337, 343; promise and threat of, 270, 271; religion and, xii; systems and, 249, 289; theology of, 26, 36–37; theopoetic, 21–22, 25. *See also* deconstruction; Derrida; open-endedness
evil. *See* Schelling; Tillich, Paul
existence: essence and, 11, 112, 141, 145–46, 169–71, 181, 230; of God, 76–77, 80–81, 119, 147–52, 179, 180, 187–89, 256–57, 263, 365–66n4; not a predicate, 46–47, 154; philosophy of, 140–41; system of, 140. *See also* Aquinas; insistence; Kant; Schelling; Tillich, Paul

facticity: of being, 142, 161, 177–78; of the future, 179–80; of God, 178–79; Heidegger and, 7, 140, 177, 362n11; Kierkegaard and, 11, 140–41. *See also* Schelling
Fichte, Johann Gottlieb, 106, 134, 139, 158
Frank, Manfred, 116
Freud, Sigmund, 10, 105, 156, 211

fundamentalism, 163, 221–28; Christian nationalism and, 223–24; ground of being and, 225–28; visceral nature of, 225. *See also* violence

Gadamer, Hans-Georg, 87, 157, 267
Galileo, 96, 310
Gandhi, Mahatma, 237
Gelassenheit. *See* Eckhart; Schelling
German Idealism, 10, 12, 31, 36, 76, 180, 219, 247, 266–67, 270, 313; end of, 106, 136, 139–52; essence of 133–34
ghost, 3, 4, 6, 8, 13, 15, 36, 278; believing in, 1–2; as call, 338; *Geist* and, 99, 180, 243; "Ghost Dance" (film), 1, 292, 304; holy, 1, 15; story, 2; of the unconditional, 36; of undecidability, 5–8, 217, 236. *See also* hauntology; specter
gift, the, 37, 159, 177, 200; of death, 331–32; love as, 235, 328; pure, 114–15, 327–28, 381–82n17. *See also* death; Derrida; economy
Gödelian problem, 131, 140, 144, 289
Grant, Iain Hamilton, 111

Habermas, Jürgen, 111, 119, 130, 150, 154, 173–74, 232, 260, 271
Hamlet, 21, 86
Haraway, Donna, 13, 279–81, 284–85, 287, 291, 298–300
Harman, Graham, 291
harmony of the spheres, 15, 341–43
Hartmann, Eduard von, 105
hauntology, 4–5, 8, 252, 272, 338; as approach to God, 3, 5, 3; materialism and, 294; quantum, 8, 13, 290–92; reduction of ontology and, 11–12, 99, 243, 308; Spirit (*Geist*) and, 180. *See also* cyborgs; ghost; posthumanism; reduction; specter; transhumanism

Hegel, Georg W. F. 10–13, 47, 52, 102, 155, 158–59, 193, 280, 268, 271, 310, 315; alliance with classical theology, 92–94; anti-apophatic, 93; Aquinas and, 93; Aristotle and, 79, 97, 142; *Aufhebung*, 31, 269; Concept (*Begriff*), 52, 91, 93, 98–100, 141, 143, 149, 176, 364n13; death of God, 74, 78, 94–98, 257, 318; edification, 93–94; the finite and the infinite, 80–84; headless Hegelianism, 99; Jesus, 95–97; mysticism and, 80, 83–84; pantheism and panentheism, 78, 109–15, 186, 266, 307; proofs for the existence of God, 80–84; revelation, 84–92; as revolutionary, 76–80; Schelling and, 103, 105, 107, 124–25, 134, 139–42, 149, 152–53, 161, 165, 169–77; theopoetics and, 85, 90, 93; Tillich and, 91, 186, 193–95, 198–99, 211, 242, 270; young Hegelians and, 139. See also apophatic imagination; atheism; creation of the world; death of God; Incarnation; mysticism; New Testament; panentheism; pantheism; reason; revelation; Schelling; Tillich, Paul; *Vorstellung*

Heidegger, Martin, ix, 5, 7, 49, 160, 162, 208, 249, 291, 306; anxiety, 71, 93, 331; *Befindlichkeit*, 93; Being, 26, 28–29, 47, 200, 228–29, 297; being-in-the-world, 225, 290, 310–11; Carnap and, 29, 208, 306; consciousness, 302; *Kampf*, 332; language, 252; *lethe*, 102, 269; metaphysics, 35, 173; ontological difference, 26–37, 47, 76, 112, 204, 229; ontological reduction, 9, 10, 12, 16, 26–27, 82, 174, 211, 242, 307–8; Schelling and, 11, 103, 111–13, 117, 135, 138, 140, 143, 149, 157; Tillich and, 259; "without why," 323–24. See also anxiety; hermeneutics

hermeneutics: devilish, 272; of facticity, 140, 143, 177; radical, 4, 99, 177, 200, 339–40, 362n11; speculative, 74–75, 76, 81, 86, 91; *subtilitas intelligendi*, 19, 23, 91, 157, 232, 314, 337, 345n2. See also Heidegger; Schelling

Hitchens, Christopher, 231
Hölderlin, Friedrich, 31
Hopkins, Gerard Manley, 337
humanism, critique of, 265, 302–3, 376–77n6. See also inhuman
Hume, David, 207–8, 291
Husserl, Edmund, 26–27, 30, 34–35, 44, 71–72, 75, 143, 156, 225, 310. See also *epochē*; phenomenology; reduction

imagination. See apophatic imagination
Incarnation, the, 281, 298–99; Eckhart and, 60–61; Hegel and, 85–87, 95; Schelling and, 124–25, 164, 199; theopoetics and, 23–24; Tillich and, 195
information: age, 34, 227, 283, 301; Derrida and, 294; disinformation and, 297; systems, 53, 277–78, 286, 287, 289, 294; technology, 1–2, 53, 296. See also posthumanism
inhuman, the, 14, 376–77n6; posthuman and, 304–5. See also humanism; posthumanism; transhumanism
insistence, 79, 181; of the call, 261–62; existence and, 79, 181, 261, 263; of God, 148, 179, 256–57, 261; of the kingdom, 21, 173–74, 263; of the unconditional, 36–37, 262–63. See also existence
intellectualism and voluntarism, 54–56, 67–72, 103, 105, 142, 159, 163, 172, 174–77, 327, 349n21, 364n10, 364n13, 367n12
intervolution, 290
Irigaray, Luce, 210, 280, 332

James, William, 310
Jaspers, Karl, 283
Jesus, iv, 24, 42, 63, 114, 166, 180, 187, 213, 234, 237, 306; angelology and, 279, 297, 299; Hegel on, 78, 86–87, 95–98; as poet, 19–20, 22–23; Schelling on, 121–22, 124–25, 137, 260; violence and, 215, 220, 222–24, 227; as Yeshua, 23–24, 261, 312. *See also* Christ; kingdom of God; New Testament
Joachim of Fiore, 120, 308
John of the Cross, 6
joy: axiology of, 325–32; cosmic, 332; unshakeable, 331–32. *See also* axiology; Porete
Joyce, James, 249
justice, 37, 197; deconstruction and, 240, 250–53, 255; God of, 209; prophetic, 215, 220, 259

Kafka, Franz, 4, 9, 44, 71
Kähler, Martin, 198
Kangas, David, 326
Kant, Immanuel, 4, 53–54, 81, 84, 148, 177–78, 198, 307, 330; existence not a predicate, 46, 52; Schelling and, 105, 130, 136, 143–44, 158; thing–in–itself, 63–64. *See also* Enlightenment; reason
Kearney, Richard, 313
Keats, John, 77
Keller, Catherine, 6, 132, 208, 313, 332, 371n6
Kennedy, Robert, 233
kenotic, versus pleromatic, 97, 114, 125, 146, 151, 172
Kierkegaard, Søren, 11, 85–86, 94, 272, 289, 299; freedom, 128, 256; pseudonyms, 33, 64 (Johannes Climacus), 92, 161 (Constantine Constantius), 170, 218; Schelling and, 139–41, 143–44, 147
King, Martin Luther, Jr., 41, 209, 215, 233, 237

kingdom of God, 20–21, 24, 101, 122, 137, 154–55, 166, 174, 223–24, 260, 328; not a reward, 262, 263; without sovereignty, 262. *See also* insistence; Jesus; theopoetics
Kuhn, Thomas, 29, 249
Kurzweil, Ray, 285, 295–96, 299

Lacan, Jacques, 105, 219, 355n3
Latour, Bruno, 132, 291, 312
Lawrence, Joseph, 133
Leibniz, G. W., 14, 113, 145, 199, 219, 306
Levinas, Emmanuel, 72, 142, 147, 156–57, 178, 233, 241, 361n9
Lewis, John, 233, 237
Lonergan, Bernard, 54
love. *See* axiology; Eckhart; gift; Porete; unconditional; violence; without why
Luther, Martin, 21, 23, 29, 41, 43, 70, 95, 102, 175, 198, 232, 272; *Deus absconditus*, xi, 10, 44, 63–70, 150, 173, 219, 260, 273, 305, 327; theology of the cross, 31, 33, 273; theology of glory, 30
Lyotard, Jean-François, 14, 99, 305

Malabou, Catherine, 312
Marcel, Gabriel, 361n10
Maritain, Jacques, 47, 54, 200
Martensen, Hans, 151
Marx, Karl, 156, 179, 211, 253, 271
materialism, 308, Derrida and, 378n18; old versus new, 278; posthumanism and, 278, 294; quantum physics and, 292–94; Schelling and, 111. *See also* Habermas; Žižek
McGrath, Alistair, 68–69
Merleau-Ponty, Maurice, 225, 311
messianic, the 35, 137, 257; Benjamin and, 36, 174, 233; Derrida and, 217, 240, 250–53, 300; time, 137; weak, 250, 253

Miles, Jack, 220
Montaigne, Michel de, 253
Moravec, Hans, 285, 296
Müller, Max, 29–30
mysterium tremendum et fascinans, 68, 113, 147, 316; universe as, 300–302, 305, 322, 341–43. *See also* mystery
mystery, xi, xiii, 64–65, 68, 178, 199, 230; cosmic, 256, 300, 306, 310, 312, 322, 338, 341–43; distinguished from problem, 306; Hegel and, 88–89; mythology and, 161–63, 167–68; openness to, 55; posthumanism and, 300–301; of the unconditional, 229. *See also* apophatic; *mysterium tremendum et fascinans*
mysticism, ix–x, 34, 42–43, 55–56, 312; Aquinas and, 55; differentiated from mystical force, 246–47; Hegel and, 80, 83–84; mystical element, ix, 43, 56, 199–200, 321, 342, 373n26; mystical rose, 322–25; mystical theology, 66, 254; Schelling and, 134, 150–51; science and, 302; Tillich and, 188, 199–203, 369n37; Wittgenstein and, 145. *See also* Eckhart; Porete; theology
myth, 4, 101–2; broken and unbroken, 222; cyborg as, 279–80, 300; in Genesis, 309. *See also* Haraway; New Testament; Schelling

natura naturans, 256, 288; Eriugena, 113; Schelling, 108, 113; technology and, 288; Tillich, 206, 210
negative theology, 34–36, 42–43, 51–52, 104, 145, 193. *See also* apophatic; mysticism
Neoplatonism, 23, 36, 317; Aquinas and, 51, 58, 193; Christianity and, 35, 66, 328; Eckhart and, 57–58, 60–62, 63, 273; *exitus* and *reditus*, 134, 172, 202, 247, 309, 313–14; mysticism

and, 36, 313, 325; the One and, x, 248; Schelling and, 134
New Testament, the, 3–4, 22, 126–29, 208, 220; Anselm and, 123, 166; Eckhart and, 61–62; fundamentalism and, 223–24; God of, 61; Hegel and, 86–88; poetics of, 19–20, 342; powers and principalities, 3–4, 12, 25, 101, 122–23, 137, 185, 208, 212, 271, 342; as story, 86–87, 101, 121, 312; temptations of Jesus, 121, 260. *See also* Jesus; myth; Schelling; theopoetics
Nicholas of Cusa, 113, 206, 313, 320
Nietzsche, Friedrich, 10, 37, 69, 156, 158, 163, 211, 271, 299; Hegel and, 74, 95; Schelling and, 115, 123, 160
nihilism, 278; of grace, 328–30. *See also* gift; without why
Novalis (Freiherr von Hardenberg, G.P.F.), 228
Nuovo, Victor, 175

ontological difference, 27–34, 36, 76, 112, 204; Aquinas and, 47. *See also* Heidegger
open-endedness: of the future, 35, 257, 311; of the promise, 37; of systems, 132, 141, 144, 244, 289. *See also* event
Otto, Rudolf, 68, 113

panentheism, 14, 27, 49, 92, 100, 210, 248, 256, 266, 282, 303, 305, 307–8, 338, 370n50; distinguished from pantheism, 78, 105, 110, 203–4; Eckhart and, 57; Hegel and, 78, 84, 92, 173, 186; limits of, 303, 307–8; mortal God and, 100, 318–19; quantum field and, 208; Schelling and, 105, 109, 111, 130, 173; Tillich and, 193–94, 203–4, 208, 210, 243. *See also* atheism; pantheism; post-theism

pantheism, 49, 308; Hegel and, 76, 78; Schelling and, 105, 109–11, 152, 186, 193, 357n21. *See also* atheism; panentheism; Rubenstein; post-theism
Parks, Rosa, 237
Parmenides, 103, 199
Pattison, George, 258
Paul, the Apostle, 5, 24, 33, 83, 86, 97, 116, 125, 127, 168
personification. *See* apophatic imagination
phenomenology, xi, xii, 28, 27; of ambiguity, 131; apophatic imagination and, 71–72, 137; dissemination and, 267; hermeneutic, 153–57, 161, 358n31; metaphysical empiricism as, 136–37, 153, 156, 161; noetic and noematic, 75; ontological difference and, 28; onto-phenomenology of the Spirit, 10–11, 98, 175, 180, 254; theopoetics as, 8–9, 16, 18, 137–38; transhumanism and, 376n5. See also *epochē*; Husserl; reduction
piety, xi, 5–6, 42–43, 51–52, 58, 84–85, 93, 141, 171, 174, 186, 188–89, 191, 193, 270, 272, 327, 360n18; austere, 32; of thinking, 323–25
Plait, Phillip, 304
Plato, 4, 48–50, 79, 107, 293, 311
poetics, 18–19, 88; of the deep, 273; imagination and 4, 322, 335–36; prosaic and, 20; theopoetics and, 16, 322, 336–37; theology and, 17, 18, 316; of the world, 309–15. *See also* theopoetics
Polanyi, Michael, 53
political, the: apophatic and, 7, 213–14; archipolitical and, 230–31; art of the impossible, 214, 235; cyborg and, 279–280, 286; mystical and, 201; political theology, 208–11, 213–15; radical theology as, 12; religion and politics of the Left, 175, 221, 228, 233–35; religion and politics of the Right, 175, 225–26, 233–35, 314; unconditional and, 12, 213–14, 252–53. *See also* religion; violence
Pope Francis, 234
Porete, Marguerite, 325, 329, 331, 333; joy and, 326–27
posthumanism, 13–15, 179, 228; angels and, 277–78, 295–97; apophatic and, 321–22, 341–42; biology and, 287–88, 298; Cartesianism and, 295; Derrida and, 264; hardline, 280–83; inhuman and, 304–5; religion and, 281–83, 321–22; theology and, 278–79, 297–303, 321, 341. *See also* cyborg; transhumanism; upload
post-theism, 10, 110, 243, 370n50; German Idealism and, 180; Hegel and, 75, 242; posthumanism and, 302–3; Schelling and, 152. *See also* atheism; panentheism; pantheism
prayer, 20–21, 42, 43, 59, 64, 137, 171, 174, 188, 223, 245, 150; theopoetic, 323–34
programs, 287; grammatology and, 34, 289; information, 287, 294; open and closed, 289. *See also* open-endedness
proofs: for God's existence, 80–85, 147–52, 187, 198–99, 315–17; ontological argument, 169–71
providence, divine, 219, 329; cosmic destruction and, 306–7; Derrida and, 271–72; Hegel and, 172, 270–71; Schelling and, 11, 130, 142, 157, 172–73, 270–71, 355n3; Tillich and, 271–72. *See also* Habermas
pure act (*actus purus*): Aquinas and, 45, 47, 194; Aristotle and, 49; Schelling and, 145, 147, 151, 164, 172, 180, 357n21, 363n37

quantum: computers, 289; entanglement, 4, 207, 291–92; field, 207–8, 231, 291; hauntology, 290–92; panentheism and, 208; physics, 311. *See also* Barad

quasi-transcendental. *See* transcendental

radical thinking, xiii, 41, 69, 71, 94, 100, 211. *See also* apophatic imagination; hermeneutics; theology

Rambach, J. J., 19, 252

reason: ecstatic, 54, 104, 200, 235, 268; faculty of principles, 54; principle of distinguished from letting-be, 323–24; *ratio* and *intellectus*, 52–56; revelation and, 84–92, 98; *Vernunft* and *Verstand*, 77–78, 81–84, 89. *See also* Hegel; Schelling; Tillich, Paul

reduction: hauntological, 27, 34–37, 242, 308; ontological, 26–34, 82, 308; theopoetic, 17–26, 310; transcendental, 310. *See also epochē*; phenomenology

religion: ambiguity of, 217–21; confessional, xiii, 69, 105, 130, 143, 187, 221, 228, 230, 238, 245, 323; deconstructibility of, 229; economy of, 240–41, 328; feeling and, 80; hypocrisy of, 315–16; imagination and, 75; religious orders and, ix–x, xii, 10, 42, 65; secular and, 34, 130, 167–68, 201, 214–17, 226, 232–33, 245, 250; violence and, 37, 214–21, 223, 227, 231–35, 236–37, 340; visceral, 225–27. *See also* cyborgs; fundamentalism; piety; political; posthumanism; theology; Tillich, Paul; violence

Resurrection, the, 85, 86, 96, 286, 333; uploads and, 297. *See also* risen body

revelation: Eckhart and, 60, 65, 70, 150; Hegel and, 84–92, 93; Luther and, 68; reason and, 80, 302, 324, 326; Schelling and, 105–6, 121, 124–25, 129, 153, 155, 161–68, 175, 205; special, 25, 313; supernatural, 9, 16, 329; theopoetics and, 17–18. *See also* Hegel; Schelling

Ricoeur, Paul, 156, 266

risen body: theopoetic space and, 24; upload and, 13, 295, 297; as *Vorstellung*, 24, 85–86, 96, 286, 295–97, 333. *See also* Resurrection

risk: beautiful, 7, 241; call as, 258; freedom and, 176; life as, 8, 158; love as, 236-37; measure of radicality, xii, 41, 94, 104, 121, 141, 268, 272, 273; religion as, 219–20; subjecting God to, 11, 94, 98, 115–19, 123, 128, 134, 150, 152, 155, 172, 174, 180, 197, 256, 260; subjecting history to, 119, 130, 155, 157, 280; unconditional and, 214, 217, 243; undecidability and, 7. *See also* Habermas; providence

Rist, Johannes, 95

Robinson, John, 186

Rousseau, Jean-Jacques, 246

Rousselot, S.J., Pierre, 53–56, 195

Rovelli, Carlo, 314

Rubenstein, Mary-Jane, 110, 203, 208

ruinology, 14–15, 268–69, 278, 305, 309

Sagan, Carl, 314, 328

Sartre, Jean-Paul, 117, 128, 156, 256

Satan, 10, 68, 126, 180, 232, 256, 297, 306, 339; Schelling and, 260, 268–70, 272. *See also* Christ; Schelling

Saussure, Ferdinand de, 264

Schelling, Friedrich W. J., 10–14, 64, 70, 218, 242, 248, 252, 254; ages of the church, 129–30; ages of the world, 119–20, 122–23, 126, 129, 137, 164–65, 180, 253, 305, 309, 355n3; *alter Deus*, 108, 116, 117, 119, 223, 268; angels and demons, 128–29; anthropology,

Schelling (*Cont.*)
358n31; apophatic philosophy, 102–3, 104, 140, 143, 177–80; Aquinas and, 102, 104, 123, 148, 171, 173, 193; *Aufhebung*, 269; barbarian principle, 119, 128, 175, 214, 268, 273; Berlin Lectures, 139–52; blind being, 145–47, 148, 149, 164, 362n19; bold theology, 147–52, 174; Catholicism and, 170, 173, 193, 367n3; Christology, 124–26, 164–66; critique of Hegel on the ontological argument, 169–71, 175; critique of Hegel on a personal God, 172–74; critique of Hegel's circularity, 171–72; critique of Hegel's Concept, 141–43; critique of Hegel's intellectualism, 174–77; death of God, 110, 120, 257; deconstruction and, 269; ecstatic reason, 104–5, 141, 200; edifying versus radical, 104–6, 112, 114–15, 120, 121, 129–36, 136–39, 150–52, 173–74, 360n18; either/or, 158–61, 176–77; evil and freedom, 11, 115–17, 118–19, 127–28, 131, 271; evil and God, 117–20; existence of God, 119, 147–52, 179–80; facticity, 11, 140–41, 142, 144, 150, 154, 157, 161, 164, 173, 176–79, 312; freedom and system, 131–33, 140–41, 340; freedom as eternal decision, 130–31; *Gelassenheit*, 133, 138, 147, 151, 180; God and, 57, 299, 308, 315, 338; Gödelian paradox of the system, 131, 140, 144, 289; ground and existence, 111–15, 124, 126, 131–34; *Indifferenz*, critique of, 133–38, 146, 147; Luther and, 232, 272; materialism, 111; metaphysical empiricism, 153, 155–57; mythology, 101–2, 153; mythology and revelation, 101, 164–68, 228, 335; panentheism, 105, 109–11, 173–74; pantheism, 105, 109–11, 152, 186, 193, 357n21; philosophical religion, 153–58, 161–62, 166–67; philosophy of mythology, 161–64; positive philosophy and negative philosophy, 11, 46, 132, 140–41, 143–44, 150, 169, 250, 312; potencies, 113, 124–25, 151, 219, 231, 296, 355n3, 363n37; *Potenzlehre*, 122–25, 127, 180; *prius*, the, 142, 145, 148, 154, 157, 159, 176, 179, 191, 199, 233; pure act, differs from Aristotle and Aquinas, 147, 151; radicalized, 103–4, 244–45; reason, 54, 235, 268; revelation, 164–68, 164–66, 164–68; Satanology, 11, 104, 106, 117, 121–38, 256, 269; speculative hermeneutics, 156–7, 158, 161, 170, 175; Spirit, 265–66, 272, 294; system of freedom, 109, 118; theopoetics and, 18, 119, 136–38, 153, 311; Tillich and, 31, 104, 185–88, 191, 193–96, 198–200, 202, 204–6, 208, 211, 213, 219, 222, 225, 243, 260, 270, 272, 317, 320; unconditional, 142, 233, 239; unprethinkable, 11, 141–44, 151, 158, 162, 164, 165, 181, 310, 337, 363n37. *See also* Habermas; Hegel; pantheism; pure act; Tillich; *Vorstellung*; Žižek

Schopenhauer, Arthur, 10, 64, 124, 156, 163

Serres, Michel, 2, 291, 296–97

Shelley, Mary, 286

Socrates, 51, 85–86, 124, 171, 325

specter: apophatic imagination and, 3, 5; of the call, 9, 12; characterized, 1–3, 7, 12, 338; exorcising, 10; of God, 3, 5, 8, 15, 17, 262, 343; of the inhuman, 14, 179, 304, 306; of justice, 253; of the posthuman, 13, 278; quantum physics and, 4, 291, 292; spectralization, 8, 13, 27, 37, 242; Spirit and, 36, 99, 180, 243; of the system, 289; of theology, 278, 302; of the unconditional, 12; of the world (cosmos), 2, 278, 301, 332, 339. *See also* ghost; hauntology

Spinoza, Baruch, 47, 76, 109, 113, 158, 179, 206
Spirit. *See* Hegel; Schelling; specter
Stirner, Max, 2, 294
subjunctive, the, 4, 20, 24, 235
superintelligence, 45, 53, 282–83, 294, 296–97, 377n9
supernatural attitude, suspension of, 9, 16, 17, 21, 153 , 161, 215, 232. See also *epochē*; phenomenology; reduction
supernaturalism, xiii, 17–18, 23, 84, 86–87, 90, 92, 95, 196, 211, 232–33, 270, 272, 349n30
Supreme Being, critique of God as, 9, 10, 16, 26, 31–32, 37, 50, 74, 84, 92, 174, 187, 189, 191, 193, 196, 199, 201, 243, 251, 254, 256, 261, 303, 307. *See also* theism; Tillich, Paul
systems, 248–49, 265; coded, 34, 277, 294; formal, 143, 289; information, 277, 284, 287, 296; open versus closed, 142–44, 249, 289; philosophical, 283; planetary, 277; totalitarian, 175. *See also* Hegel; open-endedness; Schelling; Tillich, Paul

Tauler, Johannes, 67
Taylor, Mark C., 284, 288, 290
theism, 10, 243, 245, 248, 256, 266, 307–8, 338; anthropocentrism of, 299, 302–3; destruction of the universe and, 307, 379n5; Hegel and, 92–93; monotheism, 163; politics of, 209–10; Schelling and, 105, 107, 111, 130, 132, 356n7; Tillich and, 185–212. *See also* atheism; panentheism; pantheism; post-theism; Schelling; Supreme Being; Tillich, Paul
theology, 47; biology and, 298–302, 341; bold, 147–52, 174; classical, 5, 9, 11, 13–14, 16, 76, 79, 81, 84, 92–94, 98, 104, 114, 186–88, 254, 272, 283, 295, 298, 302, 307, 330; correlational, 228– 31; of the cross (*theologia crucis*), 31, 33, 263, 273; debate between Barth and Tillich, 32–33; end of, 13, 32, 188, 263, 299; metaphysical, 9, 18, 23, 42, 43, 44, 49, 56, 60, 114, 137; of perhaps, 255–58; process, 47, 147, 155, 170, 208, 210, 353n5; radical, xiii, 11, 12, 69, 71, 105, 115, 149, 153, 177, 179, 186, 188, 195, 213, 245, 263, 323; to-come, 297–303; weak, xiii, 8–9, 16–17, 24, 26, 27, 37, 95, 196, 215, 254–55. *See also* negative theology; posthumanism; radical thinking; theopoetics; Tillich, Paul; transhumanism
theopoetics, 8–9, 13, 16–37, 107, 137, 311, 322, 337; Aquinas and, 54; *epochē* and, 17–26; Hegel and, 90, 93, 99; time in, 137; weak theology and, 17. *See also* cosmopoetics; *epochē*; reduction; Schelling; theology
Thweatt-Bates, Jennifer, 279, 378n26
Tillich, Hannah, 209
Tillich, Paul, xiii, 10, 11–14, 27, 122, 221, 253, 260; apophatic imagination and, 242, 245, 271; Aquinas and, 50–51, 192–94, 195; art, 313; atheism in theology, 187–89, 245; being-itself, 33, 92, 185, 187, 189, 190, 192–98, 199, 200–201, 202, 205–6, 207, 208, 308; boundary, the, 199–200, 242; correlational, 245; cosmological way, 192–96; cosmological way reconsidered, 205–8; courage to be, 159, 198–99, 210–12, 239–40, 244, 263, 373n25; critique of theism, 188–89, 211; death of God, 257; demonic, the, 188, 204, 208, 232, 238, 271–72; Derrida and, 216–17, 221, 233, 239–40, 242–63; eschatology versus ontology, 258–61; ethics, 239–40, 369n39; existence of God, 189, 198; faith, 196, 197–98, 201, 239–40, 244, 271; God beyond God, 186–87, 210;

Tillich, Paul (*Cont.*)
God differentiated from being-itself, 196–98; ground of being, 9, 12, 17, 31–33, 36, 37, 101, 126, 160, 168, 174, 190, 194, 196, 202, 207, 216, 219, 225 229, 235, 242–44, 245, 251, 254, 257, 259, 261, 263, 265, 271, 273, 300, 315, 316, 318, 322, 338, 363n35; Hegel and, 75, 80, 91–92; Holy, the, 185, 188–89, 219; mystical element in, 199–203, 206, 373n26; National Socialism, critique of, 185, 208, 258–59, 373n25; ontological argument, 198–99; ontological way, 189–92; panentheism, 203–4; political theology, 208–11; post-theism, 186–89, 200, 210–12, 242; *prius*, 191, 200, 202, 205, 233, 238, 324, 337, 343; Protestant Principle, 129, 229, 204–5, 210, 252–53; quantum physics and, 207–8; radicalized, 243–45, 258–61; religion as ultimate concern, xiii, 33–34, 185, 201, 213–14, 363n35; Schelling and, 185–86, 188, 191, 195, 196, 198, 200, 202, 204; socialism, Christian, 209–10, 259–60; supernaturalism, critique of, 196, 211; symbol, 13, 32–33, 162–63, 186, 187, 191, 193, 196–97, 201, 205, 208, 210, 211, 222, 242, 252, 266, 317, 335; theology of culture, 26, 91, 167, 201, 205–6, 215, 217, 337, 363n35; theology of nature, 205–8, 210, 245–47; theonomy, 201, 321; transcending theism, 186–89; unconditional, 36, 143, 214, 216, 232–33, 238, 240, 242, 245, 317. See also Derrida; Hegel; providence; Schelling; unconditional

transcendental, 28, 29, 51; attitude, 26; consciousness, 71–72, 232–33; difference, 29, 34; illusions, 313; quasi-transcendental, 34, 72, 133, 134, 144, 229, 267, 289; reduction, 35, 310–11; signified, suspension of, 21–22, 215, 232–33, 255; signifier, 5, 35. See also *epochē*; phenomenology; reduction

transhumanism: angels and, 295–97; apophatic and, 321–22; distinguished from post-humanism, 286, 376n1; as enhancement, 281, 283; first use of the word, 377n8; inhuman and, 305. *See also* cyborg; posthumanism; upload

Trinity, the Holy: Eckhart and, 60–63; Hegel and, 83–85, 86, 87, 89, 90, 353n5; paradigm for German Idealism, 170; Schelling and, 125, 165, 357n22

Tritten, Tyler, 163

Trump, Donald, 212, 222, 226, 234, 237

Tutu, Desmond, 233

unconditional: affirmation of, 197, 217, 257, 312, 319, 324, 330, 333, 338; ambiguity of, 213–16, 219, 227, 232; being and, 14, 142, 167, 189, 199, 243; call of, 37, 243, 255, 263, 301; claim of, 232–33; compared to the undeconstructible, 249–52; concern, 12, 185, 213, 215; correlation of conditional and, 228–30, 245, 251; distinguished from the conditional, 204, 208, 216; ethics and, 238–39; faith, 205; freedom, 132; God and, 189, 191, 196, 255, 317, 319; insistence of, 263; justice and, 259; as love, 235–38, 328; loyalty to, 242, 249, 254, 261–63; not confined to religion, 230, 245; as poison, 231–35; possibility of, 261–63; as promise and memory, 36; Protestant Principle and, 252–53; the perhaps and, 255–56; radicalizing, 243–45, 258–61; Tillich and Derrida compared on, 216, 229, 240–41, 242; violence of, 217–21; weakening of,

254–55; without being, 257; without sovereignty; 12, 36, 216–17, 240, 243, 257, 261–63; worth, 214, 240, 319–20. *See also* Derrida; fundamentalism; political; Schelling; Tillich, Paul; undeconstructible; violence; without sovereignty

undecidability, 1, 41; 58; of being, 1; of the divine and the demonic, 217, 271; of Eckhart's Godhead, 64–65; ghost of, 5–7, 236; of God and Satan, 10; of systems, 289; of the Holy, 219; of the two apophatics, 5–7, 14, 42, 64, 72, 325; of the unconditional, 214, 236. *See also* Derrida

undeconstructible, 252; impossible and, 217–18, 255–56; unconditional and, 36, 228–29, 232, 243, 245, 249–52. *See also* Derrida

universe, expansion of, 14, 256, 304–5, 308, 312, 322, 332. *See also* cosmic rose; cosmopoetics; *mysterium tremendum et fascinans*

upload, the, 279, 281, 282, 283–90; immortality and, 13; liberal individual and, 295; risen body and, 295. *See also* cyborg

Vaihinger, Hans, 63
Van Gogh, Vincent, 20
Vattimo, Gianni, 54, 120, 145
violence, 12; ethics and, 218–19; fundamentalism and, 221–28; Hegel and, 37; love and, 235–36; nonviolence and, 37; passage to the limits and, 235, 237; religious, 214, 217–21, 231; Schelling and, 103, 119; unconditional and, 214, 232. *See also* religion; unconditional

virtual reality, 2, 278, 292–94, 297, 300, 341; angelology and, 2; reality+, 293–94; textualism, and 294. *See also* Chalmers; information; posthumanism

voluntarism. *See* intellectualism and voluntarism

Vorstellung: defined, 74–75; Hegel and, 10, 74–75, 78, 81, 86–90, 93, 98–99, 162–63, 171–72, 213, 335, 338; Schelling and, 122, 124, 127, 213, 335, 338

Wayne, John, 222
Whitehead, A. N., 186, 208, 211, 312. *See also* theology
without being: the call, 263, 338; God, 255; unconditional, 12, 216, 243,
without sovereignty: kingdom of God, 262; unconditional, 12, 36, 216–17, 240, 243, 257, 263
without why: the call and, 263; Eckhart, 61, 73; Heidegger, 322–24; love, 236–39; Porete, 326–28; world as, 181, 343. *See also* nihilism: of grace
Wittgenstein, Ludwig, 145, 225

year of Jubilee, 20, 137, 299, 306, 316

Zarathustra, 108, 299
Zen Buddhism, 321
Žižek, Slavoj: scarecrow Hegel, xii, 11, 141, 170, 365–66n4; Schelling, 105, 111, 173–74, 118, 355n3

JOHN D. CAPUTO is the Thomas J. Watson Professor of Religion Emeritus at Syracuse University and the David R. Cook Professor of Philosophy Emeritus at Villanova University. His many books include *The Weakness of God*, *The Insistence of God*, and *Cross and Cosmos*.

www.ingramcontent.com/pod-product-compliance
Lightning Source LLC
Chambersburg PA
CBHW021239240426
43673CB00057B/631